SQL For Dummies
6th Edition

Criteria for Normal Forms

First Normal Form (1NF)

Table must be two-dimensional, with rows and columns.

Each row contains data that pertains to one thing or one portion of a thing.

Each column contains data for a single attribute of the thing being described.

Each cell (intersection of row and column) of the table must be single-valued.

All entries in a column must be of the same kind.

Each column must have a unique name.

No two rows may be identical.

The order of the columns and of the rows does not matter.

Second Normal Form (2NF)

Table must be in first normal form (1NF).

All nonkey attributes (columns) must be dependent on the entire key.

Third Normal Form (3NF)

Table must be in second normal form (2NF).

Table has no transitive dependencies.

Domain-Key Normal Form (DK/NF)

Every constraint on the table is a logical consequence of the definition of keys and domains.

SQL Data Types

Exact Numerics

INTEGER

SMALLINT

BIGINT

NUMERIC

DECIMAL

Approximate Numerics

REAL

DOUBLE PRECISION

FLOAT

Boolean

BOOLEAN

Character Strings

CHARACTER

CHARACTER VARYING (VARCHAR)

NATIONAL CHARACTER

NATIONAL CHARACTER VARYING

Datetimes

DATE

TIME

TIMESTAMP

TIME WITH TIMEZONE

TIMESTAMP WITH TIMEZONE

Intervals

INTERVAL DAY

INTERVAL YEAR

Large Objects

BLOB

CLOB

Collection Types

ARRAY

MULTISET

Other Types

ROW

XML

Set Functions

COUNT	Returns the number of rows in the specified table
MAX	Returns the maximum value that occurs in the specified table
MIN	Returns the minimum value that occurs in the specified table
SUM	Adds up the values in a specified column
AVG	Returns the average of all the values in the specified column

For Dummies: Bestselling Book Series for Beginners

SQL For Dummies
6th Edition

Cheat Sheet

Value Functions

String Value Functions	Effect
SUBSTRING	Extracts a substring from a source string
UPPER	Converts a character string to all uppercase
LOWER	Converts a character string to all lowercase
TRIM	Trims off leading or trailing blanks
TRANSLATE	Transforms a source string from one character set to another
CONVERT	Transforms a source string from one character set to another

Numeric Value Functions	Effect
POSITION	Returns the starting position of a target string within a source string
CHARACTER_LENGTH	Returns the number of characters in a string
OCTET_LENGTH	Returns the number of octets (bytes) in a character string
EXTRACT	Extracts a single field from a datetime or interval

Datetime Value Functions	Effect
CURRENT_DATE	Returns the current date
CURRENT_TIME(p)	Returns the current time; (p) is precision of seconds
CURRENT_TIMESTAMP(p)	Returns the current date and the current time; (p) is precision of seconds

WHERE Clause Predicates

Comparison Predicates	
=	Equal
<>	Not equal
<	Less than
<=	Less than or equal
>	Greater than
>=	Greater than or equal

Other Predicates
BETWEEN
IN
NOT IN
LIKE
NOT LIKE
NULL
ALL
SOME, ANY
EXISTS
UNIQUE
OVERLAPS
MATCH
SIMILAR
DISTINCT

For Dummies: Bestselling Book Series for Beginners

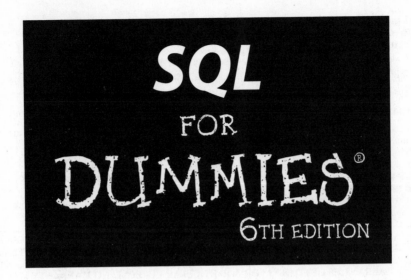

by Allen G. Taylor

Author of *Database Development For Dummies*®
and *Crystal Reports*® *10 For Dummies*®

WILEY

Wiley Publishing, Inc.

SQL For Dummies,® 6th Edition

Published by
Wiley Publishing, Inc.
111 River Street
Hoboken, NJ 07030-5774
www.wiley.com

Copyright © 2006 by Wiley Publishing, Inc., Indianapolis, Indiana

Published by Wiley Publishing, Inc., Indianapolis, Indiana

Published simultaneously in Canada

For general information on our other products and services, please contact our Customer Care Department within the U.S. at 800-762-2974, outside the U.S. at 317-572-3993, or fax 317-572-4002.

For technical support, please visit www.wiley.com/techsupport.

Wiley also publishes its books in a variety of electronic formats. Some content that appears in print may not be available in electronic books.

Library of Congress Control Number: 2006926171

ISBN-13: 978-0-470-04652-4

ISBN-10: 0-470-04652-X

Manufactured in the United States of America

10 9 8 7 6 5 4 3 2

6B/SX/QX/QW/IN

WILEY

About the Author

Allen G. Taylor is a 30-year veteran of the computer industry and the author of 24 books, including *Crystal Reports 10 For Dummies, Database Development For Dummies, Access Power Programming with VBA,* and *SQL Weekend Crash Course.* He lectures internationally on databases, networks, innovation, and entrepreneurship. He also teaches database development through a leading online education provider and teaches digital electronics and computer architecture at Portland State University. He teaches computer hardware via distance learning at the International Institute for Information Science & Technology in Shanghai, China. For the latest news on Allen's activities, check out www.DatabaseCentral.Info. You can contact Allen at allen.taylor@ieee.org.

Dedication

This book is dedicated to Georgina Taylor, my mom.

Author's Acknowledgments

First and foremost, I would like to acknowledge the help of Jim Melton, editor of the ISO/ANSI specification for SQL. Without his untiring efforts, this book, and indeed SQL itself as an international standard, would be of much less value. Andrew Eisenberg has also contributed to my knowledge of SQL through his writing. I would also like to thank my project editor, Nicole Haims, and my acquisitions editor, Tiffany Ma, for their key contributions to the production of this book. Thanks also to my agent, Carole McClendon of Waterside Productions, for her support of my career.

Publisher's Acknowledgments

We're proud of this book; please send us your comments through our online registration form located at www.dummies.com/register/.

Some of the people who helped bring this book to market include the following:

Acquisitions, Editorial, and Media Development

Project Editor: Nicole Haims

(Previous Edition: Kala Schrager)

Acquisitions Editor: Tiffany Ma

Technical Editor: Greg Guntle

Editorial Manager: Jodi Jensen

Media Development Manager:
Laura VanWinkle

Editorial Assistant: Amanda Foxworth

Sr. Editorial Assistant: Cherie Case

Cartoons: Rich Tennant
(www.the5thwave.com)

Composition Services

Project Coordinator: Tera Knapp

Layout and Graphics: Carl Byers, Andrea Dahl, Barbara Moore, Heather Ryan

Proofreaders: Leeann Harney, Christy Pingleton, Techbooks

Indexer: Techbooks

Publishing and Editorial for Technology Dummies

Richard Swadley, Vice President and Executive Group Publisher

Andy Cummings, Vice President and Publisher

Mary Bednarek, Executive Acquisitions Director

Mary C. Corder, Editorial Director

Publishing for Consumer Dummies

Diane Graves Steele, Vice President and Publisher

Joyce Pepple, Acquisitions Director

Composition Services

Gerry Fahey, Vice President of Production Services

Debbie Stailey, Director of Composition Services

Contents at a Glance

Introduction **1**

Part I: Basic Concepts **5**

Chapter 1: Relational Database Fundamentals 7

Chapter 2: SQL Fundamentals 21

Chapter 3: The Components of SQL 47

Part II: Using SQL to Build Databases **73**

Chapter 4: Building and Maintaining a Simple Database Structure 75

Chapter 5: Building a Multitable Relational Database 91

Part III: Storing and Retrieving Data **121**

Chapter 6: Manipulating Database Data 123

Chapter 7: Specifying Values 141

Chapter 8: Using Advanced SQL Value Expressions 163

Chapter 9: Zeroing In on the Data You Want 175

Chapter 10: Using Relational Operators 201

Chapter 11: Delving Deep with Nested Queries 225

Chapter 12: Recursive Queries 243

Part IV: Controlling Operations **253**

Chapter 13: Providing Database Security 255

Chapter 14: Protecting Data 269

Chapter 15: Using SQL within Applications 287

Part V: Taking SQL to the Real World **301**

Chapter 16: Accessing Data with ODBC and JDBC 303

Chapter 17: Operating on XML Data with SQL 313

Part VI: Advanced Topics **333**

Chapter 18: Stepping through a Dataset with Cursors 335

Chapter 19: Adding Procedural Capabilities with Persistent Stored Modules 345

Chapter 20: Handling Errors 361

Part VII: The Part of Tens 373
Chapter 21: Ten Common Mistakes 375
Chapter 22: Ten Retrieval Tips 379

Part VIII: Appendixes 383
Appendix A: SQL:2003 Reserved Words 385
Appendix B: Glossary 389

Index 397

Table of Contents

Introduction *1*

About This Book..1
Who Should Read This Book?...2
How This Book Is Organized...2
    Part I: Basic Concepts 2
    Part II: Using SQL to Build Databases 2
    Part III: Storing and Retrieving Data......................3
    Part IV: Controlling Operations 3
    Part V: Taking SQL to the Real World......................3
    Part VI: Advanced Topics 3
    Part VII: The Part of Tens 4
    Part VIII: Appendixes 4
Icons Used in This Book...4
Getting Started 4

Part 1: Basic Concepts *5*

Chapter 1: Relational Database Fundamentals *7*

Keeping Track of Things 7
What Is a Database?..8
Database Size and Complexity 9
What Is a Database Management System?......................9
Flat Files 10
Database Models 12
    Relational model...12
    Why relational is better 13
    Components of a relational database 13
    Holidays bring families together 13
    Enjoy the view..15
    Schemas, domains, and constraints 18
    The object model challenges the relational model........19
    The object-relational model 19
Database Design Considerations 20

Chapter 2: SQL Fundamentals *21*

What SQL Is and Isn't..21
A (Very) Little History 23
SQL Commands 24
Reserved Words 25

Data Types 26
    Exact numerics 26
    Approximate numerics 28
    Character strings 30
    Booleans 32
    Datetimes 32
    Intervals 34
    XML type 34
    ROW types 35
    Collection types 36
    REF types 37
    User-defined types 37
    Data type summary 40
Null Values..42
Constraints..42
Using SQL in a Client/Server System 43
    The server 43
    The client 44
Using SQL on the Internet/Intranet.................................45

Chapter 3: The Components of SQL **47**
Data Definition Language 48
    When "Just do it!" is not good advice 48
    Creating tables..49
    A room with a view...51
    Collecting tables into schemas.................................56
    Ordering by catalog..57
    Getting familiar with DDL commands........................58
Data Manipulation Language 59
    Value expressions...60
    Predicates..63
    Logical connectives..64
    Set functions...64
    Subqueries...66
Data Control Language..66
    Transactions..66
    Users and privileges...67
    Referential integrity constraints can jeopardize your data...........70
    Delegating responsibility for security 72

Part II: Using SQL to Build Databases 73

**Chapter 4: Building and Maintaining a Simple
Database Structure** **75**
Building a Simple Database Using a RAD Tool 76
    Deciding what to track..76
    Creating a table with Design View............................77

Altering the table structure 80
Identifying a primary key 82
Creating an index 83
Deleting a table 85
Building PowerDesign with SQL's DDL 86
Using SQL with Microsoft Access 87
Creating a table 87
Creating an index 88
Altering the table structure 89
Deleting a table 89
Deleting an index 90
Portability Considerations 90

Chapter 5: Building a Multitable Relational Database **91**

Designing a Database 91
Step 1: Defining objects 92
Step 2: Identifying tables and columns 92
Step 3: Defining tables 93
Domains, character sets, collations, and translations 97
Getting into your database fast with keys 98
Working with Indexes 100
What's an index, anyway? 101
Why you should want an index 102
Maintaining an index 103
Maintaining Integrity 104
Entity integrity 104
Domain integrity 105
Referential integrity 106
Just when you thought it was safe 109
Potential problem areas 109
Constraints 111
Normalizing the Database 114
First normal form 116
Second normal form 117
Third normal form 118
Domain-key normal form (DK/NF) 119
Abnormal form 120

Part III: Storing and Retrieving Data *121*

Chapter 6: Manipulating Database Data **123**

Retrieving Data 124
Creating Views 125
From tables 126
With a selection condition 127
With a modified attribute 128
Updating Views 129

Adding New Data 130
    Adding data one row at a time 130
    Adding data only to selected columns 132
    Adding a block of rows to a table 132
Updating Existing Data 135
Transferring Data 138
Deleting Obsolete Data 139

Chapter 7: Specifying Values 141

Values 141
    Row values 142
    Literal values 142
    Variables 144
    Special variables 146
    Column references 146
Value Expressions 147
    String value expressions 148
    Numeric value expressions 149
    Datetime value expressions 149
    Interval value expressions 150
    Conditional value expressions 150
Functions 151
    Summarizing by using set functions 151
    Value functions 154

Chapter 8: Using Advanced SQL Value Expressions 163

CASE Conditional Expressions 163
    Using CASE with search conditions 164
    Using CASE with values 166
    A special CASE — NULLIF 168
    Another special CASE — COALESCE 170
CAST Data-Type Conversions 170
    Using CAST within SQL 172
    Using CAST between SQL and the host language 172
Row Value Expressions 173

Chapter 9: Zeroing In on the Data You Want 175

Modifying Clauses 175
FROM Clauses 177
WHERE Clauses 177
    Comparison predicates 179
    BETWEEN 180
    IN and NOT IN 181
    LIKE and NOT LIKE 182
    SIMILAR 184
    NULL 184
    ALL, SOME, ANY 185
    EXISTS 188

UNIQUE 189
DISTINCT 189
OVERLAPS 190
MATCH 190
    Referential integrity rules and the MATCH predicate..................192
Logical Connectives...194
    AND 194
    OR..195
    NOT 195
GROUP BY Clauses...196
HAVING Clauses..197
ORDER BY Clauses...198

Chapter 10: Using Relational Operators 201
UNION 201
    The UNION ALL operation..203
    The CORRESPONDING operation 203
INTERSECT 204
EXCEPT..205
Various Joins..206
    Basic join 206
    Equi-join..208
    Cross join..210
    Natural join...210
    Condition join 211
    Column-name join 211
    Inner join 212
    Outer join 213
    Union join 216
ON versus WHERE..223

Chapter 11: Delving Deep with Nested Queries 225
What Subqueries Do 226
    Nested queries that return sets of rows....................227
    Nested queries that return a single value 230
    The ALL, SOME, and ANY quantifiers.......................233
    Nested queries that are an existence test.................235
    Other correlated subqueries 236
    UPDATE, DELETE, and INSERT statements 240

Chapter 12: Recursive Queries 243
What Is Recursion? 243
    Houston, we have a problem 244
    Failure is not an option...244
What Is a Recursive Query?...246
Where Might You Use a Recursive Query? 247
    Querying the hard way 248
    Saving time with a recursive query...........................249
Where Else Might You Use a Recursive Query? 252

Part IV: Controlling Operations 253

Chapter 13: Providing Database Security 255

The SQL Data Control Language 256
User Access Levels 256
    The database administrator 256
    Database object owners 257
    The public 257
Granting Privileges to Users 258
    Roles...260
    Inserting data 260
    Looking at data 260
    Modifying table data 261
    Deleting obsolete rows from a table 262
    Referencing related tables..262
    Using domains, character sets, collations, and translations.......263
    Causing SQL statements to be executed 264
Granting the Power to Grant Privileges 265
Taking Privileges Away 266
Using GRANT and REVOKE Together to Save Time and Effort 268

Chapter 14: Protecting Data 269

Threats to Data Integrity..269
    Platform instability..270
    Equipment failure 270
    Concurrent access...271
Reducing Vulnerability to Data Corruption 273
    Using SQL transactions..274
    The default transaction 275
    Isolation levels 276
    The implicit transaction-starting statement 278
    SET TRANSACTION 278
    COMMIT...279
    ROLLBACK..279
    Locking database objects 280
    Backing up your data 281
    Savepoints and subtransactions 281
Constraints Within Transactions 282

Chapter 15: Using SQL within Applications 287

SQL in an Application 288
    Keeping an eye out for the asterisk 288
    SQL strengths and weaknesses 289
    Procedural language strengths and weaknesses..........289
    Problems in combining SQL with a procedural language 290

Hooking SQL into Procedural Languages..................................291
Embedded SQL 291
Module language 294
Object-oriented RAD tools 296
Using SQL with Microsoft Access......................................297

Part V: Taking SQL to the Real World 301

Chapter 16: Accessing Data with ODBC and JDBC 303
ODBC...304
The ODBC interface...304
Components of ODBC 304
ODBC in a Client/Server Environment.................................305
ODBC and the Internet 306
Server extensions 307
Client extensions 308
ODBC and an Intranet...319
JDBC...310

Chapter 17: Operating on XML Data with SQL 313
How XML Relates to SQL...313
The XML Data Type...314
When to use the XML type 314
When not to use the XML type 315
Mapping SQL to XML and XML to SQL 316
Mapping character sets 316
Mapping identifiers 316
Mapping data types..317
Mapping tables 318
Handling null values...318
Generating the XML Schema...319
SQL Functions that Operate on XML Data 320
XMLELEMENT 320
XMLFOREST 321
XMLCONCAT 321
XMLAGG 322
XMLCOMMENT 322
XMLPARSE 323
XMLPI 323
XMLQUERY..323
XMLCAST 324
Predicates 324
DOCUMENT 325
CONTENT 325

XMLEXISTS 325
VALID 326
Transforming XML Data into SQL Tables 326
Mapping Non-Predefined Data Types to XML.....................328
Domain 328
Distinct UDT 329
Row..329
Array 330
Multiset..331
The Marriage of SQL and XML..332

Part VI: Advanced Topics 333

Chapter 18: Stepping through a Dataset with Cursors 335

Declaring a Cursor 336
The query expression 337
The ORDER BY clause..337
The updatability clause 338
Sensitivity..339
Scrollability...340
Opening a Cursor 340
Fetching Data from a Single Row..342
Syntax...342
Orientation of a scrollable cursor 343
Positioned DELETE and UPDATE statements 343
Closing a Cursor 344

**Chapter 19: Adding Procedural Capabilities with
Persistent Stored Modules 345**

Compound Statements 345
Atomicity..346
Variables 347
Cursors 348
Conditions 348
Handling conditions 349
Conditions that aren't handled....................................351
Assignment...352
Flow of Control Statements...352
IF...THEN...ELSE...END IF 352
CASE...END CASE 353
LOOP...ENDLOOP..354
LEAVE 355
WHILE...DO...END WHILE...355
REPEAT...UNTIL...END REPEAT 356

FOR...DO...END FOR..356
ITERATE 356
Stored Procedures 357
Stored Functions 358
Privileges 359
Stored Modules 359

Chapter 20: Handling Errors **361**
SQLSTATE..361
WHENEVER Clause...363
Diagnostics Areas...364
The diagnostics header area..364
The diagnostics detail area 366
Constraint violation example..368
Adding constraints to an existing table.......................369
Interpreting the information returned by SQLSTATE....370
Handling Exceptions 371

Part VII: The Part of Tens................................373

Chapter 21: Ten Common Mistakes **375**
Assuming That Your Clients Know What They Need 375
Ignoring Project Scope 376
Considering Only Technical Factors....................................376
Not Asking for Client Feedback 376
Always Using Your Favorite Development Environment 377
Using Your Favorite System Architecture Exclusively 377
Designing Database Tables in Isolation................................377
Neglecting Design Reviews 378
Skipping Beta Testing 378
Not Documenting Your Process 378

Chapter 22: Ten Retrieval Tips **379**
Verify the Database Structure..379
Try Queries on a Test Database 380
Double-Check Queries That Include Joins..........................380
Triple-Check Queries with Subselects.................................380
Summarize Data with GROUP BY 380
Watch GROUP BY Clause Restrictions 381
Use Parentheses with AND, OR, and NOT...........................381
Control Retrieval Privileges 381
Back Up Your Databases Regularly......................................382
Handle Error Conditions Gracefully 382

Part VIII: Appendixes *383*

Appendix A: SQL:2003 Reserved Words .... .385

Appendix B: Glossary .... .389

Index *397*

Introduction

Welcome to database development using the industry structured query language (SQL). Many database management system (DBMS) tools run on a variety of hardware platforms. The differences among the tools can be great, but all serious products have one thing in common: They support SQL data access and manipulation. If you know SQL, you can build relational databases and get useful information out of them.

About This Book

Relational database management systems are vital to many organizations. People often think that creating and maintaining these systems are extremely complex activities — the domain of database gurus who possess enlightenment beyond that of ordinary mortals. This book sweeps away the database mystique. In this book, you

- ✔ Get to the roots of databases.
- ✔ Find out how a DBMS is structured.
- ✔ Discover the major functional components of SQL.
- ✔ Build a database.
- ✔ Protect a database from harm.
- ✔ Operate on database data.
- ✔ Determine how to get the information you want out of a database.

The purpose of this book is to help you build relational databases and get valuable information out of them by using SQL. SQL is the international standard language used around the world to create and maintain relational databases. This edition covers the latest version of the standard, SQL:2003, as augmented in 2005 with a thorough treatment of the use of XML with SQL.

This book doesn't tell you how to design a database (I do that in *Database Development For Dummies,* also published by Wiley Publishing, Inc.). Here I assume that you or somebody else has already created a valid design. I then illustrate how you implement that design by using SQL. If you suspect that you don't have a good database design, by all means, fix your design before you try to build the database. The earlier you detect and correct problems in a development project, the cheaper the corrections will be.

Who Should Read This Book?

If you need to store or retrieve data from a DBMS, you can do a much better job with a working knowledge of SQL. You don't need to be a programmer to use SQL, and you don't need to know programming languages, such as Java, C, or BASIC. SQL's syntax is like English.

If you *are* a programmer, you can incorporate SQL into your programs. SQL adds powerful data manipulation and retrieval capability to conventional languages. This book tells you what you need to know to use SQL's rich assortment of tools and features inside your programs.

How This Book Is Organized

This book contains eight major parts. Each part contains several chapters. You may want to read this book from cover to cover once, although you don't have to. After that, this book becomes a handy reference guide. You can turn to whatever section is appropriate to answer your questions.

Part 1: Basic Concepts

Part I introduces the concept of a database and distinguishes relational data-bases from other types. It describes the most popular database architectures, as well as the major components of SQL.

Part 11: Using SQL to Build Databases

You don't need SQL to build a database. This part shows how to build a data-base by using Microsoft Access, and then you get to build the same database by using SQL. In addition to defining database tables, this part covers other important database features: domains, character sets, collations, translations, keys, and indexes.

Throughout this part, I emphasize protecting your database from corruption, which is a bad thing that can happen in many ways. SQL gives you the tools to prevent corruption, but you must use them properly to prevent problems caused by bad database design, harmful interactions, operator error, and equipment failure.

Part III: Storing and Retrieving Data

After you have some data in your database, you want to do things with it: Add to the data, change it, or delete it. Ultimately, you want to retrieve useful information from the database. SQL tools enable you to do all this. These tools give you low-level, detailed control over your data.

Part IV: Controlling Operations

A big part of database management is protecting the data from harm, which can come in many shapes and forms. People may accidentally or intentionally put bad data into database tables, for example. You can protect yourself by controlling who can access your database and what they can do. Another threat to data comes from unintended interaction of concurrent users' operations. SQL provides powerful tools to prevent this too. SQL provides much of the protection automatically, but you need to understand how the protection mechanisms work so you get all the protection you need.

Part V: Taking SQL to the Real World

SQL is different from most other computer languages in that it operates on a whole set of data items at once, rather than dealing with them one at a time. This difference in operational modes makes combining SQL with other languages a challenge, but you can face it by using the information in this book. You can exchange information with nondatabase applications by using XML. I also describe in depth how to use SQL to transfer data across the Internet or an intranet.

Part VI: Advanced Topics

In this part, you discover how to include set-oriented SQL statements in your programs and how to get SQL to deal with data one item at a time.

This part also covers error handling. SQL provides you with a lot of information whenever something goes wrong in the execution of an SQL statement, and you find out how to retrieve and interpret that information.

Part VII: The Part of Tens

This section provides some important tips on what to do, and what not to do, in designing, building, and using a database.

Part VIII: Appendixes

Appendix A lists all of SQL's reserved words, as of the 2005 release of Part 14 of the ANSI/ISO SQL standard. These are words that have a very specific meaning in SQL and cannot be used for table names, column names, or anything other than their intended meaning. Appendix B gives you a basic glossary on some frequently used terms.

Icons Used in This Book

Tips save you a lot of time and keep you out of trouble.

Pay attention to the information marked by this icon — you may need it later.

Heeding the advice that this icon points to can save you from major grief. Ignore it at your peril.

This icon alerts you to the presence of technical details that are interesting but not absolutely essential to understanding the topic being discussed.

Getting Started

Now for the fun part! Databases are the best tools ever invented for keeping track of the things you care about. After you understand databases and can use SQL to make them do your bidding, you wield tremendous power. Co-workers come to you when they need critical information. Managers seek your advice. Youngsters ask for your autograph. But most importantly, you know, at a very deep level, how your organization really works.

Part I
Basic Concepts

The 5th Wave   By Rich Tennant

"We're here to clean the code."

In this part . . .

In Part I, I present the big picture. Before talking about SQL itself, I explain what databases are and how they're different from data that early humans used to store in crude, unstructured, Stone-Age computer files. I go over the most popular database models and discuss the physical systems on which these databases run. Then I move on to SQL itself. I give you a brief look at what SQL is, how the language came about, and what it is today, based on the latest version of the international standard SQL language.

Chapter 1

Relational Database Fundamentals

. . . .

In This Chapter

▶ Organizing information

▶ Defining database

▶ Defining DBMS

▶ Comparing database models

▶ Defining relational database

▶ Considering the challenges of database design

. . . .

*S*QL (pronounced *ess-que-ell,* not *see'qwl*) is an industry-standard language specifically designed to enable people to create databases, add new data to databases, maintain the data, and retrieve selected parts of the data. Various kinds of databases exist, each adhering to a different conceptual model. SQL was originally developed to operate on data in databases that follow the *relational model.* Recently, the international SQL standard has incorporated part of the *object model,* resulting in hybrid structures called object-relational databases. In this chapter, I discuss data storage, devote a section to how the relational model compares with other major models, and provide a look at the important features of relational databases.

Before I talk about SQL, however, I need to nail down what I mean by the term *database.* Its meaning has changed as computers have changed the way people record and maintain information.

Keeping Track of Things

Today, people use computers to perform many tasks formerly done with other tools. Computers have replaced typewriters for creating and modifying documents. They've surpassed electromechanical calculators as the best way to do math. They've also replaced millions of pieces of paper, file folders, and file cabinets as the principal storage medium for important information. Compared to those old tools, of course, computers do much more, much faster — and with greater accuracy. These increased benefits do come at a cost, however. Computer users no longer have direct physical access to their data.

When computers occasionally fail, office workers may wonder whether computerization really improved anything at all. In the old days, a manila file folder only "crashed" if you dropped it — then you merely knelt down, picked up the papers, and put them back in the folder. Barring earthquakes or other major disasters, file cabinets never "went down," and they never gave you an error message. A hard drive crash is another matter entirely: You can't "pick up" lost bits and bytes. Mechanical, electrical, and human failures can make your data go away into the Great Beyond, never to return.

Taking the necessary precautions to protect yourself from accidental data loss allows you to start cashing in on the greater speed and accuracy that computers provide.

If you're storing important data, you have four main concerns:

- Storing data needs to be quick and easy, because you're likely to do it often.

- The storage medium must be reliable. You don't want to come back later and find some (or all) of your data missing.

- Data retrieval needs to be quick and easy, regardless of how many items you store.

- You need an easy way to separate the exact information that you want today from the tons of data that you don't want right now.

State-of-the-art computer databases satisfy these four criteria. If you store more than a dozen or so data items, you probably want to store those items in a database.

What Is a Database?

The term *database* has fallen into loose use lately, losing much of its original meaning. To some people, a database is any collection of data items (phone books, laundry lists, parchment scrolls . . . whatever). Other people define the term more strictly.

In this book, I define a *database* as a self-describing collection of integrated records. And yes, that does imply computer technology, complete with languages such as SQL.

A *record* is a representation of some physical or conceptual object. Say, for example, that you want to keep track of a business's customers. You assign a record for each customer. Each record has multiple *attributes,* such as name, address, and telephone number. Individual names, addresses, and so on are the *data.*

A database consists of both data and *metadata*. Metadata is the data that describes the data's structure within a database. If you know how your data is arranged, then you can retrieve it. Because the database contains a description of its own structure, it's *self-describing*. The database is *integrated* because it includes not only data items but also the relationships among data items.

The database stores metadata in an area called the *data dictionary,* which describes the tables, columns, indexes, constraints, and other items that make up the database.

Because a flat file system (described later in this chapter) has no metadata, applications written to work with flat files must contain the equivalent of the metadata as part of the application program.

Database Size and Complexity

Databases come in all sizes, from simple collections of a few records to mammoth systems holding millions of records.

A *personal database* is designed for use by a single person on a single computer. Such a database usually has a rather simple structure and a relatively small size. A *departmental* or *workgroup database* is used by the members of a single department or workgroup within an organization. This type of database is generally larger than a personal database and is necessarily more complex; such a database must handle multiple users trying to access the same data at the same time. An *enterprise database* can be huge. Enterprise databases may model the critical information flow of entire large organizations.

What Is a Database Management System?

Glad you asked. A *database management system (DBMS)* is a set of programs used to define, administer, and process databases and their associated applications. The database being managed is, in essence, a structure that you build to hold valuable data. A DBMS is the tool you use to build that structure and operate on the data contained within the database.

You can find many DBMS programs on the market today. Some run only on mainframe computers, some only on minicomputers, and some only on personal computers. A strong trend, however, is for such products to work on multiple platforms or on networks that contain all three classes of machines.

A DBMS that runs on platforms of multiple classes, large and small, is called *scalable*.

The value is not in the data, but in the structure

Years ago, some clever person calculated that if you reduce human beings to their components of carbon, hydrogen, oxygen, and nitrogen atoms (plus traces of others), they would be worth only 97 cents. However droll this assessment, it's misleading. People aren't composed of mere isolated collections of atoms. Our atoms combine into enzymes, proteins, hormones, and many other substances that would cost millions of dollars per ounce on the pharmaceutical market. The precise structure of these combinations of atoms is what gives them greater value. By analogy, database structure makes possible the interpretation of seemingly meaningless data. The structure brings to the surface patterns, trends, and tendencies in the data. Unstructured data — like uncombined atoms — has little or no value.

Whatever the size of the computer that hosts the database — and regardless of whether the machine is connected to a network — the flow of information between database and user is always the same. Figure 1-1 shows that the user communicates with the database through the DBMS. The DBMS masks the physical details of the database storage so that the application only has to concern itself with the logical characteristics of the data, not how the data is stored.

Figure 1-1:
A block diagram of a DBMS-based information system.

Flat Files

Where structured data is concerned, the flat file is as simple as it gets. No, a flat file isn't a folder that's been squashed under a stack of books. *Flat files* are so called because they have minimal structure. If they were buildings, they'd barely stick up from the ground. A flat file is simply a collection of data records, one after another, in a specified format — the data, the whole data, and nothing but the data — in effect, a list. In computer terms, a flat file is simple. Because the file doesn't store structural information (metadata), its overhead (stuff in the file that is not data) is minimal.

Say that you want to keep track of the names and addresses of your company's customers in a flat file system. The system may have a structure something like this:

```
Harold Percival26262 S. Howards Mill Rd Westminster CA92683
Jerry Appel     32323 S. River Lane Rd  Santa Ana   CA92705
Adrian Hansen   232   Glenwood Court     Anaheim     CA92640
John Baker      2222  Lafayette St       Garden GroveCA92643
Michael Pens    77730 S. New Era Rd      Irvine      CA92715
Bob Michimoto   25252 S. Kelmsley Dr     Stanton     CA92610
Linda Smith     444   S.E. Seventh St    Costa Mesa  CA92635
Robert Funnell  2424  Sheri Court        Anaheim     CA92640
Bill Checkal    9595  Curry Dr           Stanton     CA92610
Jed Style       3535  Randall St         Santa Ana   CA92705
```

As you can see, the file contains nothing but data. Each field has a fixed length (the Name field, for example, is always exactly 15 characters long), and no structure separates one field from another. The person who created the database assigned field positions and lengths. Any program using this file must "know" how each field was assigned, because that information is not contained in the database itself.

Such low overhead means that operating on flat files can be very fast. On the minus side, however, application programs must include logic that manipulates the file's data at a very low level of complexity. The application must know exactly where and how the file stores its data. Thus, for small systems, flat files work fine. The larger a system is, however, the more cumbersome a flat file system becomes.

Using a database instead of a flat file system eliminates duplication of effort. Although database files themselves may have more overhead, the applications can be more portable across various hardware platforms and operating systems. A database also makes writing application programs easier because the programmer doesn't need to know the physical details of where and how the data is stored.

Databases eliminate duplication of effort, because the DBMS handles the data-manipulation details. Applications written to operate on flat files must include those details in the application code. If multiple applications all access the same flat file data, these applications must all (redundantly) include that data manipulation code. By using a DBMS, you don't need to include such code in the applications at all.

Clearly, if a flat file-based application includes data-manipulation code that only runs on a particular hardware platform, then migrating the application to a new platform is a headache waiting to happen. You have to change all the hardware-specific code — and that's just for openers. Migrating a similar DBMS-based application to another platform is much simpler — fewer complicated steps, fewer aspirin consumed.

Database Models

Different as databases may be in size, they are generally always structured according to one of three database models:

- ✔ **Relational:** Nowadays, new installations of database management systems are almost exclusively of the relational type. Organizations that already have a major investment in hierarchical or network technology may add to the existing model, but groups that have no need to maintain compatibility with so-called *legacy systems* nearly always choose the relational model for their databases.

- ✔ **Hierarchical:** Hierarchical databases are aptly named because they have a simple hierarchical structure that allows fast data access. They suffer from redundancy problems and their structural inflexibility makes database modification difficult.

- ✔ **Network:** Network databases have minimal redundancy but pay for that advantage with structural complexity.

The first databases to see wide use were large organizational databases that today would be called enterprise databases, built according to either the hierarchical or the network model. Systems built according to the relational model followed several years later. SQL is a strictly modern language; it applies only to the relational model and its descendant, the object-relational model. So here's where this book says, "So long, it's been good to know ya," to the hierarchical and network models.

New database management systems that are not based on the relational model probably conform to the newer object model or the hybrid object-relational model.

Relational model

Dr. E. F. Codd of IBM first formulated the relational database model in 1970, and this model started appearing in products about a decade later. Ironically, IBM did not deliver the first relational DBMS. That distinction went to a small start-up company, which named its product Oracle.

Relational databases have replaced earlier database types because relational databases have valuable attributes that distinguish them as superior. Probably the most important of these attributes is that relational databases enable you to change the database structure without making changes to applications that were based on the old structures. Suppose, for example, that you add one or more new columns to a database table. You don't need to change any previously written applications that will continue to process that table unless you alter one or more of the columns used by those applications.

Of course, if you remove a column that an existing application references, you experience problems no matter what database model you follow. One of the best ways to make a database application crash is to ask it to retrieve a kind of data that your database doesn't contain.

Why relational is better

In applications written with DBMSs that follow the hierarchical or network model, database structure is *hard-coded* into the application. That is, the application is dependent on the specific physical implementation of the database. If you add a new attribute to the database, you must change your application to accommodate the change, whether or not the application uses the new attribute.

Relational databases offer structural flexibility; applications written for those databases are easier to maintain than similar applications written for hierarchical or network databases. That same structural flexibility enables you to retrieve combinations of data that you may not have anticipated needing at the time of the database's design.

Components of a relational database

Relational databases gain their flexibility because their data resides in tables that are largely independent of each other. You can add, delete, or change data in a table without affecting the data in the other tables, provided that the affected table is not a *parent* of any of the other tables. (Parent-child table relationships are explained in Chapter 5, and no, they don't have anything to do with discussing allowances over dinner.) In this section, I show what these tables consist of and how they relate to the other parts of a relational database.

Holidays bring families together

At holiday time, many of my relatives come to my house and sit down at my table. Databases have relations, too, but each of their relations has its own table. A relational database is made up of one or more relations.

A *relation* is a two-dimensional array of rows and columns, containing single-valued entries and no duplicate rows. Each cell in the array can have only one value, and no two rows may be identical.

Most people are familiar with two-dimensional arrays of rows and columns, in the form of electronic spreadsheets such as Microsoft Excel. The offensive statistics listed on the back of a major-league baseball player's baseball card are another example of such an array. On the baseball card are columns for year, team, games played, at-bats, hits, runs scored, runs batted in, doubles, triples, home runs, bases on balls, steals, and batting average. A row covers each year that the player has played in the Major Leagues. You can also store this data in a relation (a table), which has the same basic structure. Figure 1-2 shows a relational database table holding the offensive statistics for a single major-league player. In practice, such a table would hold the statistics for an entire team or perhaps the whole league.

Figure 1-2:
A table showing a baseball player's offensive statistics.

Player	Year	Team	Game	At Bat	Hits	Runs	RBI	2B	3B	HR	Walk	Steals	Bat. Avg.
Roberts	1988	Padres	5	9	3	1	0	0	0	0	1	0	.333
Roberts	1989	Padres	117	329	99	81	25	15	8	3	49	21	.301
Roberts	1990	Padres	149	556	172	104	44	36	3	9	55	46	.309

Columns in the array are *self-consistent,* in that a column has the same meaning in every row. If a column contains a player's last name in one row, the column must contain a player's last name in all rows. The order in which the rows and columns appear in the array has no significance. As far as the DBMS is concerned, it doesn't matter which column is first, which is next, and which is last. The same is true of rows. The DBMS processes the table the same way regardless of the organization.

Every column in a database table embodies a single attribute of the table, just like that baseball card. The column's meaning is the same for every row of the table. A table may, for example, contain the names, addresses, and telephone numbers of all an organization's customers. Each row in the table (also called a *record,* or a *tuple*) holds the data for a single customer. Each column holds a single attribute, such as customer number, customer name, customer street, customer city, customer state, customer postal code, or customer telephone number. Figure 1-3 shows some of the rows and columns of such a table.

The *relations* in a database model correspond to *tables* in a database based on the model. Try to say that ten times fast.

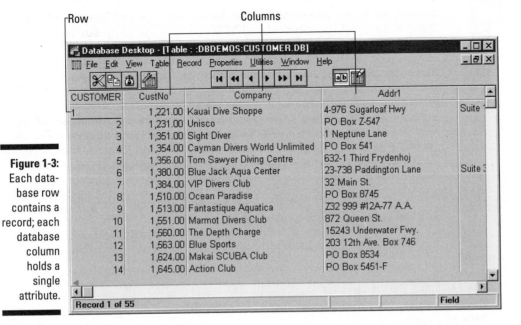

Figure 1-3:
Each data-
base row
contains a
record; each
database
column
holds a
single
attribute.

Enjoy the view

One of my favorite views is of the Yosemite Valley from the mouth of the Wawona Tunnel, late on a spring afternoon. Golden light bathes the sheer face of El Capitan, Half Dome glistens in the distance, and Bridal Veil Falls forms a silver cascade of sparkling water, while a trace of wispy clouds weaves a tapestry across the sky. Databases have views as well — even if they're not quite that picturesque. The beauty of database views is their sheer usefulness when you're working with your data.

Tables can contain many columns and rows. Sometimes all of that data interests you, and sometimes it doesn't. Only some columns of a table may interest you, or perhaps you want to see only rows that satisfy a certain condition. Some columns of one table and some other columns of a related table may interest you. To eliminate data that isn't relevant to your current needs, you can create a view. A _view_ is a subset of a database that an application can process. It may contain parts of one or more tables.

Views are sometimes called _virtual tables._ To the application or the user, views behave the same as tables. Views, however, have no independent existence. Views allow you to look at data, but views are not part of the data.

Say, for example, that you're working with a database that has a CUSTOMER table and an INVOICE table. The CUSTOMER table has the columns `CustomerID, FirstName, LastName, Street, City, State, Zipcode,` and `Phone.` The INVOICE table has the columns `InvoiceNumber, CustomerID, Date, TotalSale, TotalRemitted,` and `FormOfPayment.`

A national sales manager wants to look at a screen that contains only the customer's first name, last name, and telephone number. Creating from the CUSTOMER table a view that contains only those three columns enables the manager to view what he or she needs without having to see all the unwanted data in the other columns. Figure 1-4 shows the derivation of the national sales manager's view.

CUSTOMER Table

Customer ID
FirstName
LastName
Street
City
State
Zipcode
Phone

SALES_MGR View

FirstName
LastName
Phone

Figure 1-4: The sales manager's view derives from the CUSTOMER table.

INVOICE Table

InvoiceNumber
CustomerID
Date
TotalSale
TotalRemitted
FormOfPayment

A branch manager may want to look at the names and phone numbers of all customers whose zip codes fall between 90000 and 93999 (southern and central California). A view that places a restriction on the rows it retrieves, as well as the columns it displays, does the job. Figure 1-5 shows the sources for the branch manager's view's columns.

The accounts payable manager may want to look at customer names from the CUSTOMER table and `Date, TotalSale, TotalRemitted,` and `FormOfPayment` from the INVOICE table, where `TotalRemitted` is less than `TotalSale.` The latter would be the case if full payment hasn't yet been made. This need requires a view that draws from both tables. Figure 1-6 shows data flowing into the accounts payable manager's view from both the CUSTOMER and INVOICE tables.

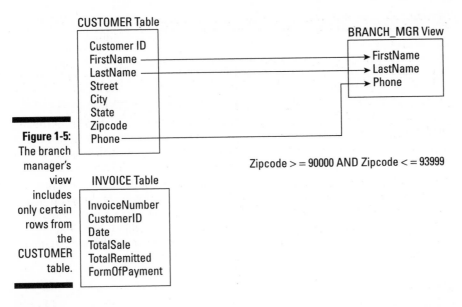

Figure 1-5:
The branch
manager's
view
includes
only certain
rows from
the
CUSTOMER
table.

 Views are useful because they enable you to extract and format database data without physically altering the stored data. Chapter 6 illustrates how to create a view by using SQL.

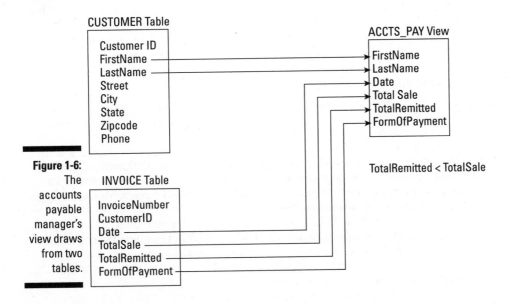

Figure 1-6:
The
accounts
payable
manager's
view draws
from two
tables.

Schemas, domains, and constraints

A database is more than a collection of tables. Additional structures, on several levels, help to maintain the data's integrity. A database's *schema* provides an overall organization to the tables. The *domain* of a table column tells you what values you may store in the column. You can apply *constraints* to a database table to prevent anyone (including yourself) from storing invalid data in the table.

Schemas

The structure of an entire database is its *schema,* or *conceptual view.* This structure is sometimes also called the *complete logical view* of the database. The schema is metadata — as such, it's part of the database. The metadata itself, which describes the database's structure, is stored in tables that are just like the tables that store the regular data. Even metadata is data; that's the beauty of it.

Domains

An attribute of a relation (that is, a column of a table) can assume some finite number of values. The set of all such values is the *domain* of the attribute.

Say, for example, that you're an automobile dealer who handles the newly introduced Curarri GT 4000 sports coupe. You keep track of the cars you have in stock in a database table that you name INVENTORY. You name one of the table columns Color, which holds the exterior color of each car. The GT 4000 comes in only four colors: blazing crimson, midnight black, snowflake white, and metallic gray. Those four colors are the domain of the Color attribute.

Constraints

Constraints are an important, although often overlooked, component of a database. Constraints are rules that determine what values the table attributes can assume.

By applying tight constraints to a column, you can prevent people from entering invalid data into that column. Of course, every value that is legitimately in the domain of the column must satisfy all the column's constraints. As I mention in the preceding section, a column's domain is the set of all values that the column can contain. A constraint is a restriction on what a column may contain. The characteristics of a table column, plus the constraints that apply to that column, determine the column's domain. By applying constraints, you can prevent users from entering data into a column that falls outside the column's domain.

In the auto dealership example, you can constrain the database to accept only those four values in the Color column. If a data entry operator then tries to enter in the Color column a value of, for example, forest green, the system refuses to accept the entry. Data entry can't proceed until the operator enters a valid value into the Color field.

You may wonder what happens when the Curarri AutoWerks decides to offer a forest green version of the GT5000 as a mid-year option. The answer is (drum roll, please) job security for database maintenance programmers. This kind of thing happens all the time and requires updates to the database structure. Only people who know how to modify the database structure (such as you) will be able to prevent a major snafu.

The object model challenges the relational model

The relational model has been fantastically successful in a wide variety of application areas. However, it is not free of its share of issues. The limitations have been made more visible by the rise in popularity of object-oriented programming languages such as C++, Java, and C#. Such languages are capable of handling more complex problems than traditional languages due to their advanced features, such as user-extensible type systems, encapsulation, inheritance, dynamic binding of methods, complex and composite objects, and object identity.

I am not going to explain all that jargon in this book (although I do touch on some of these terms later). Suffice it to say that the classic relational model doesn't mesh well with many of these features. As a result, database management systems based on the object model have been developed and are available on the market. As yet, their market share is relatively small.

The object-relational model

Database designers, like everyone else, are constantly searching for the best of all possible worlds. They mused, "Wouldn't it be great if we could have the advantages of an object-oriented database system, and still retain compatibility with the relational system that we have come to know and love?" This kind of thinking led to the hybrid object-relational model. Object-relational DBMSs extend the relational model to include support for object-oriented data modeling. Object-oriented features have been added to the international

SQL standard, allowing relational DBMS vendors to transform their products into object-relational DBMSs, while retaining compatibility with the standard. Thus, whereas the SQL-92 standard describes a purely relational database model, SQL:1999 describes an object-relational database model. SQL:2003 has even more object-oriented features. The SQL/XML:2005 update to the standard, as the name implies, is primarily concerned with XML rather than object orientation.

In this book, I describe ISO/IEC international standard SQL. This is primarily a relational database model. I also include the object-oriented extensions to the standard that were introduced in SQL:1999, and the additional extensions included in SQL:2003. The object-oriented features of the new standard allow developers to apply SQL databases to problems that are too complex to address with the older, purely relational, paradigm.

Database Design Considerations

A database is a representation of a physical or conceptual structure, such as an organization, an automobile assembly, or the performance statistics of all the major-league baseball clubs. The accuracy of the representation depends on the level of detail of the database design. The amount of effort that you put into database design should depend on the type of information you want to get out of the database. Too much detail is a waste of effort, time, and hard drive space. Too little detail may render the database worthless.

Decide how much detail you need now and how much you may need in the future — and then provide exactly that level of detail in your design (no more and no less). But don't be surprised if you have to adjust the design eventually to meet changing real-world needs.

Today's database management systems, complete with attractive graphical user interfaces and intuitive design tools, can give the would-be database designer a false sense of security. These systems make designing a database seem comparable to building a spreadsheet or engaging in some other relatively straightforward task. No such luck. Database design is difficult. If you do it incorrectly, you get a database that becomes gradually more corrupt as time goes on. Often the problem doesn't turn up until after you devote a great deal of effort to data entry. By the time you know that you have a problem, it's already serious. In many cases, the only solution is to completely redesign the database and reenter all the data. The up side is that by the time you finish your second version of the same database you realize how much better you've gotten at it.

Chapter 2

SQL Fundamentals

In This Chapter

▶ Understanding SQL

▶ Clearing up SQL misconceptions

▶ Taking a look at the different SQL standards

▶ Getting familiar with standard SQL commands and reserved words

▶ Representing numbers, characters, dates, times, and other data types

▶ Exploring null values and constraints

▶ Putting SQL to work in a client/server system

▶ Considering SQL on a network

SQL is a flexible language that you can use in a variety of ways. It's the most widely used tool for communicating with a relational database. In this chapter, I explain what SQL is and isn't — specifically, what distinguishes SQL from other types of computer languages. Then I introduce the commands and data types that standard SQL supports and explain key concepts: *null values* and *constraints*. Finally, I give an overview of how SQL fits into the client/server environment, as well as the Internet and organizational intranets.

What SQL Is and Isn't

The first thing to understand about SQL is that SQL isn't a *procedural language*, as are BASIC, C, C++, C#, and Java. To solve a problem in one of those procedural languages, you write a procedure that performs one specific operation after another until the task is complete. The procedure may be a linear sequence or may loop back on itself, but in either case, the programmer specifies the order of execution.

SQL, on the other hand, is *nonprocedural*. To solve a problem using SQL, simply tell SQL *what* you want (as if you were talking to Aladdin's genie) instead of telling the system *how to get* you what you want. The database management system (DBMS) decides the best way to get you what you request.

All right. I just told you that SQL is not a procedural language. This is essentially true. However, millions of programmers out there (and you are probably one of them) are accustomed to solving problems in a procedural manner. So, in recent years, there has been a lot of pressure to add some procedural functionality to SQL. Thus, SQL now incorporates procedural language facilities, such as BEGIN blocks, IF statements, functions, and procedures. These facilities have been added so you can store programs at the server, where multiple clients can use these programs repeatedly.

To illustrate what I mean by "tell the system what you want," suppose that you have an EMPLOYEE table and you want to retrieve from that table the rows that correspond to all your senior people. You want to define a senior person as anyone older than age 40 or anyone earning more than $60,000 per year. You can make the desired retrieval by using the following query:

```
SELECT * FROM EMPLOYEE WHERE Age>40 OR Salary>60000 ;
```

This statement retrieves all rows from the EMPLOYEE table where either the value in the Age column is greater than 40 or the value in the Salary column is greater than 60,000. In SQL, you don't need to specify how the information is retrieved. The database engine examines the database and decides for itself how to fulfill your request. You need only to specify what data you want to retrieve.

A *query* is a question you ask the database. If any of the data in the database satisfies the conditions of your query, SQL retrieves that data.

Current SQL implementations lack many of the basic programming constructs fundamental to most other languages. Real-world applications usually require at least some of these programming constructs, which is why SQL is actually a data *sublanguage*. Even with the extensions that were added in 1999, 2003, and 2005, you still need to use SQL in combination with a procedural language, such as C, to create a complete application.

You can extract information from a database in one of two ways:

✔ **Make an *ad hoc query* from a computer console by just typing an SQL statement and reading the results from the screen.** *Console* is the traditional term for the computer hardware that does the job of the keyboard and screen used in current PC-based systems. Queries from the console are appropriate when you want a quick answer to a specific question. To meet an immediate need, you may require information that you never needed before from a database. You're likely never to need that information again either, but you need it now. Enter the appropriate SQL query statement from the keyboard, and in due time, the result appears on your screen.

✔ **Execute a program that collects information from the database and then reports on the information, either on-screen or in a printed report.** Incorporating an SQL query directly into a program is a good way to run a complex query that you're likely to run again in the future. That way, you can formulate a query just once for use as often as you want. Chapter 15 explains how to incorporate SQL code into programs written in another language.

A (Very) Little History

SQL originated in one of IBM's research laboratories, as did relational database theory. In the early 1970s, as IBM researchers performed early development on relational DBMS (or RDBMS) systems, they created a data sublanguage to operate on these systems. They named the prerelease version of this sublanguage *SEQUEL* (*S*tructured *E*nglish *QUE*ry *L*anguage). However, when it came time to formally release their query language as a product, they wanted to make sure that people understood that the released product was different from and superior to the prerelease DBMS. Therefore, the whiz kids at IBM decided to give the released product a name that was different from SEQUEL but still recognizable as a member of the same family. So they named it SQL (pronounced *ess-que-ell*).

IBM's work with relational databases and SQL was well known in the industry even before IBM introduced its SQL/DS RDBMS in 1981. By that time, Relational Software, Inc. (now Oracle Corporation) had already released its first relational database management system (RDBMS). These early products immediately set the standard for a new class of database management systems. They incorporated SQL, which became the de facto standard for data sublanguages. Vendors of other relational database management systems came out with their own versions of SQL. These other implementations typically contained all the core functionality of the IBM products but were extended in ways that took advantage of the particular strengths of the underlying RDBMS. As a result, although nearly all vendors used some form of SQL, compatibility across platforms was poor.

An *implementation* is a particular RDBMS running on a specific hardware platform.

Soon, a movement began to create a universally recognized SQL standard to which everyone could adhere. In 1986, ANSI (the American National Standards Institute) released a formal standard it named *SQL-86*. ANSI updated that standard in 1989 to *SQL-89* and again in 1992 to *SQL-92*. As DBMS vendors proceed through new releases of their products, they try to bring their implementations ever closer to this standard. This effort has brought the goal of true SQL portability much closer to reality.

The most recent full version of the SQL standard is SQL:2003 (ISO/IEC 9075-X: 2003), although corrections and extensions were added in 2005. In this book, I describe SQL as SQL:2003 defines the language, including the 2005 extensions. Every specific SQL implementation differs from the standard to a certain extent. Because the complete SQL standard is comprehensive, currently available implementations are unlikely to support it fully. However, DBMS vendors are working to support a core subset of the standard SQL language. The full ISO/IEC standard is available for purchase at webstore.ansi.org.

SQL Commands

The SQL command language consists of a limited number of commands that specifically relate to data handling. Some of these commands perform data-definition functions; some perform data-manipulation functions; and others perform data-control functions. I cover the data-definition commands and data-manipulation commands in Chapters 4 through 12, and the data-control commands in Chapters 13 and 14.

To comply with SQL:2003, an implementation must include all the core features. It may also include extensions to the core set (which the SQL:2003 specification also describes). But back to basics. Table 2-1 lists the core SQL:2003 commands.

Table 2-1	Core SQL:2003 Commands	
ALTER DOMAIN	DECLARE CURSOR	FREE LOCATOR
ALTER TABLE	DECLARE TABLE	GET DIAGNOSTICS
CALL	DELETE	GRANT
CLOSE	DISCONNECT	HOLD LOCATOR
COMMIT	DROP ASSERTION	INSERT
CONNECT	DROP CHARACTER SET	OPEN
CREATE ASSERTION	DROP COLLATION	RELEASE SAVEPOINT
CREATE CHARACTER	DROP DOMAIN	RETURN
CREATE COLLATION	DROP ORDERING	REVOKE
CREATE DOMAIN	DROP ROLE	ROLLBACK

CREATE FUNCTION	DROP SCHEMA	SAVEPOINT
CREATE METHOD	DROP SPECIFIC FUNCTION	SELECT
CREATE ORDERING	DROP SPECIFIC PROCEDURE	SET CONNECTION
CREATE PROCEDURE	DROP SPECIFIC ROUTINE	SET CONSTRAINTS
CREATE ROLE	DROP TABLE	SET ROLE
CREATE SCHEMA	DROP TRANSFORM	SET SESSION AUTHORIZATION
CREATE TABLE	DROP TRANSLATION	SET SESSION CHARACTERISTICS
CREATE TRANSFORM	DROP TRIGGER	SET TIME ZONE
CREATE TRANSLATION	DROP TYPE	SET TRANSACTION
CREATE TRIGGER	DROP VIEW	START TRANSACTION
CREATE TYPE	FETCH	UPDATE
CREATE VIEW		

If you're among those programmers who love to try out new capabilities, rejoice.

Reserved Words

In addition to the commands, a number of other words have a special significance within SQL. These words, along with the commands, are reserved for specific uses, so you can't use them as variable names or in any other way that differs from their intended use. You can easily see why tables, columns, and variables should not be given names that appear on the reserved word list. Imagine the confusion that a statement such as the following would cause:

```
SELECT SELECT FROM SELECT WHERE SELECT = WHERE ;
```

A complete list of SQL reserved words appears in Appendix A.

Data Types

Depending on their histories, different SQL implementations support a variety of data types. The SQL specification recognizes six predefined general types:

- ✔ Numerics
- ✔ Strings
- ✔ Booleans
- ✔ Datetimes
- ✔ Intervals
- ✔ XML

Within each of these general types may be several subtypes (exact numerics, approximate numerics, character strings, bit strings, large object strings). In addition to the built-in, predefined types, SQL supports collection types, constructed types, and user-defined types, all of which I discuss later in this chapter.

If you use an SQL implementation that supports data types that aren't described in the SQL specification, you can keep your database more portable by avoiding these undescribed data types. Before you decide to create and use a user-defined data type, make sure that any DBMS you may want to port to in the future also supports user-defined types.

Exact numerics

As you can probably guess from the name, the *exact numeric* data types enable you to express the value of a number exactly. Five data types fall into this category:

- ✔ INTEGER
- ✔ SMALLINT
- ✔ BIGINT
- ✔ NUMERIC
- ✔ DECIMAL

INTEGER data type

Data of the INTEGER type has no fractional part, and its precision depends on the specific SQL implementation. As the database developer, you can't specify the precision.

The *precision* of a number is the maximum number of digits the number can have.

SMALLINT data type

The SMALLINT data type is also for integers, but the precision of a SMALLINT in a specific implementation can't be any larger than the precision of an INTEGER on the same implementation. Implementations on IBM System/370 computers commonly represent SMALLINT and INTEGER with 16-bit and 32-bit binary numbers respectively. In many implementations, SMALLINT and INTEGER are the same.

If you're defining a database table column to hold integer data and you know that the range of values in the column won't exceed the precision of SMALLINT data on your implementation, assign the column the SMALLINT type rather than the INTEGER type. This assignment may enable your DBMS to conserve storage space.

BIGINT data type

The BIGINT data type is defined as a type whose precision is at least as great as that of the INTEGER type (it may be greater). The exact precision of a BIGINT data type is implementation dependent.

NUMERIC data type

NUMERIC data can have a fractional component in addition to its integer component. You can specify both the precision and the scale of NUMERIC data. (Precision, remember, is the maximum number of digits possible.)

The *scale* of a number is the number of digits in its fractional part. The scale of a number can't be negative or larger than that number's precision.

If you specify the NUMERIC data type, your SQL implementation gives you exactly the precision and scale that you request. You may specify NUMERIC and get a default precision and scale, or NUMERIC (p) and get your specified precision and the default scale, or NUMERIC (p, s) and get both your specified precision and your specified scale. The parameters p and s are placeholders that would be replaced by actual values in a data declaration.

Say, for example, that the NUMERIC data type's default precision for your SQL implementation is 12 and the default scale is 6. If you specify a database column as having a NUMERIC data type, the column can hold numbers up to 999,999.999999. If, on the other hand, you specify a data type of NUMERIC (10) for a column, that column can hold only numbers with a maximum value of 9,999.999999. The parameter (10) specifies the maximum number of digits possible in the number. If you specify a data type of NUMERIC (10,2) for a column, that column can hold numbers with a maximum value of 99,999,999.99. In this case, you may still have ten total digits, but only two of the digits can fall to the right of the decimal point.

NUMERIC data is used for values such as 595.72. That value has a precision of 5 (the total number of digits) and a scale of 2 (the number of digits to the right of the decimal point). A data type of NUMERIC (5,2) is appropriate for such numbers.

DECIMAL data type

The DECIMAL data type is similar to NUMERIC. This data type can have a fractional component, and you can specify its precision and scale. The difference is that the precision your implementation supplies may be greater than what you specify, and if so, the implementation uses the greater precision. If you do not specify precision or scale, the implementation uses default values, as it does with the NUMERIC type.

An item that you specify as NUMERIC (5,2) can never contain a number with an absolute value greater than 999.99. An item that you specify as DECIMAL (5,2) can always hold values up to 999.99, but if the implementation permits larger values, the DBMS doesn't reject values larger than 999.99.

Use the NUMERIC or DECIMAL type if your data has fractional positions, and use the INTEGER, SMALLINT, or BIGINT type if your data always consists of whole numbers. Use the NUMERIC type if you want to maximize portability, because a value that you define as NUMERIC (5,2), for example, holds the same range of values on all systems.

Approximate numerics

Some quantities have such a large range of possible values (many orders of magnitude) that a computer with a given register size can't represent all the values exactly. (Examples of *register sizes* are 32 bits, 64 bits, and 128 bits.) Usually in such cases, exactness isn't necessary, and a close approximation is acceptable. SQL defines three approximate numeric data types to handle this kind of data.

REAL data type

The REAL data type gives you a single-precision floating-point number, the precision of which depends on the implementation. In general, the hardware you use determines precision. A 64-bit machine, for example, gives you more precision than does a 32-bit machine.

A *floating-point number* is a number that contains a decimal point. The decimal point "floats" or appears in different locations in the number, depending on the number's value. 3.1, 3.14, and 3.14159 are examples of floating-point numbers.

DOUBLE PRECISION data type

The DOUBLE PRECISION data type gives you a double-precision floating-point number, the precision of which again depends on the implementation. Surprisingly, the meaning of the word DOUBLE also depends on the implementation. Double-precision arithmetic is primarily employed by scientific users. Different scientific disciplines have different needs in the area of precision. Some SQL implementations cater to one category of users, and other implementations cater to other categories of users.

In some systems, the DOUBLE PRECISION type has exactly twice the capacity of the REAL data type for both mantissa and exponent. (In case you've forgotten what you learned in high school, you can represent any number as a *mantissa* multiplied by ten raised to the power given by an exponent. You can write 6,626, for example, as 6.626E3. The number 6.626 is the mantissa, which you multiply by ten raised to the third power; in that case, *3* is the exponent.)

You gain no benefit by representing numbers that are fairly close to one (such as 6,626 or even 6,626,000) with an approximate numeric data type. Exact numeric types work just as well, and after all, they're exact. For numbers that are either very near zero or much larger than one, however, such as 6.626E-34 (a very small number), you must use an approximate numeric type. The exact numeric types can't hold such numbers. On other systems, the DOUBLE PRECISION type gives you somewhat more than twice the mantissa capacity and somewhat less than twice the exponent capacity as the REAL type. On yet another type of system, the DOUBLE PRECISION type gives double the mantissa capacity but the same exponent capacity as the REAL type. In this case, accuracy doubles, but range does not.

The SQL specification doesn't try to arbitrate or establish by fiat what DOUBLE PRECISION means. The specification requires only that the precision of a DOUBLE PRECISION number be greater than the precision of a REAL number. Although it's rather weak, this constraint is probably the best possible in light of the great differences you encounter in hardware.

FLOAT data type

The FLOAT data type is most useful if you think that you may someday migrate your database to a hardware platform with different register sizes than your current platform. By using the FLOAT data type, you can specify a precision — for example, FLOAT (5). If your hardware supports the specified precision with its single-precision circuitry, single-precision arithmetic is what your system uses. If the specified precision requires double-precision arithmetic, the system uses double-precision arithmetic.

Using FLOAT rather than REAL or DOUBLE PRECISION makes porting your databases to other hardware easier, because the FLOAT data type enables you to specify precision. The precision of REAL and DOUBLE PRECISION numbers is hardware-dependent.

If you aren't sure whether to use the exact numeric data types (NUMERIC/ DECIMAL) or the approximate numeric data types (FLOAT/REAL), use the exact numeric types. The exact data types demand fewer system resources and, of course, give exact (rather than approximate) results. If the range of possible values of your data is large enough to require you to use approximate data types, you can probably determine this fact in advance.

Character strings

Databases store many types of data, including graphic images, sounds, and animations. I expect odors to come next. Can you imagine a three-dimensional 1600-x-1200, 24-bit color image of a large slice of pepperoni pizza on your screen, while an odor sample taken at DiFilippi's Pizza Grotto replays through your super-multimedia card? Such a setup may get frustrating — at least until you can afford to add taste-type data to your system as well. Alas, you can expect to wait a long time before odor and taste become standard SQL data types. These days, the data types that you use most commonly — after the numeric types, of course — are the character-string types.

You have three main types of character data: fixed character data (CHARACTER or CHAR), varying character data (CHARACTER VARYING or VARCHAR), and character large object data (CHARACTER LARGE OBJECT or CLOB). You also have three variants of these types of character data: NATIONAL CHARACTER, NATIONAL CHARACTER VARYING, and NATIONAL CHARACTER LARGE OBJECT.

CHARACTER data type

If you define the data type of a column as CHARACTER or CHAR, you can specify the number of characters the column holds by using the syntax CHARACTER (*x*), where *x* is the number of characters. If you specify a column's data type as CHARACTER (16), for example, the maximum length of any data you can enter in the column is 16 characters. If you don't specify an argument (that is, you don't provide a value in place of the *x*), SQL assumes a field length of one character. If you enter data into a CHARACTER field of a specified length and you enter fewer characters than the specified number, SQL fills the remaining character spaces with blanks.

CHARACTER VARYING data type

The CHARACTER VARYING data type is useful if entries in a column can vary in length, but you don't want SQL to pad the field with blanks. This data type enables you to store exactly the number of characters that the user enters. No default value exists for this data type. To specify this data type, use the form CHARACTER VARYING (x) or VARCHAR (x), where x is the maximum number of characters permitted.

CHARACTER LARGE OBJECT data type

The CHARACTER LARGE OBJECT (CLOB) data type was introduced with SQL:1999. As its name implies, it is used with huge character strings that are too large for the CHARACTER type. CLOBs behave much like ordinary character strings, but there are a number of restrictions on what you can do with them.

For one thing, a CLOB may not be used in a PRIMARY KEY, FOREIGN KEY, or UNIQUE predicate. Furthermore, it may not be used in a comparison other than one for either equality or inequality. Because of their large size, applications generally do not transfer CLOBs to or from a database. Instead, a special client-side type called a *CLOB locator* is used to manipulate the CLOB data. It is a parameter whose value identifies a character large object.

NATIONAL CHARACTER, NATIONAL CHARACTER VARYING, and NATIONAL CHARACTER LARGE OBJECT data types

Various languages have some characters that differ from any characters in another language. For example, German has some special characters not present in the English language character set. Some languages, such as Russian, have a very different character set than the English one. For example, if you specify the English character set as the default for your system, you can use alternate character sets because the NATIONAL CHARACTER, NATIONAL CHARACTER VARYING, and NATIONAL CHARACTER LARGE OBJECT data types function the same as the CHARACTER, CHARACTER VARYING, and CHARACTER LARGE OBJECT data types, except that the character set you're specifying is different from the default character set. You can specify the character set as you define a table column. If you want, each column can use a different character set. The following example of a table-creation statement uses multiple character sets:

```
CREATE TABLE XLATE (
   LANGUAGE_1 CHARACTER (40),
   LANGUAGE_2 CHARACTER VARYING (40) CHARACTER SET GREEK,
   LANGUAGE_3 NATIONAL CHARACTER (40),
   LANGUAGE_4 CHARACTER (40)    CHARACTER SET KANJI
   ) ;
```

The LANGUAGE_1 column contains characters in the implementation's default character set. The LANGUAGE_3 column contains characters in the implementation's national character set. The LANGUAGE_2 column contains Greek characters. And the LANGUAGE_4 column contains kanji characters.

Booleans

The BOOLEAN data type comprises the distinct truth values *true* and *false,* as well as *unknown.* If either a Boolean *true* or *false* value is compared to a NULL or *unknown* truth value, the result will have the *unknown* value.

Datetimes

The SQL standard defines five data types that deal with dates and times. These data types are called *datetime data types,* or simply *datetimes.* Considerable overlap exists among these data types, so some implementations you encounter may not support all five.

Implementations that do not fully support all five data types for dates and times may experience problems with databases that you try to migrate from another implementation. If you have trouble with a migration, check the source and the destination implementations to see how they represent dates and times.

DATE data type

The DATE type stores year, month, and day values of a date, in that order. The year value is four digits long, and the month and day values are both two digits long. A DATE value can represent any date from the year 0001 to the year 9999. The length of a DATE is ten positions, as in 1957-08-14.

TIME WITHOUT TIME ZONE data type

The TIME WITHOUT TIME ZONE data type stores hour, minute, and second values of time. The hours and minutes occupy two digits. The seconds value may be only two digits but may also expand to include an optional fractional part. This data type, therefore, represents a time of 32 minutes and 58.436 seconds past 9 a.m., for example, as 09:32:58.436.

The precision of the fractional part is implementation-dependent but is at least six digits long. A TIME WITHOUT TIME ZONE value takes up eight positions (including colons) when the value has no fractional part, or nine positions (including the decimal point) plus the number of fractional digits when the value does include a fractional part. You specify TIME WITHOUT TIME ZONE type data either as TIME, which gives you the default of no fractional digits, or as TIME WITHOUT TIME ZONE (p), where p is the number of digit positions to the right of the decimal. The example in the preceding paragraph represents a data type of TIME WITHOUT TIME ZONE (3).

TIMESTAMP WITHOUT TIME ZONE data type

TIMESTAMP WITHOUT TIME ZONE data includes both date and time information. The lengths and the restrictions on the values of the components of TIMESTAMP WITHOUT TIME ZONE data are the same as they are for DATE and TIME WITHOUT TIME ZONE data, except for one difference: The default length of the fractional part of the time component of a TIMESTAMP WITHOUT TIME ZONE is six digits rather than zero.

If the value has no fractional digits, the length of a TIMESTAMP WITHOUT TIME ZONE is 19 positions — ten date positions, one space as a separator, and eight time positions, in that order. If fractional digits are present (six digits is the default), the length is 20 positions plus the number of fractional digits. The 20th position is for the decimal point. You specify a field as TIMESTAMP WITHOUT TIME ZONE type by using either TIMESTAMP WITHOUT TIME ZONE or TIMESTAMP WITHOUT TIME ZONE (p), where p is the number of fractional digit positions. The value of p can't be negative, and the implementation determines its maximum value.

TIME WITH TIME ZONE data type

The TIME WITH TIME ZONE data type is the same as the TIME WITHOUT TIME ZONE data type except this type adds information about the offset from *universal time* (UTC, also known as Greenwich Mean Time or GMT). The value of the offset may range anywhere from –12:59 to +13:00. This additional information takes up six more digit positions following the time — a hyphen as a separator, a plus or minus sign, and then the offset in hours (two digits) and minutes (two digits) with a colon in between the hours and minutes. A TIME WITH TIME ZONE value with no fractional part (the default) is 14 positions long. If you specify a fractional part, the field length is 15 positions plus the number of fractional digits.

TIMESTAMP WITH TIME ZONE data type

The TIMESTAMP WITH TIME ZONE data type functions the same as the TIMESTAMP WITHOUT TIME ZONE data type except that this data type also adds information about the offset from universal time. The additional information takes up six more digit positions following the timestamp (see the preceding section for the form of the time zone information). Including time zone data sets up 25 positions for a field with no fractional part and 26 positions plus the number of fractional digits for fields that do include a fractional part (six digits is the default number of fractional digits).

Intervals

The *interval* data types relate closely to the datetime data types. An interval is the difference between two datetime values. In many applications that deal with dates, times, or both, you sometimes need to determine the interval between two dates or two times.

SQL recognizes two distinct types of intervals: the *year-month* interval and the *day-time* interval. A year-month interval is the number of years and months between two dates. A day-time interval is the number of days, hours, minutes, and seconds between two instants within a month. You can't mix calculations involving a year-month interval with calculations involving a day-time interval, because months come in varying lengths (28, 29, 30, or 31 days long).

XML type

The *XML data type* is the newest predefined type. XML data has a tree structure, so a root node may have child nodes, which may, in turn, have children of their own. First introduced in SQL:2003, the XML type has been fleshed out in SQL/XML:2005. The 2005 edition defines five parameterized subtypes, while retaining the original plain-vanilla XML type. XML values can exist as instances of two or even more types, because some of the subtypes are subtypes of other subtypes. Maybe I should call them sub-subtypes, or even sub-sub-subtypes.

Here's a rundown of the XML types you should be familiar with. I've organized this list to begin with the most basic types and end with the most complicated:

- ✔ XML (SEQUENCE): Every value in XML is either an SQL NULL value or an XQuery sequence. That way, every XML value is an instance of the XML (SEQUENCE) type. *XQuery* is a query language specifically designed to extract information from XML data. This is the most basic XML type.

    XML (SEQUENCE) is the least restrictive of the XML types. It can accept values that are not well-formed XML values. The other XML types, on the other hand, aren't quite so forgiving.

- ✔ XML (ANY CONTENT): This is a slightly more restrictive type than XML (SEQUENCE). Every XML value that is either a NULL value or an XQuery document node (or a child of that document node) is an instance of this type. Every instance of XML (ANY CONTENT) is also an instance of XML (SEQUENCE). XML values of the XML (ANY CONTENT) type are not necessarily well formed, either. Such values may be intermediate results in a query that are later reduced to well-formed values.

- ✔ XML (UNTYPED CONTENT): This is more restrictive than XML (ANY CONTENT), and thus any value of the XML (UNTYPED CONTENT) type is also an instance of the XML (ANY CONTENT) type and the XML (SEQUENCE) type. If XML values have undergone some form of schema validation, and at least one has gained a type annotation, then the value is an instance of the XML (ANY CONTENT) type, but not of the XML (UNTYPED CONTENT) type.

✔ XML (ANY DOCUMENT): This is another variant of the XML type. It is a subtype of the XML (ANY CONTENT) type with the added restriction that instances of XML (ANY DOCUMENT) are document nodes that have exactly one element child.

✔ XML (UNTYPED DOCUMENT): This type is the fifth and last XML subtype. Every value that is either the NULL value or an XQuery document node that has exactly one child is an instance of this type. All instances of XML (UNTYPED DOCUMENT) are also instances of XML (UNTYPED CONTENT). Furthermore, all instances of XML (UNTYPED DOCUMENT) are also instances of XML (ANY DOCUMENT). XML (UNTYPED DOCUMENT) is the most restrictive of the subtypes, sharing the restrictions of all the other subtypes. Any document that qualifies as an XML (UNTYPED DOCUMENT) is also an instance of all the other XML subtypes.

ROW types

The ROW data type was introduced with SQL:1999. It's not that easy to understand, and as a beginning to intermediate SQL programmer, you may never use it. After all, people got by without it just fine between 1986 and 1999.

One notable thing about the ROW data type is that it violates the rules of normalization that E. F. Codd declared in the early days of relational database theory. I talk more about those rules in Chapter 5. One of the defining characteristics of first normal form is that a field in a table row may not be multivalued. A field may contain one and only one value. However, the ROW data type allows you to declare an entire row of data to be contained within a single field in a single row of a table — in other words, a row nested within a row.

The *normal forms,* first articulated by Dr. Codd, are defining characteristics of relational databases. Inclusion of the ROW type in the SQL standard was the first attempt to broaden SQL beyond the pure relational model.

Consider the following SQL statement, which defines a ROW type for a person's address information:

```
CREATE ROW TYPE addr_typ (
    Street      CHARACTER VARYING (25),
    City        CHARACTER VARYING(20),
    State       CHARACTER (2),
    PostalCode  CHARACTER VARYING (9)
    ) ;
```

After it's defined, the new ROW type can be used in a table definition:

```
CREATE TABLE CUSTOMER (
    CustID          INTEGER         PRIMARY KEY,
    LastName        CHARACTER VARYING (25),
    FirstName       CHARACTER VARYING (20),
    Address         addr_typ,
    Phone           CHARACTER VARYING (15)
    ) ;
```

The advantage here is that if you are maintaining address information for multiple entities — such as customers, vendors, employees, and stockholders — you only have to define the details of the address specification once, in the ROW type definition.

Collection types

After SQL broke out of the relational straightjacket with SQL:1999, types that violate first normal form became possible. It became possible for a field to contain a whole collection of objects rather than just one. The ARRAY type was introduced in SQL:1999, and the MULTISET type was introduced in SQL:2003.

Two collections may be compared to each other only if they are both the same type, either ARRAY or MULTISET, and if their element types are comparable. Because arrays have a defined element order, corresponding elements from the arrays can be compared. Multisets do not have a defined element order, but can be compared if an enumeration exists for each multiset being compared and the enumerations can be paired.

ARRAY type

The ARRAY data type violates first normal form (1NF), but in a different way than the way the ROW type violates 1NF. The ARRAY type, a collection type, is not a distinct type in the same sense that CHARACTER and NUMERIC are distinct data types. An ARRAY type merely allows one of the other types to have multiple values within a single field of a table. For example, say your organization needs to be able to contact customers whether they are at work, at home, or on the road. You want to maintain multiple telephone numbers for them. You can do this by declaring the Phone attribute as an array, as shown in the following code:

```
CREATE TABLE CUSTOMER (
    CustID          INTEGER         PRIMARY KEY,
    LastName        CHARACTER VARYING (25),
    FirstName       CHARACTER VARYING (20),
    Address         addr_typ,
    Phone           CHARACTER VARYING (15) ARRAY [3]
    ) ;
```

The ARRAY [3] notation allows you to store up to three telephone numbers in the CUSTOMER table. The three telephone numbers represent an example of a repeating group. *Repeating groups* are a no-no according to classical relational database theory, but this is one of several examples of cases where SQL:1999 broke the rules. When Dr. Codd first specified the rules of normalization, he traded off functional flexibility for data integrity. SQL:1999 took back some of that functional flexibility, at the cost of some added structural complexity.

 The increased structural complexity could translate into compromised data integrity if you are not fully aware of all the effects of actions you perform on your database. Arrays are ordered in that each element in an array is associated with exactly one ordinal position in the array.

Multiset type

A multiset is an unordered collection. Specific elements of the multiset may not be referenced, because they are not assigned a specific ordinal position in the multiset.

REF types

REF types are not part of core SQL. This means that a DBMS may claim compliance with the SQL standard without implementing REF types at all. The REF type is not a distinct data type in the sense that CHARACTER and NUMERIC are. Instead, it is a pointer to a data item, row type, or abstract data type that resides in a row of a table (a site). Dereferencing the pointer can retrieve the value stored at the target site.

If you're confused, don't worry, because you're not alone. Using the REF types requires a working knowledge of object-oriented programming (OOP) principles. This book refrains from wading too deeply into the murky waters of OOP. In fact — because the REF types are not a part of core SQL — you may be better off if you don't use them. If you want maximum portability across DBMS platforms, stick to core SQL.

User-defined types

User-defined types (UDTs) represent another example of features that arrived in SQL:1999 that come from the object-oriented programming world. As an SQL programmer, you are no longer restricted to the data types defined in the SQL specification. You can define your own data types, using the principles of abstract data types (ADTs) found in such object-oriented programming languages as C++.

One of the most important benefits of UDTs is the fact that you can use them to eliminate the *impedance mismatch* between SQL and the host language that is "wrapped around" the SQL. A long-standing problem with SQL has been the fact the SQL's predefined data types do not match the data types of the host languages within which SQL statements are embedded. Now, with UDTs, a database programmer can create data types within SQL that match the data types of the host language.

A UDT has attributes and methods, which are encapsulated within the UDT. The outside world can see the attribute definitions and the results of the methods, but the specific implementations of the methods are hidden from view. Access to the attributes and methods of a UDT can be further restricted by specifying that they are public, private, or protected. *Public* attributes or methods are available to all users of a UDT. *Private* attributes or methods are available only to the UDT itself. *Protected* attributes or methods are available only to the UDT itself or its subtypes. You see from this that a UDT in SQL behaves much like a class in an object-oriented programming language. Two forms of user-defined types exist: distinct types and structured types.

Distinct types

Distinct types are the simpler of the two forms of user-defined types. A distinct type's defining feature is that it is expressed as a single data type. It is constructed from one of the predefined data types, called the *source type*. Multiple distinct types that are all based on a single source type are distinct from each other and are thus not directly comparable. For example, you can use distinct types to distinguish between different currencies. Consider the following type definition:

```
CREATE DISTINCT TYPE USdollar AS DECIMAL (9,2) ;
```

This definition creates a new data type for U.S. dollars, based on the predefined `DECIMAL` data type. You can create another distinct type in a similar manner:

```
CREATE DISTINCT TYPE Euro AS DECIMAL (9,2) ;
```

You can now create tables that use these new types:

```
CREATE TABLE USInvoice (
    InvID        INTEGER       PRIMARY KEY,
    CustID       INTEGER,
    EmpID        INTEGER,
    TotalSale    USdollar,
    Tax          USdollar,
    Shipping     USdollar,
    GrandTotal   USdollar
    ) ;
```

```
CREATE TABLE EuroInvoice (
    InvID        INTEGER      PRIMARY KEY,
    CustID       INTEGER,
    EmpID        INTEGER,
    TotalSale    Euro,
    Tax          Euro,
    Shipping     Euro,
    GrandTotal   Euro
    ) ;
```

The USdollar type and the Euro type are both based on the DECIMAL type, but instances of one cannot be directly compared with instances of the other or with instances of the DECIMAL type. In SQL, as in the real world, it is possible to convert U.S. dollars into euros, but doing so requires a special operation (CAST). After the conversion has been made, comparisons become possible.

Structured types

The second form of user-defined type, the structured type, is expressed as a list of attribute definitions and methods instead of being based on a single predefined source type.

Constructors

When you create a structured UDT, the DBMS automatically creates a constructor function for it, giving it the same name as the UDT. The constructor's job is to initialize the attributes of the UDT to their default values.

Mutators and observers

When you create a structured UDT, the DBMS automatically creates a mutator function and an observer function. A *mutator,* when invoked, changes the value of an attribute of a structured type. An *observer* function is the opposite of a mutator function. Its job is to retrieve the value of an attribute of a structured type. You can include observer functions in SELECT statements to retrieve values from a database.

Subtypes and supertypes

A hierarchical relationship can exist between two structured types. For example, a type named MusicCDudt has a subtype named RockCDudt and another subtype named ClassicalCDudt. MusicCDudt is the supertype of those two subtypes. RockCDudt is a *proper subtype* of MusicCDudt if there is no subtype of MusicCDudt that is a supertype of RockCDudt. If RockCDudt has a subtype named HeavyMetalCDudt, HeavyMetalCDudt is also a subtype of MusicCDudt, but it is not a proper subtype of MusicCDudt.

A structured type that has no supertype is called a *maximal supertype,* and a structured type that has no subtypes is called a *leaf subtype.*

Example of a structured type

You can create structured UDTs in the following way:

```
/* Create a UDT named MusicCDudt */
CREATE TYPE MusicCDudt AS
/* Specify attributes */
Title                    CHAR(40),
Cost                     DECIMAL(9,2),
SuggestedPrice           DECIMAL(9,2)
/* Allow for subtypes */
NOT FINAL ;
```

```
CREATE TYPE RockCDudt UNDER MusicCDudt NOT FINAL ;
```

The subtype RockCDudt inherits the attributes of its supertype MusicCDudt.

```
CREATE TYPE HeavyMetalCDudt UNDER RockCDudt FINAL ;
```

Now that you have the types, you can create tables that use them. For example:

```
CREATE TABLE METALSKU (
        Album        HeavyMetalCDudt,
        SKU          INTEGER) ;
```

Now you can add rows to the new table:

```
BEGIN
        /* Declare a temporary variable a */
        DECLARE a = HeavyMetalCDudt ;
        /* Execute the constructor function */
        SET a = HeavyMetalCDudt() ;
            /* Execute first mutator function */
            SET a = a.title('Edward the Great') ;
            /* Execute second mutator function */
            SET a = a.cost(7.50) ;
            /* Execute third mutator function */
            SET a = a.suggestedprice(15.99) ;
            INSERT INTO METALSKU VALUES (a, 31415926) ;
        END
```

Data type summary

Table 2-2 lists various data types and displays literals that conform to each type.

Table 2-2	Data Types
Data Type	*Example Value*
CHARACTER (20)	'Amateur Radio '
VARCHAR (20)	'Amateur Radio'
CLOB (1000000)	'This character string is a million characters long . . .'
SMALLINT, BIGINT, or INTEGER	7500
NUMERIC or DECIMAL	3425.432
REAL, FLOAT, or DOUBLE PRECISION	6.626E-34
BLOB (1000000)	'1001001110101011010101010101. . .'
BOOLEAN	'true'
DATE	DATE '1957-08-14'
TIME (2) WITHOUT TIME ZONE [1]	TIME '12:46:02.43' WITHOUT TIME ZONE
TIME (3) WITH TIME ZONE	TIME '12:46:02.432-08:00' WITH TIME ZONE
TIMESTAMP WITHOUT TIME ZONE (0)	TIMESTAMP '1957-08-14 12:46:02' WITHOUT TIME ZONE
TIMESTAMP WITH TIME ZONE (0)	TIMESTAMP '1957-08-14 12:46:02-08:00' WITH TIME ZONE
INTERVAL DAY	INTERVAL '4' DAY
XML (SEQUENCE)	<Client>Vince Tenetria</Client>
ROW	ROW (Street VARCHAR (25), City VARCHAR (20), State CHAR (2), PostalCode VARCHAR (9))
ARRAY	INTEGER ARRAY [15]
MULTISET	No literal applies to the MULTISET type.
REF	Not a type, but a pointer
USER DEFINED TYPE	Currency type based on DECIMAL

1 Argument specifies number of fractional digits.

Your SQL implementation may not support all the data types that I describe in this section. Furthermore, your implementation may support nonstandard data types that I don't describe here. (Your mileage may vary, and so on. You know the drill.)

Null Values

If a database field contains a data item, that field has a specific value. A field that does not contain a data item is said to have a *null value*. In a numeric field, a null value is not the same as a value of zero. In a character field, a null value is not the same as a blank. Both a numeric zero and a blank character are definite values. A null value indicates that a field's value is undefined — its value is not known.

A number of situations exist in which a field may have a null value. The following list describes a few of these situations and gives an example of each:

- ✔ **The value exists, but you don't know what the value is yet.** You set MASS to null in the Higgs boson row of the ELEMENTARY_PARTICLE table before the mass of the Higgs boson is accurately determined.

- ✔ **The value doesn't exist yet.** You set TOTAL_SOLD to null in the SQL For Dummies, 6th Edition row of the BOOKS table because the first set of quarterly sales figures is not yet reported.

- ✔ **The field isn't applicable for this particular row.** You set SEX to null in the C-3PO row of the EMPLOYEE table because C-3PO is a droid that has no gender.

- ✔ **The value is out of range.** You set SALARY to null in the Oprah Winfrey row of the EMPLOYEE table because you designed the SALARY column as type NUMERIC (8,2) and Oprah's contract calls for pay in excess of $999,999.99.

A field can have a null value for many different reasons. Don't jump to any hasty conclusions about what any particular null value means.

Constraints

Constraints are restrictions that you apply to the data that someone can enter into a database table. You may know, for example, that entries in a particular numeric column must fall within a certain range. If anyone makes an entry that falls outside that range, then that entry must be an error. Applying a range constraint to the column prevents this type of error from happening.

Traditionally, the application program that uses the database applies any constraints to a database. The most recent DBMS products, however, enable you to apply constraints directly to the database. This approach has several advantages. If multiple applications use the same database, you need to apply the constraints only once rather than multiple times. Additionally, adding constraints at the database level is usually simpler than adding them to an application. In many cases, you need only to tack a clause onto your CREATE statement.

I discuss constraints and *assertions* (which are constraints that apply to more than one table) in detail in Chapter 5.

Using SQL in a Client/Server System

SQL is a data sublanguage that works on a stand-alone system or on a multiuser system. SQL works particularly well on a client/server system. On such a system, users on multiple client machines that connect to a server machine can access — via a local area network (LAN) or other communications channel — a database that resides on the server to which they're connected. The application program on a client machine contains SQL data-manipulation commands. The portion of the DBMS residing on the client sends these commands to the server across the communications channel that connects the server to the client. At the server, the server portion of the DBMS interprets and executes the SQL command and then sends the results back to the client across the communication channel. You can encode very complex operations into SQL at the client, and then decode and perform those operations at the server. This type of setup results in the most effective use of the bandwidth of that communication channel.

If you retrieve data by using SQL on a client/server system, only the data you want travels across the communication channel from the server to the client. In contrast, a simple resource-sharing system, with minimal intelligence at the server, must send huge blocks of data across the channel to give you the small piece of data that you want. This sort of massive transmission can slow operations considerably. The client/server architecture complements the characteristics of SQL to provide good performance at a moderate cost on small, medium, and large networks.

The server

Unless it receives a request from a client, the server does nothing. It just stands around and waits. If multiple clients require service at the same time, however, servers need to respond quickly. Servers generally differ from client machines in that they have large amounts of very fast disk storage. Servers are optimized for fast data access and retrieval. And because they must handle traffic coming in simultaneously from multiple client machines, servers need a fast processor, or even multiple processors.

What the server is

The *server* (short for *database server*) is the part of a client/server system that holds the database. The server also holds the server portion of a database management system. This part of the DBMS interprets commands coming in from the clients and translates these commands into operations in the database. The server software also formats the results of retrieval requests and sends the results back to the requesting client.

What the server does

The server's job is relatively simple and straightforward. All a server needs to do is read, interpret, and execute commands that come to it across the network from clients. Those commands are in one of several data sublanguages.

A sublanguage doesn't qualify as a complete language — it implements only part of a language. A data sublanguage deals only with data handling. The sublanguage has operations for inserting, updating, deleting, and selecting data, but may not have flow control structures such as DO loops, local variables, functions, procedures, or input/output to printers. SQL is the most common data sublanguage in use today and has become an industry standard. Proprietary data sublanguages have been supplanted by SQL on machines in all performance classes. With SQL:1999, SQL acquired many of the features missing from traditional sublanguages. However, SQL is still not a complete general-purpose programming language, so it must be combined with a host language to create a database application.

The client

The *client* part of a client/server system consists of a hardware component and a software component. The hardware component is the client computer and its interface to the local area network. This client hardware may be very similar or even identical to the server hardware. The software is the distinguishing component of the client.

What the client is

The client's primary job is to provide a user interface. As far as the user is concerned, the client machine *is* the computer, and the user interface *is* the application. The user may not even realize that the process involves a server. The server is usually out of sight — often in another room. Aside from the user interface, the client also contains the application program and the client part of the DBMS. The application program performs the specific task you require, such as accounts receivable or order entry. The client part of the DBMS executes the application program's commands and exchanges data and SQL data-manipulation commands with the server part of the DBMS.

What the client does

The client part of a DBMS displays information on the screen and responds to user input transmitted via the keyboard, mouse, or other input device. The client may also process data coming in from a telecommunications link or from other stations on the network. The client part of the DBMS does all the application-specific "thinking." To a developer, the client part of a DBMS is the interesting part. The server part just handles the requests of the client part in a repetitive, mechanical fashion.

Using SQL on the Internet/Intranet

Database operation on the Internet and on intranets differs fundamentally from operation in a traditional client/server system. The difference is primarily on the client end. In a traditional client/server system, much of the functionality of the DBMS resides on the client machine. On an Internet-based database system, most or all of the DBMS resides on the server. The client may host nothing more than a Web browser. At most, the client holds a browser and a browser extension, such as a Netscape plug-in or an ActiveX control. Thus, the conceptual "center of mass" of the system shifts toward the server. This shift has several advantages:

- ✔ The client portion of the system (browser) is low cost or even free.
- ✔ You have a standardized user interface.
- ✔ The client is easy to maintain.
- ✔ You have a standardized client/server relationship.
- ✔ You have a common means of displaying multimedia data.

The main disadvantages of performing database manipulations over the Internet involve security and data integrity:

- ✔ To protect information from unwanted access or tampering, both the Web server and the client browser must support strong encryption.
- ✔ Browsers don't perform adequate data-entry validation checks.
- ✔ Database tables residing on different servers may become desynchronized.

Client and server extensions designed to address these concerns make the Internet a feasible location for production database applications. The architecture of an intranet is similar to that of the Internet, but security is less of a concern. Because the organization maintaining the intranet has physical control over all the client machines as well as the servers and the network that connects these components together, an intranet suffers much less exposure to the efforts of malicious hackers. Data-entry errors and database desynchronization, however, do remain concerns.

Chapter 3

The Components of SQL

In This Chapter
▶ Creating databases
▶ Manipulating data
▶ Protecting databases

SQL is a special-purpose language designed for the creation and mainte-nance of data in relational databases. Although the vendors of relational database management systems have their own SQL implementations, an ISO/ANSI standard (revised in 2003 and updated in 2005) defines and controls what SQL is. All implementations differ from the standard to varying degrees. Close adherence to the standard is the key to running a database (and its associated applications) on more than one platform.

Although SQL isn't a general-purpose programming language, it contains some impressive tools. Three languages within a language offer everything you need to create, modify, maintain, and provide security for a relational database:

✔ **The Data Definition Language (DDL):** The part of SQL that you use to create (completely define) a database, modify its structure, and destroy it when you no longer need it.

✔ **The Data Manipulation Language (DML):** The part of SQL that performs database maintenance. Using this powerful tool, you can specify what you want to do with the data in your database — enter it, change it, or extract it.

✔ **The Data Control Language (DCL):** The part of SQL that protects your database from becoming corrupted. Used correctly, the DCL provides security for your database; the amount of protection depends on the implementation. If your implementation doesn't provide sufficient pro-tection, you must add that protection to your application program.

This chapter introduces the DDL, DML, and DCL.

Data Definition Language

The Data Definition Language (DDL) is the part of SQL you use to create, change, or destroy the basic elements of a relational database. Basic elements include tables, views, schemas, catalogs, clusters, and possibly other things as well. In this section, I discuss the containment hierarchy that relates these elements to each other and look at the commands that operate on these elements.

In Chapter 1, I mention tables and schemas, noting that a *schema* is an overall structure that includes tables within it. Tables and schemas are two elements of a relational database's *containment hierarchy*. You can break down the containment hierarchy as follows:

- Tables contain columns and rows.
- Schemas contain tables and views.
- Catalogs contain schemas.

The database itself contains catalogs. Sometimes the database is referred to as a *cluster*.

When "Just do it!" is not good advice

Say that you need to create a database for your organization. Excited by the prospect of building a useful, valuable, and totally righteous structure of great importance to your company's future, you sit down at your computer and start entering SQL CREATE commands. Right?

Well, no. Not quite. In fact, that's a prescription for disaster. Many database development projects go awry from the start as excitement and enthusiasm overtake careful planning. Even if you have a clear idea of how to structure your database, write everything down on paper before touching your keyboard.

Database development bears some relationship to a game of chess. In the middle of a complicated and competitive chess game, you may see what looks like a good move. The urge to make that move can be overwhelming. However, the odds are good that you have missed something. Grandmasters advise newer players, only partly in jest, to sit on their hands. If sitting on your hands prevents you from making an ill-advised move, then so be it. Sit on your hands. If you study the position a little longer, you might find an even better move — or you might even see a brilliant counter move that your opponent can make. Plunging into creating a database without sufficient forethought can lead to a database structure that, at best, is suboptimal. At worst, it could be disastrous, an open invitation to data corruption. Sitting on your hands probably won't help, but it *will* help to pick up a pencil in one of those hands and start mapping your database plan on paper.

Keep in mind the following procedures when planning your database:

- ✔ Identify all tables.
- ✔ Define the columns that each table must contain.
- ✔ Give each table a *primary key* that you can guarantee is unique. (I discuss primary keys in Chapters 4 and 5.)
- ✔ Make sure that every table in the database has at least one column in common with one other table in the database. These shared columns serve as logical links that enable you to relate information in one table to the corresponding information in another table.
- ✔ Put each table in *third normal form* (3NF) or better to ensure the prevention of insertion, deletion, and update anomalies. (I discuss database normalization in Chapter 5.)

After you complete the design on paper and verify that it is sound, you're ready to transfer the design to the computer by using SQL CREATE commands.

Creating tables

A database table is a two-dimensional array made up of rows and columns. You can create a table by using the SQL CREATE TABLE command. Within the command, you specify the name and data type of each column.

After you create a table, you can start loading it with data. (Loading data is a DML, not a DDL, function.) If requirements change, you can change a table's structure by using the ALTER TABLE command. If a table outlives its usefulness or becomes obsolete, you can eliminate it with the DROP command. The various forms of the CREATE and ALTER commands, together with the DROP command, make up SQL's DDL.

Say that you're a database designer and you don't want your database tables to turn to guacamole as you make updates over time. You decide to structure your database tables according to the best normalized form so that you can maintain data integrity.

Normalization, an extensive field of study in its own right, is a way of structuring database tables so that updates don't introduce anomalies. Each table you create contains columns that correspond to attributes that are tightly linked to each other.

You may, for example, create a CUSTOMER table with the attributes CUSTOMER.CustomerID, CUSTOMER.FirstName, CUSTOMER.LastName, CUSTOMER.Street, CUSTOMER.City, CUSTOMER.State, CUSTOMER.Zipcode, and CUSTOMER.Phone. All of these attributes are more closely related to the customer entity than to any other entity in a database that may contain many tables. These attributes contain all the relatively permanent customer information that your organization keeps on file.

Most database management systems provide a graphical tool for creating database tables. You can also create such tables by using an SQL command. The following example demonstrates a command that creates your CUSTOMER table:

```
CREATE TABLE CUSTOMER (
    CustomerID       INTEGER              NOT NULL,
    FirstName        CHARACTER (15),
    LastName         CHARACTER (20)       NOT NULL,
    Street           CHARACTER (25),
    City             CHARACTER (20),
    State            CHARACTER (2),
    Zipcode          CHARACTER (10),
    Phone            CHARACTER (13) ) ;
```

For each column, you specify its name (for example, CustomerID), its data type (for example, INTEGER), and possibly one or more constraints (for example, NOT NULL).

Figure 3-1 shows a portion of the CUSTOMER table with some sample data.

Figure 3-1:
Use the
CREATE
TABLE
command to
create this
CUSTOMER
table.

File	Edit	View	Insert	Format	Records	Tools	Window	Help	Type a question for help

CUSTOMER : Table

CustomerID	FirstName	LastName	Street	City	State	Zipcode	Phone
1	Bruce	Chickenson	3330 Mentone Street	San Diego	CA	92025	619-555-1234
2	Mini	Murray	3330 Pheasant Run	Jefferson	ME	04380	207-555-2345
3	Nikki	McBurrain	3330 Waldoboro Road	E. Kingston	NH	03827	603-555-3456
4	Adrianne	Smith	3330 Foxhall Road	Morton	IL	61550	309-555-4567
5	Steph	Harris	3330 W. Victoria Circle	Irvine	CA	92612	714-555-5678
(AutoNumber)							

Record: |◄| ◄ | 6 ► |►I|►*| of 6

Datasheet View

If the SQL implementation you use doesn't fully implement the latest version of ANSI/ISO standard SQL, the syntax you need to use may differ from the syntax that I give in this book. Read your DBMS's user documentation for specific information.

A room with a view

At times, you want to retrieve specific information from the CUSTOMER table. You don't want to look at everything — only specific columns and rows. What you need is a view.

A *view* is a virtual table. In most implementations, a view has no independent physical existence. The view's definition exists only in the database's metadata, but the data comes from the table or tables from which you derive the view. The view's data is not physically duplicated somewhere else in online disk storage. Some views consist of specific columns and rows of a single table. Others, known as *multitable views,* draw from two or more tables.

Single-table view

Sometimes when you have a question, the data that gives you the answer resides in a single table in your database. If the information you want exists in a single table, you can create a single-table view of the data. For example, say that you want to look at the names and telephone numbers of all customers who live in the state of New Hampshire. You can create a view from the CUSTOMER table that contains only the data you want. The following SQL command creates this view:

```
CREATE VIEW NH_CUST AS
    SELECT CUSTOMER.FirstName,
           CUSTOMER.LastName,
           CUSTOMER.Phone
       FROM CUSTOMER
       WHERE CUSTOMER.State = 'NH' ;
```

Figure 3-2 shows how you derive the view from the CUSTOMER table.

Figure 3-2:
You derive the NH_ CUST view from the CUSTOMER table.

This code is correct, but a little on the wordy side. You can accomplish the same task with less typing if your SQL implementation assumes that all table references are the same as the ones in the FROM clause. If your system makes that reasonable default assumption, you can reduce the command to the following lines:

```
CREATE VIEW NH_CUST AS
    SELECT FirstName, LastName, Phone
        FROM CUSTOMER
        WHERE STATE = 'NH';
```

Although the second version is easier to write and read, it's more vulnerable to disruption from ALTER TABLE commands. Such disruption isn't a problem for this simple case, which has no join, but views with joins are more robust when they use fully qualified names. I cover joins in Chapter 10.

Creating a multitable view

More often than not, you need to pull data from two or more tables to answer your question. For example, say that you work for a sporting goods store, and you want to send a promotional mailing to all the customers who have bought ski equipment since the store opened last year. You need information from the CUSTOMER table, the PRODUCT table, the INVOICE table, and the INVOICE_LINE table. You can create a multitable view that shows the data you need. After you create the view, you can use that same view again and again. Each time you use the view, it reflects any changes that occurred in the underlying tables since you last used the view.

The sporting goods store database contains four tables: CUSTOMER, PRODUCT, INVOICE, and INVOICE_LINE. The tables are structured as shown in Table 3-1.

Table 3-1	Sporting Goods Store Database Tables		
Table	**Column**	**Data Type**	**Constraint**
CUSTOMER	CustomerID	INTEGER	NOT NULL
	FirstName	CHARACTER (15)	
	LastName	CHARACTER (20)	NOT NULL
	Street	CHARACTER (25)	
	City	CHARACTER (20)	
	State	CHARACTER (2)	
	Zipcode	CHARACTER (10)	
	Phone	CHARACTER (13)	

Table	Column	Data Type	Constraint
PRODUCT	ProductID	INTEGER	NOT NULL
	Name	CHARACTER (25)	
	Description	CHARACTER (30)	
	Category	CHARACTER (15)	
	VendorID	INTEGER	
	VendorName	CHARACTER (30)	
INVOICE	InvoiceNumber	INTEGER	NOT NULL
	CustomerID	INTEGER	
	InvoiceDate	DATE	
	TotalSale	NUMERIC (9,2)	
	TotalRemitted	NUMERIC (9,2)	
	FormOfPayment	CHARACTER (10)	
INVOICE_LINE	LineNumber	INTEGER	NOT NULL
	InvoiceNumber	INTEGER	
	ProductID	INTEGER	
	Quantity	INTEGER	
	SalePrice	NUMERIC (9,2)	

Notice that some of the columns in Table 3-1 contain the constraint NOT NULL. These columns are either the primary keys of their respective tables or columns that you decide must contain a value. A table's primary key must uniquely identify each row. To do that, the primary key must contain a non-null value in every row. (I discuss keys in detail in Chapter 5.)

The tables relate to each other through the columns that they have in common. The following list describes these relationships (as shown in Figure 3-3):

✔ The CUSTOMER table bears a *one-to-many relationship* to the INVOICE table. One customer can make multiple purchases, generating multiple invoices. Each invoice, however, deals with one and only one customer.

✔ The INVOICE table bears a one-to-many relationship to the INVOICE_LINE table. An invoice may have multiple lines, but each line appears on one and only one invoice.

✔ The PRODUCT table also bears a one-to-many relationship to the INVOICE_LINE table. A product may appear on more than one line on one or more invoices. Each line, however, deals with one, and only one, product.

The CUSTOMER table links to the INVOICE table by the common `CustomerID` column. The INVOICE table links to the INVOICE_LINE table by the common `InvoiceNumber` column. The PRODUCT table links to the INVOICE_LINE table by the common `ProductID` column. These links are what makes this database a *relational* database.

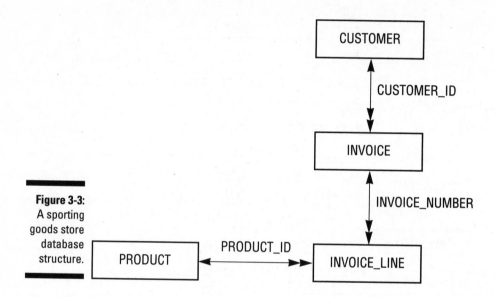

Figure 3-3:
A sporting goods store database structure.

To access the information about customers who bought ski equipment, you need `FirstName`, `LastName`, `Street`, `City`, `State`, and `Zipcode` from the CUSTOMER table; `Category` from the PRODUCT table; `InvoiceNumber` from the INVOICE table; and `LineNumber` from the INVOICE_LINE table. You can create the view you want in stages by using the following commands:

```
CREATE VIEW SKI_CUST1 AS
    SELECT FirstName,
        LastName,
        Street,
        City,
        State,
        Zipcode,
        InvoiceNumber
    FROM CUSTOMER JOIN INVOICE
    USING (CustomerID) ;
CREATE VIEW SKI_CUST2 AS
    SELECT FirstName,
        LastName,
        Street,
```

```
        City,
        State,
        Zipcode,
        ProductID
    FROM SKI_CUST1 JOIN INVOICE_LINE
    USING (InvoiceNumber) ;
CREATE VIEW SKI_CUST3 AS
    SELECT FirstName,
        LastName,
        Street,
        City,
        State,
        Zipcode,
        Category
    FROM SKI_CUST2 JOIN PRODUCT
    USING (ProductID) ;
CREATE VIEW SKI_CUST AS
    SELECT DISTINCT FirstName,
        LastName,
        Street,
        City,
        State,
        Zipcode
    FROM SKI_CUST3
    WHERE CATEGORY = 'Ski' ;
```

These CREATE VIEW statements combine data from multiple tables by using the JOIN operator. Figure 3-4 diagrams the process.

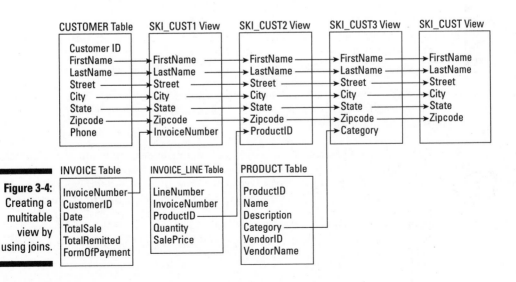

Figure 3-4: Creating a multitable view by using joins.

Here's a rundown of the four CREATE VIEW statements:

- ✔ The first statement combines columns from the CUSTOMER table with a column of the INVOICE table to create the SKI_CUST1 view.

- ✔ The second statement combines SKI_CUST1 with a column from the INVOICE_LINE table to create the SKI_CUST2 view.

- ✔ The third statement combines SKI_CUST2 with a column from the PRODUCT table to create the SKI_CUST3 view.

- ✔ The fourth statement filters out all rows that don't have a category of Ski. The result is a view (SKI_CUST) that contains the names and addresses of all customers who bought at least one product in the Ski category.

  The DISTINCT keyword in the fourth CREATE VIEW's SELECT clause ensures that you have only one entry for each customer, even if some customers made multiple purchases of ski items.

Collecting tables into schemas

A table consists of rows and columns and usually deals with a specific type of entity, such as customers, products, or invoices. Useful work generally requires information about several (or many) related entities. Organizationally, you collect the tables that you associate with these entities according to a logical schema. A *logical schema* is the organizational structure of a collection of related tables.

A database also has a *physical schema*. The physical schema is the way the data and its associated items, such as indexes, are physically arranged on the system's storage devices. When I mention the schema of a database, I'm referring to the logical schema, not the physical schema.

On a system where several unrelated projects may co-reside, you can assign all related tables to one schema. You can collect other groups of tables into schemas of their own.

Be sure to name schemas to ensure that no one accidentally mixes tables from one project with tables of another. Each project has its own associated schema, which you can distinguish from other schemas by name. Seeing certain table names (such as CUSTOMER, PRODUCT, and so on) appear in multiple projects, however, is common. If any chance exists of a naming ambiguity, qualify your table name by using its schema name as well (as in SCHEMA_NAME.TABLE_NAME). If you don't qualify a table name, SQL assigns that table to the default schema.

Ordering by catalog

For really large database systems, multiple schemas may not be sufficient. In a large distributed database environment with many users, you may even find duplicated schema names. To prevent this situation, SQL adds another level to the containment hierarchy: the catalog. A *catalog* is a named collection of schemas.

You can qualify a table name by using a catalog name and a schema name. This safeguard is the best way to ensure that no one confuses that table with a table of the same name in a schema with the same schema name. The catalog-qualified name appears in the following format:

```
CATALOG_NAME.SCHEMA_NAME.TABLE_NAME
```

At the top of the database containment hierarchy are *clusters*. Systems rarely require use of the full scope of the containment hierarchy, however. Going to the catalog level is enough in most cases. A catalog contains schemas; a schema contains tables and views; tables and views contain columns and rows.

The catalog also contains the *information schema*. The information schema contains the system tables. The system tables hold the metadata associated with the other schemas. In Chapter 1, I define a database as a self-describing collection of integrated records. The metadata contained in the system tables is what makes the database self-describing.

Because catalogs are identified by name, you can have multiple catalogs in a database. Each catalog can have multiple schemas, and each schema can have multiple tables. Of course, each table can have multiple columns and rows. The hierarchical relationships are shown in Figure 3-5.

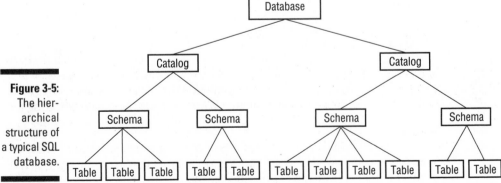

Figure 3-5:
The hierarchical structure of a typical SQL database.

Getting familiar with DDL commands

SQL's Data Definition Language (DDL) deals with the structure of a database, whereas the Data Manipulation Language (described later in this chapter) deals with the data contained within that structure. The DDL consists of these three commands:

- ✔ CREATE: You use the various forms of this command to build the essential structures of the database.
- ✔ ALTER: You use this command to change structures that you have created.
- ✔ DROP: You apply this command to a table to destroy not only the table's data, but its structure as well.

In the following sections, I give you brief descriptions of the DDL commands. In Chapters 4 and 5, I use these commands in examples.

CREATE

You can apply the SQL CREATE command to several SQL objects, including schemas, domains, tables, and views. By using the CREATE SCHEMA statement, you can create a schema, identify its owner, and specify a default character set. Here's an example of such a statement:

```
CREATE SCHEMA SALES
   AUTHORIZATION SALES_MGR
   DEFAULT CHARACTER SET ASCII_FULL ;
```

Use the CREATE DOMAIN statement to apply constraints to column values or to specify a collation order. The constraints you apply to a domain determine what objects the domain can and cannot contain. You can create domains after you establish a schema. The following example shows how to use this command:

```
CREATE DOMAIN Age AS INTEGER
   CHECK (AGE > 20) ;
```

You create tables by using the CREATE TABLE statement, and you create views by using the CREATE VIEW statement. Earlier in this chapter, I show you examples of these two statements. When you use the CREATE TABLE command, you can specify constraints on the new table's columns at the same time.

Sometimes, you may want to specify constraints that don't specifically attach to a table but that apply to an entire schema. You can use the CREATE ASSERTION statement to specify such constraints.

You also have CREATE CHARACTER SET, CREATE COLLATION, and CREATE TRANSLATION statements, which give you the flexibility of creating new character sets, collation sequences, or translation tables. (*Collation sequences* define the order in which you carry out comparisons or sorts. *Translation tables* control the conversion of character strings from one character set to another.)

ALTER

After you create a table, you're not necessarily stuck with that exact table forever. As you use the table, you may discover that it's not everything you need it to be. You can use the ALTER TABLE command to change the table by adding, changing, or deleting a column in the table. In addition to tables, you can also ALTER columns and domains.

DROP

Removing a table from a database schema is easy. Just use a DROP TABLE <*tablename*> command. You erase all the table's data as well as the metadata that defines the table in the data dictionary. It's almost as if the table never existed.

Data Manipulation Language

While the DDL is the part of SQL that creates, modifies, or destroys database structures, it doesn't deal with the data itself. Handling data is the job of the Data Manipulation Language (DML). Some DML statements read like ordinary English-language sentences and are easy to understand. Unfortunately, because SQL gives you very fine grained control of data, other DML statements can be fiendishly complex.

If a DML statement includes multiple expressions, clauses, predicates, or subqueries, understanding what that statement is trying to do can be a challenge. After you deal with some of these statements, you may even consider switching to an easier line of work, such as brain surgery or quantum electrodynamics. Fortunately, such drastic action isn't necessary. You can understand complex SQL statements by breaking them down into their basic components and analyzing them one chunk at a time.

The DML statements you can use are INSERT, UPDATE, DELETE, and SELECT. These statements can consist of a variety of parts, including multiple clauses. Each clause may incorporate value expressions, logical connectives, predicates, aggregate functions, and subqueries. You can make fine discriminations among database records and extract more information from your data by including these clauses in your statements. In Chapter 6, I discuss the operation of the DML commands, and in Chapters 7 through 12, I delve into the details of these commands.

Value expressions

You can use *value expressions* to combine two or more values. Several kinds of value expressions exist, corresponding to the different data types:

- ✔ Numeric
- ✔ String
- ✔ Datetime
- ✔ Interval
- ✔ Boolean
- ✔ User-defined
- ✔ Row
- ✔ Collection

The Boolean, user-defined, row, and collection types were introduced with SQL:1999. Some implementations may not support them all yet. If you want to use one of these data types, make sure your implementation includes it.

Numeric value expressions

To combine numeric values, use the addition (+), subtraction (–), multiplication (*), and division (/) operators. The following lines are examples of numeric value expressions:

```
12 - 7
15/3 - 4
6 * (8 + 2)
```

The values in these examples are *numeric literals*. These values may also be column names, parameters, host variables, or subqueries — provided that those column names, parameters, host variables, or subqueries evaluate to a numeric value. The following are some examples:

```
SUBTOTAL + TAX + SHIPPING
6 * MILES/HOURS
:months/12
```

The colon in the last example signals that the following term (months) is either a parameter or a host variable.

String value expressions

String value expressions may include the *concatenation operator* (| |). Use concatenation to join two text strings, as shown in Table 3-2.

Table 3-2	Examples of String Concatenation
Expression	*Result*
`'military ' || 'intelligence'`	`'military intelligence'`
`'oxy' || 'moron'`	`'oxymoron'`
`CITY|| ' ' ||STATE|| ' '||ZIP`	A single string with city, state, and zip code, each separated by a single space.

Some SQL implementations use + as the concatenation operator rather than ||. Check your documentation to see which operator your implementation uses.

Some implementations may include string operators other than concatenation, but ISO-standard SQL doesn't support such operators.

Datetime and interval value expressions

Datetime value expressions deal with (surprise!) dates and times. Data of DATE, TIME, TIMESTAMP, and INTERVAL types may appear in datetime value expressions. The result of a datetime value expression is always another datetime. You can add or subtract an interval from a datetime and specify time zone information.

Here's an example of a datetime value expression:

```
DueDate + INTERVAL '7' DAY
```

A library may use such an expression to determine when to send a late notice. The following example specifies a time rather than a date:

```
TIME '18:55:48' AT LOCAL
```

The AT LOCAL keywords indicate that the time refers to the local time zone.

Interval value expressions deal with the difference (how much time passes) between one datetime and another. You have two kinds of intervals: *year-month* and *day-time*. You can't mix the two in an expression.

As an example of an interval, say that someone returns a library book after the due date. By using an interval value expression such as that of the following example, you can calculate how many days late the book is and assess a fine accordingly:

```
(DateReturned - DateDue) DAY
```

Because an interval may be of either the year-month or the day-time variety, you need to specify which kind to use. In the preceding example, I specify DAY.

Boolean value expressions

A Boolean value expression tests the truth value of a predicate. The following is an example of a Boolean value expression:

```
(Class = SENIOR) IS TRUE
```

If this was a condition on the retrieval of rows from a student table, only rows containing the records of seniors would be retrieved. To retrieve the records of all non-seniors, you could use the following:

```
NOT (Class = SENIOR) IS TRUE
```

Alternatively, you could use:

```
(Class = SENIOR) IS FALSE
```

To retrieve all rows that have a null value in the CLASS column, use

```
(Class = SENIOR) IS UNKNOWN
```

User-defined type value expressions

User-defined types are described in Chapter 2. With this facility, you can define your own data types instead of having to settle for those provided by "stock" SQL. Expressions that incorporate data elements of such a user-defined type must evaluate to an element of the same type.

Row value expressions

A row value expression, not surprisingly, specifies a row value. The row value may consist of one value expression, or two or more comma-delimited value expressions. For example:

```
('Joseph Tykociner', 'Professor Emeritus', 1918)
```

This is a row in a faculty table, showing a faculty member's name, rank, and year of hire.

Collection value expressions

A collection value expression evaluates to an array.

Reference value expressions

A reference value expression evaluates to a value that references some other database component, such as a table column.

Predicates

Predicates are SQL equivalents of logical propositions. The following statement is an example of a proposition:

"The student is a senior."

In a table containing information about students, the domain of the CLASS column may be SENIOR, JUNIOR, SOPHOMORE, FRESHMAN, or NULL. You can use the predicate CLASS = SENIOR to filter out rows for which the predicate is false, retaining only those for which the predicate is true. Sometimes, the value of a predicate in a row is unknown (NULL). In those cases, you may choose either to discard the row or to retain it. (After all, the student *could* be a senior.) The correct course depends on the situation.

Class = SENIOR is an example of a *comparison predicate*. SQL has six comparison operators. A simple comparison predicate uses one of these operators. Table 3-3 shows the comparison predicates and some legitimate as well as bogus examples of their use.

Table 3-3	Comparison Operators and Comparison Predicates	
Operator	*Comparison*	*Expression*
=	Equal to	Class = SENIOR
<>	Not equal to	Class <> SENIOR
<	Less than	Class < SENIOR
>	Greater than	Class > SENIOR
<=	Less than or equal to	Class <= SENIOR
>=	Greater than or equal to	Class >= SENIOR

In the preceding example, only the first two entries in Table 3-3 (Class = SENIOR and Class < > SENIOR) make sense. SOPHOMORE is considered greater than SENIOR because SO comes after SE in the default collation sequence, which sorts in ascending alphabetical order. This interpretation, however, is probably not the one you want.

Logical connectives

Logical connectives enable you to build complex predicates out of simple ones. Say, for example, that you want to identify child prodigies in a database of high-school students. Two propositions that could identify these students may read as follows:

"The student is a senior."

"The student's age is less than 14 years."

You can use the logical connective AND to create a compound predicate that isolates the student records that you want, as in the following example:

```
Class = SENIOR AND Age < 14
```

If you use the AND connective, both component predicates must be true for the compound predicate to be true. Use the OR connective when you want the compound predicate to evaluate to true if either component predicate is true. NOT is the third logical connective. Strictly speaking, NOT doesn't connect two predicates, but instead reverses the truth value of the single predicate to which you apply it. Take, for example, the following expression:

```
NOT (Class = SENIOR)
```

This expression is true only if Class is not equal to SENIOR.

Set functions

Sometimes, the information that you want to extract from a table doesn't relate to individual rows but rather to sets of rows. SQL provides five *set* (or *aggregate*) *functions* to deal with such situations. These functions are COUNT, MAX, MIN, SUM, and AVG. Each function performs an action that draws data from a set of rows rather than from a single row.

COUNT

The COUNT function returns the number of rows in the specified table. To count the number of precocious seniors in my example high-school database, use the following statement:

```
SELECT COUNT (*)
     FROM STUDENT
     WHERE Grade = 12 AND Age < 14 ;
```

MAX

Use the MAX function to return the maximum value that occurs in the specified column. Say that you want to find the oldest student enrolled in your school. The following statement returns the appropriate row:

```
SELECT FirstName, LastName, Age
    FROM STUDENT
    WHERE Age = (SELECT MAX(Age) FROM STUDENT);
```

This statement returns all students whose ages are equal to the maximum age. That is, if the age of the oldest student is 23, this statement returns the first and last names and the age of all students who are 23 years old.

This query uses a subquery. The subquery SELECT MAX(Age) FROM STUDENT is embedded within the main query. I talk about subqueries (also called *nested queries*) in Chapter 11.

MIN

The MIN function works just like MAX except that MIN looks for the minimum value in the specified column rather than the maximum. To find the youngest student enrolled, you can use the following query:

```
SELECT FirstName, LastName, Age
    FROM STUDENT
    WHERE Age = (SELECT MIN(Age) FROM STUDENT);
```

This query returns all students whose age is equal to the age of the youngest student.

SUM

The SUM function adds up the values in a specified column. The column must be one of the numeric data types, and the value of the sum must be within the range of that type. Thus, if the column is of type SMALLINT, the sum must be no larger than the upper limit of the SMALLINT data type. In the retail database from earlier in this chapter, the INVOICE table contains a record of all sales. To find the total dollar value of all sales recorded in the database, use the SUM function as follows:

```
SELECT SUM(TotalSale) FROM INVOICE;
```

AVG

The AVG function returns the average of all the values in the specified column. As does the SUM function, AVG applies only to columns with a numeric data type. To find the value of the average sale, considering all transactions in the database, use the AVG function like this:

```
SELECT AVG(TotalSale) FROM INVOICE
```

Nulls have no value, so if any of the rows in the `TotalSale` column contain null values, those rows are ignored in the computation of the value of the average sale.

Subqueries

Subqueries, as you can see in the "Set functions" section earlier in this chapter, are queries within a query. Anywhere you can use an expression in an SQL statement, you can also use a subquery. Subqueries are powerful tools for relating information in one table to information in another table because you can embed (or *nest*) a query into one table, within a query to another table. By nesting one subquery within another, you enable the access of information from two or more tables to generate a final result. When you use subqueries correctly, you can retrieve just about any information you want from a database.

Data Control Language

The Data Control Language (DCL) has four commands: `COMMIT`, `ROLLBACK`, `GRANT`, and `REVOKE`. These commands protect the database from harm, both accidental or intentional.

Transactions

Your database is most vulnerable to damage while you or someone else is changing it. Even in a single-user system, making a change can be dangerous to a database. If a software or hardware failure occurs while the change is in progress, a database may be left in an indeterminate state that's somewhere between where it was before the change operation started and where it would be if the change operation completed successfully.

SQL protects your database by restricting operations that can change the database so that these operations occur only within transactions. During a transaction, SQL records every operation on the data in a log file. If anything interrupts the transaction before the `COMMIT` statement ends the transaction, you can restore the system to its original state by issuing a `ROLLBACK` statement. The `ROLLBACK` processes the transaction log in reverse, undoing all the actions that took place in the transaction. After you roll back the database to its state before the transaction began, you can clear up whatever caused the problem and attempt the transaction again.

As long as a hardware or software problem can possibly occur, your database is susceptible to damage. To minimize the chance of damage, today's DBMSs close the window of vulnerability as much as possible by performing all operations that affect the database within a transaction and then committing all these operations at one time. Modern database management systems use logging in conjunction with transactions to guarantee that hardware, software, or operational problems won't damage data. After a transaction has been committed, it's safe from all but the most catastrophic of system failures. Prior to commitment, incomplete transactions can be rolled back to their starting point and applied again, after the problem is corrected.

In a multiuser system, database corruption or incorrect results are possible even if no hardware or software failures occur. Interactions between two or more users who access the same table at the same time can cause serious problems. By restricting changes so that they occur only within transactions, SQL addresses these problems as well.

By putting all operations that affect the database into transactions, you can isolate the actions of one user from those of another user. Such isolation is critical if you want to make sure that the results you obtain from the database are accurate.

You may wonder how the interaction of two users can produce inaccurate results. For example, say that Donna reads a record in a database table. An instant later (more or less) David changes the value of a numeric field in that record. Now Donna writes a value back into that field, based on the value that she read initially. Because Donna is unaware of David's change, the value after Donna's write operation is incorrect.

Another problem can result if Donna writes to a record and then David reads that record. If Donna rolls back her transaction, David is unaware of the rollback and bases his actions on the value that he read, which doesn't reflect the value that's in the database after the rollback. It makes for good comedy, but lousy data management.

Users and privileges

Another major threat to data integrity is the users themselves. Some people should have no access to the data. Others should have only restricted access to some of the data but no access to the rest. Some should have unlimited access to everything in the database. You need a system for classifying users and for assigning access privileges to the users in different categories.

The creator of a schema specifies who is considered its owner. As the owner of a schema, you can grant access privileges to the users you specify. Any privileges that you don't explicitly grant are withheld. You can also revoke privileges that you've already granted. A user must pass an authentication procedure to prove his identity before he can access the files you authorize him to use. The specifics of that procedure are implementation-dependent.

SQL gives you the capability to protect the following database objects:

- ✔ Tables
- ✔ Columns
- ✔ Views
- ✔ Domains
- ✔ Character sets
- ✔ Collations
- ✔ Translations

I discuss character sets, collations, and translations in Chapter 5.

SQL supports several different kinds of protection: *seeing, adding, modifying, deleting, referencing,* and *using* databases. It also supports protections associated with the execution of external routines.

You permit access by using the GRANT statement and remove access by using the REVOKE statement. By controlling the use of the SELECT command, the DCL controls who can see a database object such as a table, column, or view. Controlling the INSERT command determines who can add new rows in a table. Restricting the use of the UPDATE command to authorized users controls who can modify table rows, and restricting the DELETE command controls who can delete table rows.

If one table in a database contains as a foreign key a column that is a primary key in another table in the database, you can add a constraint to the first table so that it references the second table. (Foreign keys are described in Chapter 5.) When one table references another, a user of the first table may be able to deduce information about the contents of the second. As the owner of the second table, you may want to prevent such snooping. The GRANT REFERENCES statement gives you that power. The following section discusses the problem of a renegade reference and how the GRANT REFERENCES statement prevents it. By using the GRANT USAGE statement, you can control who can use or even see the contents of a domain, character set, collation, or translation. (I cover provisions for security in Chapter 13.)

Table 3-4 summarizes the SQL statements that you use to grant and revoke privileges.

Table 3-4	Types of Protection
Protection Operation	*Statement*
Enable to see a table	GRANT SELECT
Prevent from seeing a table	REVOKE SELECT
Enable to add rows to a table	GRANT INSERT
Prevent from adding rows to a table	REVOKE INSERT
Enable to change data in table rows	GRANT UPDATE
Prevent from changing data in table rows	REVOKE UPDATE
Enable to delete table rows	GRANT DELETE
Prevent from deleting table rows	REVOKE DELETE
Enable to reference a table	GRANT REFERENCES
Prevent from referencing a table	REVOKE REFERENCES
Enable to use a domain, character translation, or set collation	GRANT USAGE ON DOMAIN, GRANT USAGE ON CHARACTER SET, GRANT USAGE ON COLLATION, GRANT USAGE ON TRANSLATION
Prevent the use of a domain, character set, collation, or translation	REVOKE USAGE ON DOMAIN, REVOKE USAGE ON CHARACTER SET, REVOKE USAGE ON COLLATION, REVOKE USAGE ON TRANSLATION

You can give different levels of access to different people, depending on their needs. The following commands offer a few examples of this capability:

```
GRANT SELECT
      ON CUSTOMER
      TO SALES_MANAGER;
```

The preceding example enables one person, the sales manager, to see the CUSTOMER table.

The following example enables anyone with access to the system to see the retail price list:

```
GRANT SELECT
      ON RETAIL_PRICE_LIST
      TO PUBLIC;
```

The following example enables the sales manager to modify the retail price list. She can change the contents of existing rows, but she can't add or delete rows:

```
GRANT UPDATE
      ON RETAIL_PRICE_LIST
      TO SALES_MANAGER;
```

The following example enables the sales manager to add new rows to the retail price list:

```
GRANT INSERT
      ON RETAIL_PRICE_LIST
      TO SALES_MANAGER;
```

Now, thanks to this last example, the sales manager can delete unwanted rows from the table, too:

```
GRANT DELETE
      ON RETAIL_PRICE_LIST
      TO SALES MANAGER;
```

Referential integrity constraints can jeopardize your data

You may think that if you can control who sees, creates, modifies, and deletes functions in a table, you're well protected. Against most threats, you are. A knowledgeable hacker, however, can still ransack the house by using an indirect method.

A correctly designed relational database has *referential integrity,* which means that the data in one table in the database is consistent with the data in all the other tables. To ensure referential integrity, database designers apply constraints to tables that restrict the data users can enter into the tables. If you have a database with referential integrity constraints, a user can possibly create a new table that uses a column in a confidential table as a foreign key. That column then serves as a link through which someone can possibly steal confidential information.

Say, for example, that you're a famous Wall Street stock analyst. Many people believe in the accuracy of your stock picks, so whenever you recommend a stock to your subscribers, many people buy that stock, and its value increases. You keep your analysis in a database, which contains a table named FOUR_ STAR. Your top recommendations for your next newsletter are in that table. Naturally, you restrict access to FOUR_STAR so that word doesn't leak out to the investing public before your paying subscribers receive the newsletter.

You're still vulnerable, however, if anyone else can create a new table that uses the stock name field of FOUR_STAR as a foreign key, as shown in the following command example:

```
CREATE TABLE HOT_STOCKS (
     Stock CHARACTER (30) REFERENCES FOUR_STAR
     );
```

The hacker can now try to insert the name of every stock on the New York Stock Exchange, American Stock Exchange, and NASDAQ into the table. Those inserts that succeed tell the hacker which stocks match the stocks that you name in your confidential table. It doesn't take long for the hacker to extract your entire list of stocks.

You can protect yourself from hacks such as the one in the preceding example by being very careful about entering statements similar to the following:

```
GRANT REFERENCES (Stock)
     ON FOUR_STAR
     TO SECRET_HACKER;
```

Avoid granting privileges to people who may abuse them. True, people don't come with guarantees printed on their foreheads. But if you wouldn't lend your new car to a person for a long trip, you probably shouldn't grant him the REFERENCES privilege on an important table either.

The preceding example offers one good reason for maintaining careful control of the REFERENCES privilege. Here are two other reasons why you should maintain careful control of REFERENCES:

- ✔ If the other person specifies a constraint in HOT STOCKS by using a RESTRICT option and you try to delete a row from your table, the DBMS tells you that you can't, because doing so would violate a referential constraint.

- ✔ If you want to use the DROP command to destroy your table, you find that you must get the other person to first drop his constraint (or his table).

The bottom line is that enabling another person to specify integrity constraints on your table not only introduces a potential security breach, but also means that the other user sometimes gets in your way.

Delegating responsibility for security

To keep your system secure, you must severely restrict the access privileges you grant, as well as the people to whom you grant these privileges. But people who can't do their work because they lack access are likely to hassle you constantly. To preserve your sanity, you'll probably need to delegate some of the responsibility for maintaining database security. SQL provides for such delegation through the WITH GRANT OPTION clause. Consider the following example:

```
GRANT UPDATE
    ON RETAIL_PRICE_LIST
    TO SALES_MANAGER WITH GRANT OPTION;
```

This statement is similar to the previous GRANT UPDATE example in that the statement enables the sales manager to update the retail price list. The statement also gives her the right to grant the update privilege to anyone she wants. If you use this form of the GRANT statement, you must not only trust the grantee to use the privilege wisely, but also trust her to choose wisely in granting the privilege to others.

The ultimate in trust, and therefore the ultimate in vulnerability, is to execute a statement such as the following:

```
GRANT ALL PRIVILEGES
    ON FOUR_STAR
    TO BENEDICT_ARNOLD WITH GRANT OPTION;
```

Be *extremely* careful about using statements such as this one.

Part II
Using SQL to Build Databases

"Your database is beyond repair, but before I tell you our backup recommendation, let me ask you a question. How many index cards do you think will fit on the walls of your computer room?"

In this part . . .

The database life cycle encompasses the following four important stages:

- ✔ Creating the database
- ✔ Filling the database with data
- ✔ Manipulating and retrieving selected data
- ✔ Deleting the data

I cover all these stages in this book, but in Part II, I focus on database creation. SQL includes all the facilities you need to create relational databases of any size or complexity. I explain what these facilities are and how to use them. I also describe some common problems that relational databases suffer from and tell you how SQL can help you prevent such problems — or at least minimize their effects.

Chapter 4

Building and Maintaining a Simple Database Structure

In This Chapter

▶ Using RAD to build, change, and remove a database table

▶ Using SQL to build, change, and remove a database table

▶ Migrating your database to another DBMS

Computer history changes so fast that sometimes the rapid turnover of technological generations can be confusing. High-level (so-called third-generation) languages such as FORTRAN, COBOL, BASIC, Pascal, and C were the first languages used to build and change large databases. Later, languages specifically designed for use with databases, such as dBASE, Paradox, and R:BASE (third-and-a-half-generation languages?) came into use. The latest step in this progression is the emergence of development environments such as Access, Delphi, and C++Builder (called fourth-generation languages, or *4GLs*), which build applications with little or no procedural programming. You can use these graphical object-oriented tools (also known as *rapid application development, or RAD, tools*) to assemble application components into production applications.

Because SQL is not a complete language, it doesn't fit tidily into one of the generational categories I just mentioned. It makes use of commands in the manner of a third-generation language but is essentially nonprocedural, like a fourth-generation language. No matter how you classify SQL, you can use it in conjunction with all the major third- and fourth-generation development tools. You can write the SQL code yourself, or you can move objects around on-screen and have the development environment generate equivalent code for you. The commands that go out to the remote database are pure SQL in either case.

In this chapter, I take you through the process of building, altering, and dropping a simple table by using a RAD tool, and then discuss how to build, alter, and drop the same table using SQL.

Building a Simple Database Using a RAD Tool

People use databases because they want to keep track of important information. Sometimes, the information that they want to track is simple, and sometimes it's not. A good database management system provides what you need in either case. Some DBMSs give you SQL. Others, such as RAD tools, give you an object-oriented graphical environment. Some DBMSs support both approaches. In the following sections, I show you how to build a simple single-table database by using a graphical database design tool. I use Microsoft Access in my examples, but the procedure is similar for other Windows-based development environments.

Deciding what to track

The first step when you create a database is to decide what you want to track. For example, imagine that you have just won $248 million in the Powerball lottery. (It's okay to imagine something like this. In real life, it's about as likely as finding your car squashed by a meteorite.) People you haven't heard from in years, and friends you'd forgotten you had, are suddenly coming out of the woodwork. Some have surefire, can't-miss business opportunities in which they want you to invest. Others represent worthy causes that could benefit from your support. As a good steward of your new wealth, you realize that some business opportunities aren't as good as others, and some causes aren't as worthy as others. You decide to put all the options into a database so that you can keep track of them and make fair and equitable judgments.

You decide to track the following information about your friends and relations:

- ✔ First name
- ✔ Last name
- ✔ Address
- ✔ City
- ✔ State or province
- ✔ Postal code
- ✔ Phone
- ✔ How known (your relationship to the person)
- ✔ Proposal
- ✔ Business or charity

You decide to put all the listed items into a single database table; you don't need something elaborate. You fire up your Access 2003 development environment and stare at the screen shown in Figure 4-1. Not super exciting, I agree, but keep reading.

Creating a table with Design View

The screen shown in Figure 4-1 contains much more information than previous-generation DBMS products displayed. In the old days (way back in the 1980s), the typical DBMS presented you with a blank screen punctuated by a single character prompt. Database management has come a long way since then, and determining what you should do first is much easier now. On the right side of the window, a number of options are displayed:

✔ The Microsoft Office Online pane gives you convenient access to helpful information on Microsoft's Web site.

✔ The Open pane lists databases that have been used recently.

✔ The New pane enables you to launch a new blank database or select from a library of database templates.

✔ The Create a New File option is a one-click entry point to creating a new database.

Figure 4-1:
Microsoft
Access
opening
screen.

Follow these steps to create a single database table in Access:

1. **Open Access and then select the Create a New File option.**

   The New File panel appears.

2. **Click the Blank Database option.**

   The File New Database dialog box surfaces. The dialog box asks you to name and save your new database file. The My Documents folder is the default choice for file locations, but you can save the database to any folder you want. For this example, replace the default name with POWER, because you're tracking data related to your Powerball winnings.

3. **Click the Create button.**

   The POWER Database window opens.

4. **Select the Create Table in Design View option.**

   The second choice, Create Table Using Wizard, isn't very flexible. The table-creating wizard builds tables from a list of predefined columns. The third choice, Create Table by Entering Data, makes many default assumptions about your data and is not the best choice for serious application development.

   After double-clicking the Create Table in Design View option, the table creation window appears.

5. **Fill in the Field Name, Data Type, and Description information for each attribute for your table.**

   After you make an entry in the `Field Name` column, a drop-down menu appears in the `Data Type` column. Select the appropriate data types you want to use from the drop-down menu.

   As you can see in Figure 4-2, the General tab shows the default values for some of the field properties. You may want to make entries for all the fields you can identify.

   Access uses the term *field* rather than *column*. The program's original file-processing systems weren't relational and used the file, field, and record terminology that are common for flat-file systems.

   You may want to retain these values, or change them as appropriate. For example, the default value for the `FirstName` field is 50 characters, which is probably more characters than you need. You can save storage space by changing the value to something more reasonable, such as 15 characters. Figure 4-3 shows the table creation window after all field entries are made.

6. **Save your table.**

   Choose File⇨Save or click the Save icon. The Save As dialog box appears. Enter a name for the table (I named my table PowerDesign).

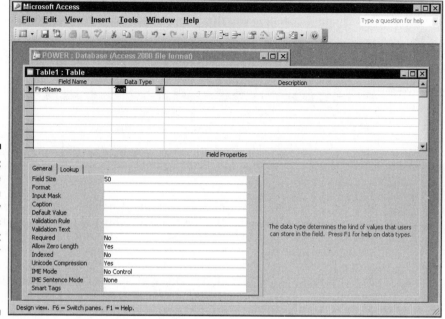

Figure 4-2:
The table creation window shows default entries for First Name field properties.

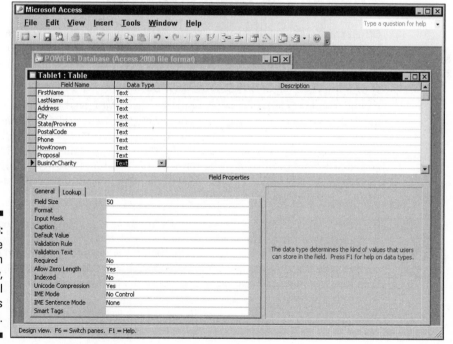

Figure 4-3:
The table creation window, with all fields defined.

When you try to save your new table, another dialog box appears (see Figure 4-4), telling you that you haven't defined a primary key and asking whether you want to define one now. I discuss primary keys in the section "Identifying a primary key," later in this chapter. For now, just click No.

Figure 4-4:
The primary
key mes-
sage box.

After you save your table, you may find that you need to tweak your original design, as I describe in the next section, "Altering the table structure." Perhaps so many people have offered you enticing business deals that a few of these folks have the same first and last names as other people in the group. To keep them straight, you decide to add a unique proposal number to each record in the database table. This way, you can tell one David Lee from another.

Altering the table structure

Often, the database tables you create need some tweaking. If you're working for someone else, your client may come to you after you create the database and tell you that she wants to keep track of another data item — perhaps several more. That means you have to go back to the drawing board.

If you're building a database for your own use, deficiencies in your structure inevitably become apparent *after* you create the structure. For example, say you start getting proposals from outside the United States and need to add a `Country` column. Or you have an older database that didn't include e-mail addresses; time to bring it up to date. In this section, I show you how to use Access to modify a table. Other RAD tools have comparable capabilities and work in a similar fashion.

If a time comes when you need to make an update, go ahead and take a moment to assess all the fields. For example, if you need to add unique proposal numbers so that you can distinguish between proposals from different people who have the same name, you may as well add a second `Address` field for people with complex addresses and a `Country` field for proposals from other countries.

To insert a new row and accommodate the changes, open the table and perform the following steps:

1. **In the table creation window, put the cursor in the top row, as shown in Figure 4-5, and choose Insert⇨Rows.**

   A blank row appears at the cursor position and pushes down all the existing rows.

2. **Enter the column headings you want to add to your table.**

   As you can see in Figure 4-6, I used `ProposalNumber` as the Field Name, `AutoNumber` as the Data Type, and `Unique identifier for each row of the PowerDesign table` as the Description. The `AutoNumber` data type is a numeric type that is automatically incremented for each succeeding row in a table. In a similar way, I added an `Address2` field below the `Address` field and a `Country` field below the `PostalCode` field.

3. **After you finish your modifications, save the table before closing it.**

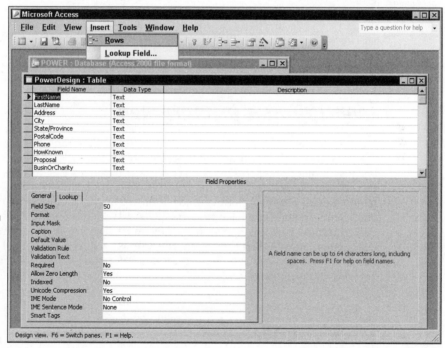

Figure 4-5: Inserting a new row into the Power Design table.

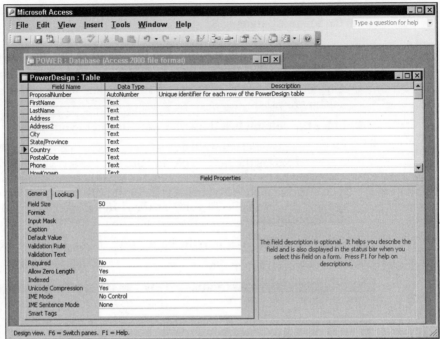

Figure 4-6:
Your revised
table defini-
tion should
look similar
to this.

Identifying a primary key

A table's primary key is a field that uniquely identifies each row.
ProposalNumber is a good candidate for PowerDesign's primary key
because it uniquely identifies each row in the table. It's the only field that you
can be sure doesn't have any duplicate entries. To designate a field as a
table's primary key, place the cursor in the appropriate row of the table creation window, and then click the Primary Key icon in the center of the Table
Design toolbar (it's the icon with the key on it). The key icon appears in the
left-most column of the table creation window, as shown in Figure 4-7, next to
the ProposalNumber field, indicating that ProposalNumber is the primary
key of the PowerDesign table.

Creating an index

In any database, you need a quick way to access records of interest. (This is
never more true than when you win the lottery — the number of investment
and charitable proposals you receive could easily grow into the thousands.)
Say, for example, that you want to look at all the proposals from people claim-
ing to be your brother. Assuming none of your brothers have changed their

last names for theatrical or professional reasons, you can isolate these offers by basing your retrieval on the contents of the `LastName` field, as shown in the following example:

```
SELECT * FROM PowerDesign
   WHERE LastName = 'Marx' ;
```

That strategy doesn't work for the proposals made by half brothers and brothers-in-law, so you need to look at a different field, as shown in the following example:

```
SELECT * FROM PowerDesign
   WHERE HowKnown = 'brother-in-law'
         OR
         HowKnown = 'half brother' ;
```

SQL scans the table a row at a time, looking for entries that satisfy the WHERE clause condition. If the PowerDesign table is large (tens of thousands of records), you may end up doing some waiting. You can speed things up by applying *indexes* to the PowerDesign table. (An *index* is a table of pointers. Each row in the index points to a corresponding row in the data table.)

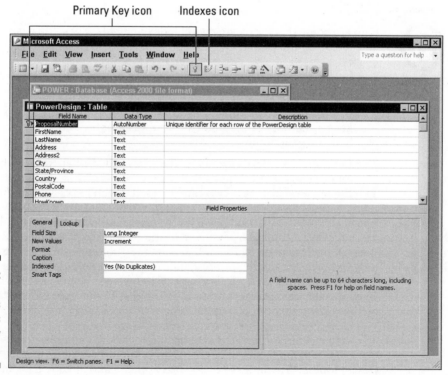

Figure 4-7:
`Proposal Number` is declared as the primary key.

You can define an index for all the different ways that you may want to access your data. If you add, change, or delete rows in the data table, you don't need to re-sort the table — you need only to update the indexes. You can update an index much faster than you can sort a table. After you establish an index with the desired ordering, you can use that index to access rows in the data table almost instantaneously.

Because the `ProposalNumber` field is unique as well as short, using that field is the quickest way to access an individual record. It is an ideal candidate to be the primary key. And because primary keys are usually the fastest way to access data, the primary key of any and every table should *always* be indexed; Access indexes primary keys automatically. To use this field, however, you must know the `ProposalNumber` of the record you want. You may want to create additional indexes based on other fields, such as `LastName`, `PostalCode`, or `HowKnown`. For a table that you index on `LastName`, after a search finds the first row containing a `LastName` of *Marx*, the search has found them all. The index keys for all the *Marx* rows are stored one right after another. You can retrieve `Chico`, `Groucho`, `Harpo`, `Zeppo`, and `Karl` almost as fast as you could get the data on `Chico` alone.

Indexes add overhead to your system, which slows down operations. You must balance this slowdown against the speed you gain by accessing records through an index.

Here are some tips for picking good indexing fields. These tips can also help you decide on the primary key:

✔ Indexing the fields you frequently use to access records is always a good idea. You can speedily access records without too much latency.

✔ Don't bother creating indexes for fields that you *never* use as retrieval keys. Creating needless indexes is a waste of time and memory space and you gain nothing.

✔ Don't create indexes for fields that don't differentiate one record from a lot of others. For example, the `BusinOrCharity` field merely divides the table records into two categories; it doesn't make a good index.

The effectiveness of an index varies from one implementation to another. If you migrate a database from one platform to another, the indexes that gave the best performance on the first system may not perform the best on the new platform. In fact, the performance may be worse than if you hadn't indexed the database at all. Try various indexing schemes to see which one gives you the best overall performance, and optimize your indexes so that neither retrieval speed nor update speed are negatively impacted.

To create indexes for the PowerDesign table, click the Indexes icon (which looks like a lightning bolt) located to the right of the Primary Key icon in the Table Design toolbar. The Indexes dialog box appears and already has entries for `PostalCode` and `ProposalNumber`. Figure 4-8 shows the Indexes dialog box.

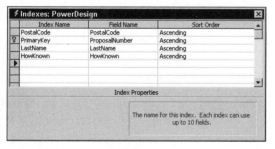

Figure 4-8:
The Indexes
dialog box.

Access automatically creates an index for `PostalCode` because that field is often used for retrievals. It automatically indexes the primary key as well.

You can see that `PostalCode` isn't a primary key and isn't necessarily unique; the opposite is true for `ProposalNumber`. Create additional indexes for `LastName` and `HowKnown`, because they're likely to be used for retrievals. Figure 4-9 shows how these new indexes are specified.

Figure 4-9:
Defining
indexes
for the
`LastName`
and
`HowKnown`
fields.

After you create all your indexes, don't forget to save the new table structure before closing it.

If you use a RAD tool other than Microsoft Access, the info in this section doesn't apply to you. However, the overall process is fairly similar.

Deleting a table

In the course of creating a table (such as the PowerDesign table I describe in this chapter) with the exact structure you want, you may create a few intermediate versions along the way. Having these variant tables on your system may confuse people later, so delete them now while they're still fresh in your mind. To do so, select the table that you want to delete and click the Delete icon in the menu bar of the database window, as shown in Figure 4-10.

Delete icon

Figure 4-10:
You can
delete a
table by
selecting its
name and
clicking
this icon.

An Access dialog box appears and asks whether you really want to delete the selected table. Say you complete the deletion by clicking Yes. You can't delete a table that's open (if you try, Access prompts you to close the table and try again).

If Access deletes a table, it deletes all subsidiary tables as well, including any indexes the table may have.

Building PowerDesign with SQL's DDL

You can accomplish all the database definition functions you perform with a RAD tool (such as Access) by using SQL. Of course, using SQL isn't as glamorous — instead of clicking menu choices with the mouse, you enter commands from the keyboard. People who prefer to manipulate visual objects find the RAD tools easy to understand and use. People who are more oriented toward stringing words together into logical statements find SQL commands easier.

Becoming proficient at using both methods is worthwhile because some things are more easily represented by using the object paradigm and others are more easily handled by using SQL.

In the following sections, I use SQL to perform the same table creation, alteration, and deletion operations that I used the RAD tool to perform in the first part of this chapter.

Using SQL with Microsoft Access

Access is designed as a rapid application development (RAD) tool that does not require programming. You can write and execute SQL statements in Access, but you have to use a back door method to do it. To open a basic editor where you can enter SQL code, follow these steps:

1. **Open your database and double-click Queries from the Objects list on the left side of the POWER dialog box.**

2. **In the task pane on the right, double-click Create Query in Design View.**

   The Show Table dialog box appears.

3. **Select any table. Click the Add button and then click the Close button.**

   The cursor blinks in the Query window that you just created, but you can ignore it.

4. **From the main Access menu, choose View⇨SQL View.**

   An editor window appears with the beginnings of an SQL SELECT statement.

5. **Delete the SELECT statement and then enter the SQL statement you want. This is where you could enter a statement such as:**

   ```
   SELECT * FROM PowerDesign
      WHERE LastName = 'Marx' ;
   ```

6. **When you're finished, click the Save icon.**

   Access asks you for a name for the query you have just created.

7. **Enter a name and then click OK.**

Your statement is saved and will be executed as a query later. Unfortunately, Access doesn't execute the full range of SQL statements. For example, it won't execute a CREATE TABLE statement. But after your table is created, you can perform just about any manipulation of your table's data that you want.

Creating a table

If you're working with a full-featured DBMS — such as Microsoft SQL Server, Oracle 9i, or IBM DB2 — to create a database table with SQL, you must enter the same information that you'd enter if you created the table with a RAD tool. The difference is that the RAD tool helps you by providing a visual interface in the form of a table creation dialog box (or some similar data-entry skeleton) and by preventing you from entering invalid field names, types, or sizes.

SQL doesn't give you as much help. You must know what you're doing at the onset; figuring things out along the way can lead to less-than-desirable database results. You must enter the entire CREATE TABLE statement before SQL even looks at it, let alone gives you any indication as to whether you made any errors in the statement.

The statement that creates a proposal-tracking table identical to the one created earlier in the chapter uses the following syntax:

```
CREATE TABLE PowerSQL (
    ProposalNumber      SMALLINT,
    FirstName           CHAR (15),
    LastName            CHAR (20),
    Address             CHAR (30),
    City                CHAR (25),
    StateProvince       CHAR (2),
    PostalCode          CHAR (10),
    Country             CHAR (30),
    Phone               CHAR (14),
    HowKnown            CHAR (30),
    Proposal            CHAR (50),
    BusinOrCharity      CHAR (1) );
```

The information in the SQL statement is essentially the same information you enter using Access's graphical user interface. The nice thing about SQL is that the language is universal. The same standard syntax works regardless of what database management system you use.

Becoming proficient in SQL has long-term payoffs because it will be around for a long time. The effort you put into becoming an expert in a particular development tool is likely to yield a lower return on investment. No matter how wonderful the latest RAD tool may be, it will be superseded by newer technology within three to five years. If you can recover your investment in the tool in that time, great! Use it. If not, you may be wise to stick with the tried and true. Train your people in SQL, and your training investment will pay dividends over a much longer period.

Creating an index

Indexes are an important part of any relational database. They serve as pointers into the tables that contain the data of interest. By using an index, you can go directly to a particular record without having to scan the table sequentially, one record at a time, to find that record. For really large tables, indexes are a necessity; without indexes, you may need to wait *years* rather than seconds for a result. (Well, I suppose you wouldn't actually wait years. Some retrievals, however, may actually take that long if you let them keep running. Unless you have nothing better to do with your computer's time, you'd probably just abort the retrieval and do without the result. Life goes on.)

Amazingly, the SQL standard doesn't provide a means to create an index. The DBMS vendors provide their own implementations of the function. Because these implementations aren't standardized, they may differ from one another. Most vendors provide the index creation function by adding a CREATE INDEX command to SQL. Even though two vendors may use the same words (CREATE INDEX), the way the command operates may not be the same. You're likely to find quite a few implementation-dependent clauses. Carefully study your DBMS documentation to determine how to use that particular DBMS to create indexes.

Altering the table structure

To change the structure of an existing table, you can use SQL's ALTER TABLE command. Interactive SQL at your client station is not as convenient as a RAD tool. The RAD tool displays your table's structure, which you can then modify. Using SQL, you must know in advance the table's structure and how you want to modify it. At the screen prompt, you must enter the appropriate command to perform the alteration. If, however, you want to embed the table alteration instructions in an application program, using SQL is usually the easiest way to do so.

To add a second address field to the PowerSQL table, use the following DDL command:

```
ALTER TABLE PowerSQL
   ADD COLUMN Address2 CHAR (30);
```

You don't need to be an SQL guru to decipher this code. Even professed computer illiterates can probably figure this one out. The command alters a table with the name PowerSQL by adding a column to the table. The column is named Address2, is of the CHAR data type, and is 30 characters long. This example demonstrates how easily you can change the structure of database tables by using SQL DDL commands.

Standard SQL provides this statement for adding a column to a table and allows you to drop an existing column in a similar manner, as in the following code:

```
ALTER TABLE PowerSQL
   DROP COLUMN Address2;
```

Deleting a table

Deleting database tables that you no longer need is easy. Just use the DROP TABLE command, as follows:

```
DROP TABLE PowerSQL ;
```

What could be simpler? If you drop a table, you erase all its data and its meta-data. No vestige of the table remains.

Deleting an index

If you delete a table by issuing a DROP TABLE command, you also delete any indexes associated with that table. Sometimes, however, you may want to keep a table but remove an index from it. The SQL standard doesn't define a DROP INDEX command, but most implementations include that command anyway. Such a command comes in handy if your system slows to a crawl and you discover that your tables aren't optimally indexed. Correcting an index problem can dramatically improve performance, which will delight users who've become accustomed to response times reminiscent of pouring molasses on a cold day in Vermont.

Portability Considerations

Any SQL implementation that you're likely to use may have extensions that give it capabilities that the SQL standard doesn't cover. Some of these features may appear in the next release of the SQL standard. Others are unique to a particular implementation and are probably destined to stay that way.

Often, extensions enable you to easily create an application that meets your needs, and you'll find yourself tempted to use them. Using the extensions may be your best course, but be aware of the trade-offs. If you ever want to migrate your application to another SQL implementation, you may need to rewrite those sections in which you used extensions that your new environment doesn't support.

The more you know about existing implementations and development trends, the better the decisions you'll make. Think about the probability of such a migration in the future and also about whether the extension you're considering is unique to your implementation or fairly widespread. Forgoing use of an extension may be better in the long run, even if its use saves you some time now. On the other hand, you may find no reason not to use the extension.

Chapter 5

Building a Multitable Relational Database

In This Chapter

▶ Deciding what to include in a database

▶ Determining relationships among data items

▶ Linking related tables with keys

▶ Designing for data integrity

▶ Normalizing the database

*I*n this chapter, I take you through an example of how to design a multitable database. The first step to designing any database is to identify what to include and what not to include. The next steps involve deciding how the included items relate to each other and setting up tables accordingly. I also discuss how to use *keys,* which enable you to access individual records and indexes quickly.

A database must do more than merely hold your data. It must also protect the data from becoming corrupted. In the latter part of this chapter, I discuss how to protect the integrity of your data. *Normalization* is one of the key methods you can use to protect the integrity of a database. I discuss the various normal forms and point out the kinds of problems that normalization solves.

Designing a Database

To design a database, follow these basic steps (I go into detail about each step in the sections that follow this list):

1. Decide what objects you want to include in your database.

2. **Determine which of these objects should be tables and which should be columns within those tables.**

3. **Define tables based on how you need to organize the objects.**

   Optionally, you may want to designate a table column or a combination of columns as a key. *Keys* provide a fast way of locating a row of interest in a table.

The following sections discuss these steps in detail, as well as some other technical issues that arise during database design.

Step 1: Defining objects

The first step in designing a database is deciding which aspects of the system are important enough to include in the model. Treat each aspect as an object and create a list of all the objects you can think of. At this stage, don't try to decide how these objects relate to each other. Just try to list them all.

You may find it helpful to gather a team of people who are familiar with the system you're modeling. These people can brainstorm and respond to each other's ideas. Working together, you'll probably develop a more complete and accurate set of objects than you would on your own.

When you have a reasonably complete set of objects, move on to the next step: deciding how these objects relate to each other. Some of the objects are *major entities*, crucial to giving you the results that you want. Others are subsidiary to those major entities. You ultimately may decide that some objects don't belong in the model at all.

Step 2: Identifying tables and columns

Major entities translate into database tables. Each major entity has a set of associated attributes, which translate into the table columns. Many business databases, for example, have a CUSTOMER table that keeps track of customers' names, addresses, and other permanent information. Each attribute of a customer, such as name, street, city, state, zip code, phone number, and e-mail address, becomes a column in the CUSTOMER table.

If you're hoping to find a set of rules to help you identify which objects should be tables and which of the attributes in the system belong to which table, think again. You may have some reasons for assigning a particular attribute to one table and other reasons for assigning the attribute to another table. You must make your judgment based on what information you want to get from the database and how you want to use that information.

When deciding how to structure database tables, involve the future users of the database as well as the people who will make decisions based on database information. If you come up with what you think is a reasonable structure, but it isn't consistent with the way that people will use the information, your system will be frustrating to use at best — and could even produce wrong information, which is even worse. Don't let this happen! Put careful effort into deciding how to structure your tables.

Take a look at an example to demonstrate the thought process that goes into creating a multitable database. Say that you just established VetLab, a clinical microbiology laboratory that tests biological specimens sent in by veterinarians. You want to track several things, including the following:

- ✔ Clients
- ✔ Tests that you perform
- ✔ Employees
- ✔ Orders
- ✔ Results

Each of these entities has associated attributes. Each client has a name, address, and other contact information. Each test has a name and a standard charge. Employees have contact information as well as a job classification and pay rate. For each order, you need to know who ordered it, when it was ordered, and what test was ordered. For each test result, you need to know the outcome of the test, whether the results were preliminary or final, and the test order number.

Step 3: Defining tables

Now you want to define a table for each entity and a column for each attribute. Table 5-1 shows how you may define the VetLab tables I introduce in the previous section.

Table 5-1	VetLab Tables
Table	*Columns*
CLIENT	Client Name
	Address 1
	Address 2

(continued)

Table 5-1 *(continued)*

Table	Columns
CLIENT	City
	State
	Postal Code
	Phone
	Fax
	Contact Person
TESTS	Test Name
	Standard Charge
EMPLOYEE	Employee Name
	Address 1
	Address 2
	City
	State
	Postal Code
	Home Phone
	Office Extension
	Hire Date
	Job Classification
	Hourly/Salary/Commission
ORDERS	Order Number
	Client Name
	Test Ordered
	Responsible Salesperson
	Order Date
RESULTS	Result Number
	Order Number
	Result

Table	Columns
RESULTS	Date Reported
	Preliminary/Final

You can create the tables defined in Table 5-1 by using either a rapid application development (RAD) tool or by using SQL's Data Definition Language (DDL), as shown in the following code:

```
CREATE TABLE CLIENT (
     ClientName       CHARACTER (30)      NOT NULL,
     Address1         CHARACTER (30),
     Address2         CHARACTER (30),
     City             CHARACTER (25),
     State            CHARACTER (2),
     PostalCode       CHARACTER (10),
     Phone            CHARACTER (13),
     Fax              CHARACTER (13),
     ContactPerson    CHARACTER (30) ) ;

CREATE TABLE TESTS (
     TestName         CHARACTER (30)      NOT NULL,
     StandardCharge   CHARACTER (30) ) ;

CREATE TABLE EMPLOYEE (
     EmployeeName     CHARACTER (30)      NOT NULL,
     Address1         CHARACTER (30),
     Address2         CHARACTER (30),
     City             CHARACTER (25),
     State            CHARACTER (2),
     PostalCode       CHARACTER (10),
     HomePhone        CHARACTER (13),
     OfficeExtension  CHARACTER (4),
     HireDate         DATE,
     JobClassification CHARACTER (10),
     HourSalComm      CHARACTER (1) ) ;

CREATE TABLE ORDERS (
     OrderNumber      INTEGER             NOT NULL,
     ClientName       CHARACTER (30),
     TestOrdered      CHARACTER (30),
     Salesperson      CHARACTER (30),
     OrderDate        DATE ) ;

CREATE TABLE RESULTS (
     ResultNumber     INTEGER             NOT NULL,
     OrderNumber      INTEGER,
     Result           CHARACTER(50),
     DateReported     DATE,
     PrelimFinal      CHARACTER (1) ) ;
```

These tables relate to each other by the attributes (columns) that they share, as the following list describes:

- The CLIENT table links to the ORDERS table by the `ClientName` column.
- The TESTS table links to the ORDERS table by the `TestName` (`TestOrdered`) column.
- The EMPLOYEE table links to the ORDERS table by the `EmployeeName` (`Salesperson`) column.
- The RESULTS table links to the ORDERS table by the `OrderNumber` column.

For a table to serve as an integral part of a relational database, link that table to at least one other table in the database by using a common column. Figure 5-1 illustrates the relationships between the tables.

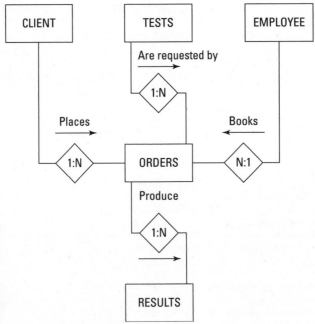

Figure 5-1: VetLab database tables and links.

The links in Figure 5-1 illustrate four different one-to-many relationships. The diamond in the middle of each relationship shows the maximum cardinality of each end of the relationship. The number 1 denotes the "one" side of the relationship and N denotes the "many" side.

- ✔ One client can make many orders, but each order is made by one, and only one, client.

- ✔ Each test can appear on many orders, but each order calls for one, and only one, test.

- ✔ Each order is taken by one, and only one, employee (or salesperson), but each salesperson can (and, you hope, does) take multiple orders.

- ✔ Each order can produce several preliminary test results and a final result, but each result is associated with one, and only one, order.

As you can see in the code, the attribute that links one table to another can have a different name in each table. Both attributes must, however, have matching data types.

Domains, character sets, collations, and translations

Although tables are the main components of a database, additional elements play a part, too. In Chapter 1, I define the *domain* of a column in a table as the set of all values that the column may assume. Establishing clear-cut domains for the columns in a table, through the use of constraints, is an important part of designing a database.

People who communicate in standard American English aren't the only ones who use relational databases. Other languages — even some that use other character sets — work equally well. Even if your data is in English, some applications may still require a specialized character set. SQL enables you to specify the character set you want to use. In fact, you can use a different character set for each column in a table. This flexibility is generally unavailable in languages other than SQL.

A *collation,* or *collating sequence,* is a set of rules that determines how strings in a character set compare with one another. Every character set has a default collation. In the default collation of the ASCII character set, *A* comes before *B,* and *B* comes before *C.* A comparison, therefore, considers *A* as less than *B* and considers *C* as greater than *B.* SQL enables you to apply different collations to a character set. This degree of flexibility isn't generally available in other languages, so you now have another reason to love SQL.

Sometimes, you encode data in a database in one character set, but you want to deal with the data in another character set. Perhaps you have data in the German character set, for example, but your printer doesn't support German characters that aren't included in the ASCII character set. A *translation* is an

SQL facility that enables you to translate character strings from one character set to another. The translation may translate one character into two, such as a German *ü* to an ASCII *ue,* or the translation may translate lowercase characters to uppercase. You can even translate one alphabet into another, such as Hebrew into ASCII.

Getting into your database fast with keys

A good rule for database design is to make sure that every row in a database table is distinguishable from every other row; each row should be unique. Sometimes, you may want to extract data from your database for a specific purpose, such as a statistical analysis, and in doing so, you create tables where rows aren't necessarily unique. For your limited purpose, this sort of duplication doesn't matter. Tables that you may use in more than one way, however, should not contain duplicate rows.

A *key* is an attribute or a combination of attributes that uniquely identifies a row in a table. To access a row in a database, you must have some way of distinguishing that row from all the other rows. Because keys must be unique, they provide such an access mechanism.

Furthermore, a key must never contain a null value. If you use null keys, you may not be able to distinguish between two rows that contain a null key field.

In the veterinary lab example, you can designate appropriate columns as keys. In the CLIENT table, ClientName is a good key. This key can distinguish each individual client from all other clients. Entering a value in this column becomes mandatory for every row in the table. TestName and EmployeeName make good keys for the TESTS and EMPLOYEE tables. OrderNumber and ResultNumber make good keys for the ORDERS and RESULTS tables. Make sure that you enter a unique value for every row.

You can have two kinds of keys: *primary keys* and *foreign keys.* The keys that I discuss in the preceding paragraph are primary keys. Primary keys guarantee uniqueness. I discuss primary and foreign keys in the next two sections.

Primary keys

A *primary key* is a column in a table with values that uniquely identify the rows in the table. To incorporate the idea of keys into the VetLab database, you can specify the primary key of a table as you create the table. In the following example, a single column is sufficient (assuming that all of VetLab's clients have unique names):

```
CREATE TABLE CLIENT (
   ClientName          CHARACTER (30)     PRIMARY KEY,
   Address1            CHARACTER (30),
   Address2            CHARACTER (30),
   City                CHARACTER (25),
   State               CHARACTER (2),
   PostalCode          CHARACTER (10),
   Phone               CHARACTER (13),
   Fax                 CHARACTER (13),
   ContactPerson       CHARACTER (30)
   ) ;
```

The constraint PRIMARY KEY replaces the constraint NOT NULL, given in the earlier definition of the CLIENT table. The PRIMARY KEY constraint implies the NOT NULL constraint, because a primary key can't have a null value.

Although most DBMSs allow you to create a table without a primary key, all tables in a database should have one. With that in mind, replace the NOT NULL constraint in all your tables. In my example, the TESTS, EMPLOYEE, ORDERS, and RESULTS tables should have the PRIMARY KEY constraint, as in the following example:

```
CREATE TABLE TESTS (
    TestName          CHARACTER (30)      PRIMARY KEY,
    StandardCharge    CHARACTER (30) ) ;
```

Sometimes, no single column in a table can guarantee uniqueness. In such cases, you can use a *composite key*. A composite key is a combination of columns, which, together, guarantee uniqueness. Imagine that some of VetLab's clients are chains that have offices in several cities. ClientName isn't sufficient to distinguish between two branch offices of the same client. To handle this situation, you can define a composite key as follows:

```
CREATE TABLE CLIENT (
   ClientName          CHARACTER (30)     NOT NULL,
   Address1            CHARACTER (30),
   Address2            CHARACTER (30),
   City                CHARACTER (25)     NOT NULL,
   State               CHARACTER (2),
   PostalCode          CHARACTER (10),
   Phone               CHARACTER (13),
   Fax                 CHARACTER (13),
   ContactPerson       CHARACTER (30),
   CONSTRAINT BranchPK    PRIMARY KEY
     (ClientName, City)
   ) ;
```

Foreign keys

A *foreign key* is a column or group of columns in a table that corresponds to or references a primary key in another table in the database. A foreign key doesn't have to be unique, but it must uniquely identify the column(s) in the table that the key references.

If the ClientName column is the primary key in the CLIENT table, every row in the CLIENT table must have a unique value in the ClientName column. ClientName is a foreign key in the ORDERS table. This foreign key corresponds to the primary key of the CLIENT table, but the key doesn't have to be unique in the ORDERS table. In fact, you hope the foreign key *isn't* unique. If each of your clients gave you only one order and then never ordered again, you'd go out of business rather quickly. You hope that many rows in the ORDERS table correspond with each row in the CLIENT table, indicating that nearly all your clients are repeat customers.

The following definition of the ORDERS table shows how you can add the concept of foreign keys to a CREATE statement:

```
CREATE TABLE ORDERS (
    OrderNumber         INTEGER             PRIMARY KEY,
    ClientName          CHARACTER (30),
    TestOrdered         CHARACTER (30),
    Salesperson         CHARACTER (30),
    OrderDate           DATE,
    CONSTRAINT BRANCHFK FOREIGN KEY (ClientName)
      REFERENCES CLIENT (ClientName),
    CONSTRAINT TestFK FOREIGN KEY (TestOrdered)
      REFERENCES TESTS (TestName),
    CONSTRAINT SalesFK FOREIGN KEY (Salesperson)
      REFERENCES EMPLOYEE (EmployeeName)
    ) ;
```

In this example, foreign keys in the ORDERS table link that table to the primary keys of the CLIENT, TESTS, and EMPLOYEE tables.

Working with Indexes

The SQL specification doesn't address the topic of indexes, but that omission doesn't mean that indexes are rare or even optional parts of a database system. Every SQL implementation supports indexes, but you'll find no universal agreement on how to support them. In Chapter 4, I show you how to create an index by using Microsoft Access, a rapid application development (RAD) tool. You must refer to the documentation for your particular database management system (DBMS) to see how the system implements indexes.

What's an index, anyway?

Data generally appears in a table in the order in which you originally entered the information. That order may have nothing to do with the order in which you later want to process the data. Say, for example, that you want to process your CLIENT table in `ClientName` order. The computer must first sort the table in `ClientName` order. Sorting the data this way takes time. The larger the table, the longer the sort takes. What if you have a table with 100,000 rows? Or a table with a million rows? In some applications, such table sizes are not rare. The best sort algorithms would have to make some 20 million comparisons and millions of swaps to put the table in the desired order. Even with a very fast computer, you may not want to wait that long.

Indexes can be a great timesaver. An *index* is a subsidiary or support table that goes along with a data table. For every row in the data table, you have a corresponding row in the index table. The order of the rows in the index table is different.

Table 5-2 shows a small example data table.

Table 5-2		CLIENT Table		
ClientName	*Address1*	*Address2*	*City*	*State*
Butternut Animal Clinic	5 Butternut Lane		Hudson	NH
Amber Veterinary, Inc.	470 Kolvir Circle		Amber	MI
Vets R Us	2300 Geoffrey Road	Suite 230	Anaheim	CA
Doggie Doctor	32 Terry Terrace		Nutley	NJ
The Equestrian Center	Veterinary	7890 Paddock Parkway	Gallup	NM
Dolphin Institute	1002 Marine Drive		Key West	FL
J. C. Campbell, Credit Vet	2500 Main Street		Los Angeles	CA
Wenger's Worm Farm	15 Bait Boulevard		Sedona	AZ

The rows are not in alphabetical order by `ClientName`. In fact, they aren't in any useful order at all. The rows are simply in the order in which somebody entered the data.

An index for this CLIENT table may look like Table 5-3.

Table 5-3	Client Name Index for the CLIENT Table
ClientName	*Pointer to Data Table*
Amber Veterinary, Inc.	2
Butternut Animal Clinic	1
Doggie Doctor	4
Dolphin Institute	6
J. C. Campbell, Credit Vet	7
The Equestrian Center	5
Vets R Us	3
Wenger's Worm Farm	8

The index contains the field that forms the basis of the index (in this case, `ClientName`) and a pointer into the data table. The pointer in each index row gives the row number of the corresponding row in the data table.

Why you should want an index

If you want to process a table in `ClientName` order, and you have an index arranged in `ClientName` order, you can perform your operation almost as fast as you could if the data table itself was in `ClientName` order. You can work through the index, moving immediately to each index row's corresponding data record by using the pointer in the index.

If you use an index, the table processing time is proportional to N, where N is the number of records in the table. Without an index, the processing time for the same operation is proportional to $N \lg N$, where $\lg N$ is the logarithm of N to the base 2. For small tables, the difference is insignificant, but for large tables, the difference is great. On large tables, some operations aren't practical to perform without the help of indexes.

Say that you have a table containing 1,000,000 records (N = 1,000,000), and processing each record takes one millisecond (one-thousandth of a second). If you have an index, processing the entire table takes only 1,000 seconds — less than 17 minutes. Without an index, you need to go through the table approximately 1,000,000 × 20 times to achieve the same result. This process would take 20,000 seconds — more than five and a half hours. I think you can agree that the difference between 17 minutes and five and a half hours is substantial. That's the difference that indexing makes on processing records.

Maintaining an index

After you create an index, you must maintain it. Fortunately, you don't have to think too much about maintenance — your DBMS maintains your indexes for you automatically, by updating them every time you update the corresponding data tables. This process takes some extra time, but it's worth it. After you create an index and your DBMS maintains it, the index is always available to speed up your data processing, no matter how many times you need to call on it.

The best time to create an index is at the same time you create its corresponding data table. If you create the index early and begin maintaining it at the same time, you don't need to undergo the pain of building the index later, with the entire operation taking place in a single, long session. Try to anticipate all the ways that you may want to access your data, and then create an index for each possibility.

Some DBMS products give you the capability to turn off index maintenance. You may want to do so in some real-time applications where updating indexes takes a great deal of time and you have precious little to spare. You may even elect to update the indexes as a separate operation during off-peak hours.

Don't fall into the trap of creating an index for retrieval orders that you're unlikely ever to use. Index maintenance is an extra operation that the computer must perform every time it modifies the index field or adds or deletes a data table row, and this operation affects performance. For optimal performance, create only those indexes that you expect to use as retrieval keys — and only for tables containing a large number of rows. Otherwise, indexes can degrade performance.

You may need to compile something such as a monthly or quarterly report that requires the data in an odd order that you don't ordinarily need. Create an index just before running that periodic report, run the report, and then drop the index so that the DBMS isn't burdened with maintaining the index during the long period between reports.

Maintaining Integrity

A database is valuable only if you're reasonably sure that the data it contains is correct. In medical, aircraft, and spacecraft databases, for example, incorrect data can lead to loss of life. Incorrect data in other applications may have less severe consequences but can still prove damaging. The database designer must do her best to make sure that incorrect data never enters the database. This isn't always possible, but it *is* possible to at least make sure the data that is entered is valid. Maintaining data integrity means making sure any data that is entered into a database system satisfies the constraints that have been established for it. For example, if a database field is of the Date type, the DBMS should reject any entry into that field that is not a valid date.

Some problems can't be stopped at the database level. The application programmer must intercept these problems before they can damage the database. Everyone responsible for dealing with the database in any way must remain conscious of the threats to data integrity and take appropriate action to nullify those threats.

Databases can experience several distinctly different kinds of integrity — and a number of problems that can affect integrity. In the following sections, I discuss three types of integrity: *entity, domain,* and *referential.* I also look at some of the problems that can threaten database integrity.

Entity integrity

Every table in a database corresponds to an entity in the real world. That entity may be physical or conceptual, but in some sense, the entity's existence is independent of the database. A table has *entity integrity* if the table is entirely consistent with the entity that it models. To have entity integrity, a table must have a primary key. The primary key uniquely identifies each row in the table. Without a primary key, you can't be sure that the row retrieved is the one you want.

To maintain entity integrity, you need to specify that the column or group of columns that comprise the primary key is NOT NULL. In addition, you must constrain the primary key to be UNIQUE. Some SQL implementations enable you to add such a constraint to the table definition. With other implementations, you must apply the constraint later, after you specify how to add, change, or delete data from the table. The best way to ensure that your primary key is both NOT NULL and UNIQUE is to give the key the PRIMARY KEY constraint when you create the table, as shown in the following example:

```
CREATE TABLE CLIENT (
    ClientName          CHARACTER (30)      PRIMARY KEY,
    Address1            CHARACTER (30),
```

```
    Address2              CHARACTER (30),
    City                  CHARACTER (25),
    State                 CHARACTER (2),
    PostalCode            CHARACTER (10),
    Phone                 CHARACTER (13),
    Fax                   CHARACTER (13),
    ContactPerson         CHARACTER (30)
    ) ;
```

An alternative is to use NOT NULL in combination with UNIQUE, as shown in the following example:

```
CREATE TABLE CLIENT (
    ClientName            CHARACTER (30)        NOT NULL,
    Address1              CHARACTER (30),
    Address2              CHARACTER (30),
    City                  CHARACTER (25),
    State                 CHARACTER (2),
    PostalCode            CHARACTER (10),
    Phone                 CHARACTER (13),
    Fax                   CHARACTER (13),
    ContactPerson         CHARACTER (30),
    UNIQUE (ClientName) ) ;
```

Domain integrity

You usually can't guarantee that a particular data item in a database is correct, but you *can* determine whether a data item is valid. Many data items have a limited number of possible values. If you make an entry that is not one of the possible values, that entry must be an error. The United States, for example, has 50 states plus the District of Columbia, Puerto Rico, and a few possessions. Each of these areas has a two-character code that the U.S. Postal Service recognizes. If your database has a State column, you can enforce *domain integrity* by requiring that any entry into that column be one of the recognized two-character codes. If an operator enters a code that's not on the list of valid codes, that entry breaches domain integrity. If you test for domain integrity, you can refuse to accept any operation that causes such a breach.

Domain integrity concerns arise if you add new data to a table by using either the INSERT statement or the UPDATE statement. You can specify a domain for a column by using a CREATE DOMAIN statement before you use that column in a CREATE TABLE statement, as shown in the following example:

```
CREATE DOMAIN LeagueDom CHAR (8)
    CHECK (VALUE IN ('American', 'National'));
CREATE TABLE TEAM (
    TeamName              CHARACTER (20)        NOT NULL,
    League                LeagueDom             NOT NULL
    ) ;
```

The domain of the League column includes only two valid values: American and National. Your DBMS doesn't enable you to commit an entry or update to the TEAM table unless the League column of the row you're adding has a value of either 'American' or 'National'.

Referential integrity

Even if every table in your system has entity integrity and domain integrity, you may still have a problem because of inconsistencies in the way one table relates to another. In most well-designed databases, every table contains at least one column that refers to a column in another table in the database. These references are important for maintaining the overall integrity of the database. The same references, however, make update anomalies possible.

Update anomalies are problems that can occur after you update the data in a row of a database table.

The relationships among tables are generally not bidirectional. One table is usually dependent on the other. Say, for example, that you have a database with a CLIENT table and an ORDERS table. You may conceivably enter a client into the CLIENT table before she makes any orders. You can't, however, enter an order into the ORDERS table unless you already have an entry in the CLIENT table for the client who's making that order. The ORDERS table is dependent on the CLIENT table. This kind of arrangement is often called a *parent-child relationship,* where CLIENT is the parent table and ORDERS is the child table. The child is dependent on the parent.

Generally, the primary key of the parent table is a column (or group of columns) that appears in the child table. Within the child table, that same column (or group) is a foreign key. A foreign key may contain nulls and need not be unique.

Update anomalies arise in several ways. A client moves away, for example, and you want to delete her from your database. If she has already made some orders, which you recorded in the ORDERS table, deleting her from the CLIENT table could present a problem. You'd have records in the ORDERS (child) table for which you have no corresponding records in the CLIENT (parent) table. Similar problems can arise if you add a record to a child table without making a corresponding addition to the parent table. The corresponding foreign keys in all child tables must reflect any changes to the primary key of a row in a parent table; otherwise, an update anomaly results.

You can eliminate most referential integrity problems by carefully controlling the update process. In some cases, you need to *cascade* deletions from a parent table to its children. To cascade a deletion, when you delete a row from a parent table, you also delete all the rows in its child tables that have foreign keys that match the primary key of the deleted row in the parent table. Take a look at the following example:

```
CREATE TABLE CLIENT (
    ClientName          CHARACTER (30)      PRIMARY KEY,
    Address1            CHARACTER (30),
    Address2            CHARACTER (30),
    City                CHARACTER (25)      NOT NULL,
    State               CHARACTER (2),
    PostalCode          CHARACTER (10),
    Phone               CHARACTER (13),
    Fax                 CHARACTER (13),
    ContactPerson       CHARACTER (30)
    ) ;

CREATE TABLE TESTS (
    TestName            CHARACTER (30)      PRIMARY KEY,
    StandardCharge      CHARACTER (30)
    ) ;

CREATE TABLE EMPLOYEE (
    EmployeeName        CHARACTER (30)      PRIMARY KEY,
    ADDRESS1            CHARACTER (30),
    Address2            CHARACTER (30),
    City                CHARACTER (25),
    State               CHARACTER (2),
    PostalCode          CHARACTER (10),
    HomePhone           CHARACTER (13),
    OfficeExtension     CHARACTER (4),
    HireDate            DATE,
    JobClassification   CHARACTER (10),
    HourSalComm         CHARACTER (1)
    ) ;

CREATE TABLE ORDERS (
    OrderNumber         INTEGER             PRIMARY KEY,
    ClientName          CHARACTER (30),
    TestOrdered         CHARACTER (30),
    Salesperson         CHARACTER (30),
    OrderDate           DATE,
    CONSTRAINT NameFK FOREIGN KEY (ClientName)
      REFERENCES CLIENT (ClientName)
        ON DELETE CASCADE,
    CONSTRAINT TestFK FOREIGN KEY (TestOrdered)
      REFERENCES TESTS (TestName)
        ON DELETE CASCADE,
    CONSTRAINT SalesFK FOREIGN KEY (Salesperson)
      REFERENCES EMPLOYEE (EmployeeName)
        ON DELETE CASCADE
    ) ;
```

The constraint `NameFK` names `ClientName` as a foreign key that references the `ClientName` column in the CLIENT table. If you delete a row in the CLIENT table, you also automatically delete all rows in the ORDERS table that have the same value in the `ClientName` column as those in the `ClientName` column of the CLIENT table. The deletion cascades down from the CLIENT table to the ORDERS table. The same is true for the foreign keys in the ORDERS table that refer to the primary keys of the TESTS and EMPLOYEE tables.

You may not want to cascade a deletion. Instead, you may want to change the child table's foreign key to a `NULL` value. Consider the following variant of the previous example:

```
CREATE TABLE ORDERS (
    OrderNumber         INTEGER             PRIMARY KEY,
    ClientName          CHARACTER (30),
    TestOrdered         CHARACTER (30),
    SalesPerson         CHARACTER (30),
    OrderDate           DATE,
    CONSTRAINT NameFK FOREIGN KEY (ClientName)
      REFERENCES CLIENT (ClientName),
    CONSTRAINT TestFK FOREIGN KEY (TestOrdered)
      REFERENCES TESTS (TestName),
    CONSTRAINT SalesFK FOREIGN KEY (Salesperson)
      REFERENCES EMPLOYEE (EmployeeName)
        ON DELETE SET NULL
    ) ;
```

The constraint `SalesFK` names the `Salesperson` column as a foreign key that references the `EmployeeName` column of the EMPLOYEE table. If a salesperson leaves the company, you delete her row in the EMPLOYEE table. New salespeople are eventually assigned to her accounts, but for now, deleting her name from the EMPLOYEE table causes all of her orders in the ORDER table to receive a null value in the `Salesperson` column.

You can also keep inconsistent data out of a database by using one of these methods:

- ✔ **Refuse to permit an addition to a child table until a corresponding row exists in its parent table.** If you refuse to permit rows in a child table without a corresponding row in a parent table, you prevent the occurrence of "orphan" rows in the child table. This refusal helps maintain consistency across tables.

- ✔ **Refuse to permit changes to a table's primary key.** If you refuse to permit changes to a table's primary key, you don't need to worry about updating foreign keys in other tables that depend on that primary key.

Just when you thought it was safe

The one thing you can count on in databases (as in life) is change. Wouldn't you know? You create a database, complete with tables, constraints, and rows and rows of data. Then word comes down from management that the structure needs to be changed. How do you add a new column to a table that already exists? How do you delete one that you don't need any more? SQL to the rescue!

Adding a column to an existing table

Suppose your company institutes a policy of having a party for every employee on his or her birthday. To give the party coordinator the advance warning she needs to plan these parties, you need to add a Birthday column to the EMPLOYEE table. As they say in the Bahamas, "No problem!" Just use the ALTER TABLE statement. Here's how:

```
ALTER TABLE EMPLOYEE
   ADD COLUMN Birthday DATE ;
```

Now all you need to do is add the birthday information to each row in the table, and you can party on.

Deleting a column from an existing table

Now suppose that an economic downturn hits your company and it can no longer afford to fund lavish birthday parties. Even in a bad economy, DJ fees have gone through the roof. No more parties means no more need to retain birthday data. With the ALTER TABLE statement, you can handle this situation too.

```
ALTER TABLE EMPLOYEE
   DROP COLUMN Birthday ;
```

Ah, well, it was fun while it lasted.

Potential problem areas

Data integrity is subject to assault from a variety of quarters. Some of these problems arise only in multitable databases, whereas others can happen even in databases that contain only a single table. You want to recognize and minimize all these potential threats.

Bad input data

The source documents or data files that you use to populate your database may contain bad data. This data may be a corrupted version of the correct data, or it may not be the data you want. A *range check* tells you whether the data has domain integrity. This type of check catches some — but not all — problems. Field values that are within the acceptable range, but are nonetheless incorrect, aren't identified as problems.

Operator error

Your source data may be correct, but the data entry operator may incorrectly transcribe the data. This type of error can lead to the same kinds of problems as bad input data. Some of the solutions are the same, too. Range checks help, but they're not foolproof. Another solution is to have a second operator independently validate all the data. This approach is costly, because independent validation takes twice the number of people and twice the time. But in some cases where data integrity is critical, the extra effort and expense may prove worthwhile.

Mechanical failure

If you experience a mechanical failure, such as a disk crash, the data in the table may be destroyed. Good backups are your main defense against this problem.

Malice

Consider the possibility that someone may want to intentionally corrupt your data. Your first line of defense is to deny database access to anyone who may have a malicious intent, and restrict authorized users so that they can access only the data they need. Your second defense is to maintain data backups in a safe place. Periodically reevaluate the security features of your installation. Being just a little paranoid doesn't hurt.

Data redundancy

Data redundancy is a big problem with the hierarchical database model, but the problem can plague relational databases, too. Not only does such redundancy waste storage space and slow down processing, but it can also lead to serious data corruption. If you store the same data item in two different tables in a database, the item in one of those tables may change, while the corresponding item in the other table remains the same. This situation generates a discrepancy, and you may have no way of determining which version is correct. Keep data redundancy to a minimum.

Although a certain amount of redundancy is necessary for the primary key of one table to serve as a foreign key in another, you should try to avoid any redundancy beyond that.

After you eliminate most redundancy from a database design, you may find that performance is now unacceptable. Operators often purposefully use redundancy to speed up processing. In the VetLab database, the ORDERS table contains only the client's name to identify the source of each order. If you prepare an order, you must join the ORDERS table with the CLIENT table to get the client's address. If this joining of tables makes the program that prints orders run too slowly, you may decide to store the client's address redundantly in the ORDERS table. This redundancy offers the advantage of printing the orders faster but at the expense of slowing down and complicating any updating of the client's address.

A common practice is to initially design a database with little redundancy and with high degrees of normalization, and then, after finding that important applications run slowly, to selectively add redundancy and denormalize. The key word here is *selectively*. The redundancy that you add back in must have a specific purpose, and because you're acutely aware of both the redundancy and the hazard it represents, you take appropriate measures to ensure that the redundancy doesn't cause more problems than it solves. For more information, see the section later in this chapter, "Normalizing the Database."

Exceeding the capacity of your DBMS

A database system might work properly for years and then start experiencing intermittent errors that become progressively more serious. This may be a sign that you are approaching one of the system's capacity limits. There are limits to the number of rows that a table may have. There are also limits on columns, constraints, and more. Check the current size and content of your database against the specifications of your DBMS. If you're near the limit in any area, consider upgrading to a system with a higher capacity. Or, you may want to archive older data that is no longer active and then delete it from your database.

Constraints

Earlier in this chapter, I talk about constraints as mechanisms for ensuring that the data you enter into a table column falls within the domain of that column. A *constraint* is an application rule that the DBMS enforces. After you define a database, you can include constraints (such as NOT NULL) in a table definition. The DBMS makes sure that you can never commit any transaction that violates a constraint.

You have three different kinds of constraints:

✔ A **column constraint** imposes a condition on a column in a table.

✔ A **table constraint** is a constraint on an entire table.

✔ An **assertion** is a constraint that can affect more than one table.

Column constraints

An example of a column constraint is shown in the following Data Definition Language (DDL) statement:

```
CREATE TABLE CLIENT (
    ClientName        CHARACTER (30)      NOT NULL,
    Address1          CHARACTER (30),
    Address2          CHARACTER (30),
    City              CHARACTER (25),
    State             CHARACTER (2),
    PostalCode        CHARACTER (10),
    Phone             CHARACTER (13),
    Fax               CHARACTER (13),
    ContactPerson     CHARACTER (30)
    ) ;
```

The statement applies the constraint NOT NULL to the ClientName column, specifying that ClientName may not assume a null value. UNIQUE is another constraint that you can apply to a column. This constraint specifies that every value in the column must be unique. The CHECK constraint is particularly useful because it can take any valid expression as an argument. Consider the following example:

```
CREATE TABLE TESTS (
    TestName          CHARACTER (30)      NOT NULL,
    StandardCharge    NUMERIC (6,2)
        CHECK (StandardCharge >= 0.0
          AND StandardCharge <= 200.0)
    ) ;
```

VetLab's standard charge for a test must always be greater than or equal to zero. And none of the standard tests costs more than $200. The CHECK clause refuses to accept any entries that fall outside the range 0 <= StandardCharge <= 200. Another way of stating the same constraint is as follows:

```
CHECK (StandardCharge BETWEEN 0.0 AND 200.0)
```

Table constraints

The PRIMARY KEY constraint specifies that the column to which it applies is a primary key. This constraint is thus a constraint on the entire table and is equivalent to a combination of the NOT NULL and the UNIQUE column constraints. You can specify this constraint in a CREATE statement, as shown in the following example:

```
CREATE TABLE CLIENT (
    ClientName      CHARACTER (30)    PRIMARY KEY,
    Address1        CHARACTER (30),
    Address2        CHARACTER (30),
    City            CHARACTER (25),
    State           CHARACTER (2),
    PostalCode      CHARACTER (10),
    Phone           CHARACTER (13),
    Fax             CHARACTER (13),
    ContactPerson   CHARACTER (30)
    ) ;
```

Assertions

An *assertion* specifies a restriction for more than one table. The following example uses a search condition drawn from two tables to create an assertion:

```
CREATE TABLE ORDERS (
    OrderNumber       INTEGER          NOT NULL,
    ClientName        CHARACTER (30),
    TestOrdered       CHARACTER (30),
    Salesperson       CHARACTER (30),
    OrderDate         DATE
    ) ;

CREATE TABLE RESULTS (
    ResultNumber      INTEGER       NOT NULL,
    OrderNumber       INTEGER,
    Result            CHARACTER(50),
    DateOrdered       DATE,
    PrelimFinal       CHARACTER (1)
    ) ;

CREATE ASSERTION
  CHECK (NOT EXISTS (SELECT * FROM ORDERS, RESULTS
    WHERE ORDERS.OrderNumber = RESULTS.OrderNumber
    AND ORDERS.OrderDate > RESULTS.DateReported)) ;
```

This assertion ensures that test results aren't reported before the test is ordered.

Normalizing the Database

Some ways of organizing data are better than others. Some are more logical. Some are simpler. Some are better at preventing inconsistencies when you start using the database.

A host of problems — called *modification anomalies* — can plague a database if you don't structure the database correctly. To prevent these problems, you can *normalize* the database structure. Normalization generally entails splitting one database table into two simpler tables.

Modification anomalies are so named because they are generated by the addition of, change to, or deletion of data from a database table.

To illustrate how modification anomalies can occur, consider the table shown in Figure 5-2.

Figure 5-2:
This SALES
table leads
to modi-
fication
anomalies.

SALES		
Customer_ID	Product	Price
1001	Laundry detergent	12
1007	Toothpaste	3
1010	Chlorine bleach	4
1024	Toothpaste	3

Your company sells household cleaning and personal-care products, and you charge all customers the same price for each product. The SALES table keeps track of everything for you. Now assume that customer 1001 moves out of the area and no longer is a customer. You don't care what he's bought in the past, because he's not going to buy anything from your company again. You want to delete his row from the table. If you do so, however, you don't just lose the fact that customer 1001 has bought laundry detergent; you also lose the fact that laundry detergent costs $12. This situation is called a *deletion anomaly*. In deleting one fact (that customer 1001 bought laundry detergent), you inadvertently delete another fact (that laundry detergent costs $12).

You can use the same table to illustrate an insertion anomaly. For example, say that you want to add stick deodorant to your product line at a price of $2. You can't add this data to the SALES table until a customer buys stick deodorant.

The problem with the SALES table in the figure is that this table deals with more than one thing: It covers not just which products customers buy, but also what the products cost. You need to split the SALES table into two tables, each dealing with only one theme or idea, as shown in Figure 5-3.

CUST_PURCH		PROD_PRICE	
Customer_ID	Product	Product	Price
1001	Laundry detergent	Laundry detergent	12
1007	Toothpaste	Toothpaste	3
1010	Chlorine bleach	Chlorine bleach	4
1024	Toothpaste		

Figure 5-3: The SALES table is split into two tables.

Figure 5-3 shows that the SALES table is divided into two tables:

- CUST_PURCH, which deals with the single idea of customer purchases.
- PROD_PRICE, which deals with the single idea of product pricing.

You can now delete the row for customer 1001 from CUST_PURCH without losing the fact that laundry detergent costs $12 (the cost of laundry detergent is now stored in PROD_PRICE). You can also add stick deodorant to PROD_PRICE, whether anyone has bought the product or not. Purchase information is stored elsewhere, in the CUST_PURCH table.

The process of breaking up a table into multiple tables, each of which has a single theme, is called *normalization.* A normalization operation that solves one problem may not affect other problems. You may need to perform several successive normalization operations to reduce each resulting table to a single theme. Each database table should deal with one — and only one — main theme. Sometimes, determining that a table really deals with two or more themes is difficult.

You can classify tables according to the types of modification anomalies to which they're subject. In a 1970 paper, E. F. Codd, the first to describe the relational model, identified three sources of modification anomalies and defined first, second, and third *normal forms* (1NF, 2NF, 3NF) as remedies to those types of anomalies. In the ensuing years, Codd and others discovered additional types of anomalies and specified new normal forms to deal with them. The Boyce-Codd normal form (BCNF), the fourth normal form (4NF), and the fifth normal form (5NF) each afforded a higher degree of protection against modification anomalies. Not until 1981, however, did a paper, written by Ronald Fagin, describe domain-key normal form (DK/NF). Using this last normal form enables you to guarantee that a table is free of modification anomalies.

The normal forms are *nested* in the sense that a table that's in 2NF is automatically also in 1NF. Similarly, a table in 3NF is automatically in 2NF, and so on. For most practical applications, putting a database in 3NF is sufficient to ensure a high degree of integrity. To be absolutely sure of its integrity, you must put the database into DK/NF.

After you normalize a database as much as possible, you may want to make selected denormalizations to improve performance. If you do, be aware of the types of anomalies that may now become possible.

First normal form

To be in first normal form (1NF), a table must have the following qualities:

- ✔ The table is two-dimensional, with rows and columns.
- ✔ Each row contains data that pertains to some thing or portion of a thing.
- ✔ Each column contains data for a single attribute of the thing it's describing.
- ✔ Each cell (intersection of a row and a column) of the table must have only a single value.
- ✔ Entries in any column must all be of the same kind. If, for example, the entry in one row of a column contains an employee name, all the other rows must contain employee names in that column, too.
- ✔ Each column must have a unique name.
- ✔ No two rows may be identical (that is, each row must be unique).
- ✔ The order of the columns and the order of the rows is not significant.

A table (relation) in first normal form is immune to some kinds of modification anomalies but is still subject to others. The SALES table shown in Figure 5-2 is in first normal form, and as discussed previously, the table is subject to deletion and insertion anomalies. First normal form may prove useful in some applications but unreliable in others.

Second normal form

To appreciate second normal form, you must understand the idea of functional dependency. A *functional dependency* is a relationship between or among attributes. One attribute is functionally dependent on another if the value of the second attribute determines the value of the first attribute. If you know the value of the second attribute, you can determine the value of the first attribute.

Suppose, for example, that a table has attributes (columns) StandardCharge, NumberOfTests, and TotalCharge that relate through the following equation:

```
TotalCharge = StandardCharge * NumberOfTests
```

TotalCharge is functionally dependent on both StandardCharge and NumberOfTests. If you know the values of StandardCharge and NumberOfTests, you can determine the value of TotalCharge.

Every table in first normal form must have a unique primary key. That key may consist of one or more than one column. A key consisting of more than one column is called a *composite key.* To be in second normal form (2NF), all non-key attributes (columns) must depend on the entire key. Thus, every relation that is in 1NF with a single attribute key is automatically in second normal form. If a relation has a composite key, all non-key attributes must depend on all components of the key. If you have a table where some non-key attributes don't depend on all components of the key, break the table up into two or more tables so that, in each of the new tables, all non-key attributes depend on all components of the primary key.

Sound confusing? Look at an example to clarify matters. Consider a table like the SALES table back in Figure 5-2. Instead of recording only a single purchase for each customer, you add a row every time a customer buys an item for the first time. An additional difference is that charter customers (those with Customer_ID values of 1001 to 1007) get a discount off the normal price. Figure 5-4 shows some of this table's rows.

SALES_TRACK		
Customer_ID	Product	Price
1001	Laundry detergent	11.00
1007	Toothpaste	2.70
1010	Chlorine bleach	4.00
1024	Toothpaste	3.00
1010	Laundry detergent	12.00
1001	Toothpaste	2.70

Figure 5-4:
In the
SALES_
TRACK
table, the
Customer
ID and
Product
columns
constitute a
composite
key.

In Figure 5-4, Customer_ID does not uniquely identify a row. In two rows, Customer_ID is 1001. In two other rows, Customer_ID is 1010. The combination of the Customer_ID column and the Product column uniquely identifies a row. These two columns together are a composite key.

If not for the fact that some customers qualify for a discount and others don't, the table wouldn't be in second normal form, because Price (a non-key attribute) would depend only on part of the key (Product). Because some customers do qualify for a discount, Price depends on both CustomerID and Product, and the table is in second normal form.

Third normal form

Tables in second normal form are subject to some types of modification anomalies. These anomalies come from transitive dependencies.

A *transitive dependency* occurs when one attribute depends on a second attribute, which depends on a third attribute. Deletions in a table with such a dependency can cause unwanted information loss. A relation in third normal form is a relation in second normal form with no transitive dependencies.

Look again at the SALES table in Figure 5-2, which you know is in first normal form. As long as you constrain entries to permit only one row for each Customer_ID, you have a single-attribute primary key, and the table is in second normal form. However, the table is still subject to anomalies. What if customer 1010 is unhappy with the chlorine bleach, for example, and returns the item for a refund? You want to remove the third row from the table, which records the fact that customer 1010 bought chlorine bleach.

You have a problem: If you remove that row, you also lose the fact that chlorine bleach has a price of $4. This situation is an example of a transitive dependency. `Price` depends on `Product`, which, in turn, depends on the primary key `Customer_ID`.

Breaking the SALES table into two tables solves the transitive dependency problem. The two tables shown in Figure 5-3, CUST_PURCH and PROD_PRICE, make up a database that's in third normal form.

Domain-key normal form (DK/NF)

After a database is in third normal form, you've eliminated most, but not all, chances of modification anomalies. Normal forms beyond the third are defined to squash those few remaining bugs. Boyce-Codd normal form (BCNF), fourth normal form (4NF), and fifth normal form (5NF) are examples of such forms. Each form eliminates a possible modification anomaly but doesn't guarantee prevention of all possible modification anomalies. Domain-key normal form (DK/NF), however, provides such a guarantee.

A relation is in *domain-key normal form (DK/NF)* if every constraint on the relation is a logical consequence of the definition of keys and domains. A *constraint* in this definition is any rule that's precise enough that you can evaluate whether or not it's true. A *key* is a unique identifier of a row in a table. A *domain* is the set of permitted values of an attribute.

Look again at the database in Figure 5-2, which is in 1NF, to see what you must do to put that database in DK/NF.

Table: SALES (`Customer_ID`, `Product`, `Price`)

Key: `Customer_ID`

Constraints: 1. `Customer_ID` determines `Product`
                  2. `Product` determines `Price`
                  3. `Customer_ID` must be an integer > 1,000

To enforce Constraint 3 (that `Customer_ID` must be an integer greater than 1,000), you can simply define the domain for `Customer_ID` to incorporate this constraint. That makes the constraint a logical consequence of the domain of the `CustomerID` column. `Product` depends on `Customer_ID`, and `Customer_ID` is a key, so you have no problem with Constraint 1, which is a logical consequence of the definition of the key. Constraint 2 *is* a problem. `Price` depends on (is a logical consequence of) `Product`, and `Product` isn't a key. The solution is to divide the SALES table into two tables. One table uses `Customer_ID` as a key, and the other uses `Product` as a key. This setup is what you have in Figure 5-3. The database in Figure 5-3, besides being in 3NF, is also in DK/NF.

Design your databases so they're in DK/NF if possible. If you do so, enforcing key and domain restrictions causes all constraints to be met, and modification anomalies aren't possible. If a database's structure is designed so that you can't put it into domain-key normal form, you must build the constraints into the application program that uses the database. The database doesn't guarantee that the constraints will be met.

Abnormal form

Sometimes being abnormal pays off. You can get carried away with normalization and go too far. You can break up a database into so many tables that the entire thing becomes unwieldy and inefficient. Performance can plummet. Often, the optimal structure is somewhat denormalized. In fact, practical databases are almost never normalized all the way to DK/NF. You want to normalize the databases you design as much as possible, however, to eliminate the possibility of data corruption that results from modification anomalies.

After you normalize the database as far as you can, make some retrievals. If performance isn't satisfactory, examine your design to see whether selective denormalization would improve performance without sacrificing integrity. By carefully adding redundancy in strategic locations and denormalizing, you can arrive at a database that's both efficient and safe from anomalies.

Part III
Storing and Retrieving Data

The 5th Wave   By Rich Tennant

"Well, isn't this festive – a miniature intranet amidst a swirl of Java applets."

In this part . . .

SQL provides a rich set of tools for manipulating data in a relational database. As you may expect, SQL has mechanisms for adding new data, updating existing data, retrieving data, and deleting obsolete data. Nothing's particularly extraordinary about these capabilities (heck, human brains use 'em all the time). Where SQL shines is in its capability to isolate the *exact* data you want from all the rest — and present that data to you in an understandable form. SQL's comprehensive Data Manipulation Language (DML) provides this critically important capability.

In this part, I delve deep into the riches of DML. You discover how to use SQL tools to massage raw data into a form suitable for your purposes — and then to retrieve the result as useful information (what a concept).

Chapter 6

Manipulating Database Data

· ·

In This Chapter

▶ Dealing with data

▶ Retrieving the data you want from a table

▶ Displaying only selected information from one or more tables

▶ Updating the information in tables and views

▶ Adding a new row to a table

▶ Changing some or all of the data in a table row

▶ Deleting a table row

· ·

*C*hapters 3 and 4 reveal that creating a sound database structure is critical to maintaining data integrity. The stuff that you're really interested in, however, is the data itself — not its structure. You want to do four things with data: add it to tables, retrieve and display it, change it, and delete it from tables.

In principle, database manipulation is quite simple. Understanding how to add data to a table isn't difficult — you can add your data either one row at a time or in a batch. Changing, deleting, or retrieving table rows is also easy in practice. The main challenge to database manipulation is *selecting* the rows that you want to change, delete, or retrieve. The data that you want may reside in a database containing a large volume of data that you don't want. Fortunately, if you can specify what you want by using an SQL SELECT statement, the computer does all the searching for you. I guess that means manipulating a database with SQL is a piece of cake. Adding, changing, deleting, and retrieving are all easy! Hmmm. Perhaps that might be a slight exaggeration. At least let's start off easy, with a simple data retrieval.

Retrieving Data

The data manipulation task that users perform most frequently is retrieving selected information from a database. You may want to retrieve the contents of one row out of thousands in a table. You may want to retrieve all the rows that satisfy a condition or a combination of conditions. You may even want to retrieve all the rows in the table. One particular SQL statement, the SELECT statement, performs all these tasks for you.

The simplest use of the SELECT statement is to retrieve all the data in all the rows of a specified table. To do so, use the following syntax:

```
SELECT * FROM CUSTOMER ;
```

The asterisk (*) is a wildcard character that means *everything*. In this context, the asterisk is a shorthand substitute for a listing of all the column names of the CUSTOMER table. As a result of this statement, all the data in all the rows and columns of the CUSTOMER table appear on-screen.

SELECT statements can be much more complicated than the statement in this example. In fact, some SELECT statements can be so complicated that they're virtually indecipherable. This potential complexity is a result of the fact that you can tack multiple modifying clauses onto the basic statement. Chapter 9 covers modifying clauses in detail. In this chapter, I briefly discuss the WHERE clause, which is the most commonly used method to restrict the rows that a SELECT statement returns.

A SELECT statement with a WHERE clause has the following general form:

```
SELECT column_list FROM table_name
    WHERE condition ;
```

The column list specifies which columns you want to display. The statement displays only the columns that you list. The FROM clause specifies from which table you want to display columns. The WHERE clause excludes rows that do not satisfy a specified condition. The condition may be simple (for example, WHERE CUSTOMER_STATE = 'NH'), or it may be compound (for example, WHERE CUSTOMER_STATE='NH' AND STATUS='Active').

The following example shows a compound condition inside a SELECT statement:

```
SELECT FirstName, LastName, Phone FROM CUSTOMER
    WHERE State = 'NH'
    AND Status = 'Active' ;
```

SQL in proprietary tools

Using SQL `SELECT` statements is not the only way to retrieve data from a database. If you're interacting with your database through a DBMS, this system probably already has proprietary tools for manipulating data. You can use these tools (many of which are quite intuitive) to add to, delete from, change, or query your database.

Many DBMS front ends give you the choice of using either their proprietary tools or SQL. In some cases, the proprietary tools can't express everything that you can express by using SQL. If you need to perform an operation that the proprietary tool can't handle, you may need to use SQL. So becoming familiar with SQL is a good idea, even if you use a proprietary tool most of the time. To successfully perform an operation that's too complex for your proprietary tool, you need a clear understanding of how SQL works and what it can do.

This statement returns the names and phone numbers of all active customers living in New Hampshire. The `AND` keyword means that for a row to qualify for retrieval, that row must meet both conditions: `State = 'NH'` and `Status = 'Active'`.

Creating Views

The structure of a database that's designed according to sound principles — including appropriate normalization — maximizes the integrity of the data. This structure, however, is often not the best way to look at the data. Several applications may use the same data, but each application may have a different emphasis. One of the most powerful features of SQL is its capability to display views of the data that are structured differently from how the database tables store the data. The tables you use as sources for columns and rows in a view are the *base tables.* Chapter 3 discusses views as part of the Data Definition Language (DDL). This section looks at views in the context of retrieving and manipulating data.

A `SELECT` statement always returns a result in the form of a virtual table. A *view* is a special kind of virtual table. You can distinguish a view from other virtual tables because the database's metadata holds the definition of a view. This distinction gives a view a degree of persistence that other virtual tables don't possess.

You can manipulate a view just as you can manipulate a real table. The difference is that a view's data doesn't have an independent existence. The view derives its data from the table or tables from which you draw the view's columns. Each application can have its own unique views of the same data.

Consider the VetLab database that I describe in Chapter 5. That database contains five tables: CLIENT, TESTS, EMPLOYEE, ORDERS, and RESULTS. Suppose the national marketing manager wants to see from which states the company's orders are coming. Some of this information lies in the CLIENT table; some lies in the ORDERS table. Suppose the quality-control officer wants to compare the order date of a test to the date on which the final test result came in. This comparison requires some data from the ORDERS table and some from the RESULTS table. To satisfy needs such as these, you can create views that give you exactly the data you want in each case.

From tables

For the marketing manager, you can create the view shown in Figure 6-1.

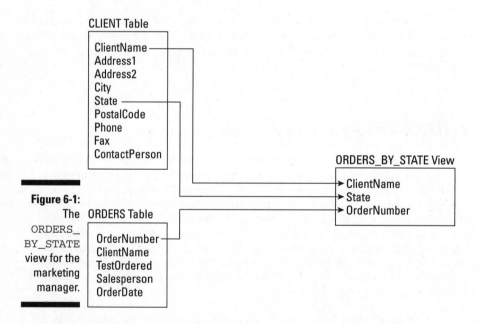

Figure 6-1: The ORDERS_ BY_STATE view for the marketing manager.

The following statement creates the marketing manager's view:

```
CREATE VIEW ORDERS_BY_STATE
    (ClientName, State, OrderNumber)
  AS SELECT CLIENT.ClientName, State, OrderNumber
  FROM CLIENT, ORDERS
  WHERE CLIENT.ClientName = ORDERS.ClientName ;
```

The new view has three columns: ClientName, State, and OrderNumber. ClientName appears in both the CLIENT and ORDERS tables and serves as the link between the two tables. The new view draws State information from the CLIENT table and takes the OrderNumber from the ORDERS table. In the preceding example, you explicitly declare the names of the columns in the new view.

You don't need this declaration if the names are the same as the names of the corresponding columns in the source tables. The example in the following section shows a similar CREATE VIEW statement, except that the view column names are implied rather than explicitly stated.

With a selection condition

The quality-control officer requires a different view from the one that the marketing manager uses, as shown by the example in Figure 6-2.

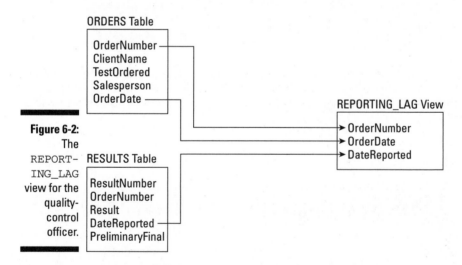

Figure 6-2: The REPORT-ING_LAG view for the quality-control officer.

Here's the code that creates the view in Figure 6-2:

```
CREATE VIEW REPORTING_LAG
   AS SELECT ORDERS.OrderNumber, OrderDate, DateReported
   FROM ORDERS, RESULTS
   WHERE ORDERS.OrderNumber = RESULTS.OrderNumber
   AND RESULTS.PreliminaryFinal = 'F' ;
```

This view contains order-date information from the ORDERS table and final-report-date information from the RESULTS table. Only rows that have an `'F'` in the `PreliminaryFinal` column of the RESULTS table appear in the `REPORTING LAG` view. Note also that the column list in the ORDERS_BY_STATE view is optional. The REPORTING_LAG view works fine without such a list.

With a modified attribute

The `SELECT` clauses in the examples in the two preceding sections contain only column names. You can include expressions in the `SELECT` clause as well. Suppose VetLab's owner is having a birthday and wants to give all his customers a 10-percent discount to celebrate. He can create a view based on the ORDERS table and the TESTS table. He may construct this table as shown in the following code example:

```
CREATE VIEW BIRTHDAY
    (ClientName, Test, OrderDate, BirthdayCharge)
    AS SELECT ClientName, TestOrdered, OrderDate,
        StandardCharge * .9
    FROM ORDERS, TESTS
    WHERE TestOrdered = TestName ;
```

Notice that the second column in the `BIRTHDAY` view — `Test` — corresponds to the `TestOrdered` column in the ORDERS table, which also corresponds to the `TestName` column in the TESTS table. Figure 6-3 shows how to create this view.

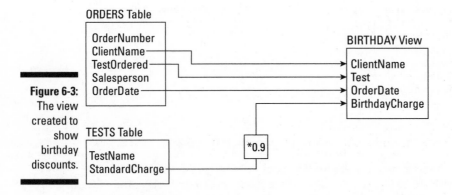

Figure 6-3:
The view created to show birthday discounts.

You can build a view based on multiple tables, as shown in the preceding examples, or you can build a view based on a single table. If you don't need some of the columns or rows in a table, create a view to remove these elements from sight and then deal with the view rather than the original table. This approach ensures that users see only the parts of the table that are relevant to the task at hand.

Another reason for creating a view is to provide security for its underlying tables. You may want to make some columns in your tables available for inspection while hiding others. You can create a view that includes only those columns that you want to make available and then grant broad access to that view, while restricting access to the tables from which you draw the view. Chapter 13 explores database security and describes how to grant and revoke data-access privileges.

Updating Views

After you create a table, that table is automatically capable of accommodating insertions, updates, and deletions. Views don't necessarily exhibit the same capability. If you update a view, you're actually updating its underlying table. Here are a few potential problems you may encounter when you update views:

- **Some views may draw components from two or more tables.** If you update such a view, the underlying tables may not be updated properly.

- **A view may include an expression in a SELECT list.** Since expressions don't map directly to rows in tables, your DBMS won't know how to update an expression.

Suppose that you create a view by using the following statement:

```
CREATE VIEW COMP (EmpName, Pay)
    AS SELECT EmpName, Salary+Comm AS Pay
    FROM EMPLOYEE ;
```

You may think that you can update Pay by using the following statement:

```
UPDATE COMP SET Pay = Pay + 100 ;
```

Unfortunately, this approach doesn't make any sense because the underlying table has no Pay column. You can't update something that doesn't exist in the base table.

Keep the following rule in mind whenever you consider updating views: You can't update a column of a view unless it corresponds to a column of an underlying base table.

Adding New Data

Every database table starts out empty. After you create a table, either by using SQL's DDL or a RAD tool, that table is nothing but a structured shell containing no data. To make the table useful, you must put some data into it. You may or may not have that data already stored in digital form. Your data may appear in one of the following forms:

- ✔ **Not yet compiled in any digital format:** If your data is not already in digital form, someone will probably have to enter the data manually, one record at a time. You can also enter data by using optical scanners and voice recognition systems, but the use of such devices for data entry is relatively rare.

- ✔ **Compiled in some sort of digital format:** If your data is already in digital form but perhaps not in the format of the database tables that you use, you need to translate the data into the appropriate format and then insert the data into the database.

- ✔ **Compiled in the correct digital format:** If your data is already in digital form and in the correct format, you're ready to transfer it to a new database.

The following sections address adding data to a table when it exists in each of these three forms. Depending on the current form of the data, you may be able to transfer it to your database in one operation, or you may need to enter the data one record at a time. Each data record that you enter corresponds to a single row in a database table.

Adding data one row at a time

Most DBMSs support form-based data entry. This feature enables you to create a screen form that has a field for every column in a database table. Field labels on the form enable you to determine easily what data goes into each field. The data-entry operator enters all the data for a single row into the form. After the DBMS accepts the new row, the system clears the form to accept another row. In this way, you can easily add data to a table one row at a time.

Form-based data entry is easy and less susceptible to data-entry errors than using a list of *comma-delimited values*. The main problem with form-based data entry is that it is nonstandard; each DBMS has its own method of creating forms. This diversity, however, is not a problem for the data-entry operator.

You can make the form look generally the same from one DBMS to another. (The data-entry operator may not suffer too much, but the application developer must return to the bottom of the learning curve every time he or she changes development tools.) Another possible problem with form-based data entry is that some implementations may not permit a full range of validity checks on the data that you enter.

The best way to maintain a high level of data integrity in a database is to keep bad data out of the database. You can prevent the entry of some bad data by applying constraints to the fields on a data-entry form. This approach enables you to make sure that the database accepts only data values of the correct type and within a predefined range. Applying such constraints can't prevent all possible errors, but they can catch some errors.

If the form-design tool in your DBMS doesn't enable you to apply all the validity checks that you need to ensure data integrity, you may want to build your own screen, accept data entries into variables, and check the entries by using application program code. After you're sure that all the values entered for a table row are valid, you can then add that row by using the SQL INSERT command.

If you enter the data for a single row into a database table, the INSERT command uses the following syntax:

```
INSERT INTO table_1 [(column_1, column_2, ..., column_n)]
   VALUES (value_1, value_2, ..., value_n) ;
```

As indicated by the square brackets ([ ]), the listing of column names is optional. The default column list order is the order of the columns in the table. If you put the VALUES in the same order as the columns in the table, these elements go into the correct columns — whether you explicitly specify those columns or not. If you want to specify the VALUES in some order other than the order of the columns in the table, you must list the column names, putting the columns in an order that corresponds to the order of the VALUES.

To enter a record into the CUSTOMER table, for example, use the following syntax:

```
INSERT INTO CUSTOMER (CustomerID, FirstName, LastName,
   Street, City, State, Zipcode, Phone)
   VALUES (:vcustid, 'David', 'Taylor', '235 Nutley Ave.',
   'Nutley', 'NJ', '07110', '(201) 555-1963') ;
```

The first VALUE, vcustid, is a variable that you increment with your program code after you enter each new row of the table. This approach guarantees that you have no duplication of the CustomerID. CustomerID is the primary key for this table and, therefore, must be unique. The rest of the values are data items rather than variables that contain data items. Of course, you can hold the data for these columns in variables, too, if you want. The `INSERT` statement works equally well either with variables or with an explicit copy of the data itself as arguments of the `VALUES` keyword.

Adding data only to selected columns

Sometimes you want to note the existence of an object, even if you don't have all the facts on it yet. If you have a database table for such objects, you can insert a row for the new object without filling in the data in all the columns. If you want the table in first normal form, you must insert enough data to distinguish the new row from all the other rows in the table. (For a discussion of first normal form, see Chapter 5.) Inserting the new row's primary key is sufficient for this purpose. In addition to the primary key, insert any other data that you have about the object. Columns in which you enter no data contain nulls.

The following example shows such a partial row entry:

```
INSERT INTO CUSTOMER (CustomerID, FirstName, LastName)
    VALUES (:vcustid, 'Tyson', 'Taylor') ;
```

You insert only the customer's unique identification number and name into the database table. The other columns in this row contain null values.

Adding a block of rows to a table

Loading a database table one row at a time by using `INSERT` statements can be tedious, particularly if that's all you do. Even entering the data into a care- fully human-engineered ergonomic screen form gets tiring after a while. Clearly, if you have a reliable way to enter the data automatically, you'll find occasions in which automatic entry is better than having a person sit at a keyboard and type.

Automatic data entry is feasible, for example, if the data already exists in electronic form because somebody has already manually entered the data. If so, there is no reason to repeat history. The transfer of data from one data file to another is a task that a computer can perform with a minimum of human involvement. If you know the characteristics of the source data and the desired form of the destination table, a computer can (in principle) per- form the data transfer automatically.

Copying from a foreign data file

Suppose that you're building a database for a new application. Some data that you need already exists in a computer file. The file may be a flat file or a table in a database created by a DBMS different from the one you use. The data may be in ASCII or EBCDIC code or in some arcane proprietary format. What do you do?

The first things you do are hope and pray that the data you want is in a widely used format. If the data is in a popular format, you have a good chance of finding a format conversion utility that can translate the data into one or more other popular formats. Your development environment can probably import at least one of these formats, and if you're really lucky, your development environment can handle the current data format directly. On personal computers, the Access, xBASE, and MySQL formats are the most widely used. If the data that you want is in one of these formats, conversion should be easy. If the format of the data is less common, you may need to go through a two-step conversion.

If the data is in an old, proprietary, or defunct format, as a last resort, you can turn to a professional data-translation service. These businesses specialize in translating computer data from one format to another. They deal with hundreds of formats — most of which nobody has ever heard of. Give one of these services a tape or disk containing the data in its original format, and you get back the same data translated into whatever format you specify.

Transferring all rows between tables

A less severe problem than dealing with foreign data is taking data that already exists in one table in your database and combining that data with compatible data in another table. This process works great if the structure of the second table is identical to the structure of the first table — that is, every column in the first table has a corresponding column in the second table, and the data types of the corresponding columns match. If so, you can combine the contents of the two tables by using the UNION relational operator. The result is a virtual table containing data from both source tables. I discuss the relational operators, including UNION, in Chapter 10.

Transferring selected columns and rows between tables

Generally, the structure of the data in the source table isn't identical to the structure of the table into which you want to insert the data. Perhaps only some of the columns match — and these are the columns that you want to transfer. By combining SELECT statements with a UNION, you can specify which columns from the source tables to include in the virtual result table. By including WHERE clauses in the SELECT statements, you can restrict the rows that you place into the result table to those that satisfy specific conditions. I cover WHERE clauses extensively in Chapter 9.

Suppose that you have two tables, PROSPECT and CUSTOMER, and you want to list everyone living in the state of Maine who appears in either table. You can create a virtual result table with the desired information by using the following command:

```
SELECT FirstName, LastName
    FROM PROSPECT
    WHERE State = 'ME'
UNION
SELECT FirstName, LastName
    FROM CUSTOMER
    WHERE State = 'ME' ;
```

Here's a closer look:

- ✔ The SELECT statements specify that the columns included in the result table are FirstName and LastName.

- ✔ The WHERE clauses restrict the rows included to those with the value 'ME' in the State column.

- ✔ The State column isn't included in the results table but is present in both the PROSPECT and CUSTOMER tables.

- ✔ The UNION operator combines the results from the SELECT statement on PROSPECT with the results of the SELECT on CUSTOMER, deletes any duplicate rows, and then displays the result.

Another way to copy data from one table in a database to another is to nest a SELECT statement within an INSERT statement. This method (a *subselect*) doesn't create a virtual table but instead duplicates the selected data. You can take all the rows from the CUSTOMER table, for example, and insert those rows into the PROSPECT table. Of course, this only works if the structures of the CUSTOMER and PROSPECT tables are identical. If you want to place only those customers who live in Maine into the PROSPECT table, a simple SELECT with one condition in the WHERE clause does the trick, as shown in the following example:

```
INSERT INTO PROSPECT
    SELECT * FROM CUSTOMER
    WHERE State = 'ME' ;
```

Even though this operation creates redundant data (you're now storing customer data in both the PROSPECT table and the CUSTOMER table), you may want to do it anyway to improve the performance of retrievals. Beware of the redundancy, however! To maintain data consistency, make sure that you don't insert, update, or delete rows in one table without inserting, updating, or deleting the corresponding rows in the other table. Another potential problem is the possibility that the INSERT statement might generate duplicate primary keys. If even one pre-existing prospect has a primary key of `ProspectID` that matches the corresponding primary key, `CustomerID`, of a customer that you are trying to insert into the PROSPECT table, the insert operation will fail.

Updating Existing Data

You can count on one thing in this world — change. If you don't like the current state of affairs, just wait a while. Before long, things will be different. Because the world is constantly changing, the databases used to model aspects of the world also need to change. A customer may change her address. The quantity of a product in stock may change (because, you hope, someone buys an item now and then). A basketball player's season performance statistics change each time he plays in another game. These are the kinds of events that require you to update a database.

SQL provides the UPDATE statement for changing data in a table. By using a single UPDATE statement, you can change one, some, or all the rows in a table. The UPDATE statement uses the following syntax:

```
UPDATE table_name
    SET column_1 = expression_1, column_2 = expression_2,
    ..., column_n = expression_n
    [WHERE predicates] ;
```

The WHERE clause is optional. This clause specifies the rows that you're updating. If you don't use a WHERE clause, all the rows in the table are updated. The SET clause specifies the new values for the columns that you're changing.

Consider the CUSTOMER table shown in Table 6-1.

Table 6-1	CUSTOMER Table		
Name	*City*	*Area Code*	*Telephone*
Abe Abelson	Springfield	(714)	555-1111
Bill Bailey	Decatur	(714)	555-2222
Chuck Wood	Philo	(714)	555-3333
Don Stetson	Philo	(714)	555-4444
Dolph Stetson	Philo	(714)	555-5555

Customer lists change occasionally — as people move, change their phone numbers, and so on. Suppose that Abe Abelson moves from Springfield to Kankakee. You can update his record in the table by using the following UPDATE statement:

```
UPDATE CUSTOMER
   SET City = 'Kankakee', Telephone = '666-6666'
   WHERE Name = 'Abe Abelson' ;
```

This statement causes the changes shown in Table 6-2.

Table 6-2   CUSTOMER Table after UPDATE to One Row

Name	City	Area Code	Telephone
Abe Abelson	Kankakee	(714)	666-6666
Bill Bailey	Decatur	(714)	555-2222
Chuck Wood	Philo	(714)	555-3333
Don Stetson	Philo	(714)	555-4444
Dolph Stetson	Philo	(714)	555-5555

You can use a similar statement to update multiple rows. Assume that Philo is experiencing explosive population growth and now requires its own area code. You can change all rows for customers who live in Philo by using a single UPDATE statement, as follows:

```
UPDATE CUSTOMER
   SET AreaCode = '(619)'
   WHERE City = 'Philo' ;
```

The table now looks like the one shown in Table 6-3.

Table 6-3   CUSTOMER Table after UPDATE to Several Rows

Name	City	Area Code	Telephone
Abe Abelson	Kankakee	(714)	666-6666
Bill Bailey	Decatur	(714)	555-2222
Chuck Wood	Philo	(619)	555-3333
Don Stetson	Philo	(619)	555-4444
Dolph Stetson	Philo	(619)	555-5555

Updating all the rows of a table is even easier than updating only some of the rows. You don't need to use a WHERE clause to restrict the statement. Imagine that the city of Rantoul has acquired major political clout and has now annexed not only Kankakee, Decatur, and Philo, but also all the cities and towns in the database. You can update all the rows by using a single statement, as follows:

```
UPDATE CUSTOMER
   SET City = 'Rantoul' ;
```

Table 6-4 shows the result.

Table 6-4	CUSTOMER Table after UPDATE to All Rows		
Name	**City**	**Area Code**	**Telephone**
Abe Abelson	Rantoul	(714)	666-6666
Bill Bailey	Rantoul	(714)	555-2222
Chuck Wood	Rantoul	(619)	555-3333
Don Stetson	Rantoul	(619)	555-4444
Dolph Stetson	Rantoul	(619)	555-5555

When you use the WHERE clause with the UPDATE statement to restrict which rows are updated, the contents of the WHERE clause can be a *subselect*. A subselect enables you to update rows in one table based on the contents of another table.

For example, suppose that you're a wholesaler and your database includes a VENDOR table containing the names of all the manufacturers from whom you buy products. You also have a PRODUCT table containing the names of all the products that you sell and the prices that you charge for them. The VENDOR table has columns VendorID, VendorName, Street, City, State, and Zip. The PRODUCT table has ProductID, ProductName, VendorID, and SalePrice.

Your vendor, Cumulonimbus Corporation, decides to raise the prices of all its products by 10 percent. To maintain your profit margin, you must raise your prices on the products that you obtain from Cumulonimbus by 10 percent. You can do so by using the following UPDATE statement:

```
UPDATE PRODUCT
   SET SalePrice = (SalePrice * 1.1)
   WHERE VendorID IN
      (SELECT VendorID FROM VENDOR
      WHERE VendorName = 'Cumulonimbus Corporation') ;
```

The subselect finds the VendorID that corresponds to Cumulonimbus. You can then use the VendorID field in the PRODUCT table to find the rows that you need to update. The prices on all Cumulonimbus products increase by 10 percent, whereas the prices on all other products stay the same. I discuss subselects more extensively in Chapter 11.

Transferring Data

In addition to using the INSERT and UPDATE statements, you can add data to a table or view by using the MERGE statement. You can MERGE data from a source table or view into a destination table or view. The MERGE can either insert new rows into the destination table or update existing rows. MERGE is a convenient way to take data that already exists somewhere in a database and copy it to a new location.

For example, consider the VetLab database that I describe in Chapter 5. Suppose some people in the EMPLOYEE table are salespeople who have taken orders, whereas others are nonsales employees or salespeople who have not yet taken an order. The year just concluded has been profitable, and you want to share some of that success with the employees. You decide to give a bonus of $100 to everyone who has taken at least one order and a bonus of $50 to everyone else. First, you create a BONUS table and insert into it a record for each employee who appears at least once in the ORDERS table, assigning each record a default bonus value of $100.

Next, you want to use the MERGE statement to insert new records for those employees who have not taken orders, giving them $50 bonuses. Here's some code that builds and fills the BONUS table:

```
CREATE TABLE BONUS (
    EmployeeName CHARACTER (30)        PRIMARY KEY,
    Bonus        NUMERIC               DEFAULT 100 ) ;

INSERT INTO BONUS (EmployeeName)
    (SELECT EmployeeName FROM EMPLOYEE, ORDERS
    WHERE EMPLOYEE.EmployeeName = ORDERS.Salesperson
    GROUP BY EMPLOYEE.EmployeeName) ;
```

You can now query the BONUS table to see what it holds:

```
SELECT * FROM BONUS ;

EmployeeName              Bonus
-----------       -------------
Brynna Jones              100
Chris Bancroft            100
Greg Bosser               100
Kyle Weeks                100
```

Now by executing a MERGE statement, you can give $50 bonuses to the rest of the employees:

```
MERGE INTO BONUS
   USING EMPLOYEE
   ON (BONUS.EmployeeName = EMPLOYEE.EmployeeName)
   WHEN NOT MATCHED THEN INSERT
      (BONUS.EmployeeName, BONUS.bonus)
      VALUES (EMPLOYEE.EmployeeName, 50) ;
```

Records for people in the EMPLOYEE table that do not match records for people already in the BONUS table are now inserted into the BONUS table. Now a query of the BONUS table gives the following:

```
SELECT * FROM BONUS ;

EmployeeName              Bonus
--------------       -----------
Brynna Jones                100
Chris Bancroft              100
Greg Bosser                 100
Kyle Weeks                  100
Neth Doze                    50
Matt Bak                     50
Sam Saylor                   50
Nic Foster                   50
```

The first four records, which were created with the INSERT statement, are in alphabetical order by employee name. The rest of the records, added by the MERGE statement, appear in whatever order they were listed in the EMPLOYEE table.

Deleting Obsolete Data

As time passes, data can get old and lose its usefulness. You may want to remove this outdated data from its table. Unneeded data in a table slows performance, consumes memory, and can confuse users. You may want to transfer older data to an archive table and then take the archive offline. That way, in the unlikely event that you ever need to look at that data again, you can recover it. In the meantime, it doesn't slow down your everyday processing. Whether you decide that obsolete data is worth archiving or not, you eventually come to the point where you want to delete that data. SQL provides for the removal of rows from database tables by use of the DELETE statement.

You can delete all the rows in a table by using an unqualified DELETE statement, or you can restrict the deletion to only selected rows by adding a WHERE clause. The syntax is similar to the syntax of a SELECT statement, except that you don't need to specify columns. After all, if you want to delete a table row, you probably want to remove all the data in that row's columns.

For example, suppose that your customer, David Taylor, just moved to Tahiti and isn't going to buy anything from you anymore. You can remove him from your CUSTOMER table by using the following statement:

```
DELETE FROM CUSTOMER
    WHERE FirstName = 'David' AND LastName = 'Taylor' ;
```

Assuming that you have only one customer named David Taylor, this statement makes the intended deletion. If you have two or more customers who share the name David Taylor, you can add more conditions to the WHERE clause (such as STREET or PHONE or CUSTOMER_ID) to make sure that you delete only the customer you want to remove. If you don't add a WHERE clause, all customers named David Taylor will be deleted.

Chapter 7

Specifying Values

In This Chapter

▶ Using variables to eliminate redundant coding

▶ Extracting frequently required information from a database table field

▶ Combining simple values to form complex expressions

This book emphasizes the importance of database structure for maintaining database integrity. Although the significance of database structure is often overlooked, you must never forget that the most important thing is the data itself. After all, the values held in the cells that form the intersections of the database table's rows and columns are the raw materials from which you can derive meaningful relationships and trends.

You can represent values in several ways. You can represent them directly, or you can derive them with functions or expressions. This chapter describes the various kinds of values, as well as functions and expressions.

Functions examine data and calculate a value based on the data. *Expressions* are combinations of data items that SQL evaluates to produce a single value.

Values

SQL recognizes several kinds of values:

- �' Row values
- ▶ Literal values
- ▶ Variables
- ▶ Special variables
- ▶ Column references

Atoms aren't indivisible either

In the 19th century, scientists believed that an atom was the irreducible smallest possible piece of matter. That's why they named it *atom,* which comes from the Greek word *atomos,* which means *indivisible.* Now scientists know that atoms aren't indivisible — they're made up of protons, neutrons, and electrons. Protons and neutrons, in turn, are made up of quarks, gluons, and virtual quarks. Even these things may not be indivisible. Who knows?

The value of a field in a database table is called *atomic,* even though many fields aren't indivisible. A DATE value has components of month, year, and day. A TIMESTAMP value has components of hour, minute, second, and so on. A REAL or FLOAT value has components of *exponent* and *mantissa.* A CHAR value has components that you can access by using SUBSTRING. Therefore, calling database field values *atomic* is true to the analogy of atoms of matter. Neither modern application of the term *atomic,* however, is true to the word's original meaning.

Row values

The most visible values in a database are table *row values.* These are the values that each row of a database table contains. A row value is typically made up of multiple components, because each column in a row contains a value. A *field* is the intersection of a single column with a single row. A field contains a *scalar,* or *atomic,* value. A value that's scalar or atomic has only a single component.

Literal values

In SQL, either a variable or a constant may represent a *value.* Logically enough, the value of a *variable* may change from time to time, but the value of a *constant* never changes. An important kind of constant is the *literal value.* You may consider a *literal* to be a *WYSIWYG* value, because *What You See Is What You Get.* The representation is itself the value.

Just as SQL has many data types, it also has many types of literals. Table 7-1 shows some examples of literals of the various data types.

Notice that single quotes enclose the literals of the nonnumeric types. These marks help to prevent confusion; they can, however, also cause problems, as you can see in Table 7-1.

Table 7-1	**Example Literals of Various Data Types**
Data Type	*Example Literal*
BIGINT	8589934592
INTEGER	186282
SMALLINT	186
NUMERIC	186282.42
DECIMAL	186282.42
REAL	6.02257E23
DOUBLE PRECISION	3.1415926535897E00
FLOAT	6.02257E23
CHARACTER(15)	'GREECE '
Note: Fifteen total characters and spaces are between the quote marks above.	
VARCHAR (CHARACTER VARYING)	'lepton'
NATIONAL CHARACTER(15)	'ΕΛΛΑΣ '[1]
Note: Fifteen total characters and spaces are between the quote marks above.	
NATIONAL CHARACTER VARYING	'@@lclam@@lceps@@lcpi@@ lctau@@lcomi@@lcnu'[2]
CHARACTER LARGE OBJECT (CLOB)	(A really long character string)
BINARY LARGE OBJECT (BLOB)	(A really long string of ones and zeros)
DATE	DATE '1969-07-20'
TIME(2)	TIME '13.41.32.50'
TIMESTAMP(0)	TIMESTAMP '2006-02-25-13. 03.16.000000'
TIME WITH TIMEZONE(4)	TIME '13.41.32.5000- 08.00'
TIMESTAMP WITH TIMEZONE(0)	TIMESTAMP '2006-02-25-13. 03.16.0000+02.00'
INTERVAL DAY	INTERVAL '7' DAY

[1] This term is the word that Greeks use to name their own country in their own language. (The English equivalent is Hellas.)

[2] This term is the word lepton in Greek national characters.

What if a literal is a character string that itself contains a single quote? In that case, you must type two single quotes to show that one of the quote marks that you're typing is a part of the character string and not an indicator of the end of the string. You'd type `'Earth''s atmosphere'`, for example, to represent the character literal `'Earth's atmosphere'`.

Variables

Although being able to manipulate literals and other kinds of constants while dealing with a database gives you great power, having variables is helpful, too. In many cases, you'd need to do much more work if you didn't have variables. A *variable,* by the way, is a quantity that has a value that can change. Look at the following example to see why variables are valuable.

Suppose that you're a retailer who has several classes of customers. You give your high-volume customers the best price, your medium-volume customers the next best price, and your low-volume customers the highest price. You want to index all prices to your cost of goods. For your F-117A product, you decide to charge your high-volume customers (Class C) 1.4 times your cost of goods. You charge your medium-volume customers (Class B) 1.5 times your cost of goods, and you charge your low-volume customers (Class A) 1.6 times your cost of goods.

You store the cost of goods and the prices that you charge in a table named PRICING. To implement your new pricing structure, you issue the following SQL commands:

```
UPDATE PRICING
    SET Price = Cost * 1.4
    WHERE Product = 'F-117A'
       AND Class = 'C' ;
UPDATE PRICING
    SET Price = Cost * 1.5
    WHERE Product = 'F-117A'
       AND Class = 'B' ;
UPDATE PRICING
    SET Price = Cost * 1.6
    WHERE Product = 'F-117A'
       AND Class = 'A' ;
```

This code is fine and meets your needs — for now. But if aggressive competition begins to eat into your market share, you may need to reduce your margins to remain competitive. To change your margins, you need to enter code something like this:

```
UPDATE PRICING
   SET Price = Cost * 1.25
   WHERE Product = 'F-117A'
      AND Class = 'C' ;
UPDATE PRICING
   SET Price = Cost * 1.35
   WHERE Product = 'F-117A'
      AND Class = 'B' ;
UPDATE PRICING
   SET Price = Cost * 1.45
   WHERE Product = 'F-117A'
      AND Class = 'A' ;
```

If you're in a volatile market, you may need to rewrite your SQL code repeatedly. This task can become tedious, particularly if prices appear in multiple places in your code. You can minimize your work by replacing literals (such as 1.45) with variables (such as :multiplierA). Then you can perform your updates as follows:

```
UPDATE PRICING
   SET Price = Cost * :multiplierC
   WHERE Product = 'F-117A'
      AND Class = 'C' ;
UPDATE PRICING
   SET Price = Cost * :multiplierB
   WHERE Product = 'F-117A'
      AND Class = 'B' ;
UPDATE PRICING
   SET Price = Cost * :multiplierA
   WHERE Product = 'F-117A'
      AND Class = 'A' ;
```

Now whenever market conditions force you to change your pricing, you need to change only the values of the variables :multiplierC, :multiplierB, and :multiplierA. These variables are parameters that pass to the SQL code, which then uses the variables to compute new prices.

Sometimes, when variables are used in this way they're called *parameters*. Other times they're referred to as *host variables*. Variables are called *parameters* if they appear in applications written in SQL module language. They're called *host variables* when they're used in embedded SQL.

Embedded SQL means that SQL statements are embedded into the code of an application written in a host language. Alternatively, you can use SQL module language to create an entire module of SQL code. The host language application then calls the module. Either method can give you the capabilities that you want. The approach that you use depends on your SQL implementation.

Special variables

If a user on a client machine connects to a database on a server, this connection establishes a *session*. If the user connects to several databases, the session associated with the most recent connection is considered the *current session;* *previous sessions* are considered *dormant.* SQL defines several *special variables* that are valuable on multiuser systems. These variables keep track of the different users. Here's a list of the special variables:

- ✔ SESSION_USER: The special variable SESSION_USER holds a value that's equal to the user authorization identifier of the current SQL session. If you write a program that performs a monitoring function, you can interrogate SESSION_USER to find out who is executing SQL statements.

- ✔ CURRENT_USER: An SQL module may have a user-specified authorization identifier associated with it. The CURRENT_USER variable stores this value. If a module has no such identifier, CURRENT_USER has the same value as SESSION_USER.

- ✔ SYSTEM_USER: The SYSTEM_USER variable contains the operating system's user identifier. This identifier may differ from that user's identifier in an SQL module. A user may log onto the system as LARRY, for example, but identify himself to a module as PLANT_MGR. The value in SESSION_USER is PLANT_MGR. If he makes no explicit specification of the module identifier, and CURRENT_USER also contains PLANT_MGR, SYSTEM_USER holds the value LARRY.

The SYSTEM_USER, SESSION_USER, and CURRENT_USER special variables track who is using the system. You can maintain a log table and periodically insert into that table the values that SYSTEM_USER, SESSION_USER, and CURRENT_USER contain. The following example shows how:

```
INSERT INTO USAGELOG (SNAPSHOT)
    VALUES ('User ' || SYSTEM_USER ||
        ' with ID ' || SESSION_USER ||
        ' active at ' || CURRENT_TIMESTAMP) ;
```

This statement produces log entries similar to the following example:

```
User LARRY with ID PLANT_MGR active at 2006-03-07-23.50.00
```

Column references

Every column contains one value for each row of a table. SQL statements often refer to such values. A fully qualified column reference consists of the table name, a period, and then the column name (for example, PRICING. Product). Consider the following statement:

```
SELECT PRICING.Cost
   FROM PRICING
   WHERE PRICING.Product = 'F-117A' ;
```

PRICING.Product is a column reference. This reference contains the value 'F-117A'. PRICING.Cost is also a column reference, but you don't know its value until the preceding SELECT statement executes.

Because it only makes sense to reference columns in the current table, you don't generally need to use fully qualified column references. The following statement, for example, is equivalent to the previous one:

```
SELECT Cost
   FROM PRICING
   WHERE Product = 'F-117A' ;
```

Sometimes, you may be dealing with more than one table. Two tables in a database may contain one or more columns with the same name. If so, you must fully qualify column references for those columns to guarantee that you get the column you want.

For example, suppose that your company maintains facilities in both Kingston and Jefferson, and you maintain separate employee records for each site. You name the Kingston employee table EMP_KINGSTON, and you name the Jefferson employee table EMP_JEFFERSON. You want a list of employees who work at both sites, so you need to find the employees whose names appear in both tables. The following SELECT statement gives you what you want:

```
SELECT EMP_KINGSTON.FirstName, EMP_KINGSTON.LastName
   FROM EMP_KINGSTON, EMP_JEFFERSON
   WHERE EMP_KINGSTON.EmpID = EMP_JEFFERSON.EmpID ;
```

Because each employee's ID number is unique and remains the same regardless of the work site, you can use this ID as a link between the two tables. This retrieval returns only the names of employees who appear in both tables.

Value Expressions

An expression may be simple or complex. The expression can contain literal values, column names, parameters, host variables, subqueries, logical connectives, and arithmetic operators. Regardless of its complexity, an expression must reduce to a single value.

For this reason, SQL expressions are commonly known as *value expressions*. Combining multiple value expressions into a single expression is possible, as long as the component value expressions reduce to values of compatible data types.

SQL has five kinds of value expressions:

- ✔ String value expressions
- ✔ Numeric value expressions
- ✔ Datetime value expressions
- ✔ Interval value expressions
- ✔ Conditional value expressions

String value expressions

The simplest *string value expression* is a single string value specification. Other possibilities include a column reference, a set function, a scalar sub-query, a CASE expression, a CAST expression, or a complex string value expression. (I discuss CASE and CAST value expressions in Chapter 8.)

Only one operator is possible in a string value expression: the *concatenation operator.* You may concatenate any of the value expressions I mention in the bulleted list in the previous section with another expression to create a more complex string value expression. A pair of vertical lines (| |) represents the concatenation operator. The following table shows some examples of string value expressions.

Expression	*Produces*
`'Peanut ' || 'brittle'`	`'Peanut brittle'`
`'Jelly' || ' ' || 'beans'`	`'Jelly beans'`
`FIRST_NAME || ' ' || LAST_NAME`	`'Joe Smith'`
`B'1100111' || B'01010011'`	`B'110011101010011'`
`'' || 'Asparagus'`	`'Asparagus'`
`'Asparagus' || ''`	`'Asparagus'`
`'As' || '' || 'par' || '' || 'agus'`	`'Asparagus'`

As the table shows, if you concatenate a string to a zero-length string, the result is the same as the original string.

Numeric value expressions

In *numeric value expressions,* you can apply the addition, subtraction, multiplication, and division operators to numeric-type data. The expression must reduce to a numeric value. The components of a numeric value expression may be of different data types as long as all of the data types are numeric. The data type of the result depends on the data types of the components from which you derive the result. The SQL standard doesn't rigidly specify the type that results from any specific combination of source expression components because of differences among hardware platforms. Check the documentation for your specific platform when mixing numeric data types.

Here are some examples of numeric value expressions:

- -27
- 49 + 83
- 5 * (12 - 3)
- PROTEIN + FAT + CARBOHYDRATE
- FEET/5280
- COST * :multiplierA

Datetime value expressions

Datetime value expressions perform operations on data that deals with dates and times. These value expressions can contain components that are of the types DATE, TIME, TIMESTAMP, or INTERVAL. The result of a date time value expression is always a datetime type (DATE, TIME, or TIMESTAMP). The following expression, for example, gives the date one week from today:

```
CURRENT_DATE + INTERVAL '7' DAY
```

Times are maintained in Universal Time Coordinated (UTC) — known in Great Britain as Greenwich Mean Time — but you can specify an offset to make the time correct for any particular time zone. For your system's local time zone, you can use the simple syntax given in the following example:

```
TIME '22:55:00' AT LOCAL
```

Alternatively, you can specify this value the long way:

```
TIME '22:55:00' AT TIME ZONE INTERVAL '-08.00' HOUR TO
        MINUTE
```

This expression defines the local time as the time zone for Portland, Oregon, which is eight hours earlier than that of Greenwich, England.

Interval value expressions

If you subtract one datetime from another, you get an *interval*. Adding one datetime to another makes no sense, so SQL doesn't permit you to do so. If you add two intervals together or subtract one interval from another interval, the result is an interval. You can also either multiply or divide an interval by a numeric constant.

SQL has two types of intervals: *year-month* and *day-time*. To avoid ambiguities, you must specify which to use in an interval expression. The following expression, for example, gives the interval in years and months until you reach retirement age:

```
(BIRTHDAY_65 - CURRENT_DATE) YEAR TO MONTH
```

The following example gives an interval of 40 days:

```
INTERVAL '17' DAY + INTERVAL '23' DAY
```

The example that follows approximates the total number of months that a mother of five has been pregnant (assuming that she's not currently expecting number six!):

```
INTERVAL '9' MONTH * 5
```

Intervals can be negative as well as positive and may consist of any value expression or combination of value expressions that evaluates to an interval.

Conditional value expressions

The value of a *conditional value expression* depends on a condition. The conditional value expressions CASE, NULLIF, and COALESCE are significantly more complex than the other kinds of value expressions. In fact, these three conditional value expressions are so complex that I don't have enough room to talk about them here. I give conditional value expressions extensive coverage in Chapter 8.

Functions

A *function* is a simple to moderately complex operation that the usual SQL commands don't perform but that comes up often in practice. SQL provides functions that perform tasks that the application code in the host language (within which you embed your SQL statements) would otherwise need to perform. SQL has two main categories of functions: *set* (or *aggregate*) *functions* and *value functions*.

Summarizing by using set functions

Set functions apply to *sets* of rows in a table rather than to a single row. These functions summarize some characteristic of the current set of rows. The set may include all the rows in the table or a subset of rows that are specified by a WHERE clause. (I discuss WHERE clauses extensively in Chapter 9.) Programmers sometimes call set functions *aggregate functions* because these functions take information from multiple rows, process that information in some way, and deliver a single-row answer. That answer is an *aggregation* of the information in the rows making up the set.

To illustrate the use of the set functions, consider Table 7-2, a list of nutrition facts for 100 grams of selected foods.

Table 7-2	Nutrition Facts for 100 Grams of Selected Foods			
Food	*Calories*	*Protein (grams)*	*Fat (grams)*	*Carbohydrate (grams)*
Almonds, roasted	627	18.6	57.7	19.6
Asparagus	20	2.2	0.2	3.6
Bananas, raw	85	1.1	0.2	22.2
Beef, lean hamburger	219	27.4	11.3	
Chicken, light meat	166	31.6	3.4	
Opossum, roasted	221	30.2	10.2	
Pork, ham	394	21.9	33.3	
Beans, lima	111	7.6	0.5	19.8
Cola	39			10.0
Bread, white	269	8.7	3.2	50.4

(continued)

Table 7-2 (continued)

Food	Calories	Protein (grams)	Fat (grams)	Carbohydrate (grams)
Bread, whole wheat	243	10.5	3.0	47.7
Broccoli	26	3.1	0.3	4.5
Butter	716	0.6	81.0	0.4
Jelly beans	367		0.5	93.1
Peanut brittle	421	5.7	10.4	81.0

A database table named FOODS stores the information in Table 7-2. Blank fields contain the value NULL. The set functions COUNT, AVG, MAX, MIN, and SUM can tell you important facts about the data in this table.

COUNT

The COUNT function tells you how many rows are in the table or how many rows in the table meet certain conditions. The simplest usage of this function is as follows:

```
SELECT COUNT (*)
   FROM FOODS ;
```

This function yields a result of 15, because it counts all rows in the FOODS table. The following statement produces the same result:

```
SELECT COUNT (Calories)
   FROM FOODS ;
```

Because the Calories column in every row of the table has an entry, the count is the same. If a column contains nulls, however, the function doesn't count the rows corresponding to those nulls.

The following statement returns a value of 11, because 4 of the 15 rows in the table contain nulls in the Carbohydrate column.

```
SELECT COUNT (Carbohydrate)
   FROM FOODS ;
```

A field in a database table may contain a null value for a variety of reasons. A common reason for this is that the actual value is not known or not yet known. Or the value may be known but not yet entered. Sometimes, if a value is known to be zero, the data-entry operator doesn't bother entering anything in a field — leaving that field a null. This is not a good practice because zero is a definite value, and you can include it in computations. Null is *not* a definite value, and SQL doesn't include null values in computations.

You can also use the COUNT function, in combination with DISTINCT, to determine how many distinct values exist in a column. Consider the following statement:

```
SELECT COUNT (DISTINCT Fat)
   FROM FOODS ;
```

The answer that this statement returns is 12. You can see that a 100-gram serving of asparagus has the same fat content as 100 grams of bananas (0.2 grams) and that a 100-gram serving of lima beans has the same fat content as 100 grams of jelly beans (0.5 grams). Thus the table has a total of only 12 distinct fat values.

AVG

The AVG function calculates and returns the average of the values in the specified column. Of course, you can use the AVG function only on columns that contain numeric data, as in the following example:

```
SELECT AVG (Fat)
   FROM FOODS ;
```

The result is 15.37. This number is so high primarily because of the presence of butter in the database. You may wonder what the average fat content may be if you didn't include butter. To find out, you can add a WHERE clause to your statement, as follows:

```
SELECT AVG (Fat)
   FROM FOODS
   WHERE Food <> 'Butter' ;
```

The average fat value drops down to 10.32 grams per 100 grams of food.

MAX

The MAX function returns the maximum value found in the specified column. The following statement returns a value of 81 (the fat content in 100 grams of butter):

```
SELECT MAX (Fat)
   FROM FOODS ;
```

MIN

The MIN function returns the minimum value found in the specified column. The following statement returns a value of 0.4, because the function doesn't treat the nulls as zeros:

```
SELECT MIN (Carbohydrate)
   FROM FOODS ;
```

SUM

The SUM function returns the sum of all the values found in the specified column. The following statement returns 3,924, which is the total caloric content of all 15 foods:

```
SELECT SUM (Calories)
   FROM FOODS ;
```

Value functions

A number of operations apply in a variety of contexts. Because you need to use these operations so often, incorporating them into SQL as value functions makes good sense. SQL offers relatively few value functions compared to PC database management systems such as Access or FoxPro, but the few that SQL does have are probably the ones that you'll use most often. SQL uses the following four types of value functions:

- ✔ String value functions
- ✔ Numeric value functions
- ✔ Datetime value functions
- ✔ Internal value functions

String value functions

String value functions take one character string as an input and produce another character string as an output. SQL has eight such functions:

- ✔ SUBSTRING
- ✔ SUBSTRING SIMILAR
- ✔ OVERLAY
- ✔ UPPER
- ✔ LOWER
- ✔ TRIM
- ✔ TRANSLATE
- ✔ CONVERT

SUBSTRING

Use the SUBSTRING function to extract a substring from a source string. The extracted substring is of the same type as the source string. If the source string is a CHARACTER VARYING string, for example, the substring is also a CHARACTER VARYING string. Following is the syntax of the SUBSTRING function:

```
SUBSTRING (string_value FROM start [FOR length])
```

The clause in square brackets ([ ]) is optional. The substring extracted from string_value begins with the character that start represents and continues for length characters. If the FOR clause is absent, the substring extracted extends from the start character to the end of the string. Consider the following example:

```
SUBSTRING ('Bread, whole wheat' FROM 8 FOR 7)
```

The substring extracted is 'whole w'. This substring starts with the eighth character of the source string and has a length of seven characters. On the surface, SUBSTRING doesn't seem like a very valuable function; if you have a literal like 'Bread, whole wheat', you don't need a function to figure out characters 8 through 14. SUBSTRING really is a valuable function, however, because the string value doesn't need to be a literal. The value can be any expression that evaluates to a character string. Thus, you could have a variable named fooditem that takes on different values at different times. The following expression would extract the desired substring regardless of what character string the fooditem variable currently represents:

```
SUBSTRING (:fooditem FROM 8 FOR 7)
```

All the value functions are similar in that these functions can operate on expressions that evaluate to values as well as on the literal values themselves.

You need to watch out for a couple of things if you use the SUBSTRING function. Make sure that the substring that you specify actually falls within the source string. If you ask for a substring starting at character eight but the source string is only four characters long, you get a null result. You must, therefore, have some idea of the form of your data before you specify a substring function. You also don't want to specify a negative substring length, because the end of a string can't precede the beginning.

If a column is of the VARCHAR type, you may not know how far the field extends for a particular row. This lack of knowledge doesn't present a problem for the SUBSTRING function. If the length that you specify goes beyond the right edge of the field, SUBSTRING returns whatever it finds. It doesn't return an error.

Say that you have the following statement:

```
SELECT * FROM FOODS
   WHERE SUBSTRING (Food FROM 8 FOR 7) = 'white' ;
```

This statement returns the row for white bread from the FOODS table, even though the value in the Food column ('Bread, white') is less than 14 characters long.

If any *operand* (value from which an operator derives another value) in the substring function has a null value, SUBSTRING returns a null result.

UPPER

The UPPER value function converts a character string to all uppercase characters, as in the examples shown in the following table.

This Statement	Returns
UPPER ('e. e. cummings')	'E. E. CUMMINGS'
UPPER ('Isaac Newton, Ph.D.')	'ISAAC NEWTON, PH.D.'

The UPPER function doesn't affect a string that's already in all uppercase characters.

LOWER

The LOWER value function converts a character string to all lowercase characters, as in the examples in the following table.

This Statement	Returns
LOWER ('TAXES')	'taxes'
LOWER ('E. E. Cummings')	'e. e. cummings'

The LOWER function doesn't affect a string that's already in all lowercase characters.

TRIM

Use the TRIM function to trim off leading or trailing blanks (or other characters) from a character string. The following examples show how to use TRIM.

This Statement	Returns
TRIM (LEADING ' ' FROM ' treat ')	'treat '
TRIM (TRAILING ' ' FROM ' treat ')	' treat'
TRIM (BOTH ' ' FROM ' treat ')	'treat'
TRIM (BOTH 't' from 'treat')	'rea'

The default trim character is the blank, so the following syntax also is legal:

```
TRIM (BOTH FROM ' treat ')
```

This syntax gives you the same result as the third example in the table —
`'treat'`.

TRANSLATE and CONVERT

The `TRANSLATE` and `CONVERT` functions take a source string in one character
set and transform the original string into a string in another character set.
Examples may be English to Kanji or Hebrew to French. The conversion functions that specify these transformations are implementation-specific. Consult
the documentation of your implementation for details.

If translating from one language to another was as easy as invoking an SQL
`TRANSLATE` function, that would be great. Unfortunately, the task is not that
easy. All `TRANSLATE` does is translate a character in the first character set to
the corresponding character in the second character set. The function can,
for example, translate 'Ελλασ' to 'Ellas'. But it can't translate 'Ελλασ'
to 'Greece'.

Numeric value functions

Numeric value functions can take a variety of data types as input, but the output
is always a numeric value. SQL has 13 types of numeric value functions:

- ✔ Position expression (`POSITION`)
- ✔ Extract expression (`EXTRACT`)
- ✔ Length expression (`CHAR_LENGTH`, `CHARACTER_LENGTH`, `OCTET_LENGTH`)
- ✔ Cardinality expression (`CARDINALITY`)
- ✔ Absolute value expression (`ABS`)
- ✔ Modulus expression (`MOD`)
- ✔ Natural logarithm (`LN`)
- ✔ Exponential function (`EXP`)
- ✔ Power function (`POWER`)
- ✔ Square root (`SQRT`)
- ✔ Floor function (`FLOOR`)
- ✔ Ceiling function (`CEIL`, `CEILING`)
- ✔ Width bucket function (`WIDTH_BUCKET`)

POSITION

POSITION searches for a specified target string within a specified source string and returns the character position where the target string begins. The syntax looks like this:

```
POSITION (target IN source)
```

The following table shows a few examples.

This Statement	Returns
POSITION ('B' IN 'Bread, whole wheat')	1
POSITION ('Bre' IN 'Bread, whole wheat')	1
POSITION ('wh' IN 'Bread, whole wheat')	8
POSITION ('whi' IN 'Bread, whole wheat')	0
POSITION ('' IN 'Bread, whole wheat')	1

If the function doesn't find the target string, the POSITION function returns a zero value. If the target string has zero length (as in the last example), the POSITION function always returns a value of one. If any operand in the function has a null value, the result is a null value.

EXTRACT

The EXTRACT function extracts a single field from a datetime or an interval. The following statement, for example, returns 08:

```
EXTRACT (MONTH FROM DATE '2006-08-20')
```

CHARACTER_LENGTH

The CHARACTER_LENGTH function returns the number of characters in a character string. The following statement, for example, returns 16:

```
CHARACTER_LENGTH ('Opossum, roasted')
```

As I note in regard to the SUBSTRING function (in the "Substring" section, earlier in the chapter), this function is not particularly useful if its argument is a literal like 'Opossum, roasted'. I can just as easily write 16 as I can CHARACTER_LENGTH ('Opossum, roasted'). In fact, writing 16 is easier. This function is more useful if its argument is an expression rather than a literal value.

OCTET_LENGTH

In music, a vocal ensemble made up of eight singers is called an *octet*. Typically, the parts that the ensemble represents are first and second soprano, first and second alto, first and second tenor, and first and second bass. In computer terminology, an ensemble of eight data bits is called a *byte*. The word *byte* is clever in that the term clearly relates to *bit* but implies something larger than a bit. A nice wordplay — but, unfortunately, nothing in the word *byte* conveys the concept of "eightness." By borrowing the musical term, a more apt description of a collection of eight bits becomes possible.

Practically all modern computers use eight bits to represent a single alphanumeric character. More complex character sets (such as Chinese) require 16 bits to represent a single character. The OCTET_LENGTH function counts and returns the number of octets (bytes) in a string. If the string is a bit string, OCTET_LENGTH returns the number of octets you need to hold that number of bits. If the string is an English-language character string (with one octet per character), the function returns the number of characters in the string. If the string is a Chinese character string, the function returns a number that is twice the number of Chinese characters. The following string is an example:

```
OCTET_LENGTH ('Beans, lima')
```

This function returns 11, because each character takes up one octet.

Some character sets use a variable number of octets for different characters. In particular, some character sets that support mixtures of Kanji and Latin characters use *escape* characters to switch between the two character sets. A string that contains both Latin and Kanji may have, for example, 30 characters and require 30 octets if all the characters are Latin; 62 characters if all the characters are Kanji (60 characters plus a leading and trailing shift character); and 150 characters if the characters alternate between Latin and Kanji (because each Kanji character needs two octets for the character and one octet each for the leading and trailing shift characters). The OCTET_LENGTH function returns the number of octets you need for the current value of the string.

CARDINALITY

Cardinality deals with collections of elements such as arrays or multisets, where each element is a value of some data type. The cardinality of the collection is the number of elements that it contains. One use of the CARDINALITY function might be:

```
CARDINALITY (TeamRoster)
```

This function would return 12, for example, if there were 12 team members on the roster. `TeamRoster`, a column in the TEAM table, can be either an array or a multiset. An *array* is an ordered collection of elements, and a *multiset* is an unordered collection of elements. For a team roster, which changes frequently, multiset makes more sense.

ABS

The ABS function returns the absolute value of a numeric value expression.

```
ABS (-273)
```

This returns 273.

MOD

The MOD function returns the *modulus* of two numeric value expressions.

```
MOD (3,2)
```

This function returns 1, the modulus of three divided by two.

LN

The LN function returns the natural logarithm of a numeric value expression.

```
LN (9)
```

This function returns something like 2.197224577. The number of digits beyond the decimal point is implementation dependent.

EXP

The EXP function raises the base of the natural logarithms *e* to the power specified by a numeric value expression.

```
EXP (2)
```

This function returns something like 7.389056. The number of digits beyond the decimal point is implementation dependent.

POWER

The POWER function raises the value of the first numeric value expression to the power of the second numeric value expression.

```
POWER (2,8)
```

This function returns 256, which is two raised to the eighth power.

SQRT

The SQRT function returns the square root of the value of the numeric value expression.

```
SQRT (4)
```

This function returns 2, the square root of four.

FLOOR

The FLOOR function rounds the numeric value expression to the largest integer not greater than the expression.

```
FLOOR (3.141592)
```

This function returns 3.0.

CEIL or CEILING

The CEIL or CEILING function rounds the numeric value expression to the smallest integer not less than the expression.

```
CEIL (3.141592)
```

This function returns 4.0.

WIDTH_BUCKET

The WIDTH_BUCKET function, used in *online application processing* (OLAP), is a function of four arguments, returning an integer between 0 (zero) and the value of the final argument plus 1 (one). It assigns the first argument to an *equiwidth partitioning* of the range of numbers between the second and third arguments. Values outside this range are assigned to either 0 (zero) or the value of the third argument plus 1 (one).

For example:

```
WIDTH_BUCKET ( PI, 0, 10, 5)
```

Suppose PI is a numeric value expression with a value of 3.141592. The example partitions the interval from zero to nine into five equal *buckets,* each with a width of two. The function returns a value of 2, because 3.141592 falls into the second bucket, which covers the range from two to four.

Datetime value functions

SQL includes three functions that return information about the current date, current time, or both. CURRENT_DATE returns the current date; CURRENT_TIME returns the current time; and CURRENT_TIMESTAMP returns (surprise!) both the current date and the current time. CURRENT_DATE doesn't take an argument, but CURRENT_TIME and CURRENT_TIMESTAMP both take a single argument. The argument specifies the precision for the seconds part of the time value that the function returns. Datetime data types and the precision concept are described in Chapter 2.

The following table offers some examples of these datetime value functions.

This Statement	*Returns*
CURRENT_DATE	2006-12-31
CURRENT_TIME (1)	08:36:57.3
CURRENT_TIMESTAMP (2)	2006-12-31 08:36:57.38

The date that CURRENT_DATE returns is DATE type data. The time that CURRENT_TIME (p) returns is TIME type data, and the timestamp that CURRENT_TIMESTAMP(p) returns is TIMESTAMP type data. Because SQL retrieves date and time information from your computer's system clock, the information is correct for the time zone in which the computer resides.

In some applications, you may want to deal with dates, times, or timestamps as character strings to take advantage of the functions that operate on character data. You can perform a type conversion by using the CAST expression, which I describe in Chapter 8.

Interval value functions

An interval value function named ABS was introduced in SQL:1999. It is similar to the ABS numeric value function, but operates on interval type data rather than numeric type data. ABS takes a single operand and returns an interval of the identical precision that is guaranteed not to have a negative value. Here's an example:

```
ABS ( TIME '11:31:00' - TIME '12:31:00' )
```

The result is:

```
INTERVAL +'1:00:00' HOUR TO SECOND
```

Chapter 8

Using Advanced SQL Value Expressions

· ·

In This Chapter

▶ Using the CASE conditional expressions

▶ Converting a data item from one data type to another

▶ Saving data entry time by using row value expressions

· ·

SQL is described in Chapter 2 as a *data sublanguage*. In fact, the sole function of SQL is to operate on data in a database. SQL lacks many of the features of a conventional procedural language. As a result, developers who use SQL must switch back and forth between SQL and its host language to control the flow of execution. This repeated switching complicates matters at development time and negatively affects performance at run time.

The performance penalty exacted by SQL's limitations prompts the addition of new features to SQL every time a new version of the international specification is released. One of those added features, the CASE expression, provides a long-sought conditional structure. A second feature, the CAST expression, facilitates data conversion in a table from one type of data to another. A third feature, the row value expression, enables you to operate on a list of values where, previously, only a single value was possible. For example, if your list of values is a list of columns in a table, you can now perform an operation on all those columns by using a very simple syntax.

CASE Conditional Expressions

Every complete computer language has some kind of conditional statement or command. In fact, most have several kinds. Probably the most common conditional statement or command is the IF...THEN...ELSE...ENDIF structure. If the condition following the IF keyword evaluates to True, the block of commands following the THEN keyword executes. If the condition doesn't evaluate to True, the block of commands after the ELSE keyword executes. The ENDIF keyword signals the end of the structure. This structure is great for any decision that goes one of two ways. The structure doesn't work as well for decisions that can have more than two outcomes.

Most complete languages have a CASE statement that handles situations in which you may want to perform more than two tasks based on more than two conditions.

SQL has a CASE statement and a CASE *expression.* A CASE expression is only part of a statement — not a statement in its own right. In SQL, you can place a CASE expression almost anywhere a value is legal. At run time, a CASE expression evaluates to a value. SQL's CASE statement doesn't evaluate to a value; rather, it executes a block of statements.

The CASE expression searches a table, one row at a time, taking on the value of a specified result whenever one of a list of conditions is TRUE. If the first condition is not satisfied for a row, the second condition is tested, and if it is TRUE, the result specified for it is given to the expression, and so on until all conditions are processed. If no match is found, the expression takes on a NULL value. Processing then moves to the next row.

You can use the CASE expression in the following two ways:

- ✔ **Use the expression with search conditions.** CASE searches for rows in a table where specified conditions are True. If CASE finds a search condition to be True for a table row, the statement containing the CASE expression makes a specified change to that row.

- ✔ **Use the expression to compare a table field to a specified value.** The outcome of the statement containing the CASE expression depends on which of several specified values in the table field is equal to each table row.

The next two sections, "Using CASE with search conditions" and "Using CASE with values," help make these concepts more clear. In the first section, two examples use CASE with search conditions. One example searches a table and makes changes to table values, based on a condition. The second section explores two examples of the value form of CASE.

Using CASE with search conditions

One powerful way to use the CASE expression is to search a table for rows in which a specified search condition is True. If you use CASE this way, the expression uses the following syntax:

```
CASE
    WHEN condition1 THEN result1
    WHEN condition2 THEN result2
    ...
    WHEN conditionn THEN resultn
    ELSE resultx
END
```

CASE examines the first *qualifying row* (the first row that meets the conditions of the enclosing WHERE clause, if any) to see whether condition1 is True. If it is, the CASE expression receives a value of result1. If condition1 is not True, CASE evaluates the row for condition2. If condition2 is True, the CASE expression receives the value of result2, and so on. If none of the stated conditions are True, the CASE expression receives the value of resultx. The ELSE clause is optional. If the expression has no ELSE clause and none of the specified conditions are True, the expression receives a null value. After the SQL statement containing the CASE expression applies itself to the first qualifying row in a table and takes the appropriate action, it processes the next row. This sequence continues until the SQL statement finishes processing the entire table.

Updating values based on a condition

Because you can embed a CASE expression within an SQL statement almost anywhere a value is possible, this expression gives you tremendous flexibility. You can use CASE within an UPDATE statement, for example, to make changes to table values — based on certain conditions. Consider the following example:

```
UPDATE FOODS
   SET RATING = CASE
                   WHEN FAT < 1
                       THEN 'very low fat'
                   WHEN FAT < 5
                       THEN 'low fat'
                   WHEN FAT < 20
                       THEN 'moderate fat'
                   WHEN FAT < 50
                       THEN 'high fat'
                   ELSE 'heart attack city'
                END ;
```

This statement evaluates the WHEN conditions in order until the first True value is returned, after which the statement ignores the rest of the conditions.

Table 7-2 in Chapter 7 shows the fat content of 100 grams of certain foods. A database table holding this information can contain a RATING column that gives a quick assessment of the fat content's meaning. If you run the preceding UPDATE on the FOODS table in Chapter 7, the statement assigns asparagus a value of very low fat, gives chicken a value of low fat, and puts roasted almonds into the heart attack city category.

Avoiding conditions that cause errors

Another valuable use of CASE is *exception avoidance* — checking for conditions that cause errors.

Consider a case that determines compensation for salespeople. Companies that compensate their salespeople by straight commission often pay their new employees by giving them a *draw* against the future commissions they're expected to earn. In the following example, new salespeople receive a draw against commission; the draw is phased out gradually as their commissions rise:

```
UPDATE SALES_COMP
   SET COMP = COMMISSION + CASE
                         WHEN COMMISSION <> 0
                            THEN DRAW/COMMISSION
                         WHEN COMMISSION = 0
                            THEN DRAW
                      END ;
```

If the salesperson's commission is zero, the structure in this example avoids a division by zero operation, which causes an error. If the salesperson has a nonzero commission, the total compensation is the commission plus a draw that is reduced proportionately to the size of the commission.

All of the THEN expressions in a CASE expression must be of the same type — all numeric, all character, or all date. The result of the CASE expression is also of the same type.

Using CASE with values

You can use a more compact form of the CASE expression if you're comparing a test value for equality with a series of other values. This form is useful within a SELECT or UPDATE statement if a table contains a limited number of values in a column and you want to associate a corresponding result value to each of those column values. If you use CASE in this way, the expression has the following syntax:

```
CASE valuet
   WHEN value1 THEN result1
   WHEN value2 THEN result2
   ...
   WHEN valuen THEN resultn
   ELSE resultx
END
```

If the test value (valuet) is equal to value1, the expression takes on the value result1. If valuet is not equal to value1 but is equal to value2, the expression takes on the value result2. The expression tries each comparison value in turn, all the way down to valuen, until it achieves a match. If none of the comparison values equal the test value, the expression takes on the value resultx. Again, if the optional ELSE clause isn't present and none of the comparison values match the test value, the expression receives a null value.

To understand how the value form works, consider a case in which you have a table containing the names and ranks of various military officers. You want to list the names preceded by the correct abbreviation for each rank. The following statement does the job:

```
SELECT CASE RANK
        WHEN 'general'           THEN 'Gen.'
        WHEN 'colonel'           THEN 'Col.'
        WHEN 'lieutenant colonel' THEN 'Lt. Col.'
        WHEN 'major'             THEN 'Maj.'
        WHEN 'captain'           THEN 'Capt.'
        WHEN 'first lieutenant'  THEN '1st. Lt.'
        WHEN 'second lieutenant' THEN '2nd. Lt.'
        ELSE NULL
    END,
        LAST_NAME
    FROM OFFICERS ;
```

The result is a list similar to the following example:

```
Capt.  Midnight
Col.   Sanders
Gen.   Schwarzkopf
Maj.   Disaster
       Nimitz
```

Chester Nimitz was an admiral in the United States Navy during World War II. Because his rank isn't listed in the CASE expression, the ELSE clause doesn't give him a title.

For another example, suppose that Captain Midnight gets a promotion to major and you want to update the OFFICERS database accordingly. Assume that the variable officer_last_name contains the value 'Midnight' and that the variable new_rank contains an integer (4) that corresponds to Midnight's new rank, according to the following table.

new_rank	Rank
1	general
2	colonel
3	lieutenant colonel
4	major
5	captain
6	first lieutenant
7	second lieutenant
8	NULL

You can record the promotion by using the following SQL code:

```
UPDATE OFFICERS
   SET RANK = CASE :new_rank
                  WHEN 1 THEN 'general'
                  WHEN 2 THEN 'colonel'
                  WHEN 3 THEN 'lieutenant colonel'
                  WHEN 4 THEN 'major'
                  WHEN 5 THEN 'captain'
                  WHEN 6 THEN 'first lieutenant'
                  WHEN 7 THEN 'second lieutenant'
                  WHEN 8 THEN NULL
              END
   WHERE LAST_NAME = :officer_last_name ;
```

An alternative syntax for the CASE with values is:

```
CASE
   WHEN valuet = value1 THEN result1
   WHEN valuet = value2 THEN result2
   ...
   WHEN valuet = valuen THEN resultn
   ELSE resultx
END
```

A special CASE — NULLIF

The one thing you can be sure of in this world is change. Sometimes things change from one known state to another. Other times, you think that you know something but later you find out that you didn't know it after all. Classical thermodynamics and modern chaos theory both tell us that systems naturally migrate from a well-known, ordered state into a disordered state that no one can predict. Anyone who has ever monitored the status of a teenager's room for a one-week period after the room is cleaned can vouch for the accuracy of these theories.

Database tables have definite values in fields containing known contents. Usually, if the value of a field is unknown, the field contains the null value. In SQL, you can use a CASE expression to change the contents of a table field from a definite value to a null. The null indicates that you no longer know the field's value. Consider the following example.

Imagine that you own a small airline that offers flights between southern California and Washington state. Until recently, some of your flights stopped at San Jose International Airport to refuel before continuing on. Unfortunately, you just lost your right to fly into San Jose. From now on, you must make your refueling stop at either San Francisco International Airport or Oakland

International Airport. At this point, you don't know which flights stop at which airport, but you do know that none of the flights are stopping at San Jose. You have a FLIGHT database that contains important information about your routes, and now you want to update the database to remove all references to San Jose. The following example shows one way to do this:

```
UPDATE FLIGHT
   SET RefuelStop = CASE
                        WHEN RefuelStop = 'San Jose'
                           THEN NULL
                        ELSE RefuelStop
                     END ;
```

Because occasions like this one, in which you want to replace a known value with a null value, frequently arise, SQL offers a shorthand notation to accomplish this task. The preceding example, expressed in this shorthand form, looks like this:

```
UPDATE FLIGHT
   SET RefuelStop = NULLIF(RefuelStop, 'San Jose') ;
```

You can translate this expression to English as, "Update the FLIGHT table by setting the RefuelStop column to null if the existing value of RefuelStop is 'San Jose'. Otherwise, make no change."

NULLIF is even handier if you're converting data that you originally accumulated for use with a program written in a standard programming language such as COBOL or FORTRAN. Standard programming languages don't have nulls, so a common practice is to represent the "not known" or "not applicable" concept by using special values. A numeric -1 may represent a not known value for SALARY, for example, and a character string "***" may represent a not known or not applicable value for JOBCODE. If you want to represent these not known and not applicable states in an SQL-compatible database by using nulls, you need to convert the special values to nulls. The following example makes this conversion for an employee table, in which some salary values are unknown:

```
UPDATE EMP
   SET Salary = CASE Salary
                   WHEN -1 THEN NULL
                   ELSE Salary
                END ;
```

You can perform this conversion more conveniently by using NULLIF, as follows:

```
UPDATE EMP
   SET Salary = NULLIF(Salary, -1) ;
```

Another special CASE — COALESCE

COALESCE, like NULLIF, is a shorthand form of a particular CASE expression. COALESCE deals with a list of values that may or may not be null. Here's how it works:

- ✔ **If one of the values in the list is non-null:** The COALESCE expression takes on that value.

- ✔ **If more than one value in the list is non-null:** The expression takes on the value of the first non-null item in the list.

- ✔ **If all the values in the list are null:** The expression takes on the null value.

A CASE expression with this function has the following form:

```
CASE
    WHEN value1 IS NOT NULL
        THEN value1
    WHEN value2 IS NOT NULL
        THEN value2
    ...
    WHEN valuen IS NOT NULL
        THEN valuen
    ELSE NULL
END
```

The corresponding COALESCE shorthand looks like this:

```
COALESCE(value1, value2, ..., valuen)
```

You may want to use a COALESCE expression after you perform an OUTER JOIN operation (discussed in Chapter 10). In such cases, COALESCE can save you a lot of typing.

CAST Data-Type Conversions

Chapter 2 covers the data types that SQL recognizes and supports. Ideally, each column in a database table has a perfect choice of data type. In this non-ideal world, however, exactly what that perfect choice may be isn't always clear. In defining a database table, suppose you assign a data type to a column that works perfectly for your current application. Later, you want to expand your application's scope or write an entirely new application that uses the data differently. This new use could require a data type different from the one you originally chose.

You may want to compare a column of one type in one table with a column of a different type in a different table. For example, you could have dates stored as character data in one table and as date data in another table. Even if both columns contain the same sort of information (dates, for example), the fact that the types are different may prevent you from making the comparison. In the earliest SQL standards, SQL-86 and SQL-89, type incompatibility posed a big problem. SQL-92, however, introduced an easy-to-use solution in the CAST expression.

The CAST expression converts table data or host variables of one type to another type. After you make the conversion, you can proceed with the operation or analysis that you originally envisioned.

Naturally, you face some restrictions when using the CAST expression. You can't just indiscriminately convert data of any type into any other type. The data that you're converting must be compatible with the new data type. You can, for example, use CAST to convert the CHAR(10) character string '2007-04-26' to the DATE type. But you can't use CAST to convert the CHAR(10) character string 'rhinoceros' to the DATE type. You can't convert an INTEGER to the SMALLINT type if the former exceeds the maximum size of a SMALLINT.

You can convert an item of any character type to any other type (such as numeric or date) provided that the item's value has the form of a literal of the new type. Conversely, you can convert an item of any type to any of the character types, provided that the value of the item has the form of a literal of the original type.

The following list describes some additional conversions you can make:

✔ Any numeric type to any other numeric type. If converting to a less fractionally precise type, the system rounds or truncates the result.

✔ Any exact numeric type to a single component interval, such as INTERVAL DAY or INTERVAL SECOND.

✔ Any DATE to a TIMESTAMP. The time part of the TIMESTAMP fills in with zeros.

✔ Any TIME to a TIME with a different fractional-seconds precision or a TIMESTAMP. The date part of the TIMESTAMP fills in with the current date.

✔ Any TIMESTAMP to a DATE, a TIME, or a TIMESTAMP with a different fractional-seconds precision.

✔ Any year-month INTERVAL to an exact numeric type or another year-month INTERVAL with different leading-field precision.

✔ Any day-time INTERVAL to an exact numeric type or another day-time INTERVAL with different leading-field precision.

Using CAST within SQL

Suppose that you work for a company that keeps track of prospective employees as well as employees whom you've actually hired. You list the prospective employees in a table named PROSPECT, and you distinguish them by their Social Security numbers, which you store as a CHAR(9) type. You list the employees in a table named EMPLOYEE, and you distinguish them by their Social Security numbers, which are of the INTEGER type. You now want to generate a list of all people who appear in both tables. You can use CAST to perform the task:

```
SELECT * FROM EMPLOYEE
    WHERE EMPLOYEE.SSN =
        CAST(PROSPECT.SSN AS INTEGER) ;
```

Using CAST between SQL and the host language

The key use of CAST is to deal with data types that are available in SQL but not in the host language that you use. The following list offers some examples of these data types:

- ✔ SQL has DECIMAL and NUMERIC, but FORTRAN and Pascal don't.
- ✔ SQL has FLOAT and REAL, but standard COBOL doesn't.
- ✔ SQL has DATETIME, which no other language has.

Suppose that you want to use FORTRAN or Pascal to access tables with DECIMAL(5,3) columns, and you don't want any inaccuracies to result from converting those values to the REAL data type used by FORTRAN and Pascal. You can perform this task by CASTing the data to and from character-string host variables. You retrieve a numeric salary of 198.37 as a CHAR(10) value of '0000198.37'. Then if you want to update that salary to 203.74, you can place that value in a CHAR(10) as '0000203.74'. First, you use CAST to change the SQL DECIMAL(5,3) data type to the CHAR(10) type for the employee whose ID number you're storing in the host variable :emp_id_var, as follows:

```
SELECT CAST(Salary AS CHAR(10)) INTO :salary_var
        FROM EMP
        WHERE EmpID = :emp_id_var ;
```

The application examines the resulting character string value in :salary_var, possibly sets the string to a new value of '000203.74', and then updates the database by using the following SQL code:

```
UPDATE EMP
   SET Salary = CAST(:salary_var AS DECIMAL(5,3))
      WHERE EmpID = :emp_id_var ;
```

Dealing with character-string values like '000198.37' is awkward in FORTRAN or Pascal, but you can write a set of subroutines to do the necessary manipulations. You can then retrieve and update any SQL data from any host language and get and set exact values.

The general idea is that CAST is most valuable for converting between host types and the database rather than for converting within the database.

Row Value Expressions

In the original SQL standards, such as SQL-86 and SQL-89, most operations dealt with a single value or a single column in a table row. To operate on multiple values, you must build complex expressions by using logical *connectives* (which I discuss in Chapter 9).

SQL-92 introduced *row value expressions*, which operate on a list of values or columns rather than a single value or column. A row value expression is a list of value expressions that you enclose in parentheses and separate by commas. You can operate on an entire row at once or on a selected subset of the row.

Chapter 6 covers how to use the INSERT statement to add a new row to an existing table. To do so, the statement uses a row value expression. Consider the following example:

```
INSERT INTO FOODS
   (FOODNAME, CALORIES, PROTEIN, FAT, CARBOHYDRATE)
   VALUES
   ('Cheese, cheddar', 398, 25, 32.2, 2.1) ;
```

In this example, ('Cheese, cheddar', 398, 25, 32.2, 2.1) is a row value expression. If you use a row value expression in an INSERT statement this way, it can contain null and default values. (A *default value* is the value that a table column assumes if you specify no other value.) The following line, for example, is a legal row value expression:

```
('Cheese, cheddar', 398, NULL, 32.2, DEFAULT)
```

You can add multiple rows to a table by putting multiple row value expressions in the VALUES clause, as follows:

```
INSERT INTO FOODS
   (FOODNAME, CALORIES, PROTEIN, FAT, CARBOHYDRATE)
   VALUES
   ('Lettuce', 14, 1.2, 0.2, 2.5),
   ('Margarine', 720, 0.6, 81.0, 0.4),
   ('Mustard', 75, 4.7, 4.4, 6.4),
   ('Spaghetti', 148, 5.0, 0.5, 30.1) ;
```

You can use row value expressions to save yourself from having to enter comparisons manually. Suppose you have two tables of nutritional values, one compiled in English and the other in Spanish. You want to find those rows in the English language table that correspond exactly to the rows in the Spanish language table. Without a row value expression, you may need to formulate something like the following example:

```
SELECT * FROM FOODS
   WHERE FOODS.CALORIES = COMIDA.CALORIA
      AND FOODS.PROTEIN = COMIDA.PROTEINA
      AND FOODS.FAT = COMIDA.GORDO
      AND FOODS.CARBOHYDRATE = COMIDA.CARBOHIDRATO ;
```

Row value expressions enable you to code the same logic, as follows:

```
SELECT * FROM FOODS
   WHERE (FOODS.CALORIES, FOODS.PROTEIN, FOODS.FAT,
         FOODS.CARBOHYDRATE)
      =
      (COMIDA.CALORIA, COMIDA.PROTEINA, COMIDA.GORDO,
      COMIDA.CARBOHIDRATO) ;
```

In this example, you don't save much typing. You would benefit slightly more if you were comparing more columns. In cases of marginal benefit like this example, you may be better off sticking with the older syntax because its meaning is clearer.

You gain one benefit by using a row value expression instead of its coded equivalent — the row value expression is much faster. In principle, a clever implementation can analyze the coded version and implement it as the row value version. In practice, this operation is a difficult optimization that no DBMS currently on the market can perform.

Chapter 9

Zeroing In on the Data You Want

....

In This Chapter

▶ Specifying the tables you want to work with

▶ Separating rows of interest from the rest

▶ Building effective WHERE clauses

▶ Handling null values

▶ Building compound expressions with logical connectives

▶ Grouping query output by column

▶ Putting query output in order

....

A database management system has two main functions: storing data and providing easy access to that data. Storing data is nothing special; a file cabinet can perform that chore. The hard part of data management is providing easy access. For data to be useful, you must be able to separate the (usually) small amount you want from the huge amount you don't want.

SQL enables you to use some characteristics of the data to determine whether a particular table row is of interest to you. The SELECT, DELETE, and UPDATE statements convey to the database *engine* (the part of the DBMS that directly interacts with the data) which rows to select, delete, or update. You add modifying clauses to the SELECT, DELETE, and UPDATE statements to refine the search to your specifications.

Modifying Clauses

The modifying clauses available in SQL are FROM, WHERE, HAVING, GROUP BY, and ORDER BY. The FROM clause tells the database engine which table or tables to operate on. The WHERE and HAVING clauses specify a data characteristic that determines whether or not to include a particular row in the current operation. The GROUP BY and ORDER BY clauses specify how to display the retrieved rows. Table 9-1 provides a summary.

Table 9-1	Modifying Clauses and Functions
Modifying Clause	*Function*
FROM	Specifies from which tables data should be taken
WHERE	Filters out rows that don't satisfy the search condition
GROUP BY	Separates rows into groups based on the values in the grouping columns
HAVING	Filters out groups that don't satisfy the search condition
ORDER BY	Sorts the results of prior clauses to produce final output

If you use more than one of these clauses, they must appear in the following order:

```
SELECT column_list
   FROM table_list
   [WHERE search_condition]
   [GROUP BY grouping_column]
   [HAVING search_condition]
   [ORDER BY ordering_condition] ;
```

Here's the lowdown on the execution of these clauses:

- The WHERE clause is a filter that passes rows that meet the search condition and rejects rows that don't meet the condition.

- The GROUP BY clause rearranges the rows that the WHERE clause passes according to the value of the grouping column.

- The HAVING clause is another filter that takes each group that the GROUP BY clause forms and passes those groups that meet the search condition, rejecting the rest.

- The ORDER BY clause sorts whatever remains after all the preceding clauses process the table.

As the square brackets ([ ]) indicate, the WHERE, GROUP BY, HAVING, and ORDER BY clauses are optional.

SQL evaluates these clauses in the order FROM, WHERE, GROUP BY, HAVING, and finally SELECT. The clauses operate like a pipeline — each clause receives the result of the prior clause and produces an output for the next clause. In functional notation, this order of evaluation appears as follows:

```
SELECT(HAVING(GROUP BY(WHERE(FROM...))))
```

ORDER BY operates after SELECT, which explains why ORDER BY can only reference columns in the SELECT list. ORDER BY can't reference other columns in the FROM table(s).

FROM Clauses

The FROM clause is easy to understand if you specify only one table, as in the following example:

```
SELECT * FROM SALES ;
```

This statement returns all the data in all the rows of every column in the SALES table. You can, however, specify more than one table in a FROM clause. Consider the following example:

```
SELECT *
   FROM CUSTOMER, SALES ;
```

This statement forms a virtual table that combines the data from the CUSTOMER table with the data from the SALES table. Each row in the CUSTOMER table combines with every row in the SALES table to form the new table. The new virtual table that this combination forms contains the number of rows in the CUSTOMER table multiplied by the number of rows in the SALES table. If the CUSTOMER table has 10 rows and the SALES table has 100, then the new virtual table has 1,000 rows.

This operation is called the *Cartesian product* of the two source tables. The Cartesian product is a type of join. I cover join operations in detail in Chapter 10.

In most applications, when you take the Cartesian product of two tables, most of the rows that are formed are meaningless. In the case of the virtual table that forms from the CUSTOMER and SALES tables, only the rows where the CustomerID from the CUSTOMER table matches the CustomerID from the SALES table are of interest. You can filter out the rest of the rows by using a WHERE clause.

WHERE Clauses

I use the WHERE clause many times throughout this book without really explaining it because its meaning and use are obvious: A statement performs an operation (such as SELECT, DELETE, or UPDATE) only on table rows WHERE a stated condition is True. The syntax of the WHERE clause is as follows:

```
SELECT column_list
   FROM table_name
   WHERE condition ;

DELETE FROM table_name
   WHERE condition ;

UPDATE table_name
   SET column₁=value₁, column₂=value₂, ..., columnₙ=valueₙ
   WHERE condition ;
```

The condition in the WHERE clause may be simple or arbitrarily complex. You may join multiple conditions together by using the logical connectives AND, OR, and NOT (which I discuss later in this chapter) to create a single condition.

The following are some typical examples of WHERE clauses:

```
WHERE CUSTOMER.CustomerID = SALES.CustomerID
WHERE FOODS.Calories = COMIDA.Caloria
WHERE FOODS.Calories < 219
WHERE FOODS.Calories > 3 * base_value
WHERE FOODS.Calories < 219 AND FOODS.Protein > 27.4
```

The conditions that these WHERE clauses express are known as predicates. A *predicate* is an expression that asserts a fact about values.

The predicate FOODS.Calories < 219, for example, is True if the value for the current row of the column FOODS.Calories is less than 219. If the assertion is True, it satisfies the condition. An assertion may be True, False, or unknown. The unknown case arises if one or more elements in the assertion are null. The *comparison predicates* (=, <, >, <>, <=, and >=) are the most common, but SQL offers several others that greatly increase your capability to filter out a desired data item from others in the same column. The following list notes the predicates that give you that filtering capability:

- Comparison predicates
- BETWEEN
- IN [NOT IN]
- LIKE [NOT LIKE]
- NULL

- ✔ ALL, SOME, ANY
- ✔ EXISTS
- ✔ UNIQUE
- ✔ OVERLAPS
- ✔ MATCH
- ✔ SIMILAR
- ✔ DISTINCT

Comparison predicates

The examples in the preceding section show typical uses of comparison predicates in which you compare one value to another. For every row in which the comparison evaluates to a True value, that value satisfies the WHERE clause, and the operation (SELECT, UPDATE, DELETE, or whatever) executes upon that row. Rows that the comparison evaluates to FALSE are skipped. Consider the following SQL statement:

```
SELECT * FROM FOODS
   WHERE Calories < 219 ;
```

This statement displays all rows from the FOODS table that have a value of less than 219 in the Calories column.

Six comparison predicates are listed in Table 9-2.

Table 9-2	SQL's Comparison Predicates
Comparison	*Symbol*
Equal	=
Not equal	<>
Less than	<
Less than or equal	<=
Greater than	>
Greater than or equal	>=

BETWEEN

Sometimes, you want to select a row if the value in a column falls within a specified range. One way to make this selection is by using comparison predicates. For example, you can formulate a WHERE clause to select all the rows in the FOODS table that have a value in the Calories column greater than 100 and less than 300, as follows:

```
WHERE FOODS.Calories > 100 AND FOODS.Calories < 300
```

This comparison doesn't include foods with a calorie count of exactly 100 or 300 — only those values that fall in between these two numbers. To include the end points, you can write the statement as follows:

```
WHERE FOODS.Calories >= 100 AND FOODS.Calories <= 300
```

Another way of specifying a range that includes the end points is to use a BETWEEN predicate in the following manner:

```
WHERE FOODS.Calories BETWEEN 100 AND 300
```

This clause is functionally identical to the preceding example, which uses comparison predicates. This formulation saves some typing and is a little more intuitive than the one that uses two comparison predicates joined by the logical connective AND.

The BETWEEN keyword may be confusing because it doesn't tell you explicitly whether the clause includes the end points. In fact, the clause *does* include these end points. When you use the BETWEEN keyword, a little birdy doesn't swoop down to remind you that the first term in the comparison must be equal to or less than the second. If, for example, FOODS.Calories contains a value of 200, the following clause returns a True value:

```
WHERE FOODS.Calories BETWEEN 100 AND 300
```

However, a clause that you may think is equivalent to the preceding example returns the opposite result, False:

```
WHERE FOODS.Calories BETWEEN 300 AND 100
```

If you use BETWEEN, you must be able to guarantee that the first term in your comparison is always equal to or less than the second term.

You can use the BETWEEN predicate with character, bit, and datetime data types as well as with the numeric types. You may see something like the following example:

```
SELECT FirstName, LastName
   FROM CUSTOMER
   WHERE CUSTOMER.LastName BETWEEN 'A' AND 'Mzzz' ;
```

This example returns all customers whose last names are in the first half of the alphabet.

IN and NOT IN

The IN and NOT IN predicates deal with whether specified values (such as OR, WA, and ID), are contained within a particular set of values (such as the states of the United States). You may, for example, have a table that lists suppliers of a commodity that your company purchases on a regular basis. You want to know the phone numbers of the suppliers located in the Pacific Northwest. You can find these numbers by using comparison predicates, such as those shown in the following example:

```
SELECT Company, Phone
   FROM SUPPLIER
   WHERE State = 'OR' OR State = 'WA' OR State = 'ID' ;
```

You can also use the IN predicate to perform the same task, as follows:

```
SELECT Company, Phone
   FROM SUPPLIER
   WHERE State IN ('OR', 'WA', 'ID') ;
```

This formulation is a bit more compact than the one using comparison predicates and logical OR. It also eliminates any possible confusion between the logical OR operator and the abbreviation for the state of Oregon.

The NOT IN version of this predicate works the same way. Say that you have locations in California, Arizona, and New Mexico, and to avoid paying sales tax, you want to consider using suppliers located anywhere except in those states. Use the following construction:

```
SELECT Company, Phone
   FROM SUPPLIER
   WHERE State NOT IN ('CA', 'AZ', 'NM') ;
```

Using the IN keyword this way saves you a little typing. Saving a little typing, however, isn't that great of an advantage. You can do the same job by using comparison predicates as shown in this section's first example.

You may have another good reason to use the IN predicate rather than comparison predicates, even if using IN doesn't save much typing. Your DBMS probably implements the two methods differently, and one of the methods may be significantly faster than the other on your system. You may want to run a performance comparison on the two ways of expressing inclusion in (or exclusion from) a group and then use the technique that produces the quicker result. A DBMS with a good optimizer will probably choose the more efficient method, regardless of which predicate you use.

The IN keyword is valuable in another area, too. If IN is part of a subquery, the keyword enables you to pull information from two tables to obtain results that you can't derive from a single table. I cover subqueries in detail in Chapter 11, but here's an example that shows how a subquery uses the IN keyword.

Suppose that you want to display the names of all customers who've bought the F-117A product in the last 30 days. Customer names are in the CUSTOMER table, and sales transaction data is in the TRANSACT table. You can use the following query:

```
SELECT FirstName, LastName
    FROM CUSTOMER
    WHERE CustomerID IN
        (SELECT CustomerID
            FROM TRANSACT
            WHERE ProductID = 'F-117A'
            AND TransDate >= (CurrentDate - 30)) ;
```

The inner SELECT of the TRANSACT table nests within the outer SELECT of the CUSTOMER table. The inner SELECT finds the CustomerID numbers of all customers who bought the F-117A product in the last 30 days. The outer SELECT displays the first and last names of all customers whose CustomerID is retrieved by the inner SELECT.

LIKE and NOT LIKE

You can use the LIKE predicate to compare two character strings for a partial match. Partial matches are valuable if you don't know the exact form of the string for which you're searching. You can also use partial matches to retrieve multiple rows that contain similar strings in one of the table's columns.

To identify partial matches, SQL uses two wildcard characters. The percent sign (%) can stand for any string of characters that have zero or more characters. The underscore (_) stands for any single character. Table 9-3 provides some examples that show how to use LIKE.

Table 9-3	SQL's LIKE Predicate
Statement	*Values Returned*
WHERE Word LIKE 'intern%'	intern
	internal
	international
	internet
	interns
WHERE Word LIKE '%Peace%'	Justice of the Peace
	Peaceful Warrior
WHERE Word LIKE 't_p_'	tape
	taps
	tipi
	tips
	tops
	type

The NOT LIKE predicate retrieves all rows that don't satisfy a partial match, including one or more wildcard characters, as in the following example:

```
WHERE Phone NOT LIKE '503%'
```

This example returns all the rows in the table for which the phone number starts with something other than 503.

You may want to search for a string that includes a percent sign or an under-score. In this case, you want SQL to interpret the percent sign as a percent sign and not as a wildcard character. You can conduct such a search by typing an escape character just prior to the character you want SQL to take literally. You can choose any character as the escape character, as long as that character doesn't appear in the string that you're testing, as shown in the following example:

```
SELECT Quote
   FROM BARTLETTS
   WHERE Quote LIKE '20#%'
      ESCAPE '#' ;
```

The % character is escaped by the preceding # sign, so the statement interprets this symbol as a percent sign rather than as a wildcard. You can escape an underscore or the escape character itself, in the same way. The preceding query, for example, would find the following quotation in *Bartlett's Familiar Quotations:*

```
20% of the salespeople produce 80% of the results.
```

The query would also find the following:

```
20%
```

SIMILAR

SQL:1999 added the SIMILAR predicate, which offers a more powerful way of finding partial matches than the LIKE predicate provides. With the SIMILAR predicate, you can compare a character string to a regular expression. For example, say you're searching the OperatingSystem column of a software compatibility table to look for Microsoft Windows compatibility. You could construct a WHERE clause such as the following:

```
WHERE OperatingSystem SIMILAR TO
'('Windows '(3.1|95|98|ME|CE|NT|2000|XP))'
```

This predicate retrieves all rows that contain any of the specified Microsoft operating systems.

NULL

The NULL predicate finds all rows where the value in the selected column is null. In the FOODS table in Chapter 7, several rows have null values in the Carbohydrate column. You can retrieve their names by using a statement such as the following:

```
SELECT (Food)
   FROM FOODS
   WHERE Carbohydrate IS NULL ;
```

This query returns the following values:

```
Beef, lean hamburger
Chicken, light meat
Opossum, roasted
Pork, ham
```

As you may expect, including the NOT keyword reverses the result, as in the following example:

```
SELECT (Food)
   FROM FOODS
   WHERE Carbohydrate IS NOT NULL ;
```

This query returns all the rows in the table except the four that the preceding query returns.

The statement Carbohydrate IS NULL is not the same as Carbohydrate = NULL. To illustrate this point, assume that, in the current row of the FOODS table, both Carbohydrate and Protein are null. From this fact, you can draw the following conclusions:

- ✔ Carbohydrate IS NULL is True.

- ✔ Protein IS NULL is True.

- ✔ Carbohydrate IS NULL AND Protein IS NULL is True.

- ✔ Carbohydrate = Protein is unknown.

- ✔ Carbohydrate = NULL is an illegal expression.

Using the keyword NULL in a comparison is meaningless because the answer always returns as *unknown.*

Why is Carbohydrate = Protein defined as unknown, even though Carbohydrate and Protein have the same (null) value? Because NULL simply means "I don't know." You don't know what Carbohydrate is, and you don't know what Protein is; therefore, you don't know whether those (unknown) values are the same. Maybe Carbohydrate is 37, and Protein is 14, or maybe Carbohydrate is 93, and Protein is 93. If you don't know both the carbohydrate value and the protein value, you can't say whether the two are the same.

ALL, SOME, ANY

Thousands of years ago, the Greek philosopher Aristotle formulated a system of logic that became the basis for much of Western thought. The essence of this logic is to start with a set of premises that you know to be true, apply valid operations to these premises, and, thereby, arrive at new truths. An example of this procedure is as follows:

Premise 1: All Greeks are human.

Premise 2: All humans are mortal.

Conclusion: All Greeks are mortal.

ANY can be ambiguous

The original SQL used the word ANY for existential quantification. This usage turned out to be confusing and error-prone, because the English language connotations of *any* are sometimes universal and sometimes existential:

✔ "Do any of you know where Baker Street is?"

✔ "I can eat more eggs than any of you."

The first sentence is probably asking whether at least one person knows where Baker Street is. *Any* is used as an existential quantifier. The second sentence, however, is a boast that's stating that I can eat more eggs than the biggest eater among all you people can eat. In this case, *any* is used as a universal quantifier.

Thus, for the SQL-92 standard, the developers retained the word ANY for compatibility with early products, but they also added the word SOME as a less confusing synonym. SQL continues to support both existential quantifiers.

Another example:

> *Premise 1:* Some Greeks are women.
>
> *Premise 2:* All women are human.
>
> *Conclusion:* Some Greeks are human.

By way of presenting a third example, let me state the same logical idea of the second example in a slightly different way:

> If any Greeks are women and all women are human, then some Greeks are human.

The first example uses the universal quantifier ALL in both premises, enabling you to make a sound deduction about all Greeks in the conclusion. The second example uses the existential quantifier SOME in one premise, enabling you to make a deduction about some Greeks in the conclusion. The third example uses the existential quantifier ANY, which is a synonym for SOME, to reach the same conclusion you reach in the second example.

Look at how SOME, ANY, and ALL apply in SQL.

Consider an example in baseball statistics. Baseball is a physically demanding sport, especially for pitchers. A pitcher must throw the baseball from the pitcher's mound to home plate between 90 and 150 times during a game. This effort can be exhausting, and if (as is often the case) the pitcher becomes ineffective before the game ends, a relief pitcher must replace him. Pitching an entire game is an outstanding achievement, regardless of whether the effort results in a victory.

Suppose that you're keeping track of the number of complete games that all major-league pitchers pitch. In one table, you list all the American League pitchers, and in another table, you list all the National League pitchers. Both tables contain the players' first names, last names, and number of complete games pitched.

The American League permits a designated hitter (DH) (who isn't required to play a defensive position) to bat in place of any of the nine players who play defense. The National League doesn't allow designated hitters, but does allow pinch hitters. When the pinch hitter comes into the game for the pitcher, the pitcher can't play for the remainder of the game. Usually the DH bats for the pitcher, because pitchers are notoriously poor hitters. Pitchers must spend so much time and effort on perfecting their pitching that they don't have as much time to practice batting as the other players do.

Say that you have a theory that, on average, American League starting pitchers throw more complete games than do National League starting pitchers. This idea is based on your observation that designated hitters enable hard-throwing, weak-hitting, American League pitchers to keep pitching as long as they are effective, even in a close game. Because a DH is already batting for these pitchers, their poor hitting isn't a liability. In the National League, however, under everyday circumstances the pitcher would go to bat. A pinch hitter would only hit for the pitcher in a close game where getting a base hit is more crucial than keeping an effective pitcher in the game. To test your theory, you formulate the following query:

```
SELECT FirstName, LastName
    FROM AMERICAN_LEAGUER
    WHERE CompleteGames > ALL
        (SELECT CompleteGames
            FROM NATIONAL_LEAGUER) ;
```

The subquery (the inner SELECT) returns a list showing, for every National League pitcher, the number of complete games he pitched. The outer query returns the first and last names of all American Leaguers who pitched more complete games than ALL of the National Leaguers. The query returns the names of those American League pitchers who pitched more complete games than the pitcher who has thrown the most complete games in the National League.

Consider the following similar statement:

```
SELECT FirstName, LastName
    FROM AMERICAN_LEAGUER
    WHERE CompleteGames > ANY
        (SELECT CompleteGames
            FROM NATIONAL_LEAGUER) ;
```

In this case, you use the existential quantifier ANY instead of the universal quantifier ALL. The subquery (the inner, nested query) is identical to the subquery in the previous example. This subquery retrieves a complete list of the complete game statistics for all the National League pitchers. The outer query returns the first and last names of all American League pitchers who pitched more complete games than ANY National League pitcher. Because you can be virtually certain that at least one National League pitcher hasn't pitched a complete game, the result probably includes all American League pitchers who've pitched at least one complete game.

If you replace the keyword ANY with the equivalent keyword SOME, the result is the same. If the statement that at least one National League pitcher hasn't pitched a complete game is a true statement, you can then say that SOME National League pitcher hasn't pitched a complete game.

EXISTS

You can use the EXISTS predicate in conjunction with a subquery to determine whether the subquery returns any rows. If the subquery returns at least one row, that result satisfies the EXISTS condition, and the outer query executes. Consider the following example:

```
SELECT FirstName, LastName
    FROM CUSTOMER
    WHERE EXISTS
      (SELECT DISTINCT CustomerID
        FROM SALES
        WHERE SALES.CustomerID = CUSTOMER.CustomerID);
```

The SALES table contains all of your company's sales transactions. The table includes the CustomerID of the customer who makes each purchase, as well as other pertinent information. The CUSTOMER table contains each customer's first and last names, but no information about specific transactions.

The subquery in the preceding example returns a row for every customer who has made at least one purchase. The outer query returns the first and last names of the customers who made the purchases that the SALES table records.

EXISTS is equivalent to a comparison of COUNT with zero, as the following query shows:

```
SELECT FirstName, LastName
    FROM CUSTOMER
    WHERE 0 <>
      (SELECT COUNT(*)
        FROM SALES
        WHERE SALES.CustomerID = CUSTOMER.CustomerID);
```

For every row in the SALES table that contains a `CustomerID` that's equal to a `CustomerID` in the CUSTOMER table, this statement displays the `FirstName` and `LastName` columns in the CUSTOMER table. For every sale in the SALES table, therefore, the statement displays the name of the customer who made the purchase.

UNIQUE

As you do with the `EXISTS` predicate, you use the `UNIQUE` predicate with a subquery. Although the `EXISTS` predicate evaluates to True only if the subquery returns at least one row, the `UNIQUE` predicate evaluates to True only if no two rows returned by the subquery are identical. In other words, the `UNIQUE` predicate evaluates to True only if all rows that its subquery returns are unique. Consider the following example:

```
SELECT FirstName, LastName
    FROM CUSTOMER
    WHERE UNIQUE
      (SELECT CustomerID FROM SALES
          WHERE SALES.CustomerID = CUSTOMER.CustomerID);
```

This statement retrieves the names of all new customers for whom the SALES table records only one sale. Because a null value is an unknown value, two null values aren't considered equal to each other; when the `UNIQUE` keyword is applied to a result table that only contains two null rows, the `UNIQUE` predicate evaluates to True.

DISTINCT

The `DISTINCT` predicate is similar to the `UNIQUE` predicate, except in the way it treats nulls. If all the values in a result table are `UNIQUE`, then they're also `DISTINCT` from each other. However, unlike the result for the `UNIQUE` predicate, if the `DISTINCT` keyword is applied to a result table that contains only two null rows, the `DISTINCT` predicate evaluates to False. Two null values are *not* considered distinct from each other, while at the same time they are considered to be unique.

This strange situation seems contradictory, but there's a reason for it. In some situations, you may want to treat two null values as different from each other, whereas in other situations, you want to treat them as if they're the same. In the first case, use the `UNIQUE` predicate. In the second case, use the `DISTINCT` predicate.

OVERLAPS

You use the OVERLAPS predicate to determine whether two time intervals overlap each other. This predicate is useful for avoiding scheduling conflicts. If the two intervals overlap, the predicate returns a True value. If they don't overlap, the predicate returns a False value.

You can specify an interval in two ways: either as a start time and an end time or as a start time and a duration. Here are a few examples:

```
(TIME '2:55:00', INTERVAL '1' HOUR)
OVERLAPS
(TIME '3:30:00', INTERVAL '2' HOUR)
```

The preceding example returns a True, because 3:30 is less than one hour after 2:55.

```
(TIME '9:00:00', TIME '9:30:00')
OVERLAPS
(TIME '9:29:00', TIME '9:31:00')
```

The preceding example returns a True, because you have a one-minute overlap between the two intervals.

```
(TIME '9:00:00', TIME '10:00:00')
OVERLAPS
(TIME '10:15:00', INTERVAL '3' HOUR)
```

The preceding example returns a False, because the two intervals don't overlap.

```
(TIME '9:00:00', TIME '9:30:00')
OVERLAPS
(TIME '9:30:00', TIME '9:35:00')
```

This example returns a False, because even though the two intervals are contiguous, they don't overlap.

MATCH

In Chapter 5, I discuss referential integrity, which involves maintaining consistency in a multitable database. You can lose integrity by adding a row to a child table that doesn't have a corresponding row in the child's parent table. You can cause similar problems by deleting a row from a parent table if rows corresponding to that row exist in a child table.

Say that your business has a CUSTOMER table that keeps track of all your customers and a SALES table that records all sales transactions. You don't want to add a row to SALES until after you enter the customer making the purchase into the CUSTOMER table. You also don't want to delete a customer from the

CUSTOMER table if that customer made purchases that exist in the SALES table. Before you perform an insertion or deletion, you may want to check the candidate row to make sure that inserting or deleting that row doesn't cause integrity problems. The MATCH predicate can perform such a check.

Say you have a CUSTOMER table and a SALES table. CustomerID is the primary key of the CUSTOMER table and acts as a foreign key in the SALES table. Every row in the CUSTOMER table must have a unique, CustomerID that isn't null. CustomerID isn't unique in the SALES table, because repeat customers buy more than once. This situation is fine and does not threaten integrity because CustomerID is a foreign key rather than a primary key in that table.

Seemingly, CustomerID can be null in the SALES table, because someone can walk in off the street, buy something, and walk out before you get a chance to enter his or her name and address into the CUSTOMER table. This situation can create a row in the child table with no corresponding row in the parent table. To overcome this problem, you can create a generic customer in the CUSTOMER table and assign all such anonymous sales to that customer.

Say that a customer steps up to the cash register and claims that she bought an F-117A Stealth Fighter on May 18, 2006. Although she has lost her receipt, she now wants to return the plane because it shows up as an aircraft carrier on opponent radar screens. You can verify whether she bought an F-117A by searching your SALES database for a match. First, you must retrieve her CustomerID into the variable vcustid; then you can use the following syntax:

```
... WHERE (:vcustid, 'F-117A', '2006-05-18')
         MATCH
         (SELECT CustomerID, ProductID, SaleDate
            FROM SALES)
```

If the MATCH predicate returns a True value, the database contains a sale of the F-117A on May 18, 2006, to this client's CustomerID. Take back the defective product and refund the customer's money. (**Note:** If any values in the first argument of the MATCH predicate are null, a True value always returns.)

SQL's developers added the MATCH predicate and the UNIQUE predicate for the same reason — they provide a way to explicitly perform the tests defined for the implicit referential integrity (RI) and UNIQUE constraints.

The general form of the MATCH predicate is as follows:

```
Row_value MATCH   [UNIQUE] [SIMPLE|  PARTIAL  |  FULL ]
          Subquery
```

The UNIQUE, SIMPLE, PARTIAL, and FULL options relate to rules that come into play if the row value expression *R* has one or more columns that are null. The rules for the MATCH predicate are a copy of corresponding referential integrity rules.

Referential integrity rules and the MATCH predicate

Referential integrity rules require that the values of a column or columns in one table match the values of a column or columns in another table. You refer to the columns in the first table as the *foreign key* and the columns in the second table as the *primary key* or *unique key*. For example, you may declare the column EmpDeptNo in an EMPLOYEE table as a foreign key that references the DeptNo column of a DEPT table. This matchup ensures that if you record an employee in the EMPLOYEE table as working in department 123, a row appears in the DEPT table where DeptNo is 123.

If the foreign key and primary key both consist of a single column, the situation is pretty straightforward. However, the two keys can consist of multiple columns. The DeptNo value, for example, may be unique only within a Location; therefore, to uniquely identify a DEPT row, you must specify both a Location and a DeptNo. If both the Boston and Tampa offices have a department 123, you need to identify the departments as ('Boston', '123') and ('Tampa', '123'). In this case, the EMPLOYEE table needs two columns to identify a DEPT. Call those columns EmpLoc and EmpDeptNo. If an employee works in department 123 in Boston, the EmpLoc and EmpDeptNo values are 'Boston' and '123'. And the foreign key declaration in the EMPLOYEE table looks like this:

```
FOREIGN KEY (EmpLoc, EmpDeptNo)
    REFERENCES DEPT (Location, DeptNo)
```

Drawing valid conclusions from your data is complicated immensely if the data contains nulls. Sometimes you want to treat data that contains nulls one way, and sometimes you want to treat it another way. The UNIQUE, SIMPLE, PARTIAL, and FULL keywords specify different ways of treating data that contains nulls. If your data does not contain any null values, you can save yourself a lot of head scratching by merely skipping from here to the following section of this chapter, "Logical Connectives." If your data *does* contain null values, drop out of Evelyn Woods's speed-reading mode now and read the following list slowly and carefully. Each entry in the list presents a different situation with respect to null values and tells how the MATCH predicate handles it.

Here are scenarios that illustrate the rules for dealing with null values and the MATCH predicate:

- ✔ **The values are both one way or the other:** If neither of the values of EmpLoc and EmpDeptNo are null (or both are null), the referential integrity rules are the same as for single-column keys with values that are null or not null.

✔ **One value is null and one isn't:** If, for example, `EmpLoc` is null and `EmpDeptNo` is not null — or `EmpLoc` is not null and `EmpDeptNo` is null — you need new rules. When implementing rules, if you insert or update the EMPLOYEE table with `EmpLoc` and `EmpDeptNo` values of (`NULL`, `'123'`) or (`'Boston'`, `NULL`), you have six main alternatives: `SIMPLE`, `PARTIAL`, and `FULL`, each either with or without the `UNIQUE` keyword.

✔ **The `UNIQUE` keyword is present:** A matching row in the subquery result table must be unique in order for the predicate to evaluate to a True value.

✔ **Both components of the row value expression R are null:** The `MATCH` predicate returns a True value regardless of the contents of the subquery result table being compared.

✔ **Neither component of the row value expression R is null, `SIMPLE` is specified, `UNIQUE` is not specified, and at least one row in the subquery result table matches R:** The `MATCH` predicate returns a True value. Otherwise, it returns a False value.

✔ **Neither component of the row value expression R is null, `SIMPLE` is specified, `UNIQUE` is specified, and at least one row in the subquery result table is both unique and matches R:** The `MATCH` predicate returns a True value. Otherwise, it returns a False value.

✔ **Any component of the row value expression R is null and `SIMPLE` is specified:** The `MATCH` predicate returns a True value.

✔ **Any component of the row value expression R isn't null, `PARTIAL` is specified, `UNIQUE` isn't specified, and the non-null parts of at least one row in the subquery result table matches R:** The `MATCH` predicate returns a True value. Otherwise, it returns a False value.

✔ **Any component of the row value expression R is non-null, `PARTIAL` is specified, `UNIQUE` is specified, and the non-null parts of R match the non-null parts of at least one unique row in the subquery result table:** The `MATCH` predicate returns a True value. Otherwise, it returns a False value.

✔ **Neither component of the row value expression R is null, `FULL` is specified, `UNIQUE` is not specified, and at least one row in the subquery result table matches R:** The `MATCH` predicate returns a True value. Otherwise, it returns a False value.

✔ **Neither component of the row value expression R is null, `FULL` is specified, `UNIQUE` is specified, and at least one row in the subquery result table is both unique and matches R:** The `MATCH` predicate returns a True value. Otherwise, it returns a False value.

✔ **Any component of the row value expression R is null and `FULL` is specified:** The `MATCH` predicate returns a False value.

> ## Rule by committee
>
> The SQL-89 version of the standard specified the `UNIQUE` rule as the default, before anyone proposed or debated the alternatives. During development of the SQL-92 version of the standard, proposals appeared for the alternatives. Some people strongly preferred the `PARTIAL` rules and argued that they should be the only rules. These people thought that the SQL-89 (`UNIQUE`) rules were so undesirable that they wanted those rules considered a bug and the `PARTIAL` rules specified as a correction.
>
> Other people preferred the `UNIQUE` rules and thought that the `PARTIAL` rules were obscure, error-prone, and inefficient. Still other people preferred the additional discipline of the `FULL` rules. The issue was finally settled by providing all three keywords so that users could choose whichever approach they preferred. SQL:1999 added the `SIMPLE` rules. The proliferation of rules makes dealing with nulls anything but simple. If `SIMPLE`, `PARTIAL`, or `FULL` isn't specified, the `SIMPLE` rules are followed.

Logical Connectives

Often, as a number of previous examples show, applying one condition in a query isn't enough to return the rows that you want from a table. In some cases, the rows must satisfy two or more conditions. In other cases, if a row satisfies any of two or more conditions, it qualifies for retrieval. On other occasions, you want to retrieve only rows that don't satisfy a specified condition. To meet these needs, SQL offers the logical connectives AND, OR, and NOT.

AND

If multiple conditions must all be True before you can retrieve a row, use the AND logical connective. Consider the following example:

```
SELECT InvoiceNo, SaleDate, Salesperson, TotalSale
    FROM SALES
    WHERE SaleDate >= '2006-05-15'
        AND SaleDate <= '2006-05-21' ;
```

The WHERE clause must meet the following two conditions:

- ✔ SaleDate must be greater than or equal to May 15, 2006.
- ✔ SaleDate must be less than or equal to May 21, 2006.

Only rows that record sales occurring during the week of May 15 meet both conditions. The query returns only these rows.

Notice that the AND connective is strictly logical. This restriction can some-times be confusing because people commonly use the word *and* with a looser meaning. Suppose, for example, that your boss says to you, "I'd like to see the sales for Ferguson and Ford." He said, "Ferguson and Ford," so you may write the following SQL query:

```
SELECT *
    FROM SALES
    WHERE Salesperson = 'Ferguson'
        AND Salesperson = 'Ford';
```

Well, don't take that answer back to your boss. The following query is more like what he had in mind:

```
SELECT *
    FROM SALES
    WHERE Salesperson IN ('Ferguson', 'Ford') ;
```

The first query won't return anything, because none of the sales in the SALES table were made by *both* Ferguson and Ford. The second query will return the information on all sales made by *either* Ferguson *or* Ford, which is probably what the boss wanted.

OR

If any one of two or more conditions must be True to qualify a row for retrieval, use the OR logical connective, as in the following example:

```
SELECT InvoiceNo, SaleDate, Salesperson, TotalSale
    FROM SALES
        WHERE Salesperson = 'Ford'
            OR TotalSale > 200 ;
```

This query retrieves all of Ford's sales, regardless of how large, as well as all sales of more than $200, regardless of who made the sales.

NOT

The NOT connective negates a condition. If the condition normally returns a True value, adding NOT causes the same condition to return a False value. If a condition normally returns a False value, adding NOT causes the condition to return a True value. Consider the following example:

```
SELECT InvoiceNo, SaleDate, Salesperson, TotalSale
    FROM SALES
        WHERE NOT (Salesperson = 'Ford') ;
```

This query returns rows for all sales transactions completed by salespeople other than Ford.

When you use AND, OR, or NOT, sometimes the scope of the connective isn't clear. To be safe, use parentheses to make sure that SQL applies the connective to the predicate you want. In the preceding example, the NOT connective applies to the entire predicate (Salesperson = 'Ford').

GROUP BY Clauses

Sometimes, rather than retrieving individual records, you want to know something about a group of records. The GROUP BY clause is the tool you need.

Suppose you're the sales manager and you want to look at the performance of your sales force. If you do a simple SELECT, such as the following query:

```
SELECT InvoiceNo, SaleDate, Salesperson, TotalSale
    FROM SALES;
```

you receive a result similar to that shown in Figure 9-1.

This result gives you some idea of how well your salespeople are doing because so few total sales are involved. However, in real life, a company would have many more sales, and it wouldn't be as easy to tell whether sales objectives were being met. To do the real analysis you need to do, you can combine the GROUP BY clause with one of the *aggregate* functions (also called *set functions*) to get a quantitative picture of sales performance. For example, you can see which salesperson is selling more of the profitable high-ticket items by using the average (AVG) function as follows:

```
SELECT Salesperson, AVG(TotalSale)
    FROM SALES
    GROUP BY Salesperson;
```

Figure 9-1:
A result set
for retrieval
of sales
from 07/01/
2001 to
07/07/2001.

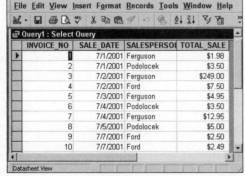

You receive a result similar to that shown in Figure 9-2.

As shown in Figure 9-2, the average value of Ferguson's sales is considerably higher than that of the other two salespeople. You compare total sales with a similar query:

```
SELECT Salesperson, SUM(TotalSale)
    FROM SALES
    GROUP BY Salesperson;
```

This query gives the result shown in Figure 9-3.

Figure 9-2:
Average sales for each salesperson.

Ferguson also has the highest total sales, which is consistent with having the highest average sales.

Figure 9-3:
Total sales for each salesperson.

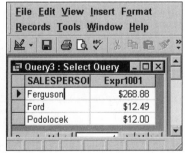

HAVING Clauses

You can analyze the grouped data further by using the HAVING clause. The HAVING clause is a filter that acts similar to a WHERE clause, but on groups of rows rather than on individual rows. To illustrate the function of the HAVING clause, suppose the sales manager considers Ferguson to be in a class by himself. His performance distorts the overall data for the other salespeople.

You can exclude Ferguson's sales from the grouped data by using a `HAVING` clause as follows:

```
SELECT Salesperson, SUM(TotalSale)
    FROM SALES
    GROUP BY Salesperson
    HAVING Salesperson <> 'Ferguson';
```

This query gives the result shown in Figure 9-4. Only rows where the sales-person is not Ferguson are considered.

Figure 9-4:
Total sales
for all
salespeople
except
Ferguson.

ORDER BY Clauses

Use the `ORDER BY` clause to display the output table of a query in either ascending or descending alphabetical order. Whereas the `GROUP BY` clause gathers rows into groups and sorts the groups into alphabetical order, `ORDER BY` sorts individual rows. The `ORDER BY` clause must be the last clause that you specify in a query. If the query also contains a `GROUP BY` clause, the clause first arranges the output rows into groups. The `ORDER BY` clause then sorts the rows within each group. If you have no `GROUP BY` clause, then the statement considers the entire table as a group, and the `ORDER BY` clause sorts all its rows according to the column (or columns) that the `ORDER BY` clause specifies.

To illustrate this point, consider the data in the SALES table. The SALES table contains columns for `InvoiceNo`, `SaleDate`, `Salesperson`, and `TotalSale`. If you use the following example, you see all the data in the SALES table, but in an arbitrary order:

```
SELECT * FROM SALES ;
```

In one implementation, this may be the order in which you inserted the rows in the table, and on another implementation, the order may be that of the most recent updates. The order can also change unexpectedly if anyone physically reorganizes the database. Usually, you ought to specify the order in which you want the rows. You may, for example, want to see the rows in order by the SaleDate like this:

```
SELECT * FROM SALES ORDER BY SaleDate ;
```

This example returns all the rows in the SALES table in order by SaleDate.

For rows with the same SaleDate, the default order depends on the implementation. You can, however, specify how to sort the rows that share the same SaleDate. You may want to see the sales for each SaleDate in order by InvoiceNo, as follows:

```
SELECT * FROM SALES ORDER BY SaleDate, InvoiceNo ;
```

This example first orders the sales by SaleDate; then for each SaleDate, it orders the sales by InvoiceNo. But don't confuse that example with the following query:

```
SELECT * FROM SALES ORDER BY InvoiceNo, SaleDate ;
```

This query first orders the sales by INVOICE_NO. Then for each different InvoiceNo, the query orders the sales by SaleDate. This probably won't yield the result you want, because it is unlikely that multiple sale dates will exist for a single invoice number.

The following query is another example of how SQL can return data:

```
SELECT * FROM SALES ORDER BY Salesperson, SaleDate ;
```

This example first orders by Salesperson and then by SaleDate. After you look at the data in that order, you may want to invert it, as follows:

```
SELECT * FROM SALES ORDER BY SaleDate, Salesperson ;
```

This example orders the rows first by SaleDate and then by Salesperson.

All these ordering examples are in ascending (ASC) order, which is the default sort order. The last SELECT shows earlier sales first and, within a given date, shows sales for 'Adams' before 'Baker'. If you prefer descending (DESC) order, you can specify this order for one or more of the order columns, as follows:

```
SELECT * FROM SALES
ORDER BY SaleDate DESC, Salesperson ASC ;
```

This example specifies a descending order for sale dates, showing the more recent sales first, and an ascending order for salespeople, putting them in alphabetical order.

Chapter 10

Using Relational Operators

In This Chapter

▶ Combining tables with similar structures

▶ Combining tables with different structures

▶ Deriving meaningful data from multiple tables

*Y*ou probably know by now that SQL is a query language for relational databases. In previous chapters, I present simple databases, and in most cases, my examples deal with only one table. In this chapter, I put the *relational* in relational database. After all, relational databases are so named because they consist of multiple related tables.

Because the data in a relational database is distributed across multiple tables, a query usually draws data from more than one table. SQL has operators that combine data from multiple sources into a single result table. These are the UNION, INTERSECTION, and EXCEPT operators, as well as a family of JOIN operators. Each operator combines data from multiple tables in a different way.

UNION

The UNION operator is the SQL implementation of relational algebra's union operator. The UNION operator enables you to draw information from two or more tables that have the same structure. *Same structure* means

▶ The tables must all have the same number of columns.

▶ Corresponding columns must all have identical data types and lengths.

When these criteria are met, the tables are *union compatible.* The union of two tables returns all the rows that appear in either table and eliminates duplicates.

Say that you create a baseball statistics database (like the one in Chapter 9). It contains two union-compatible tables named AMERICAN and NATIONAL. Both tables have three columns, and corresponding columns are all the same type. In fact, corresponding columns have identical column names (although this condition isn't required for union compatibility).

NATIONAL lists the names and number of complete games pitched by National League pitchers. AMERICAN lists the same information about pitchers in the American League. The UNION of the two tables gives you a virtual result table containing all the rows in the first table plus all the rows in the second table. For this example, I put just a few rows in each table to illustrate the operation:

```
SELECT * FROM NATIONAL ;
FirstName    LastName      CompleteGames
---------    --------      -------------
Sal          Maglie                   11
Don          Newcombe                  9
Sandy        Koufax                   13
Don          Drysdale                 12

SELECT * FROM AMERICAN ;

FirstName    LastName    CompleteGames
---------    --------    -------------
Whitey       Ford                   12
Don          Larson                 10
Bob          Turley                  8
Allie        Reynolds               14

SELECT * FROM NATIONAL
UNION
SELECT * FROM AMERICAN ;

FirstName    LastName    CompleteGames
---------    --------    -------------
Allie        Reynolds               14
Bob          Turley                  8
Don          Drysdale               12
Don          Larson                 10
Don          Newcombe                9
Sal          Maglie                 11
Sandy        Koufax                 13
Whitey       Ford                   12
```

The UNION DISTINCT operator functions identically to the UNION operator without the DISTINCT keyword. In both cases, duplicate rows are eliminated from the result set.

I've been using the asterisk (*) as shorthand for all the columns in a table. This shortcut is fine most of the time, but it can get you into trouble when you use relational operators in embedded or module-language SQL. If you add one or more new columns to one table and not to another, or you add different columns to the two tables, the two tables are no longer union-compatible, and your program will be invalid the next time it's recompiled. Even if the same new columns are added to both tables so that they are still union-compatible, your program is probably not prepared to deal with the additional data. You should explicitly list the columns that you want rather than relying on the * shorthand. When you're entering ad hoc SQL queries from the console, the asterisk probably works fine, because you can quickly display a table structure to verify union compatibility if your query isn't successful.

The UNION ALL operation

As I mention previously, the UNION operation usually eliminates any duplicate rows that result from its operation, which is the desired result most of the time. Sometimes, however, you may want to preserve duplicate rows. On those occasions, use UNION ALL.

Referring to the example, suppose that "Bullet" Bob Turley had been traded in midseason from the New York Yankees in the American League to the Brooklyn Dodgers in the National League. Now suppose that during the season, he pitched eight complete games for each team. The ordinary UNION displayed in the example throws away one of the two lines containing Turley's data. Although he seemed to pitch only 8 complete games in the season, he actually hurled a remarkable 16 complete games. The following query gives you the true facts:

```
SELECT * FROM NATIONAL
UNION ALL
SELECT * FROM AMERICAN ;
```

You can sometimes form the UNION of two tables even if they are not union-compatible. If the columns you want in your result table are present and compatible in both tables, you can perform a UNION CORRESPONDING operation. Only the specified columns are considered, and they are the only columns displayed in the result table.

The CORRESPONDING operation

Baseball statisticians keep different statistics on pitchers than they keep on outfielders. In both cases, first names, last names, putouts, errors, and fielding percentages are recorded. Outfielders, of course, don't have a won/lost record, a saves record, or a number of other stats that pertain only to pitching. You can still perform a UNION that takes data from the OUTFIELDER table and from the PITCHER table to give you some overall information about defensive skill:

```
SELECT *
   FROM OUTFIELDER
UNION CORRESPONDING
```

```
     (FirstName, LastName, Putouts, Errors, FieldPct)
SELECT *
   FROM PITCHER ;
```

The result table holds the first and last names of all the outfielders and pitchers, along with the putouts, errors, and fielding percentage of each player. As with the simple UNION, duplicates are eliminated. Thus, if a player spent some time in the outfield and also pitched in one or more games, the UNION CORRESPONDING operation loses some of his statistics. To avoid this problem, use UNION ALL CORRESPONDING.

Each column name in the list following the CORRESPONDING keyword must be a name that exists in both unioned tables. If you omit this list of names, an implicit list of all names that appear in both tables is used. But this implicit list of names may change when new columns are added to one or both tables. Therefore, you're better off explicitly listing the column names than you are omitting them.

INTERSECT

The UNION operation produces a result table containing all rows that appear in *any* of the source tables. If you want only rows that appear in *all* the source tables, you can use the INTERSECT operation, which is the SQL implementation of relational algebra's intersect operation. I illustrate INTERSECT by returning to the fantasy world in which Bob Turley was traded to the Dodgers in midseason:

```
SELECT * FROM NATIONAL;
FirstName    LastName    CompleteGames
---------    --------    -------------
Sal          Maglie               11
Don          Newcombe              9
Sandy        Koufax               13
Don          Drysdale             12
Bob          Turley                8

SELECT * FROM AMERICAN;
FIRST_NAME   LAST_NAME   COMPLETE_GAMES
----------   ---------   --------------
Whitey       Ford                 12
Don          Larson               10
Bob          Turley                8
Allie        Reynolds             14
```

Only rows that appear in all source tables show up in the INTERSECT operation's result table:

```
SELECT *
   FROM NATIONAL
INTERSECT
SELECT *
   FROM AMERICAN;

FirstName    LastName    CompleteGames
---------    --------    -------------
Bob          Turley                  8
```

The result table tells you that Bob Turley was the only pitcher to throw the same number of complete games in both leagues (a rather obscure distinction for old Bullet Bob). *Note:* As was the case with UNION, INTERSECT DISTINCT produces the same result as the INTERSECT operator used alone. In this example, only one of the identical rows featuring Bob Turley is returned.

The ALL and CORRESPONDING keywords function in an INTERSECT operation the same way they do in a UNION operation. If you use ALL, duplicates are retained in the result table. If you use CORRESPONDING, the intersected tables don't need to be union-compatible, although the corresponding columns must have matching types and lengths.

Consider another example: A municipality keeps track of the pagers carried by police officers, firefighters, street sweepers, and other city employees. A database table called PAGERS contains data on all pagers in active use. Another table named OUT, with an identical structure, contains data on all pagers that have been taken out of service. No pager should ever exist in both tables. With an INTERSECT operation, you can test to see whether such an unwanted duplication has occurred:

```
SELECT *
   FROM PAGERS
INTERSECT CORRESPONDING (PagerID)
SELECT *
   FROM OUT ;
```

If the result table contains any rows, you know you have a problem. You should investigate any PagerID entries that appear in the result table. The corresponding pager is either active or out of service; it can't be both. After you detect the problem, you can perform a DELETE operation on one of the two tables to restore database integrity.

EXCEPT

The UNION operation acts on two source tables and returns all rows that appear in either table. The INTERSECT operation returns all rows that appear in both the first and the second tables. In contrast, the EXCEPT (or EXCEPT

DISTINCT) operation returns all rows that appear in the first table but that *do not* also appear in the second table.

Returning to the municipal pager database example (see the "INTERSECT" section, earlier in this chapter), say that a group of pagers that had been declared out of service and returned to the vendor for repairs have now been fixed and placed back into service. The PAGERS table was updated to reflect the returned pagers, but the returned pagers were not removed from the OUT table as they should have been. You can display the PagerID numbers of the pagers in the OUT table, with the reactivated ones eliminated, using an EXCEPT operation:

```
SELECT *
   FROM OUT
EXCEPT CORRESPONDING (PagerID)
SELECT *
   FROM PAGERS;
```

This query returns all the rows in the OUT table whose PagerID is not also present in the PAGERS table.

Various Joins

The UNION, INTERSECT, and EXCEPT operators are valuable in multitable databases that contain union-compatible tables. In many cases, however, you want to draw data from multiple tables that have very little in common. Joins are powerful relational operators that combine data from multiple tables into a single result table. The source tables may have little (or even nothing) in common with each other.

SQL supports a number of types of joins. The best one to choose in a given situation depends on the result you're trying to achieve. The following sections give you the details.

Basic join

Any multitable query is a type of join. The source tables are joined in the sense that the result table includes information taken from all the source tables. The simplest join is a two-table SELECT that has no WHERE clause qualifiers. Every row of the first table is joined to every row of the second table. The result table is the Cartesian product of the two source tables. The number of rows in the result table is equal to the number of rows in the first source table multiplied by the number of rows in the second source table.

For example, imagine that you're the personnel manager for a company and that part of your job is to maintain employee records. Most employee data, such as home address and telephone number, is not particularly sensitive. But some data, such as current salary, should be available only to authorized personnel. To maintain security of the sensitive information, keep it in a separate table that is password protected. Consider the following pair of tables:

```
EMPLOYEE                          COMPENSATION
--------                          ------------
EmpID                             Employ
FName                             Salary
LName                             Bonus
City
Phone
```

Fill the tables with some sample data:

EmpID	FName	LName	City	Phone
1	Whitey	Ford	Orange	555-1001
2	Don	Larson	Newark	555-3221
3	Sal	Maglie	Nutley	555-6905
4	Bob	Turley	Passaic	555-8908

Employ	Salary	Bonus
1	33000	10000
2	18000	2000
3	24000	5000
4	22000	7000

Create a virtual result table with the following query

```
SELECT *
   FROM EMPLOYEE, COMPENSATION ;
```

that produces

EmpID	FName	LName	City	Phone	Employ	Salary	Bonus
1	Whitey	Ford	Orange	555-1001	1	33000	10000
1	Whitey	Ford	Orange	555-1001	2	18000	2000
1	Whitey	Ford	Orange	555-1001	3	24000	5000
1	Whitey	Ford	Orange	555-1001	4	22000	7000
2	Don	Larson	Newark	555-3221	1	33000	10000
2	Don	Larson	Newark	555-3221	2	18000	2000
2	Don	Larson	Newark	555-3221	3	24000	5000
2	Don	Larson	Newark	555-3221	4	22000	7000
3	Sal	Maglie	Nutley	555-6905	1	33000	10000
3	Sal	Maglie	Nutley	555-6905	2	18000	2000
3	Sal	Maglie	Nutley	555-6905	3	24000	5000
3	Sal	Maglie	Nutley	555-6905	4	22000	7000

```
4  Bob     Turley  Passaic  555-8908    1  33000  10000
4  Bob     Turley  Passaic  555-8908    2  18000  2000
4  Bob     Turley  Passaic  555-8908    3  24000  5000
4  Bob     Turley  Passaic  555-8908    4  22000  7000
```

The result table, which is the Cartesian product of the EMPLOYEE and COMPENSATION tables, contains considerable redundancy. Furthermore, it doesn't make much sense. It combines every row of EMPLOYEE with every row of COMPENSATION. The only rows that convey meaningful information are those in which the EmpID number that came from EMPLOYEE matches the Employ number that came from COMPENSATION. In those rows, an employee's name and address are associated with his or her compensation.

When you're trying to get useful information out of a multitable database, the Cartesian product produced by a basic join is almost never what you want, but it's almost always the first step toward what you want. By applying constraints to the JOIN with a WHERE clause, you can filter out the unwanted rows. The following section explains how to filter the stuff you don't need to see.

Equi-join

The most common join that uses the WHERE clause filter is the equi-join. An *equi-join* is a basic join with a WHERE clause containing a condition specifying that the value in one column in the first table must be equal to the value of a corresponding column in the second table. Applying an equi-join to the example tables from the previous section brings a more meaningful result:

```
SELECT *
   FROM EMPLOYEE, COMPENSATION
   WHERE EMPLOYEE.EmpID = COMPENSATION.Employ ;
```

This query produces the following results:

```
EmpID  FName   LName   City     Phone     Employ  Salary  Bonus
-----  ------  -----   ----     -----     ------  ------  -----
    1  Whitey  Ford    Orange   555-1001       1   33000  10000
    2  Don     Larson  Newark   555-3221       2   18000  2000
    3  Sal     Maglie  Nutley   555-6905       3   24000  5000
    4  Bob     Turley  Passaic  555-8908       4   22000  7000
```

In this result table, the salaries and bonuses on the right apply to the employees named on the left. The table still has some redundancy because the EmpID column duplicates the Employ column. You can fix this problem with a slight reformulation of the query:

```
SELECT EMPLOYEE.*,COMPENSATION.Salary,COMPENSATION.Bonus
   FROM EMPLOYEE, COMPENSATION
   WHERE EMPLOYEE.EmpID = COMPENSATION.Employ ;
```

This query produces the following result table:

```
EmpID FName  LName   City    Phone     Salary Bonus
----- -----  -----   ----    -----     ------ -----
    1 Whitey Ford    Orange  555-1001  33000  10000
    2 Don    Larson  Newark  555-3221  18000   2000
    3 Sal    Maglie  Nutley  555-6905  24000   5000
    4 Bob    Turley  Passaic 555-8908  22000   7000
```

This table tells you what you want to know, but doesn't burden you with any extraneous data. The query is somewhat tedious to write, however. To avoid ambiguity, you can qualify the column names with the names of the tables they came from. Typing those table names repeatedly provides good exercise for the fingers, but has no other merit.

You can cut down on the amount of typing by using aliases (or *correlation names*). An *alias* is a short name that stands for a table name. If you use aliases in recasting the preceding query, it comes out like this:

```
SELECT E.*, C.Salary, C.Bonus
    FROM EMPLOYEE E, COMPENSATION C
    WHERE E.EmpID = C.Employ ;
```

In this example, E is the alias for EMPLOYEE, and C is the alias for COMPENSA-
TION. The alias is local to the statement it's in. After you declare an alias (in
the FROM clause), you must use it throughout the statement. You can't use
both the alias and the long form of the table name in the same statement.

Even if you could mix the long form of table names with aliases, you wouldn't
want to, because doing so creates major confusion. Consider the following
example:

```
SELECT T1.C, T2.C
    FROM T1 T2, T2 T1
    WHERE T1.C > T2.C ;
```

In this example, the alias for T1 is T2, and the alias for T2 is T1. Admittedly,
this isn't a smart selection of aliases, but it isn't forbidden by the rules. If you
mix aliases with long-form table names, you can't tell which table is which.

The preceding example with aliases is equivalent to the following SELECT
statement with no aliases:

```
SELECT T2.C, T1.C
    FROM T1 , T2
    WHERE T2.C > T1.C ;
```

SQL enables you to join more than two tables. The maximum number varies from one implementation to another. The syntax is analogous to the two-table case:

```
SELECT E.*, C.Salary, C.Bonus, Y.TotalSales
   FROM EMPLOYEE E, COMPENSATION C, YTD_SALES Y
   WHERE E.EmpID = C.Employ
      AND C.Employ = Y.EmpNo ;
```

This statement performs an equi-join on three tables, pulling data from corresponding rows of each one to produce a result table that shows the salespeople's names, the amount of sales they are responsible for, and their compensation. The sales manager can quickly see whether compensation is in line with production.

Storing a salesperson's year-to-date sales in a separate YTD_SALES table ensures better performance and reliability than keeping that data in the EMPLOYEE table. The data in the EMPLOYEE table is relatively static. A person's name, address, and telephone number don't change very often. In contrast, the year-to-date sales change frequently (you hope). Because the YTD_SALES table has fewer columns than the EMPLOYEE table, you may be able to update it more quickly. If, in the course of updating sales totals, you don't touch the EMPLOYEE table, you decrease the risk of accidentally modifying employee information that should stay the same.

Cross join

CROSS JOIN is the keyword for the basic join without a WHERE clause. Therefore,

```
SELECT *
FROM EMPLOYEE, COMPENSATION ;
```

can also be written as:

```
SELECT *
FROM EMPLOYEE CROSS JOIN COMPENSATION ;
```

The result is the Cartesian product (also called the *cross product*) of the two source tables. A cross join rarely gives you the final result you want, but it can be useful as the first step in a chain of data manipulation operations that ultimately produce the desired result.

Natural join

The *natural join* is a special case of an equi-join. In the WHERE clause of an equi-join, a column from one source table is compared with a column of a second source table for equality. The two columns must be the same type and length and must have the same name. In fact, in a natural join, all columns in one table that have the same names, types, and lengths as corresponding columns in the second table are compared for equality.

Imagine that the COMPENSATION table from the preceding example has columns `EmpID`, `Salary`, and `Bonus` rather than `Employ`, `Salary`, and `Bonus`. In that case, you can perform a natural join of the COMPENSATION table with the EMPLOYEE table. The traditional join syntax would look like this:

```
SELECT E.*, C.Salary, C.Bonus
   FROM EMPLOYEE E, COMPENSATION C
   WHERE E.EmpID = C.EmpID ;
```

This query is a natural join. An alternate syntax for the same operation is the following:

```
SELECT E.*, C.Salary, C.Bonus
   FROM EMPLOYEE E NATURAL JOIN COMPENSATION C ;
```

Condition join

A *condition join* is like an equi-join, except the condition being tested doesn't have to be equality (although it can be). It can be any well-formed predicate. If the condition is satisfied, the corresponding row becomes part of the result table. The syntax is a little different from what you have seen so far, in that the condition is contained in an ON clause rather than a WHERE clause.

Say that a baseball statistician wants to know which National League pitchers have pitched the same number of complete games as one or more American League pitchers. This question is a job for an equi-join, which can also be expressed with condition join syntax:

```
SELECT *
   FROM NATIONAL JOIN AMERICAN
   ON NATIONAL.CompleteGames = AMERICAN.CompleteGames ;
```

Column-name join

The *column-name join* is like a natural join, but it's more flexible. In a natural join, all the source table columns that have the same name are compared with each other for equality. With the column-name join, you select which same-name columns to compare. You can choose them all if you want, making the column-name join effectively a natural join. Or you may choose fewer than all same-name columns. In this way, you have a great degree of control over which cross product rows qualify to be placed into your result table.

Say that you're a chess set manufacturer and have one inventory table that keeps track of your stock of white pieces and another that keeps track of black pieces. The tables contain data as follows:

```
WHITE                           BLACK
-----                           -----

Piece Quant Wood                Piece   Quant Wood
----- ----- ----                -----   ----- ----
King    502 Oak                 King      502 Ebony
Queen   398 Oak                 Queen     397 Ebony
Rook   1020 Oak                 Rook     1020 Ebony
Bishop  985 Oak                 Bishop    985 Ebony
Knight  950 Oak                 Knight    950 Ebony
Pawn    431 Oak                 Pawn      453 Ebony
```

For each piece type, the number of white pieces should match the number of black pieces. If they don't match, some chessmen are being lost or stolen, and you need to tighten security measures.

A natural join compares all columns with the same name for equality. In this case, a result table with no rows is produced because no rows in the WOOD column in the WHITE table match any rows in the WOOD column in the BLACK table. This result table doesn't help you determine whether any merchandise is missing. Instead, do a column-name join that excludes the WOOD column from consideration. It can take the following form:

```
SELECT *
    FROM WHITE JOIN BLACK
    USING (Piece, Quant) ;
```

The result table shows only the rows for which the number of white pieces in stock equals the number of black pieces:

```
Piece Quant Wood Piece   Quant Wood
----- ----- ---- -----   ----- ----
King    502 Oak  King      502 Ebony
Rook   1020 Oak  Rook     1020 Ebony
Bishop  985 Oak  Bishop    985 Ebony
Knight  950 Oak  Knight    950 Ebony
```

The shrewd person can deduce that Queen and Pawn are missing from the list, indicating a shortage somewhere for those piece types.

Inner join

By now, you're probably getting the idea that joins are pretty esoteric and that it takes an uncommon level of spiritual discernment to deal with them adequately. You may have even heard of the mysterious *inner join* and speculated that it probably represents the core or essence of relational operations.

Well, ha! The joke is on you. There's nothing mysterious about inner joins. In fact, all the joins covered so far in this chapter are inner joins. I could have formulated the column-name join in the last example as an inner join by using the following syntax:

```
SELECT *
    FROM WHITE INNER JOIN BLACK
    USING (Piece, Quant) ;
```

The result is the same.

The inner join is so named to distinguish it from the outer join. An inner join discards all rows from the result table that don't have corresponding rows in both source tables. An outer join preserves unmatched rows. That's the difference. There is nothing metaphysical about it.

Outer join

When you're joining two tables, the first one (call it the one on the left) may have rows that don't have matching counterparts in the second table (the one on the right). Conversely, the table on the right may have rows that don't have matching counterparts in the table on the left. If you perform an inner join on those tables, all the unmatched rows are excluded from the output. *Outer joins*, however, don't exclude the unmatched rows. Outer joins come in three types: the left outer join, the right outer join, and the full outer join.

Left outer join

In a query that includes a join, the left table is the one that precedes the keyword JOIN, and the right table is the one that follows it. The *left outer join* preserves unmatched rows from the left table but discards unmatched rows from the right table.

To understand outer joins, consider a corporate database that maintains records of the company's employees, departments, and locations. Tables 10-1, 10-2, and 10-3 contain the database's example data.

Table 10-1	LOCATION
LOCATION_ID	*CITY*
1	Boston
3	Tampa
5	Chicago

Table 10-2	DEPT	
DEPT_ID	LOCATION_ID	NAME
21	1	Sales
24	1	Admin
27	5	Repair
29	5	Stock

Table 10-3	EMPLOYEE	
EMP_ID	DEPT_ID	NAME
61	24	Kirk
63	27	McCoy

Now suppose that you want to see all the data for all employees, including department and location. You get this with an equi-join:

```
SELECT *
   FROM LOCATION L, DEPT D, EMPLOYEE E
   WHERE L.LocationID = D.LocationID
     AND D.DeptID = E.DeptID ;
```

This statement produces the following result:

```
1    Boston    24    1    Admin    61    24    Kirk
5    Chicago   27    5    Repair   63    27    McCoy
```

This result table gives all the data for all the employees, including their location and department. The equi-join works because every employee has a location and a department.

Suppose now that you want the data on the locations, with the related department and employee data. This is a different problem because a location without any associated departments may exist. To get what you want, you have to use an outer join, as in the following example:

```
SELECT *
   FROM LOCATION L LEFT OUTER JOIN DEPT D
      ON (L.LocationID = D.LocationID)
   LEFT OUTER JOIN EMPLOYEE E
      ON (D.DeptID = E.DeptID);
```

This join pulls data from three tables. First, the LOCATION table is joined to the DEPT table. The resulting table is then joined to the EMPLOYEE table. Rows from the table on the left of the `LEFT OUTER JOIN` operator that have no corresponding row in the table on the right are included in the result. Thus, in the first join, all locations are included, even if no department associated with them exists. In the second join, all departments are included, even if no employee associated with them exists. The result is as follows:

```
1    Boston    24    1    Admin    61    24    Kirk
5    Chicago   27    5    Repair   63    27    McCoy
3    Tampa     NULL  NULL NULL     NULL  NULL  NULL
5    Chicago   29    5    Stock    NULL  NULL  NULL
1    Boston    21    1    Sales    NULL  NULL  NULL
```

The first two rows are the same as the two result rows in the previous example. The third row (3 Tampa) has nulls in the department and employee columns because no departments are defined for Tampa and no employees are stationed there. The fourth and fifth rows (5 Chicago and 1 Boston) contain data about the Stock and the Sales departments, but the employee columns for these rows contain nulls because these two departments have no employees. This outer join tells you everything that the equi-join told you plus the following:

✔ All the company's locations, whether they have any departments or not

✔ All the company's departments, whether they have any employees or not

The rows returned in the preceding example aren't guaranteed to be in the order you want. The order may vary from one implementation to the next. To make sure that the rows returned are in the order you want, add an `ORDER BY` clause to your `SELECT` statement, like this:

```
SELECT *
   FROM LOCATION L LEFT OUTER JOIN DEPT D
      ON (L.LocationID = D.LocationID)
   LEFT OUTER JOIN EMPLOYEE E
      ON (D.DeptID = E.DeptID)
   ORDER BY L.LocationID, D.DeptID, E.EmpID;
```

You can abbreviate the left outer join language as `LEFT JOIN` because there's no such thing as a left inner join.

Right outer join

I bet you figured out how the right outer join behaves. Right! The *right outer join* preserves unmatched rows from the right table but discards unmatched rows from the left table. You can use it on the same tables and get the same result by reversing the order in which you present tables to the join:

```
SELECT *
    FROM EMPLOYEE E RIGHT OUTER JOIN DEPT D
        ON (D.DeptID = E.DeptID)
    RIGHT OUTER JOIN LOCATION L
        ON (L.LocationID = D.LocationID) ;
```

In this formulation, the first join produces a table that contains all departments, whether they have an associated employee or not. The second join produces a table that contains all locations, whether they have an associated department or not.

You can abbreviate the right outer join language as RIGHT JOIN because there's no such thing as a right inner join.

Full outer join

The *full outer join* combines the functions of the left outer join and the right outer join. It retains the unmatched rows from both the left and the right tables. Consider the most general case of the company database used in the preceding examples. It could have

- ✔ Locations with no departments
- ✔ Departments with no locations
- ✔ Departments with no employees
- ✔ Employees with no departments

To show all locations, departments, and employees, regardless of whether they have corresponding rows in the other tables, use a full outer join in the following form:

```
SELECT *
    FROM LOCATION L FULL OUTER JOIN DEPT D
        ON (L.LocationID = D.LocationID)
    FULL OUTER JOIN EMPLOYEE E
        ON (D.DeptID = E.DeptID) ;
```

You can abbreviate the full outer join language as FULL JOIN because there's no such thing as a full inner join.

Union join

Unlike the other kinds of join, the *union join* makes no attempt to match a row from the left source table with any rows in the right source table. It creates a new virtual table that contains the union of all the columns in both source tables. In the virtual result table, the columns that came from the left source table contain all the rows that were in the left source table. For those rows, the columns that came from the right source table all have the null value. Similarly, the columns that came from the right source table contain all the rows that were in the right source table. For those rows, the columns that came from the left source table all have the null value. Thus, the table resulting from a union join contains all the columns of both source tables, and the number of rows that it contains is the sum of the number of rows in the two source tables.

The result of a union join by itself is not immediately useful in most cases; it produces a result table with many nulls in it. But you can get useful information from a union join when you use it in conjunction with the COALESCE expression discussed in Chapter 8. Look at an example.

Suppose that you work for a company that designs and builds experimental rockets. You have several projects in the works. You also have several design engineers who have skills in multiple areas. As a manager, you want to know which employees, having which skills, have worked on which projects. Currently, this data is scattered among the EMPLOYEE table, the PROJECTS table, and the SKILLS table.

The EMPLOYEE table carries data about employees, and EMPLOYEE.EmpID is its primary key. The PROJECTS table has a row for each project that an employee has worked on. PROJECTS.EmpID is a foreign key that references the EMPLOYEE table. The SKILLS table shows the expertise of each employee. SKILLS.EmpID is a foreign key that references the EMPLOYEE table.

The EMPLOYEE table has one row for each employee; the PROJECTS table and the SKILLS table have zero or more rows.

Tables 10-4, 10-5, and 10-6 show example data in the three tables.

Table 10-4	EMPLOYEE Table
EmpID	*Name*
1	Ferguson
2	Frost
3	Toyon

Table 10-5	PROJECTS Table
ProjectName	*EmpID*
X-63 Structure	1
X-64 Structure	1

(continued)

Table 10-5 *(continued)*

ProjectName	EmpID
X-63 Guidance	2
X-64 Guidance	2
X-63 Telemetry	3
X-64 Telemetry	3

Table 10-6   **SKILLS Table**

Skill	EmpID
Mechanical Design	1
Aerodynamic Loading	1
Analog Design	2
Gyroscope Design	2
Digital Design	3
R/F Design	3

From the tables, you can see that Ferguson has worked on X-63 and X-64 structure design and has expertise in mechanical design and aerodynamic loading.

Now suppose that, as a manager, you want to see all the information about all the employees. You decide to apply an equi-join to the EMPLOYEE, PROJECTS, and SKILLS tables:

```
SELECT *
   FROM EMPLOYEE E, PROJECTS P, SKILLS S
   WHERE E.EmpID = P.EmpID
      AND E.EmpID = S.EmpID ;
```

You can express this same operation as an inner join by using the following syntax:

```
SELECT *
   FROM EMPLOYEE E INNER JOIN PROJECTS P
      ON (E.EmpID = P.EmpID)
   INNER JOIN SKILLS S
      ON (E.EmpID = S.EmpID) ;
```

Both formulations give the same result, as shown in Table 10-7.

Table 10-7			Result of Inner Join		
E.EmpID	*Name*	*P.EmpID*	*ProjectName*	*S.EmpID*	*Skill*
1 Design	Ferguson	1	X-63 Structure	1	Mechanical
1 Loading	Ferguson	1	X-63 Structure	1	Aerodynamic
1 Design	Ferguson	1	X-64 Structure	1	Mechanical
1 Loading	Ferguson	1	X-64 Structure	1	Aerodynamic
2	Frost	2	X-63 Guidance	2	Analog Design
2 Design	Frost	2	X-63 Guidance	2	Gyroscope
2	Frost	2	X-64 Guidance	2	Analog Design
2 Design	Frost	2	X-64 Guidance	2	Gyroscope
3	Toyon	3	X-63 Telemetry	3	Digital Design
3	Toyon	3	X-63 Telemetry	3	R/F Design
3	Toyon	3	X-64 Telemetry	3	Digital Design
3	Toyon	3	X-64 Telemetry	3	R/F Design

This data arrangement is not particularly enlightening. The employee ID numbers appear three times, and the projects and skills are duplicated for each employee. The inner joins are not well suited to answering this type of question. You can put the union join to work here, along with some strategically chosen SELECT statements, to produce a more suitable result. You begin with the basic union join:

```
SELECT *
    FROM EMPLOYEE E UNION JOIN PROJECTS P
        UNION JOIN SKILLS S ;
```

Notice that the union join has no ON clause. It doesn't filter the data, so an ON clause isn't needed. This statement produces the result shown in Table 10-8.

Table 10-8			Result of Union Join		
E.EmpID	**Name**	**P.EmpID**	**ProjectName**	**S.EmpID**	**Skill**
1	Ferguson	NULL	NULL	NULL	NULL
NULL	NULL	1	X-63 Structure	NULL	NULL
NULL	NULL	1	X-64 Structure	NULL	NULL
NULL	NULL	NULL	NULL	1	Mechanical Design
NULL	NULL	NULL	NULL	1	Aero-dynamic Loading
2	Frost	NULL	NULL	NULL	NULL
NULL	NULL	2	X-63 Guidance	NULL	NULL
NULL	NULL	2	X-64 Guidance	NULL	NULL
NULL	NULL	NULL	NULL	2	Analog Design
NULL	NULL	NULL	NULL	2	Gyroscope Design
3	Toyon	NULL	NULL	NULL	NULL
NULL	NULL	3	X-63 Telemetry	NULL	NULL
NULL	NULL	3	X-64 Telemetry	NULL	NULL
NULL	NULL	NULL	NULL	3	Digital Design
NULL	NULL	NULL	NULL	3	R/F Design

Each table has been extended to the right or left with nulls, and those null-extended rows have been unioned. The order of the rows is arbitrary and depends on the implementation. Now you can massage the data to put it in a more useful form.

Notice that the table has three ID columns, two of which are null in any row. You can improve the display by coalescing the ID columns. As I note in Chapter 8, the COALESCE expression takes on the value of the first non-null value in a list of values. In the present case, it takes on the value of the only non-null value in a column list:

```
SELECT COALESCE (E.EmpID, P.EmpID, S.EmpID) AS ID,
     E.Name, P.ProjectName, S.Skill
   FROM EMPLOYEE E UNION JOIN PROJECTS P
     UNION JOIN SKILLS S
   ORDER BY ID ;
```

The FROM clause is the same as in the previous example, but now the three EMP_ID columns are coalesced into a single column named ID. You're also ordering the result by ID. Table 10-9 shows the result.

Table 10-9	Result of Union Join with COALESCE Expression		
ID	**Name**	**ProjectName**	**Skill**
1	Ferguson	X-63 Structure	NULL
1	Ferguson	X-64 Structure	NULL
1	Ferguson	NULL	Mechanical Design
1	Ferguson	NULL	Aerodynamic Loading
2	Frost	X-63 Guidance	NULL
2	Frost	X-64 Guidance	NULL
2	Frost	NULL	Analog Design
2	Frost	NULL	Gyroscope Design
3	Toyon	X-63 Telemetry	NULL
3	Toyon	X-64 Telemetry	NULL
3	Toyon	NULL	Digital Design
3	Toyon	NULL	R/F Design

Each row in this result has data about a project or a skill, but not both. When you read the result, you first have to determine what type of information is in each row (project or skill). If the ProjectName column has a non-null value, the row names a project on which the employee has worked. If the Skill column is non-null, the row names one of the employee's skills.

You can make the result a little clearer by adding another COALESCE to the SELECT statement, as follows:

```
SELECT COALESCE (E.EmpID, P.EmpID, S.EmpID) AS ID,
     E.Name, COALESCE (P.Type, S.Type) AS Type,
     P.ProjectName, S.Skill
   FROM EMPLOYEE E
     UNION JOIN (SELECT "Project" AS Type, P.*
```

```
                      FROM PROJECTS) P
   UNION JOIN (SELECT "Skill" AS Type, S.*
                      FROM SKILLS) S
   ORDER BY ID, Type ;
```

In this union join, the PROJECTS table in the previous example is replaced with a nested SELECT that appends a column named P.Type with a constant value "Project" to the columns coming from the PROJECTS table. Similarly, the SKILLS table is replaced with a nested SELECT that appends a column named S.Type with a constant value "Skill" to the columns coming from the SKILLS table. In each row, P.Type is either null or "Project", and S.Type is either null or "Skill".

The outer SELECT list specifies a COALESCE of those two Type columns into a single column named Type. You then specify Type in the ORDER BY clause, which sorts the rows that all have the same ID so that all projects are first, followed by all the skills. The result is shown in Table 10-10.

Table 10-10		Refined Result of Union Join with COALESCE Expressions		
ID	**Name**	**Type**	**ProjectName**	**Skill**
1	Ferguson	Project	X-63 Structure	NULL
1	Ferguson	Project	X-64 Structure	NULL
1	Ferguson	Skill	NULL	Mechanical Design
1	Ferguson	Skill	NULL	Aerodynamic Loading
2	Frost	Project	X-63 Guidance	NULL
2	Frost	Project	X-64 Guidance	NULL
2	Frost	Skill	NULL	Analog Design
2	Frost	Skill	NULL	Gyroscope Design
3	Toyon	Project	X-63 Telemetry	NULL
3	Toyon	Project	X-64 Telemetry	NULL
3	Toyon	Skill	NULL	Digital Design
3	Toyon	Skill	NULL	R/F Design

The result table now presents a very readable account of the project experience and the skill sets of all the employees in the EMPLOYEE table.

Considering the number of JOIN operations available, relating data from different tables shouldn't be a problem, regardless of the tables' structure. Trust that if the raw data exists in your database, SQL has the means to get it out and display it in a meaningful form.

ON versus WHERE

The function of the ON and WHERE clauses in the various types of joins is potentially confusing. These facts may help you keep things straight:

- ✔ The ON clause is part of the inner, left, right, and full joins. The cross join and union join don't have an ON clause because neither of them does any filtering of the data.

- ✔ The ON clause in an inner join is logically equivalent to a WHERE clause; the same condition could be specified either in the ON clause or a WHERE clause.

- ✔ The ON clauses in outer joins (left, right, and full joins) are different from WHERE clauses. The WHERE clause simply filters the rows that are returned by the FROM clause. Rows that are rejected by the filter are not included in the result. The ON clause in an outer join first filters the rows of a cross product and then includes the rejected rows, extended with nulls.

Chapter 11

Delving Deep with Nested Queries

In This Chapter

▶ Pulling data from multiple tables with a single SQL statement

▶ Comparing a value from one table with a set of values from another table

▶ Using the SELECT statement to compare a value from a table with a value from another table

▶ Comparing a value from one table with all the corresponding values in another table

▶ Making queries that correlate two corresponding rows in tables

▶ Determining which rows to update, delete, or insert by using a subquery

*O*ne of the best ways to protect your data's integrity is to avoid modification anomalies by normalizing your database. *Normalization* involves breaking up a single table into multiple tables, each of which has a single theme. You don't want product information in the same table with customer information, for example, even if the customers have bought products.

If you normalize a database properly, the data is scattered across multiple tables. Most queries that you want to make need to pull data from two or more tables. One way to do this is to use a join operator or one of the other relational operators (UNION, INTERSECT, or EXCEPT). The relational operators take information from multiple tables and combine it all into a single table. Different operators combine the data in different ways.

Another way to pull data from two or more tables is to use a nested query. In SQL, a *nested query* is one in which an outer enclosing statement contains within it a subquery. That subquery may serve as an enclosing statement for a lower-level subquery that is nested within it. Although there are no theoretical limits to the number of nesting levels that a nested query may have, you do face some implementation-dependent practical limits.

Subqueries are invariably SELECT statements, but the outermost enclosing statement may also be an INSERT, UPDATE, or DELETE.

Because a subquery can operate on a different table than the table operated on by its enclosing statement, nested queries give you another way to extract information from multiple tables.

For example, suppose that you want to query your corporate database to find all department managers who are more than 50 years old. With the joins I discuss in Chapter 10, you may use a query like this:

```
SELECT D.Deptno, D.Name, E.Name, E.Age
   FROM DEPT D, EMPLOYEE E
   WHERE D.ManagerID = E.ID AND E.Age > 50 ;
```

D is the alias for the DEPT table, and E is the alias for the EMPLOYEE table. The EMPLOYEE table has an ID column that is the primary key, and the DEPT table has a column ManagerID that is the ID value of the employee who is the department's manager. A simple join (the list of tables in the FROM clause) pairs the related tables, and a WHERE clause filters all rows except those that meet the criterion. Note that the SELECT statement's parameter list includes the Deptno and Name columns from the DEPT table and the Name and Age columns from the EMPLOYEE table.

Next, suppose that you're interested in the same set of rows but you want only the columns from the DEPT table. In other words, you're interested in the departments whose managers are 50 or older, but you don't care who those managers are or exactly how old they are. You could then write the query with a *subquery* rather than a join:

```
SELECT D.Deptno, D.Name
   FROM DEPT D
   WHERE EXISTS (SELECT * FROM EMPLOYEE E
      WHERE E.ID = D.ManagerID AND E.Age > 50) ;
```

This query has two new elements: the EXISTS keyword and the SELECT * in the WHERE clause of the inner SELECT. The inner SELECT is a subquery (or *subselect*), and the EXISTS keyword is one of several tools for use with a subquery that is described in this chapter.

What Subqueries Do

Subqueries are located within the WHERE clause of their enclosing statement. Their function is to set the search conditions for the WHERE clause. Each kind of subquery produces a different result. Some subqueries produce a list of values that is then used as input by the enclosing statement. Other subqueries produce a single value that the enclosing statement then evaluates with a comparison operator. A third kind of subquery returns a value of True or False.

Nested queries that return sets of rows

To illustrate how a nested query returns a set of rows, suppose that you work for a systems integrator of computer equipment. Your company, Zetec Corporation, assembles systems from components that you buy, and then it sells them to companies and government agencies. You keep track of your business with a relational database. The database consists of many tables, but right now you're concerned with only three of them: the PRODUCT table, the COMP_USED table, and the COMPONENT table. The PRODUCT table (shown in Table 11-1) contains a list of all your standard products. The COMPONENT table (shown in Table 11-2) lists components that go into your products, and the COMP_USED table (shown in Table 11-3) tracks which components go into each product.

Table 11-1	PRODUCT Table	
Column	*Type*	*Constraints*
Model	CHAR (6)	PRIMARY KEY
ProdName	CHAR (35)	
ProdDesc	CHAR (31)	
ListPrice	NUMERIC (9,2)	

Table 11-2	COMPONENT Table	
Column	*Type*	*Constraints*
CompID	CHAR (6)	PRIMARY KEY
CompType	CHAR (10)	
CompDesc	CHAR (31)	

Table 11-3	COMP_USED Table	
Column	*Type*	*Constraints*
Model	CHAR (6)	FOREIGN KEY (for PRODUCT)
CompID	CHAR (6)	FOREIGN KEY (for COMPONENT)

A component may be used in multiple products, and a product can contain multiple components (a many-to-many relationship). This situation can cause integrity problems. To circumvent the problems, create the linking table COMP_USED to relate COMPONENT to PRODUCT. A component may appear in many COMP_USED rows, but each COMP_USED row references only one component (a one-to-many relationship). Similarly, a product may appear in many COMP_USED rows, but each COMP_USED row references only one product (another one-to-many relationship). By adding the linking table, a troublesome many-to-many relationship has been transformed into two relatively simple one-to-many relationships. This process of reducing the complexity of relationships is one example of normalization.

Subqueries introduced by the keyword IN

One form of a nested query compares a single value with the set of values returned by a SELECT statement. It uses the IN predicate with the following syntax:

```
SELECT column_list
    FROM table
    WHERE expression IN (subquery) ;
```

The expression in the WHERE clause evaluates to a value. If that value is IN the list returned by the subquery, then the WHERE clause returns a True value. The specified columns from the table row being processed are added to the result table. The subquery may reference the same table referenced by the outer query, or it may reference a different table.

In the following example, I use Zetec's database to demonstrate this type of query. Assume that there is a shortage of computer monitors in the computer industry. When you run out of monitors, you can no longer deliver products that include them. You want to know which products are affected. Enter the following query:

```
SELECT Model
    FROM COMP_USED
    WHERE CompID IN
        (SELECT CompID
            FROM COMPONENT
            WHERE CompType = 'Monitor') ;
```

SQL processes the innermost query first, so it processes the COMPONENT table, returning the value of CompID for every row where CompType is 'Monitor'. The result is a list of the ID numbers of all monitors. The outer query then compares the value of CompID in every row in the COMP_USED table against the list. If the comparison is successful, the value of the Model column for that row is added to the outer SELECT's result table. The result is a list of all product models that include a monitor. The following example shows what happens when you run the query:

```
Model
-----
CX3000
CX3010
CX3020
MB3030
MX3020
MX3030
```

You now know which products will soon be out of stock. It's time to go to the sales force and tell them to slow down on promoting these products.

When you use this form of nested query, the subquery must specify a single column, and that column's data type must match the data type of the argument preceding the IN keyword.

Subqueries introduced by the keyword NOT IN

Just as you can introduce a subquery with the IN keyword, you can do the opposite and introduce it with the NOT IN keyword. In fact, now is a great time for Zetec management to make such a query. By using the query in the preceding section, Zetec management found out what products not to sell. That is valuable information, but it doesn't pay the rent. What Zetec management really wants to know is what products *to* sell. Management wants to emphasize the sale of products that *don't* contain monitors. A nested query featuring a subquery introduced by the NOT IN keyword provides the requested information:

```
SELECT Model
    FROM COMP_USED
    WHERE Model NOT IN
        (SELECT Model
            FROM COMP_USED
            WHERE CompID IN
                (SELECT CompID
                    FROM COMPONENT
                    WHERE CompType = 'Monitor')) ;
```

This query produces the following result:

```
Model
-----
PX3040
PB3050
PX3040
PB3050
```

A couple things are worth noting here:

- ✔ **This query has two levels of nesting.** The two subqueries are identical to the previous query statement. The only difference is that a new enclosing statement has been wrapped around them. The enclosing statement takes the list of products that contain monitors and applies a SELECT introduced by the NOT IN keyword to that list. The result is another list that contains all product models except those that have monitors.

- ✔ **The result table does contain duplicates.** The duplication occurs because a product containing several components that are not monitors has a row in the COMP_USED table for each component. The query creates an entry in the result table for each of those rows.

In the example, the number of rows does not create a problem because the result table is short. In the real world, however, such a result table may have hundreds or thousands of rows. To avoid confusion, you need to eliminate the duplicates. You can do so easily by adding the DISTINCT keyword to the query. Only rows that are distinct (different) from all previously retrieved rows are added to the result table:

```
SELECT DISTINCT Model
   FROM COMP_USED
   WHERE Model NOT IN
      (SELECT Model
          FROM COMP_USED
          WHERE CompID IN
             (SELECT CompID
                 FROM COMPONENT
                 WHERE CompType = 'Monitor')) ;
```

As expected, the result is as follows:

```
Model
-----
PX3040
PB3050
```

Nested queries that return a single value

Introducing a subquery with one of the six comparison operators (=, <>, <, <=, >, >=) is often useful. In such a case, the expression preceding the operator evaluates to a single value, and the subquery following the operator must also evaluate to a single value. An exception is the case of the *quantified comparison operator,* which is a comparison operator followed by a quantifier (ANY, SOME, or ALL).

To illustrate a case in which a subquery returns a single value, look at another piece of Zetec Corporation's database. It contains a CUSTOMER table that holds information about the companies that buy Zetec products. It also contains a CONTACT table that holds personal data about individuals at each of Zetec's customer organizations. The tables are structured as shown in Tables 11-4 and 11-5.

Table 11-4	CUSTOMER Table	
Column	*Type*	*Constraints*
CustID	INTEGER	PRIMARY KEY
Company	CHAR (40)	
CustAddress	CHAR (30)	
CustCity	CHAR (20)	
CustState	CHAR (2)	
CustZip	CHAR (10)	
CustPhone	CHAR (12)	
ModLevel	INTEGER	

Table 11-5	CONTACT Table	
Column	*Type*	*Constraints*
CustID	INTEGER	FOREIGN KEY
ContFName	CHAR (10)	
ContLName	CHAR (16)	
ContPhone	CHAR (12)	
ContInfo	CHAR (50)	

Say that you want to look at the contact information for Olympic Sales, but you don't remember that company's CustID. Use a nested query like this one to recover the information you want:

```
SELECT *
   FROM CONTACT
      WHERE CustID =
         (SELECT CustID
             FROM CUSTOMER
                WHERE Company = 'Olympic Sales') ;
```

The result looks something like this:

```
CustID  ContFName   ContLName    ContPhone    ContInfo
------  ---------   ---------    ---------    --------
   118  Jerry       Attwater     505-876-3456 Will play
                                              major role in
                                              coordinating
                                              the
                                              wireless
                                              Web.
```

You can now call Jerry at Olympic and tell him about this month's special sale on Web-enabled cellphones.

When you use a subquery in an "=" comparison, the subquery's SELECT list must specify a single column (CustID in the example). When the subquery is executed, it must return a single row in order to have a single value for the comparison.

In this example, I assume that the CUSTOMER table has only one row with a Company value of 'Olympic Sales'. The CREATE TABLE statement for CUSTOMER specifies a UNIQUE constraint for Company, and this statement guarantees that the subquery in the preceding example returns a single value (or no value). Subqueries like the one in this example, however, are commonly used on columns that are not specified to be UNIQUE. In such cases, you must rely on prior knowledge of the database contents for believing that the column has no duplicates.

If more than one CUSTOMER has a value of 'Olympic Sales' in the Company column (perhaps in different states), the subquery raises an error.

If no Customer with such a company name exists, the subquery is treated as if it was null, and the comparison becomes *unknown*. In this case, the WHERE clause returns no row (because it returns only rows with the condition True and filters rows with the condition False or unknown). This would probably happen, for example, if someone misspelled the COMPANY as 'Olumpic Sales'.

Although the equals operator (=) is the most common, you can use any of the other five comparison operators in a similar structure. For every row in the table specified in the enclosing statement's FROM clause, the single value returned by the subquery is compared to the expression in the enclosing statement's WHERE clause. If the comparison gives a True value, a row is added to the result table.

You can guarantee that a subquery will return a single value if you include an aggregate function in it. *Aggregate functions* always return a single value. (Aggregate functions are described in Chapter 3.) Of course, this way of returning a single value is helpful only if you want the result of an aggregate function.

Say that you are a Zetec salesperson and you need to earn a big commission check to pay for some unexpected bills. You decide to concentrate on selling Zetec's most expensive product. You can find out what that product is with a nested query:

```
SELECT Model, ProdName, ListPrice
    FROM PRODUCT
        WHERE ListPrice =
            (SELECT MAX(ListPrice)
                FROM PRODUCT) ;
```

In the preceding nested query, both the subquery and the enclosing statement operate on the same table. The subquery returns a single value: the maximum list price in the PRODUCT table. The outer query retrieves all rows from the PRODUCT table that have that list price.

The next example shows a comparison subquery that uses a comparison operator other than =:

```
SELECT Model, ProdName, ListPrice
    FROM PRODUCT
        WHERE ListPrice <
            (SELECT AVG(ListPrice)
                FROM PRODUCT) ;
```

The subquery returns a single value: the average list price in the PRODUCT table. The outer query retrieves all rows from the PRODUCT table that have a list price less than the average list price.

In the original SQL standard, a comparison could have only one subquery, and it had to be on the right side of the comparison. SQL:1999 allowed either or both operands of the comparison to be subqueries, and later versions of SQL retain that expansion of capability.

The ALL, SOME, and ANY quantifiers

Another way to make sure that a subquery returns a single value is to introduce it with a quantified comparison operator. The universal quantifier ALL, and the existential quantifiers SOME and ANY, when combined with a comparison operator, process the list returned by a subquery, reducing it to a single value.

You'll see how these quantifiers affect a comparison by looking at the baseball pitchers' complete game database from Chapter 10, which is listed next.

The contents of the two tables are given by the following two queries:

```
SELECT * FROM NATIONAL

FirstName    LastName    CompleteGames
---------    --------    -------------
Sal          Maglie               11
Don          Newcombe              9
Sandy        Koufax               13
Don          Drysdale             12
Bob          Turley                8

SELECT * FROM AMERICAN

FirstName    LastName    CompleteGames
---------    --------    -------------
Whitey       Ford                 12
Don          Larson               10
Bob          Turley                8
Allie        Reynolds             14
```

The presumption is that the pitchers with the most complete games should be in the American League because of the presence of designated hitters in that league. One way to verify this presumption is to build a query that returns all American League pitchers who have thrown more complete games than all the National League pitchers. The query can be formulated as follows:

```
SELECT *
   FROM AMERICAN
   WHERE CompleteGames > ALL
      (SELECT CompleteGames FROM NATIONAL) ;
```

This is the result:

```
FirstName    LastName    CompleteGames
----------   ----------  ---------------
Allie        Reynolds    14
```

The subquery (`SELECT CompleteGames FROM NATIONAL`) returns the values in the `CompleteGames` column for all National League pitchers. The `> ALL` quantifier says to return only those values of `CompleteGames` in the AMERICAN table that are greater than each of the values returned by the subquery. This condition translates into "greater than the highest value returned by the subquery." In this case, the highest value returned by the subquery is 13 (Sandy Koufax). The only row in the AMERICAN table higher than that is Allie Reynolds's record, with 14 complete games.

What if your initial presumption was wrong? What if the major-league leader in complete games was a National League pitcher, in spite of the fact that the National League has no designated hitter? If that was the case, the query

```
SELECT *
    FROM AMERICAN
    WHERE CompleteGames > ALL
        (SELECT CompleteGames FROM NATIONAL) ;
```

would return a warning stating that no rows satisfy the query's conditions, meaning that no American League pitcher has thrown more complete games than the pitcher who has thrown the most complete games in the National League.

Nested queries that are an existence test

A query returns data from all table rows that satisfy the query's conditions. Sometimes many rows are returned; sometimes only one comes back. Sometimes none of the rows in the table satisfy the conditions, and no rows are returned. You can use the EXISTS and NOT EXISTS predicates to introduce a subquery. That structure tells you whether any rows in the table located in the subquery's FROM clause meet the conditions in its WHERE clause.

Subqueries introduced with EXISTS and NOT EXISTS are fundamentally different from the other subqueries in this chapter so far. In all the previous cases, SQL first executes the subquery and then applies that operation's result to the enclosing statement. EXISTS and NOT EXISTS subqueries, on the other hand, are examples of correlated subqueries.

A *correlated subquery* first finds the table and row specified by the enclosing statement and then executes the subquery on the row in the subquery's table that correlates with the current row of the enclosing statement's table.

The subquery either returns one or more rows or it returns none. If it returns at least one row, the EXISTS predicate succeeds (see the following section), and the enclosing statement performs its action. In the same circumstances, the NOT EXISTS predicate fails (see the section after that), and the enclosing statement does not perform its action. After one row of the enclosing statement's table is processed, the same operation is performed on the next row. This action is repeated until every row in the enclosing statement's table has been processed.

EXISTS

Say that you are a salesperson for Zetec Corporation and you want to call your primary contact people at all of Zetec's customer organizations in California. Try the following query:

```
SELECT *
   FROM CONTACT
   WHERE EXISTS
      (SELECT *
         FROM CUSTOMER
         WHERE CustState = 'CA'
            AND CONTACT.CustID = CUSTOMER.CustID) ;
```

Notice the reference to `CONTACT.CustID`, which is referencing a column from the outer query and comparing it with another column, `CUSTOMER.CustID` from the inner query. For each candidate row of the outer query, you evaluate the inner query, using the `CustID` value from the current `CONTACT` row of the outer query in the `WHERE` clause of the inner query.

The `CustID` column links the CONTACT table to the CUSTOMER table. SQL looks at the first record in the CONTACT table, finds the row in the CUSTOMER table that has the same `CustID`, and checks that row's `CustState` field. If `CUSTOMER.CustState = 'CA'`, then the current `CONTACT` row is added to the result table. The next `CONTACT` record is then processed in the same way, and so on, until the entire CONTACT table has been processed. Because the query specifies `SELECT * FROM CONTACT`, all the contact table's fields are returned, including the contact's name and phone number.

NOT EXISTS

In the previous example, the Zetec salesperson wants to know the names and numbers of the contact people of all the customers in California. Imagine that a second salesperson is responsible for all of the United States except California. She can retrieve her contact people by using NOT EXISTS in a query similar to the preceding one:

```
SELECT *
   FROM CONTACT
   WHERE NOT EXISTS
      (SELECT *
         FROM CUSTOMER
         WHERE CustState = 'CA'
            AND CONTACT.CustID = CUSTOMER.CustID) ;
```

Every row in CONTACT for which the subquery does not return a row is added to the result table.

Other correlated subqueries

As noted in a previous section of this chapter, subqueries introduced by IN or by a comparison operator need not be correlated queries, but they can be.

Correlated subqueries introduced with IN

In the earlier section "Subqueries introduced by the keyword IN," I discuss how a noncorrelated subquery can be used with the IN predicate. To show how a correlated subquery may use the IN predicate, ask the same question that came up with the EXISTS predicate: What are the names and phone numbers of the contacts at all of Zetec's customers in California? You can answer this question with a correlated IN subquery:

```
SELECT *
    FROM CONTACT
    WHERE 'CA' IN
        (SELECT CustState
            FROM CUSTOMER
            WHERE CONTACT.CustID = CUSTOMER.CustID) ;
```

The statement is evaluated for each record in the CONTACT table. If, for that record, the CustID numbers in CONTACT and CUSTOMER match, then the value of CUSTOMER.CustState is compared to 'CA'. The result of the subquery is a list that contains, at most, one element. If that one element is 'CA', the WHERE clause of the enclosing statement is satisfied, and a row is added to the query's result table.

Subqueries introduced with comparison operators

A correlated subquery can also be introduced by one of the six comparison operators, as shown in the next example.

Zetec pays bonuses to its salespeople based on their total monthly sales volume. The higher the volume is, the higher the bonus percentage is. The bonus percentage list is kept in the BONUSRATE table:

MinAmount	MaxAmount	BonusPct
0.00	24999.99	0.
25000.00	49999.99	0.001
50000.00	99999.99	0.002
100000.00	249999.99	0.003
250000.00	499999.99	0.004
500000.00	749999.99	0.005
750000.00	999999.99	0.006

If a person's monthly sales are between $100,000.00 and $249,999.99, the bonus is 0.3 percent of sales.

Sales are recorded in a transaction master table named TRANSMASTER:

TRANSMASTER		
Column	Type	Constraints

```
TransID        INTEGER         PRIMARY KEY
CustID         INTEGER         FOREIGN KEY
EmpID          INTEGER         FOREIGN KEY
TransDate      DATE
NetAmount      NUMERIC
Freight        NUMERIC
Tax            NUMERIC
InvoiceTotal   NUMERIC
```

Sales bonuses are based on the sum of the NetAmount field for all of a person's transactions in the month. You can find any person's bonus rate with a correlated subquery that uses comparison operators:

```
SELECT BonusPct
   FROM BONUSRATE
      WHERE MinAmount <=
         (SELECT SUM (NetAmount)
            FROM TRANSMASTER
               WHERE EmpID = 133)
         AND MaxAmount >=
            (SELECT SUM (NetAmount)
               FROM TRANSMASTER
                  WHERE EmpID = 133) ;
```

This query is interesting in that it contains two subqueries, making use of the logical connective AND. The subqueries use the SUM aggregate operator, which returns a single value: the total monthly sales of employee number 133. That value is then compared against the MinAmount and the MaxAmount columns in the BONUSRATE table, producing the bonus rate for that employee.

If you had not known the EmpID but had known the person's name, you could arrive at the same answer with a more complex query:

```
SELECT BonusPct
   FROM BONUSRATE
      WHERE MinAmount <=
         (SELECT SUM (NetAmount)
            FROM TRANSMASTER
               WHERE EmpID =
                  (SELECT EmpID
                     FROM EMPLOYEE
                        WHERE EmplName = 'Coffin'))
         AND MaxAmount >=
            (SELECT SUM (NetAmount)
               FROM TRANSMASTER
                  WHERE EmpID =
                     (SELECT EmpID
                        FROM EMPLOYEE
                           WHERE EmplName = 'Coffin'));
```

This example uses subqueries nested within subqueries, which, in turn, are nested within an enclosing query to arrive at the bonus rate for the employee named Coffin. This structure works only if you know for sure that the company has one, and only one, employee whose last name is Coffin. If you know that more than one employee has the same last name, you can add terms to the WHERE clause of the innermost subquery until you're sure that only one row of the EMPLOYEE table is selected.

Subqueries in a HAVING clause

You can have a correlated subquery in a HAVING clause just as you can in a WHERE clause. As I mention in Chapter 9, a HAVING clause is usually preceded by a GROUP BY clause. The HAVING clause acts as a filter to restrict the groups created by the GROUP BY clause. Groups that don't satisfy the condition of the HAVING clause are not included in the result. When used in this way, the HAVING clause is evaluated for each group created by the GROUP BY clause.

In the absence of a GROUP BY clause, the HAVING clause is evaluated for the set of rows passed by the WHERE clause, which is considered to be a single group. If neither a WHERE clause nor a GROUP BY clause is present, the HAVING clause is evaluated for the entire table:

```
SELECT TM1.EmpID
   FROM TRANSMASTER TM1
      GROUP BY TM1.Department
      HAVING MAX (TM1.NetAmount) >= ALL
         (SELECT 2 * AVG (TM2.NetAmount)
             FROM TRANSMASTER TM2
             WHERE TM1.EmpID <> TM2.EmpID) ;
```

This query uses two aliases for the same table, enabling you to retrieve the EmpID number of all salespeople who had a sale of at least twice the average sale of all the other salespeople. The query works as follows:

1. The outer query groups TRANSMASTER rows by the employees' department. This is done with the SELECT, FROM, and GROUP BY clauses.

2. The HAVING clause filters these groups. For each group, it calculates the MAX of the NetAmount column for the rows in that group.

3. The inner query evaluates twice the average NetAmount from all rows of TRANSMASTER whose EmpID is different from the EmpID of the current group of the outer query. Note that in the last line you need to reference two different EmpID values, so in the FROM clauses of the outer and inner queries, you use different aliases for TRANSMASTER.

4. You then use those aliases in the comparison of the query's last line to indicate that you're referencing both the EmpID from the current row of the inner subquery (TM2.EmpID) and the EmpID from the current group of the outer subquery (TM1.EmpID).

UPDATE, DELETE, and INSERT statements

In addition to SELECT statements, UPDATE, DELETE, and INSERT statements can also include WHERE clauses. Those WHERE clauses can contain subqueries in the same way that SELECT statements WHERE clauses do.

For example, Zetec has just made a volume purchase deal with Olympic Sales and wants to retroactively provide Olympic with a 10-percent credit for all its purchases in the last month. You can give this credit with an UPDATE statement:

```
UPDATE TRANSMASTER
    SET NetAmount = NetAmount * 0.9
    WHERE CustID =
        (SELECT CustID
            FROM CUSTOMER
            WHERE Company = 'Olympic Sales') ;
```

You can also have a correlated subquery in an UPDATE statement. Suppose the CUSTOMER table has a column LastMonthsMax, and Zetec wants to give such a credit for purchases that exceed LastMonthsMax for the customer:

```
UPDATE TRANSMASTER TM
    SET NetAmount = NetAmount * 0.9
    WHERE NetAmount >
        (SELECT LastMonthsMax
            FROM CUSTOMER C
            WHERE C.CustID = TM.CustID) ;
```

Note that this subquery is correlated: The WHERE clause in the last line references both the CustID of the CUSTOMER row from the subquery and the CustID of the current TRANSMASTER row that is a candidate for updating.

A subquery in an UPDATE statement can also reference the table that is being updated. Suppose that Zetec wants to give a 10-percent credit to customers whose purchases have exceeded $10,000:

```
UPDATE TRANSMASTER TM1
    SET NetAmount = NetAmount * 0.9
    WHERE 10000 < (SELECT SUM(NetAmount)
                FROM TRANSMASTER TM2
                    WHERE TM1.CustID = TM2.CustID);
```

The inner subquery calculates the SUM of the NetAmount column for all TRANSMASTER rows for the same customer. What does this mean? Suppose that the customer with CustID = 37 has four rows in TRANSMASTER with values for NetAmount: 3000, 5000, 2000, and 1000. The SUM of NetAmount for this CustID is 11000.

The order in which the UPDATE statement processes the rows is defined by your implementation and is generally not predictable. The order may differ depending on how the rows are arranged on the disk. Assume that the implementation processes the rows for this CustID in this order: first the TRANS-MASTER with a NetAmount of 3000, then the one with NetAmount = 5000, and so on. After the first three rows for CustID 37 have been updated, their NetAmount values are 2700 (90 percent of $3,000), 4500 (90 percent of $5,000), and 1800 (90 percent of $2,000). Then when you process the last TRANSMASTER row for CustID 37, whose NetAmount is 1000, the SUM returned by the subquery would seem to be 10000 — that is, the SUM of the new NetAmount values of the first three rows for CustID 37, and the old NetAmount value of the last row for CustID 37. Thus it would seem that the last row for CustID 37 isn't updated, because the comparison with that SUM is not True (10000 is not less than SELECT SUM (NetAmount)). But that is not how the UPDATE statement is defined when a subquery references the table that is being updated.

All evaluations of subqueries in an UPDATE statement reference the old values of the table being updated. In the preceding UPDATE for CustID 37, the subquery returns 11000 — the original SUM.

The subquery in a WHERE clause operates the same as a SELECT statement or an UPDATE statement. The same is true for DELETE and INSERT. To delete all of Olympic's transactions, use this statement:

```
DELETE TRANSMASTER
   WHERE CustID =
      (SELECT CustID
          FROM CUSTOMER
          WHERE Company = 'Olympic Sales') ;
```

As with UPDATE, DELETE subqueries can also be correlated and can also reference the table being deleted. The rules are similar to the rules for UPDATE subqueries. Suppose you want to delete all rows from TRANSMASTER for customers whose total NetAmount is larger than $10,000:

```
DELETE TRANSMASTER TM1
   WHERE 10000 < (SELECT SUM(NetAmount)
      FROM TRANSMASTER TM2
          WHERE TM1.CustID = TM2.CustID) ;
```

This query deletes all rows from TRANSMASTER that have CustID 37, as well as any other customers with purchases exceeding $10,000. All references to TRANSMASTER in the subquery denote the contents of TRANSMASTER before any deletes by the current statement. So even when you are deleting the last TRANSMASTER row for CustID 37, the subquery is evaluated on the original TRANSMASTER table and returns 11000.

When you update, delete, or insert database records, you risk making a table's data inconsistent with other tables in the database. Such an inconsistency is called a *modification anomaly,* discussed in Chapter 5. If you delete TRANS-MASTER records and a TRANSDETAIL table depends on TRANSMASTER, you must delete the corresponding records from TRANSDETAIL, too. This operation is called a *cascading delete,* because the deletion of a parent record must cascade to its associated child records. Otherwise, the undeleted child records become orphans. In this case, they would be invoice detail lines that are in limbo because they are no longer connected to an invoice record.

Chapter 12

Recursive Queries

In This Chapter

▶ Understanding recursive processing

▶ Defining recursive queries

▶ Finding ways to use recursive queries

*O*ne of the major criticisms of SQL, up through and including SQL-92, was its inability to implement *recursive processing*. Many important problems that are difficult to solve by other means yield readily to recursive solutions. Extensions included in SQL:1999 allow recursive queries, greatly expanding the language's power. If your SQL implementation includes the recursion extensions, you can efficiently solve a large new class of problems. However, because recursion is not a part of core SQL, many implementations currently available do not include it.

What Is Recursion?

Recursion is a feature that's been around for years in programming languages such as Logo, LISP, and C++. In these languages, you can define a *function* (a set of one or more commands) that performs a specific operation. The main program invokes the function by issuing a command called a *function call*. If the function calls itself as a part of its operation, you have the simplest form of recursion.

A simple program that uses recursion in one of its functions provides an illustration of the joys and pitfalls of recursion. The following program, written in C++, draws a spiral on the computer screen. It assumes that the drawing tool is initially pointing toward the top of the screen, and includes three functions:

▶ The function `line(n)` draws a line *n* units long.

▶ The function `left_turn(d)` rotates the drawing tool *d* degrees counter-clockwise.

✔ You can define the function `spiral(segment)` as follows:

```
void spiral(int segment)
{
    line(segment)
    left_turn(90)
    spiral(segment + 1)
} ;
```

If you call `spiral(1)` from the main program, the following actions take place:

`spiral(1)` draws a line one unit long toward the top of the screen.

`spiral(1)` turns left 90 degrees.

`spiral(1)` calls `spiral(2)`.

`spiral(2)` draws a line two units long toward the left side of the screen.

`spiral(2)` turns left 90 degrees.

`spiral(2)` calls `spiral(3)`.

And so on. . . .

Eventually the program generates the spiral shown in Figure 12-1.

Houston, we have a problem

Well, okay, the situation here is not as serious as it was for Apollo 13 when the main oxygen tank exploded while the spacecraft was en route to the moon. Your problem is that the spiral-drawing program keeps calling itself and drawing longer and longer lines. It will continue to do that until the computer executing it runs out of resources and (if you're lucky) puts an obnoxious error message on the screen. If you're unlucky, the computer just crashes.

Failure is not an option

The scenario described in the previous section shows one of the dangers of using recursion. A program written to call itself invokes a new instance of itself — which in turn calls yet another instance, *ad infinitum*. This is generally not what you want.

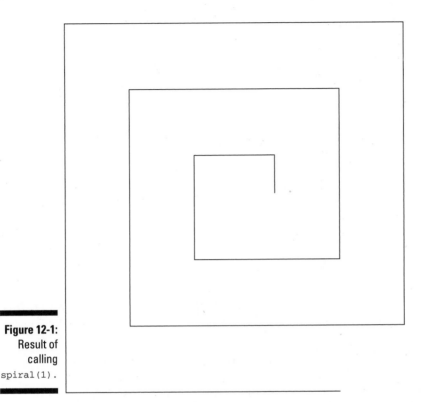

Figure 12-1:
Result of
calling
`spiral(1).`

To address this problem, programmers include a *termination condition* within the recursive function — a limit on how deep the recursion can go — so the program performs the desired action and then terminates gracefully. You can include a termination condition in your spiral-drawing program to save computer resources and prevent dizziness in programmers:

```
void spiral2(int segment)
{
    if (segment <= 10)
    {
        line(segment)
        left_turn(90)
        spiral2(segment + 1)
    }
} ;
```

When you call `spiral2(1)`, it executes and then (recursively) calls itself until the value of `segment` exceeds 10. At the point where `segment` equals 11, the `if (segment <=10)` construct returns a False value, and the code within the interior braces is skipped. Control returns to the previous invocation of `spiral2` and, from there, returns all the way up to the first invocation, after which the program terminates. Figure 12-2 shows the sequence of calls and returns that occur.

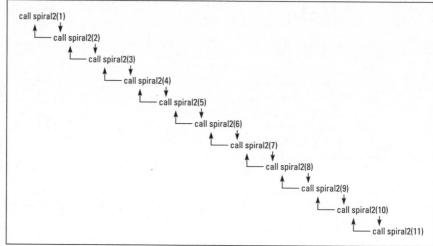

Every time a function calls itself, it takes you one level farther away from the main program that was the starting point of the operation. For the main program to continue, the deepest iteration must return control to the iteration that called it. That iteration will have to do likewise, continuing all the way back to the main program that made the first call to the recursive function.

Recursion is a powerful tool for repeatedly executing code when you don't know at the outset how many times the code should be repeated. It's ideal for searching through tree-shaped structures such as family trees, complex electronic circuits, or multilevel distribution networks.

What Is a Recursive Query?

A *recursive query* is a query that is functionally dependent upon itself. The simplest form of such functional dependence is the case where a query Q1 includes an invocation of itself in the query expression body. A more complex case is where query Q1 depends on query Q2, which in turn depends on query Q1. There is still a functional dependency, and recursion is still involved, no matter how many queries lie between the first and the second invocation of the same query.

Where Might You Use a Recursive Query?

Recursive queries may help save you time and frustration in dealing with various kinds of problems. Suppose, for example, that you have a pass that gives you free air travel on any flight of the (fictional) Vannevar Airlines. Way cool. The next question you ask is, "Where can I go for free?" The FLIGHT table contains all the flights that Vannevar runs. Table 12-1 shows the flight number and the source and destination of each flight.

Table 12-1	Flights Offered by Vannevar Airlines	
Flight No.	*Source*	*Destination*
3141	Portland	Orange County
2173	Portland	Charlotte
623	Portland	Daytona Beach
5440	Orange County	Montgomery
221	Charlotte	Memphis
32	Memphis	Champaign
981	Montgomery	Memphis

Figure 12-3 illustrates the routes on a map of the United States.

To get started on your vacation plan, create a database table for FLIGHT by using SQL as follows:

```
CREATE TABLE FLIGHT (
    FlightNo
            INTEGER
            NOT NULL,
    Source
            CHARACTER (30),
    Destination
            CHARACTER (30)
);
```

After the table is created, you can populate it with the data shown in Table 12-1.

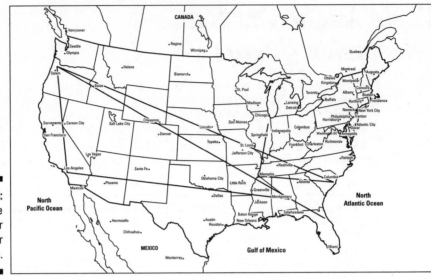

Figure 12-3:
Route
map for
Vannevar
Airlines.

Suppose you're starting from Portland and you want to visit a friend in Montgomery. Naturally you wonder, "What cities can I reach via Vannevar if I start from Portland?" and "What cities can I reach via the same airline if I start from Montgomery?" Some cities are reachable in one hop; others are not. Some might require two or more hops. You can find all the cities that Vannevar will take you to, starting from any given city on its route map — but if you do it one query at a time, you're . . .

Querying the hard way

To find out what you want to know — provided you have the time and patience — you can make a series of queries, starting with Portland as the starting city:

```
SELECT Destination FROM FLIGHT WHERE Source = 'Portland';
```

The first query returns `Orange County`, `Charlotte`, and `Daytona Beach`. Your second query uses the first of these results as a starting point:

```
SELECT Destination FROM FLIGHT WHERE Source = 'Orange
        County';
```

The second query returns `Montgomery`. Your third query returns to the results of the first query and uses the second result as a starting point:

```
SELECT Destination FROM FLIGHT WHERE Source = 'Charlotte';
```

The third query returns `Memphis`. Your fourth query goes back to the results of the first query and uses the remaining result as a starting point:

```
SELECT Destination FROM FLIGHT WHERE Source = 'Daytona
        Beach';
```

Sorry, the fourth query returns a null result because Vannevar offers no outgoing flights from Daytona Beach. But the second query returned another city (`Montgomery`) as a possible starting point, so your fifth query uses that result:

```
SELECT Destination FROM FLIGHT WHERE Source =
        'Montgomery';
```

This query returns `Memphis`, but you already know it's among the cities you can get to (in this case, via Charlotte). But you go ahead and try this latest result as a starting point for another query:

```
SELECT Destination FROM FLIGHT WHERE Source = 'Memphis';
```

The query returns `Champaign` — which you can add to the list of reachable cities (even if you have to get there in two hops). As long as you're considering multiple hops, you plug in `Champaign` as a starting point:

```
SELECT Destination FROM FLIGHT WHERE Source = 'Champaign';
```

Oops. This query returns a null value; Vannevar offers no outgoing flights from Champaign. (Seven queries so far. Are you fidgeting yet?)

Vannevar doesn't offer a flight out of Daytona Beach, either, so if you go there, you're stuck — which might not be a hardship if it's Spring Break week. (Of course, if you use up a week running individual queries to find out where to go next, you might get a worse headache than you'd get from a week of partying.) Or you might get stuck in Champaign — in which case, you could enroll in the University of Illinois and take a few database courses.

Granted, this method will (eventually) answer the question, "What cities are reachable from Portland?" But running one query after another, making each one dependent on the results of a previous query, is complicated, time-consuming, and fidgety.

Saving time with a recursive query

A simpler way to get the info you need is to craft a single recursive query that does the entire job in one operation. Here's the syntax for such a query:

```
WITH RECURSIVE
   REACHABLEFROM (Source, Destination)
```

```
        AS (SELECT Source, Destination
               FROM FLIGHT
            UNION
            SELECT in.Source, out.Destination
               FROM REACHABLEFROM in, FLIGHT out
               WHERE in.Destination = out.Source
            )
     SELECT * FROM ReachableFrom
     WHERE Source = 'Portland';
```

The first time through the recursion, FLIGHT has seven rows, and REACH-ABLEFROM has none. The UNION takes the seven rows from FLIGHT and copies them into ReachableFrom. At this point, REACHABLEFROM has the data shown in Table 12-2.

Table 12-2   ReachableFrom After One Pass through Recursion

Source	Destination
Portland	Orange County
Portland	Charlotte
Portland	Daytona Beach
Orange County	Montgomery
Charlotte	Memphis
Memphis	Champaign
Montgomery	Memphis

The second time through the recursion, things start to get interesting. The WHERE clause (WHERE in.Destination = out.Source) means that you're looking only at rows where the Destination field of the REACHABLEFROM table equals the Source field of the FLIGHT table. For those rows, you're taking the Source field from REACHABLEFROM and the Destination field from FLIGHT, and adding those two fields to REACHABLEFROM as a new row. Table 12-3 shows the result of this iteration of the recursion.

Table 12-3   REACHABLEFROM After Two Passes through the Recursion

Source	Destination
Portland	Orange County
Portland	Charlotte

Source	Destination
Portland	Daytona Beach
Orange County	Montgomery
Charlotte	Memphis
Memphis	Champaign
Montgomery	Memphis
Portland	Montgomery
Portland	Memphis
Orange County	Memphis
Charlotte	Champaign

The results are looking more useful. REACHABLEFROM now contains all the Destination cities that are reachable from any Source city in two hops or less. Next, the recursion processes three-hop trips, and so on, until all possible destination cities have been reached.

After the recursion is complete, the third and final SELECT statement (which is outside the recursion) extracts from REACHABLEFROM only those cities you can reach from Portland by flying Vannevar. In this example, all six other cities are reachable from Portland — in few enough hops that you won't feel like you're going by pogo stick.

If you scrutinize the code in the recursive query, it doesn't *look* any simpler than the seven individual queries that it replaces. It does, however, have two advantages:

- ✔ When you set it in motion, it completes the entire operation without any further intervention.
- ✔ It can do the job fast.

Imagine a real-world airline with many more cities on its route map. The more possible destinations that are available, the bigger the advantage of using the recursive method.

What makes this query recursive? The fact that you're defining REACHABLE-FROM in terms of itself. The recursive part of the definition is the second SELECT statement, the one just after the UNION. REACHABLEFROM is a temporary table that progressively is filled with data as the recursion proceeds.

Processing continues until all possible destinations have been added to REACHABLEFROM. Any duplicates are eliminated, because the UNION operator doesn't add duplicates to the result table. After the recursion completes, REACHABLEFROM contains all the cities that are reachable from any starting city. The third and final SELECT statement returns only those destination cities that you can reach from Portland. Bon voyage.

Where Else Might You Use a Recursive Query?

Any problem that you can lay out as a treelike structure can potentially be solved by using a recursive query. The classic industrial application is materials processing (the process of turning raw materials into finished goods). Suppose your company is building a new gasoline-electric hybrid car. Such a machine is built of subassemblies — engine, batteries, and so on — which are constructed from smaller subassemblies (crankshaft, electrodes, and so on) — which are made of even smaller parts.

Keeping track of all the various parts can be difficult in a relational database that does not use recursion. Recursion enables you to start with the complete machine and ferret your way along any path to get to the smallest part. Want to find out the specs for the fastening screw that holds the clamp to the negative electrode of the auxiliary battery? The WITH RECURSIVE structure gives SQL the capability to address such a problem.

Recursion is also a natural for 'What if?' processing. In the Vannevar Airlines example, what if management discontinues service from Portland to Charlotte? How does that affect the cities that are reachable from Portland? A recursive query quickly gives you the answer.

Part IV
Controlling Operations

The 5th Wave   By Rich Tennant

"You ever get the feeling this project could just up and die at any moment?"

In this part . . .

After creating a database and filling it with data, you want to protect your new database from harm or misuse. In this part, I discuss in detail SQL's tools for maintaining the safety and integrity of your data. SQL's Data Control Language (DCL) enables you to protect your data from misuse by selectively granting or denying access to the data. You can protect your database from other threats — such as interference from simultaneous access by multiple users — by using SQL's transaction-processing facilities. You can use constraints to help prevent users from entering bad data in the first place. Of course, even SQL can't defend you against bad application design — that's strictly a live-and-learn proposition. But if you take full advantage of the tools that SQL provides, SQL *can* protect your data from most problems.

Chapter 13

Providing Database Security

· ·

In This Chapter

▶ Controlling access to database tables

▶ Deciding who has access to what

▶ Granting access privileges

▶ Taking access privileges away

▶ Defeating attempts at unauthorized access

▶ Passing on the power to grant privileges

· ·

A system administrator must have special knowledge of how a database works. That's why, in preceding chapters, I discuss the parts of SQL that create databases and manipulate data — and then (in Chapter 3) introduce SQL's facilities for protecting databases from harm or misuse. In this chapter, I go into more depth on the subject of misuse.

The person in charge of a database can determine who has access to the database — and can set users' access levels, granting or revoking access to aspects of the system. The system administrator can even grant — or revoke — the right to grant and revoke access privileges. If you use them correctly, the security tools that SQL provides are powerful protectors of important data. Used incorrectly, these same tools can tie up the efforts of legitimate users in a big knot of red tape when they're just trying to do their jobs.

Because databases often contain sensitive information that you shouldn't make available to everyone, SQL provides different levels of access — from complete to none, with several levels in between. By controlling which operations each authorized user can perform, the database administrator can make available all the data that the users need to do their jobs — but restrict access to parts of the database that not everyone should see or change.

The SQL Data Control Language

The SQL statements that you use to create databases form a group known as the *Data Definition Language (DDL)*. After you create a database, you can use another set of SQL statements — known collectively as the *Data Manipulation Language (DML)* — to add, change, and remove data from the database. SQL includes additional statements that don't fall into either of these categories. Programmers sometimes refer to these statements collectively as the *Data Control Language (DCL)*. DCL statements primarily protect the database from unauthorized access, from harmful interaction among multiple database users, and from power failures and equipment malfunctions. In this chapter, I discuss protection from unauthorized access.

User Access Levels

SQL provides controlled access to nine database management functions:

- **Creating, seeing, modifying, and deleting:** These functions correspond to the INSERT, SELECT, UPDATE, and DELETE operations that I discuss in Chapter 6.

- **Referencing:** Using the REFERENCES keyword (which I discuss in Chapters 3 and 5) involves applying referential integrity constraints to a table that depends on another table in the database.

- **Using:** The USAGE keyword pertains to domains, character sets, collations, and translations. (I define domains, character sets, collations, and translations in Chapter 5.)

- **Defining new data types:** You deal with user-defined type names with the UNDER keyword.

- **Responding to an event:** The use of the TRIGGER keyword causes an SQL statement or statement block to be executed whenever a predetermined event occurs.

- **Executing:** Using the EXECUTE keyword causes a routine to be executed.

The database administrator

In most installations with more than a few users, the supreme database authority is the *database administrator (DBA)*. The DBA has all rights and privileges to all aspects of the database. Being a DBA can give you a feeling of power — and responsibility. With all that power at your disposal, you can easily mess up your database and destroy thousands of hours of work. DBAs must think clearly and carefully about the consequences of every action they perform.

The DBA not only has all rights to the database, but also controls the rights that other users have. This way, highly trusted individuals can access more functions — and, perhaps, more tables — than can the majority of users.

The best way to become a DBA is to install the database management system. The installation manual gives you an account, or *login,* and a password. That login identifies you as a specially privileged user. Sometimes, the system calls this privileged user the DBA, sometimes the *system administrator,* and sometimes the *super user* (sorry, no cape and boots provided). As your first official act after logging in, you should change your password from the default to a secret one of your own.

If you don't change the password, anyone who reads the manual can also log in with full DBA privileges. After you change the password, only people who know the new password can log in as DBA. I suggest that you share the new DBA password with only a small number of highly trusted people. After all, a falling meteor could strike you tomorrow; you could win the lottery; or you may become unavailable to the company in some other way. Your colleagues must be able to carry on in your absence. Anyone who knows the DBA login and password becomes the DBA after using that information to access the system.

If you have DBA privileges, log in as DBA only if you need to perform a specific task that requires DBA privileges. After you finish, log out. For routine work, log in by using your own personal login ID and password. This approach may prevent you from making mistakes that have serious consequences for other users' tables (as well as for your own).

Database object owners

Another class of privileged user, along with the DBA, is the *database object owner.* Tables and views, for example, are *database objects.* Any user who creates such an object can specify its owner. A table owner enjoys every possible privilege associated with that table, including the privilege to grant access to the table to other people. Because you can base views on underlying tables, someone other than a table's owner can create a view based on that owner's table. However, the view owner only receives privileges that he or she has for the underlying table. The bottom line is that a user can't circumvent the protection on another user's table simply by creating a view based on that table.

The public

In network terms, the public consists of all users who are not specially privileged users (that is, either DBAs or object owners) and to whom a privileged user hasn't specifically granted access rights. If a privileged user grants certain access rights to PUBLIC, then everyone who can access the system gains those rights.

It's a tough job, but. . . .

You're probably wondering how you can become a DBA (database administrator) and accrue for yourself all the status and admiration that goes with the title. The obvious answer is to kiss up to the boss in the hope of landing this plum assignment. Demonstrating competence, integrity, and reliability in the performance of your everyday duties may help. (Actually, the key requisite is that you're sucker enough to take the job. I was kidding when I said that stuff about status and admiration. Mostly, the DBA gets the blame if anything goes wrong with the database — and invariably, something does.) It helps to have the fortitude of a superhero, even if you don't have the cape and boots.

In most installations, a hierarchy of user privilege exists, in which the DBA stands at the highest level and the public at the lowest. Figure 13-1 illustrates the privilege hierarchy.

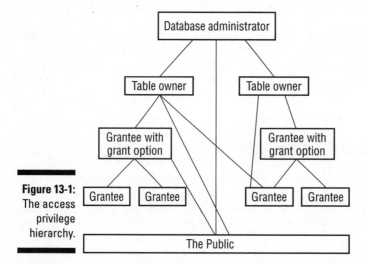

Figure 13-1: The access privilege hierarchy.

Granting Privileges to Users

The DBA, by virtue of his or her position, has all privileges on all objects in the database. After all, the owner of an object has all privileges with respect to that object — and the database itself is an object. No one else has any privileges with respect to any object, unless someone who already has those privileges (and the authority to pass them on) specifically grants the privileges. You grant privileges to someone by using the GRANT statement, which has the following syntax:

```
GRANT privilege-list
   ON object
   TO user-list
   [WITH GRANT OPTION] ;
```

In this statement, *privilege-list* is defined as follows:

```
privilege [, privilege] ...
```

or

```
ALL PRIVILEGES
```

Here *privilege* is defined as follows:

```
SELECT
 | DELETE
 | INSERT [(column-name [, column-name]...)]
 | UPDATE [(column-name [, column-name]...)]
 | REFERENCES [(column-name [, column-name]...)]
 | USAGE
 | UNDER
 | TRIGGER
 | EXECUTE
```

In the original statement, *object* is defined as follows:

```
[ TABLE ] <table name>
 | DOMAIN <domain name>
 | COLLATION <collation name>
 | CHARACTER SET <character set name>
 | TRANSLATION <transliteration name>
 | TYPE <schema-resolved user-defined type name>
 | SEQUENCE <sequence generator name>
 | <specific routine designator>
```

And *user-list* in the statement is defined as follows:

```
   login-ID [, login-ID]...
 | PUBLIC
```

The preceding syntax considers a view to be a table. The SELECT, DELETE, INSERT, UPDATE, TRIGGER, and REFERENCES privileges apply to tables and views only. The USAGE privilege applies to domains, character sets, collations, and translations. The UNDER privilege applies only to types, and the EXECUTE privilege applies only to routines. The following sections give examples of the various ways you can use the GRANT statement and the results of those uses.

Roles

A *user name* is one type of authorization identifier, but it's not the only one. It identifies a person (or a program) who is authorized to perform one or more functions on a database. In a large organization with many users, granting privileges to every individual employee can be tedious and time-consuming. SQL addresses this problem by introducing the notion of roles.

A *role,* identified by a role name, is a set of zero or more privileges that can be granted to multiple people who all require the same level of access to the database. For example, everyone who performs the role SecurityGuard has the same privileges. These privileges are different from those granted to the people who have the role SalesClerk.

As always, not every feature mentioned in the latest version of the SQL specification is available in every implementation. Check your DBMS documentation before you try to use roles.

You can create roles by using syntax similar to the following:

```
CREATE ROLE SalesClerk ;
```

After you've created a role, you can assign people to the role with the GRANT statement, similar to the following:

```
GRANT SalesClerk to Becky ;
```

You can grant privileges to a role in exactly the same way that you grant privileges to users, with one exception: It won't argue or complain.

Inserting data

To grant a role the privilege of adding data to a table, follow this example:

```
GRANT INSERT
   ON CUSTOMER
   TO SalesClerk ;
```

This privilege enables any clerk in the sales department to add new customer records to the CUSTOMER table.

Looking at data

To enable people to view the data in a table, use the following example:

```
GRANT SELECT
   ON PRODUCT
   TO PUBLIC ;
```

This privilege enables anyone with access to the system (PUBLIC) to view the contents of the PRODUCT table.

This statement can be dangerous. Columns in the PRODUCT table may contain information that not everyone should see, such as CostOfGoods. To provide access to most information while withholding access to sensitive information, define a view on the table that doesn't include the sensitive columns. Then grant SELECT privileges on the view rather than the underlying table. The following example shows the syntax for this procedure:

```
CREATE VIEW MERCHANDISE AS
   SELECT Model, ProdName, ProdDesc, ListPrice
      FROM PRODUCT ;
GRANT SELECT
   ON MERCHANDISE
   TO PUBLIC ;
```

Using the MERCHANDISE view, the public doesn't get to see the PRODUCT table's CostOfGoods column or any other column. The public sees only the four columns listed in the CREATE VIEW statement.

Modifying table data

In any active organization, table data changes over time. You need to grant to some people the right and power to make changes and to prevent everyone else from doing so. To grant change privileges, follow this example:

```
GRANT UPDATE (BonusPct)
   ON BONUSRATE
   TO SalesMgr ;
```

The sales manager can adjust the bonus rate that salespeople receive for sales (the BonusPct column), based on changes in market conditions. However, the sales manager can't modify the values in the MinAmount and MaxAmount columns that define the ranges for each step in the bonus schedule. To enable updates to all columns, you must specify either all column names or no column names, as shown in the following example:

```
GRANT UPDATE
   ON BONUSRATE
   TO VPSales ;
```

Deleting obsolete rows from a table

Customers go out of business or stop buying products for some other reason. Employees quit, retire, are laid off, or die. Products become obsolete. Life goes on, and things that you tracked in the past may no longer be of interest. Someone needs to remove obsolete records from your tables. You want to carefully control who can remove which records. Regulating such privileges is another job for the GRANT statement, as shown in the following example:

```
GRANT DELETE
   ON EMPLOYEE
   TO PersonnelMgr ;
```

The personnel manager can remove records from the EMPLOYEE table. So can the DBA and the EMPLOYEE table owner (who's probably also the DBA). No one else can remove personnel records (unless another GRANT statement gives that person the power to do so).

Referencing related tables

If one table includes a second table's primary key as a foreign key, information in the second table becomes available to users of the first table. This situation potentially creates a dangerous back door through which unauthorized users can extract confidential information. In such a case, a user doesn't need access rights to a table to discover something about its contents. If the user has access rights to a table that references the target table, those rights often enable the user to access the target table as well.

Suppose, for example, that the table LAYOFF_LIST contains the names of the employees who will be laid off next month. Only authorized management has SELECT access to the table. An unauthorized employee, however, deduces that the table's primary key is EmpID. The employee then creates a new table SNOOP, which has EmpID as a foreign key, enabling him to sneak a peek at LAYOFF_LIST. (I describe how to create a foreign key with a REFERENCES clause in Chapter 5. It's high on the list of techniques every system administrator should know.)

```
CREATE TABLE SNOOP
   (EmpID INTEGER REFERENCES LAYOFF_LIST) ;
```

Now all that the employee needs to do is try to INSERT rows corresponding to all employee ID numbers into SNOOP. The table accepts the inserts for only the employees on the layoff list. All rejected inserts are for employees not on the list.

All is not lost. You aren't at risk of exposing all private data you want to keep to yourself. The latest version of SQL prevents this security breach by requiring privileged users to explicitly grant any reference rights to other users, as shown in the following example:

```
GRANT REFERENCES (EmpID)
    ON LAYOFF_LIST
    TO PERSONNEL_CLERK ;
```

Using domains, character sets, collations, and translations

Domains, character sets, collations, and translations also have an effect on security issues. You must closely watch created domains, in particular, to avoid them being used to undermine your security measures.

You can define a domain that encompasses a set of columns. In doing so, you want all these columns to have the same type and to share the same constraints. The columns you create in your CREATE DOMAIN inherit the type and constraints of the domain. You can override these characteristics for specific columns, if you want, but domains provide a convenient way to apply numerous characteristics to multiple columns with a single declaration.

Domains come in handy if you have multiple tables that contain columns with similar characteristics. Your business database, for example, may consist of several tables, each of which contains a Price column that should have a type of DECIMAL(10,2) and values that aren't negative and are no greater than 10,000. Before you create tables that hold these columns, create a domain that specifies the columns' characteristics, like this:

```
CREATE DOMAIN PriceTypeDomain  DECIMAL (10,2)
    CHECK (Price >= 0 AND Price <= 10000) ;
```

Perhaps you identify your products in multiple tables by ProductCode, which is always of type CHAR (5), with a first character of X, C, or H and a last character of either 9 or 0. You can create a domain for these columns, too, as in the following example:

```
CREATE DOMAIN ProductCodeDomain CHAR (5)
    CHECK (SUBSTR (VALUE, 1,1) IN ('X', 'C', 'H')
    AND SUBSTR (VALUE, 5, 1) IN (9, 0) ) ;
```

With the domains in place, you can now proceed to create tables, as follows:

```
CREATE TABLE PRODUCT
   (ProductCode ProductCodeDomain,
   ProductName CHAR (30),
   Price PriceTypeDomain) ;
```

In the table definition, instead of giving the data type for `ProductCode` and `Price`, specify the appropriate domain. This action gives those columns the correct type and also applies the constraints you specify in your `CREATE DOMAIN` statements.

When you use domains, you open up your database to certain security implications. What if someone wants to use the domains you create — can this cause problems? Yes. What if someone creates a table with a column that has a domain of `PriceTypeDomain`? That person can assign progressively larger values to that column until it rejects a value. By doing so, the user can determine the upper bound on `PriceType` that you specify in the `CHECK` clause of your `CREATE DOMAIN` statement. If you consider that upper bound private information, you don't want others to access the `PriceType` domain. To protect tables in such situations, SQL allows only those to whom the domain owner explicitly grants permission to use domains. Thus, only the domain owner (as well as the DBA) can grant such permission. After you deem that it's safe to do so, you can grant users permission by using a statement such as the one shown in the following example:

```
GRANT USAGE ON DOMAIN PriceType TO SalesMgr ;
```

Different security problems may arise if you `DROP` domains. Tables that contain columns that you define in terms of a domain cause problems if you try to `DROP` the domain. You may need to `DROP` all such tables first. Or you may find yourself unable to `DROP` the domain. How a domain `DROP` is handled may vary from one implementation to another. SQL Server may do it one way, whereas Oracle does it another way. At any rate, you may want to restrict who can `DROP` domains. The same applies to character sets, collations, and translations.

Causing SQL statements to be executed

Sometimes the execution of one SQL statement triggers the execution of another SQL statement, or even a block of statements. SQL supports triggers. A *trigger* specifies a trigger event, a trigger action time, and one or more triggered actions:

✔ The *trigger event* causes the trigger to execute, or fire.

✔ The *trigger action time* determines when the triggered action occurs, either just before or just after the trigger event.

✔ The *triggered action* is the execution of one or more SQL statements.

If more than one SQL statement is triggered, the statements must all be contained within a BEGIN ATOMIC...END structure. The trigger event can be an INSERT, UPDATE, or DELETE statement.

For example, you can use a trigger to execute a statement that checks the validity of a new value before an UPDATE is allowed. If the new value is found to be invalid, the update can be aborted.

A user or role must have the TRIGGER privilege in order to create a trigger. An example might be:

```
CREATE TRIGGER CustomerDelete BEFORE DELETE
     ON CUSTOMER FOR EACH ROW
     WHEN State = NY
     INSERT INTO CUSTLOG VALUES ('deleted a NY customer') ;
```

Whenever a New York customer is deleted from the CUSTOMERS table, an entry in the log table CUSTLOG will record the deletion.

Granting the Power to Grant Privileges

The DBA can grant any privileges to anyone. An object owner can grant any privileges on that object to anyone. But users who receive privileges this way can't in turn grant those privileges to someone else. This restriction helps the DBA or table owner retain control. Only users that the DBA or object owner empowers to do so can gain access to the object in question.

From a security standpoint, putting limits on the capability to delegate access privileges makes a lot of sense. Many occasions arise, however, in which users need the power to delegate their authority. Work can't come to a screeching halt every time someone is ill, on vacation, or out to lunch.

You can trust *some* users with the power to delegate their access rights to reliable designated alternates. To pass such a right of delegation to a user, the GRANT uses the WITH GRANT OPTION clause. The following statement shows one example of how you can use this clause:

```
GRANT UPDATE (BonusPct)
   ON BONUSRATE
   TO SalesMgr
   WITH GRANT OPTION ;
```

Now the sales manager can delegate the UPDATE privilege by issuing the following statement:

```
GRANT UPDATE (BonusPct)
   ON BONUSRATE
   TO AsstSalesMgr ;
```

After the execution of this statement, the assistant sales manager can make changes to the BonusPct column in the BONUSRATE table — a power she didn't have before.

Of course, you make a tradeoff between security and convenience when you delegate access rights to a designated alternate. The owner of the BONUSRATE table relinquishes considerable control in granting the UPDATE privilege to the sales manager by using the WITH GRANT OPTION. The table owner hopes that the sales manager takes this responsibility seriously and is careful about passing on the privilege.

Taking Privileges Away

If you have a way to give access privileges to people, you should also have a way of taking those privileges away. People's job functions change, and with these changes their data access needs change. Say an employee leaves the organization to join a competitor. You should probably revoke all the access privileges to that person immediately.

SQL allows you to remove access privileges by using the REVOKE statement. This statement acts like the GRANT statement does, except that it has the reverse effect. The syntax for this statement is as follows:

```
REVOKE [GRANT OPTION FOR] privilege-list
   ON object
   FROM user-list [RESTRICT|CASCADE] ;
```

You can use this structure to revoke specified privileges while leaving others intact. The principal difference between the REVOKE statement and the GRANT statement is the presence of the optional RESTRICT or CASCADE keyword in the REVOKE statement.

For example, suppose you used WITH GRANT OPTION when you granted certain privileges to a user. Eventually, when you want to revoke those privileges, you can use CASCADE in the REVOKE statement. When you revoke a user's privileges in this way, you also yank privileges from anyone to whom that person had granted privileges.

On the other hand, the REVOKE statement with the RESTRICT option works only if the grantee *hasn't* delegated the specified privileges. In that case, the REVOKE statement revokes the grantee's privileges just fine. But if the grantee passed on the specified privileges, the REVOKE statement with the RESTRICT option doesn't revoke anything and instead returns an error code.

You can use a REVOKE statement with the optional GRANT OPTION FOR clause to revoke only the grant option for specified privileges while enabling the grantee to retain those privileges for himself. If the GRANT OPTION FOR clause and the CASCADE keyword are both present, you revoke all privileges that the grantee granted, along with the grantee's right to bestow such privileges — as if you'd never granted the grant option in the first place. If the GRANT OPTION FOR clause and the RESTRICT clause are both present, one of two things happens:

- ✔ If the grantee didn't grant to anyone else any of the privileges you're revoking, then the REVOKE statement executes and removes the grantee's ability to grant privileges.

- ✔ If the grantee has already granted at least one of the privileges you're revoking, the REVOKE statement doesn't execute and returns an error code instead.

The fact that you can grant privileges by using WITH GRANT OPTION, combined with the fact that you can also selectively revoke privileges, makes system security much more complex than it appears at first glance. Multiple grantors, for example, can conceivably grant a privilege to any single user. If one of those grantors then revokes the privilege, the user still retains that privilege because of the still-existing grant from another grantor. If a privilege passes from one user to another by way of the WITH GRANT OPTION, this situation creates a *chain of dependency,* in which one user's privileges depend on those of another user. If you're a DBA or object owner, always be aware that after you grant a privilege by using the WITH GRANT OPTION clause, that privilege may show up in unexpected places. Revoking the privilege from unwanted users while letting legitimate users retain the same privilege may prove challenging. In general, the GRANT OPTION and CASCADE clauses encompass numerous subtleties. If you use these clauses, check both the SQL standard and your product documentation carefully to ensure that you understand how the clauses work.

Using GRANT and REVOKE Together to Save Time and Effort

Enabling multiple privileges for multiple users on selected table columns may require a lot of typing. Consider this example: The vice president of sales wants everyone in the sales department to see everything in the CUSTOMER table. But only sales managers should update, delete, or insert rows. *Nobody* should update the CustID field. The sales managers' names are Tyson, Keith, and David. You can grant appropriate privileges to these managers with GRANT statements, as follows:

```
GRANT SELECT, INSERT, DELETE
    ON CUSTOMER
    TO Tyson, Keith, David ;
GRANT UPDATE
    ON CUSTOMER (Company, CustAddress, CustCity,
        CustState, CustZip, CustPhone, ModLevel)
    TO Tyson, Keith, David ;
GRANT SELECT
    ON CUSTOMER
    TO Jenny, Valerie, Melody, Neil, Robert, Sam,
        Brandon, MichelleT, Allison, Andrew,
        Scott, MichelleB, Jaime, Linleigh, Matthew, Amanda;
```

That should do the trick. Everyone has SELECT rights on the CUSTOMER table. The sales managers have full INSERT and DELETE rights on the table, and they can update any column but the CustID column.

Here's an easier way to get the same result:

```
GRANT SELECT
    ON CUSTOMER
    TO SalesReps ;
GRANT INSERT, DELETE, UPDATE
    ON CUSTOMER
    TO Tyson, Keith, David ;
REVOKE UPDATE
    ON CUSTOMER (CustID)
    FROM Tyson, Keith, David ;
```

You still take three statements in this example for the same protection of the three statements in the preceding example. No one may change data in the CustID column; only Tyson, Keith, and David have INSERT, DELETE, and UPDATE privileges. These latter three statements are significantly shorter than those in the preceding example because you don't name all the users in the sales department and all the columns in the table. (The time you spend typing names is also significantly shorter. That's the idea.)

Chapter 14

Protecting Data

· ·

In This Chapter

▶ Avoiding database damage

▶ Understanding the problems caused by concurrent operations

▶ Dealing with concurrency problems through SQL mechanisms

▶ Tailoring protection to your needs with SET TRANSACTION

▶ Protecting your data without paralyzing operations

· ·

*E*veryone has heard of Murphy's Law — usually stated, "If anything can go wrong, it will." People joke about this pseudo-law because most of the time things go fine. At times, you may feel lucky because you're untouched by one of the basic laws of the universe. When unexpected problems arise, you probably just recognize what has happened and deal with it.

In a complex structure, the potential for unanticipated problems shoots way up (a mathematician might say it "increases approximately as the square of the complexity"). Thus large software projects are almost always delivered late and are often loaded with bugs. A nontrivial, multiuser DBMS application is a large, complex structure. In the course of operation, many things can go wrong. Methods have been developed for minimizing the impact of these problems, but the problems can never be eliminated completely. This is good news for professional database maintenance and repair people, because automating them out of a job will probably never be possible. This chapter discusses the major things that can go wrong with a database and the tools that SQL provides for you to deal with the problems that arise.

Threats to Data Integrity

Cyberspace (including your network) is a nice place to visit, but for the data living there, it's no picnic. Data can be damaged or corrupted in a variety of ways. Chapter 5 discusses problems resulting from bad input data, operator error, and deliberate destruction. Poorly formulated SQL statements and improperly designed applications can also damage your data, and figuring out how doesn't take much imagination. Two relatively obvious threats — platform instability and equipment failure — can also trash your data. Both hazards are detailed in the following sections, as well as problems that can be caused by concurrent access.

Platform instability

Platform instability is a category of problem that shouldn't even exist, but alas, it does. It is most prevalent when you're running one or more new and relatively untried components in your system. Problems can lurk in a new DBMS release, a new operating system version, or new hardware. Conditions or situations that have never appeared before show up while you're running a critical job. Your system locks up, and your data is damaged. Beyond directing a few choice words at your computer and the people who built it, you can't do much except hope that your latest backup was a good one.

Never put important production work on a system that has *any* unproven components. Resist the temptation to put your bread-and-butter work on an untried beta release of the newest, most function-laden version of your DBMS or operating system. If you must gain some hands-on experience with a new software product, do so on a machine that is completely isolated from your production network.

Equipment failure

Even well-proven, highly reliable equipment fails sometimes, sending your data to the great beyond. Everything physical wears out eventually — even modern, solid-state computers. If such a failure happens while your database is open and active, you can lose data — and sometimes (even worse) not realize it. Such a failure will happen sooner or later. If Murphy's Law is in operation that day, the failure will happen at the worst possible time.

One way to protect data against equipment failure is *redundancy*. Keep extra copies of everything. For maximum safety (provided your organization can swing it financially), have duplicate hardware configured exactly like your production system. Have database and application backups that can be loaded and run on your backup hardware when needed. If cost constraints keep you from duplicating everything (which effectively doubles your costs), at least be sure to back up your database and applications frequently enough that an unexpected failure doesn't require you to reenter a large amount of data.

Another way to avoid the worst consequences of equipment failure is to use *transaction processing* — a topic that takes center stage later in this chapter. A *transaction* is an indivisible unit of work, so when you use transaction processing, either an entire transaction is executed or none of it is. This all-or-nothing approach may seem drastic, but the worst problems arise when a series of database operations is only partially processed. Thus, you are much less likely to lose or corrupt your data, even if the machine on which the database resides is crashing.

Concurrent access

Assume that you're running on proven hardware and software, your data is good, your application is bug-free, and your equipment is inherently reliable. Data utopia, right? Not quite. Problems can still arise when multiple people try to use the same database table at the same time *(concurrent access)* and their computers argue about who gets to go first *(contention)*. Multiple-user database systems must be able to handle the ruckus efficiently.

Transaction interaction trouble

Contention troubles can lurk even in applications that seem straightforward. Consider this example. You're writing an order-processing application that involves four tables: ORDER_MASTER, CUSTOMER, LINE_ITEM, and INVENTORY. The following conditions apply:

- The ORDER_MASTER table has `OrderNumber` as a primary key and `CustomerNumber` as a foreign key that references the CUSTOMER table.

- The LINE_ITEM table has `LineNumber` as a primary key, `ItemNumber` as a foreign key that references the INVENTORY table, and `Quantity` as one of its columns.

- The INVENTORY table has `ItemNumber` as a primary key; it also has a field named `QuantityOnHand`.

- All three tables have other columns, but they don't enter into this example.

Your company policy is to ship each order completely or not at all. No partial shipments or back orders are allowed. (Relax. It's a hypothetical situation.) You write the ORDER_PROCESSING application to process each incoming order in the ORDER_MASTER table as follows: It first determines whether your company can ship *all* the line items. If so, it writes the order and then decrements the `QuantityOnHand` column of the INVENTORY table as required. (This action deletes the affected entries from the ORDER_MASTER and LINE_ITEM tables.) So far, so good. You set up the application to process orders in one of two ways when users access the database concurrently:

- Method 1 processes the INVENTORY row that corresponds to each row in the LINE_ITEM table. If `QuantityOnHand` is large enough, the application decrements that field. If `QuantityOnHand` is not large enough, it rolls back the transaction to restore all inventory reductions made to other LINE_ITEMs in this order.

- Method 2 checks every INVENTORY row that corresponds to a row in the order's LINE_ITEMs. If they are *all* big enough, then it processes those items by decrementing them.

Usually, Method 1 is more efficient when you succeed in processing the order; Method 2 is more efficient when you fail. Thus, if most orders can be filled most of the time, you're better off using Method 1. If most orders can't be filled most of the time, you're better off with Method 2. Suppose this hypothetical application is up and running on a multiuser system that doesn't have adequate concurrency control. Yep. Trouble is brewing, all right. Consider this scenario:

1. **A customer contacts an order processor at your company (User 1) to order ten bolt cutters and five wide adjustable wrenches.**

2. **User 1 uses Method 1 to process the order. The first item in the order is ten pieces of Item 1 (bolt cutters).**

   As it happens, your company has ten bolt cutters in stock, and User 1's order takes them all.

   The order-processing function chugs along, decrementing the quantity of bolt cutters to zero. Then things get (as the Chinese proverb says) *interesting*. Another customer contacts your company to process an order and talks to User 2.

3. **User 2 attempts to process the customer's small order for one bolt cutter — and finds that there are no bolt cutters in stock.**

   User 2's order is rolled back because it can't be filled.

4. **Meanwhile, User 1 tries to complete his customer's order and checks the system for five pieces of Item 37 (wide adjustable wrenches).**

   Unfortunately, your company only has four wide adjustable wrenches in stock. User 1's complete order (including the bolt cutters) is rolled back because it can't be completely filled.

   The INVENTORY table is now back to the state it was in before either user started operating. Neither order has been filled, even though User 2's order could have been.

Method 2 fares no better, although for a different reason. User 1 checks all the items ordered and decides that all the items ordered *are* available. Then User 2 comes in and processes an order for one of those items *before* User 1 performs the decrement operation; User 1's transaction fails.

Serialization eliminates harmful interactions

No conflict occurs if transactions are executed *serially* rather than concurrently. (Taking turns — what a concept.) In the first example, if User 1's unsuccessful transaction was completed before User 2's transaction started, the ROLLBACK function would have made the single bolt cutter ordered by User 2 available. (The ROLLBACK function rolls back, or undoes the entire transaction.) If the transactions had run serially in the second example, User 2 would have had no opportunity to change the quantity of any item until User 1's transaction was complete. User 1's transaction completes, either successfully or unsuccessfully — and User 2 then sees how many bolt cutters are left in stock.

If transactions are executed serially, one after the other, they have no chance of interacting destructively. Execution of concurrent transactions is *serializable* if the result is the same as it would be if the transactions were executed serially.

Serializing concurrent transactions isn't a cure-all. You have to make a trade-off between performance and protection from harmful interactions. The more you isolate transactions from each other, the more time it takes to perform each function. (In cyberspace, as in real life, waiting in line takes time.) Be aware of the tradeoffs so you can configure your system for adequate protection — but not more protection than you need. Controlling concurrent access too tightly can kill overall system performance.

Reducing Vulnerability to Data Corruption

You can take precautions at several levels to reduce the chances of losing data through some mishap or unanticipated interaction. You can set up your DBMS to take some of these precautions for you. When you configure your DBMS appropriately, it acts like a guardian angel to protect you from harm, operating behind the scenes; you don't even know that the DBMS is helping you out. Your database administrator (DBA) can take other precautions at his or her discretion that you may not be aware of. As the developer, you can take precautions as you write your code.

To avoid a lot of grief, get into the habit of adhering to a few simple principles automatically so they are always included in your code or in your interactions with your database:

✔ Use SQL transactions.

✔ Tailor the level of isolation to balance performance and protection.

✔ Know when and how to set transactions, lock database objects, and perform backups.

Details coming right up.

Using SQL transactions

The transaction is one of SQL's main tools for maintaining database integrity. An *SQL transaction* encapsulates all the SQL statements that can have an effect on the database. An SQL transaction is completed with either a COMMIT or ROLLBACK statement:

- ✔ If the transaction finishes with a COMMIT, the effects of all the statements in the transaction are applied to the database in one rapid-fire sequence.
- ✔ If the transaction finishes with a ROLLBACK, the effects of all the statements are *rolled back* (that is, undone), and the database returns to the state it was in before the transaction began.

In this discussion, the term *application* means either an execution of a program (whether in COBOL, C, or some other programming language) or a series of actions performed at a terminal during a single logon.

An application can include a series of SQL transactions. The first SQL transaction begins when the application begins; the last SQL transaction ends when the application ends. Each COMMIT or ROLLBACK that the application performs ends one SQL transaction and begins the next. For example, an application with three SQL transactions has the following form:

```
Start of the application
    Various SQL statements (SQL transaction-1)
COMMIT or ROLLBACK
    Various SQL statements (SQL transaction-2)
COMMIT or ROLLBACK
    Various SQL statements (SQL transaction-3)
COMMIT or ROLLBACK
End of the application
```

I use the phrase *SQL transaction* because the application may be using other facilities (such as for network access) that do other sorts of transactions. In the following discussion, I use *transaction* to mean *SQL transaction* specifically.

A normal SQL transaction has an access mode that is either READ-WRITE or READ-ONLY; it has an isolation level that is SERIALIZABLE, REPEATABLE READ, READ COMMITTED, or READ UNCOMMITTED. (Find transaction characteristics in the "Isolation levels" section, later in this chapter.) The default characteristics are READ-WRITE and SERIALIZABLE. If you want any other characteristics, you have to specify them with a SET TRANSACTION statement such as the following:

```
SET TRANSACTION READ ONLY ;
```

or

```
SET TRANSACTION READ ONLY REPEATABLE READ ;
```

or

```
SET TRANSACTION READ COMMITTED ;
```

You can have multiple SET TRANSACTION statements in an application, but you can specify only one in each transaction — and it must be the first SQL statement executed in the transaction. If you want to use a SET TRANSACTION statement, execute it either at the beginning of the application or after a COMMIT or ROLLBACK. You must perform a SET TRANSACTION at the beginning of every transaction for which you want nondefault properties, because each new transaction after a COMMIT or ROLLBACK is automatically given the default properties.

A SET TRANSACTION statement can also specify a DIAGNOSTICS SIZE, which determines the number of error conditions for which the implementation should be prepared to save information. (Such a numerical limit is necessary because an implementation can detect more than one error during a statement.) The SQL default for this limit is implementation-defined, and that default is almost always adequate.

The default transaction

The default SQL transaction has characteristics that are satisfactory for most users most of the time. If necessary, you can specify different transaction characteristics with a SET TRANSACTION statement, as described in the previous section. (SET TRANSACTION gets its own spotlight treatment later in the chapter.)

The default transaction makes a few other implicit assumptions:

- ✔ The database will change over time.
- ✔ It's always better to be safe than sorry.

It sets the mode to READ-WRITE, which, as you may expect, enables you to issue statements that change the database. It also sets the isolation level to SERIALIZABLE, which is the highest level of isolation possible (thus the safest). The default diagnostics size is implementation-dependent. Look at your SQL documentation to see what that size is for your system.

Isolation levels

Ideally, the system handles your transactions independently from every other transaction, even if those transactions happen concurrently with yours. This concept is referred to as *isolation*. In the real world, however, complete isolation is not always feasible. Isolation may exact too large a performance penalty. A tradeoff question arises: "How much isolation do you really want, and how much are you willing to pay for it in terms of performance?"

Getting mucked up by a dirty read

The weakest level of isolation is called READ UNCOMMITTED, which allows the sometimes-problematic dirty read. A *dirty read* is a situation in which a change made by one user can be read by a second user before the first user completes her transaction with a COMMIT statement.

The problem arises when the first user aborts and rolls back the transaction. The second user's subsequent operations are now based on an incorrect value. The classic example of this foul-up can appear in an inventory application. In "Transaction interaction trouble," earlier in this chapter, I outline one possible scenario of this type, but here's another example: One user decrements inventory; a second user reads the new (lower) value. The first user rolls back her transaction (restoring the inventory to its initial value), but the second user, thinking inventory is low, orders more stock and possibly creates a severe overstock. And that's if you're lucky.

Don't use the READ UNCOMMITTED isolation level unless you don't care about accurate results.

You *can* use READ UNCOMMITTED if you want to generate approximate statistical data, such as:

- ✔ Maximum delay in filling orders
- ✔ Average age of salespeople who don't make quota
- ✔ Average age of new employees

In many such cases, approximate information is sufficient; the extra (performance) cost of the concurrency control required to give an exact result may not be worthwhile.

Getting bamboozled by a nonrepeatable read

The next highest level of isolation is READ COMMITTED: A change made by another transaction isn't visible to your transaction until the other user has finalized the other transaction with the COMMIT statement. This level gives you a better result than you can get from READ UNCOMMITTED, but it's still subject to a *nonrepeatable read* — a serious problem that happens like a comedy of errors.

Consider the classic inventory example: User 1 queries the database to see how many items of a particular product are in stock. The number is ten. At almost the same time, User 2 starts, and then finalizes, a transaction with the COMMIT statement that records an order for ten units of that same product, decrementing the inventory to zero. Now User 1, having seen that ten are available, tries to order five of them. Five are no longer left, however, because User 2 has raided the pantry. User 1's initial read of the quantity available is not repeatable. Because the quantity has changed out from under User 1, any assumptions made on the basis of the initial read are not valid.

Risking the phantom read

An isolation level of REPEATABLE READ guarantees that the nonrepeatable-read problem doesn't happen. This isolation level, however, is still haunted by the *phantom read* — a problem that arises when the data a user is reading changes in response to another transaction (and does not show the change on-screen) *while the user is reading it.*

Suppose, for example, that User 1 issues a command whose search condition (the WHERE clause or HAVING clause) selects a set of rows, and, immediately afterward, User 2 performs and commits an operation that changes the data in some of those rows. Those data items met User 1's search condition at the start of this snafu, but now they no longer do. Maybe some other rows that first did *not* meet the original search condition now *do* meet it. User 1, whose transaction is still active, has no inkling of these changes; the application behaves as if nothing has happened. The hapless User 1 issues another SQL statement with the same search conditions as the original one, expecting to retrieve the same rows. Instead, the second operation is performed on rows other than those used in the first operation. Reliable results go out the window, spirited away by the phantom read.

Getting a reliable (if slower) read

An isolation level of SERIALIZABLE is not subject to any of the problems that beset the other three levels. At this level, concurrent transactions can be run without interfering with each other, and results are the same as they would be if the transactions had been run serially — one after the other — rather than in parallel. If you're running at this isolation level, hardware or software problems can still cause your transaction to fail, but at least you don't have to worry about the validity of your results if you know that your system is functioning properly.

Of course, superior reliability may come at the price of slower performance, so we're back in Tradeoff City. Table 14-1 sums up the tradeoff terms, showing the four isolation levels and the problems they solve.

Table 14-1	Isolation Levels and Problems Solved
Isolation Level	*Problems Solved*
READ UNCOMMITTED	None
READ COMMITTED	Dirty read
REPEATABLE READ	Dirty read
	Nonrepeatable read
SERIALIZABLE	Dirty read
	Nonrepeatable read
	Phantom read

The implicit transaction-starting statement

Some SQL implementations require that you signal the beginning of a transaction with an explicit statement, such as BEGIN or BEGIN TRAN. SQL does not. If you don't have an active transaction and you issue a statement that calls for one, SQL starts a default transaction for you. CREATE TABLE, SELECT, and UPDATE are examples of statements that require the context of a transaction. Issue one of these statements, and SQL starts a transaction for you.

SET TRANSACTION

On occasion, you may want to use transaction characteristics that are different from those set by default. You can specify different characteristics with a SET TRANSACTION statement before you issue your first statement that actually requires a transaction. The SET TRANSACTION statement enables you to specify mode, isolation level, and diagnostics size.

To change all three, for example, you may issue the following statement:

```
SET TRANSACTION
    READ ONLY,
    ISOLATION LEVEL READ UNCOMMITTED,
    DIAGNOSTICS SIZE 4 ;
```

With these settings, you can't issue any statements that change the database (READ ONLY), and you have set the lowest and most hazardous isolation level (READ UNCOMMITTED). The diagnostics area has a size of 4. You are making minimal demands on system resources.

In contrast, you may issue this statement:

```
SET TRANSACTION
    READ WRITE,
    ISOLATION LEVEL SERIALIZABLE,
    DIAGNOSTICS SIZE 8 ;
```

These settings enable you to change the database, give you the highest level of isolation, and give you a larger diagnostics area. They also make larger demands on system resources. Depending on your implementation, these settings may turn out to be the same as those used by the default transaction. Naturally, you can issue SET TRANSACTION statements with other choices for isolation level and diagnostics size.

Set your transaction isolation level as high as you need to, but no higher. Always setting your isolation level to SERIALIZABLE just to be on the safe side may seem reasonable, but it isn't so for all systems. Depending on your implementation and what you're doing, you may not need to do so, and performance can suffer significantly if you do. If you don't intend to change the database in your transaction, for example, set the mode to READ ONLY. Bottom line: Don't tie up any system resources that you don't need.

COMMIT

Although SQL doesn't require an explicit transaction-starting keyword, it has two that terminate a transaction: COMMIT and ROLLBACK. Use COMMIT when you have come to the end of the transaction and you want to make permanent the changes that you have made to the database (if any). You may include the optional keyword WORK (COMMIT WORK) if you want. If the database encounters an error or the system crashes while a COMMIT is in progress, you may have to roll the transaction back and try it again.

ROLLBACK

When you come to the end of a transaction, you may decide that you don't want to make permanent the changes that have occurred during the transaction. In fact, you should restore the database to the state it was in before the transaction began. To do this, issue a ROLLBACK statement. ROLLBACK is a fail-safe mechanism.

Even if the system crashes while a ROLLBACK is in progress, you can restart the ROLLBACK after you restore the system; the rollback will continue its work, restoring the database to its pretransaction state.

Locking database objects

The isolation level set either by default or by a SET TRANSACTION statement tells the DBMS how zealous to be in protecting your work from interaction with the work of other users. The main protection from harmful transactions that the DBMS gives to you is its application of locks to the database objects you're using. Here are a few examples:

- ✔ The table row you're accessing is locked, preventing others from accessing that record while you're using it.

- ✔ An entire table is locked, if you're performing an operation that could affect the whole table.

- ✔ Reading, but not writing, is allowed. Sometimes, writing is allowed, but not reading.

Each implementation handles locking in its own way. Some implementations are more bulletproof than others, but most up-to-date systems protect you from the worst problems that can arise in a concurrent-access situation.

TECHNICAL STUFF

Having an ACID database

You may hear database designers say they want their databases to have ACID. Well, no, they're not planning to zonk their creations with a 1960s psychedelic, or dissolve the data they contain into a bubbly mess. ACID is simply an acronym for Atomicity, Consistency, Isolation, and Durability. These four characteristics are necessary to protect a database from corruption:

- ✔ **Atomicity:** Database transactions should be atomic, in the classic sense of the word: The entire transaction is treated as an indivisible unit. Either it is executed in its entirety (committed), or the database is restored (rolled back) to the state it would have been in if the transaction had not been executed.

- ✔ **Consistency:** Oddly enough, the meaning of *consistency* is not consistent; it varies from one application to another. When you transfer funds from one account to another in a banking application, for example, you want the total amount of money in both accounts

at the end of the transaction to be the same as it was at the beginning of the transaction. In a different application, your criterion for consistency might be different.

- ✔ **Isolation:** Ideally, database transactions should be totally isolated from other transactions that execute at the same time. If the transactions are serializable, then total isolation is achieved. If the system has to process transactions at top speed, sometimes lower levels of isolation can enhance performance.

- ✔ **Durability:** After a transaction has committed or rolled back, you should be able to count on the database being in the proper state: well stocked with uncorrupted, reliable, up-to-date data. Even if your system suffers a hard crash after a commit — but before the transaction is stored to disk — a durable DBMS can guarantee that upon recovery from the crash, the database can be restored to its proper state.

Backing up your data

Backing up data is a protective action that your DBA should perform on a regular basis. All system elements should be backed up at intervals that depend on how frequently they're updated. If your database is updated daily, it should be backed up daily. Your applications, forms, and reports may change, too, though less frequently. Whenever you make changes to them, your DBA should back up the new versions.

Keep several generations of backups. Sometimes, database damage doesn't become evident until some time has passed. To return to the last good version, you may have to go back several backup versions.

You can perform a backup in one of several different ways:

✔ Use SQL to create backup tables and copy data into them.

✔ Use an implementation-defined mechanism that backs up the whole database or portions of it. This mechanism is generally more convenient and efficient than using SQL.

✔ Your installation may have a mechanism in place for backing up everything, including databases, programs, documents, spreadsheets, utilities, and computer games. If so, you may not have to do anything beyond assuring yourself that the backups are performed frequently enough to protect you.

Savepoints and subtransactions

Ideally, transactions should be atomic — as indivisible as the ancient Greeks thought atoms were. However, atoms are not really indivisible, and starting with SQL:1999, database transactions are not really atomic. A transaction is divisible into multiple *subtransactions*. Each subtransaction is terminated by a SAVEPOINT statement. The SAVEPOINT statement is used in conjunction with the ROLLBACK statement. Before the introduction of *savepoints* (the point in the program where the SAVEPOINT statement takes effect), the ROLLBACK statement could be used only to cancel an entire transaction. Now it can be used to roll back a transaction to a savepoint within the transaction. What good is this, you might ask?

Granted, the primary use of the ROLLBACK statement is to prevent data corruption if a transaction is interrupted by an error condition. And no, rolling back to a savepoint does not make sense if an error occurred while a transaction was in progress; you'd want to roll back the *entire* transaction to bring the database back to the state it was in before the transaction started. But you might have other reasons for rolling back part of a transaction.

Say you're performing a complex series of operations on your data. Partway through the process, you receive results that lead you to conclude that you're going down an unproductive path. If you put a SAVEPOINT statement just before you started on that path, you can roll back to the savepoint and try another option. Provided the rest of your code was in good shape before you set the savepoint, this approach works better than aborting the current transaction and starting a new one just to try a new path.

To insert a savepoint into your SQL code, use the following syntax:

```
SAVEPOINT  savepoint_name ;
```

You can cause execution to roll back to that savepoint with code such as the following:

```
ROLLBACK TO SAVEPOINT savepoint_name ;
```

Some SQL implementations may not include the SAVEPOINT statement. If your implementation is one of those, you won't be able to use it.

Constraints Within Transactions

Ensuring the validity of the data in your database means doing more than just making sure the data is of the right type. Perhaps some columns, for example, should never hold a null value — and maybe others should hold only values that fall within a certain range. Such restrictions are *constraints,* as discussed in Chapter 5.

Constraints are relevant to transactions because they can conceivably prevent you from doing what you want. For example, suppose that you want to add data to a table that contains a column with a NOT NULL constraint. One common method of adding a record is to append a blank row to your table and then insert values into it later. The NOT NULL constraint on one column, however, causes the append operation to fail. SQL doesn't allow you to add a row that has a null value in a column with a NOT NULL constraint, even though you plan to add data to that column before your transaction ends. To address this problem, SQL enables you to designate constraints as either DEFERRABLE or NOT DEFERRABLE.

Constraints that are NOT DEFERRABLE are applied immediately. You can set DEFERRABLE constraints to be either initially DEFERRED or IMMEDIATE. If a DEFERRABLE constraint is set to IMMEDIATE, it acts like a NOT DEFERRABLE constraint — it is applied immediately. If a DEFERRABLE constraint is set to DEFERRED, it is not enforced. (No, your code doesn't have an attitude problem; it's simply following orders.)

To append blank records or perform other operations that may violate DEFERRABLE constraints, you can use a statement similar to the following:

```
SET CONSTRAINTS ALL DEFERRED ;
```

This statement puts all DEFERRABLE constraints in the DEFERRED condition. It does not affect the NOT DEFERRABLE constraints. After you have performed all operations that could violate your constraints, and the table reaches a state that doesn't violate them, you can reapply them. The statement that reapplies your constraints looks like this:

```
SET CONSTRAINTS ALL IMMEDIATE ;
```

If you made a mistake and any of your constraints are still being violated, you find out as soon as this statement takes effect.

If you do not explicitly set your DEFERRED constraints to IMMEDIATE, SQL does it for you when you attempt to COMMIT your transaction. If a violation is still present at that time, the transaction does not COMMIT; instead, SQL gives you an error message.

SQL's handling of constraints protects you from entering invalid data (or an invalid *absence* of data — which is just as important) while giving you the flexibility to violate constraints temporarily while a transaction is still active.

Consider a payroll example to see why being able to defer the application of constraints is important.

Assume that an EMPLOYEE table has columns EmpNo, EmpName, DeptNo, and Salary. EMPLOYEE.DeptNo is a foreign key referencing the DEPT table. Assume also that the DEPT table has columns DeptNo and DeptName. DeptNo is the primary key.

In addition, you want to have a table like DEPT that also contains a Payroll column that holds the sum of the Salary values for employees in each department.

You can create the equivalent of this table with the following view:

```
CREATE VIEW DEPT2 AS
    SELECT D.*, SUM(E.Salary) AS Payroll
        FROM DEPT D, EMPLOYEE E
        WHERE D.DeptNo = E.DeptNo
        GROUP BY D.DeptNo ;
```

You can also define this same view as follows:

```
CREATE VIEW DEPT3 AS
   SELECT D.*,
      (SELECT SUM(E.Salary)
         FROM EMPLOYEE E
         WHERE D.DeptNo = E.DeptNo) AS Payroll
      FROM DEPT D ;
```

But suppose that, for efficiency, you don't want to calculate the SUM every time you reference DEPT3.Payroll. Instead, you want to store an actual Payroll column in the DEPT table. You will then update that column every time you change a Salary.

To make sure that the Salary column is accurate, you can include a CONSTRAINT in the table definition:

```
CREATE TABLE DEPT
   (DeptNo CHAR(5),
   DeptName CHAR(20),
   Payroll DECIMAL(15,2),
   CHECK (Payroll = (SELECT SUM(Salary)
            FROM EMPLOYEE E
            WHERE E.DeptNo= DEPT.DeptNo)));
```

Now, suppose that you want to increase the Salary of employee 123 by 100. You can do it with the following update:

```
UPDATE EMPLOYEE
   SET Salary = Salary + 100
   WHERE EmpNo = '123' ;
```

And you must remember to do the following as well:

```
UPDATE DEPT D
   SET Payroll = Payroll + 100
   WHERE D.DeptNo = (SELECT E.DeptNo
            FROM EMPLOYEE E
            WHERE E.EmpNo = '123') ;
```

(You use the subquery to reference the DeptNo of employee 123.)

But there's a problem: Constraints are checked after each statement. In principle, *all* constraints are checked. In practice, implementations check only the constraints that reference the values modified by the statement.

After the first preceding UPDATE statement, the implementation checks all constraints that reference values that the statement modifies. This includes the constraint defined in the DEPT table, because that constraint references the Salary column of the EMPLOYEE table and the UPDATE statement is modifying that column. After the first UPDATE statement, that constraint is violated. You assume that before you execute the UPDATE statement the database is correct, and each Payroll value in the DEPT table equals the sum of the Salary values in the corresponding columns of the EMPLOYEE table. When the first UPDATE statement increases a Salary value, this equality is no longer true. The second UPDATE statement corrects this and again leaves the database values in a state for which the constraint is True. Between the two updates, the constraint is False.

The SET CONSTRAINTS DEFERRED statement lets you temporarily disable or *suspend* all constraints, or only specified constraints. The constraints are deferred until either you execute a SET CONSTRAINTS IMMEDIATE statement, or you execute a COMMIT or ROLLBACK statement. So you surround the previous two UPDATE statements with SET CONSTRAINTS statements. The code looks like this:

```
SET CONSTRAINTS DEFERRED ;
UPDATE EMPLOYEE
   SET Salary = Salary + 100
   WHERE EmpNo = '123' ;
UPDATE DEPT D
   SET Payroll = Payroll + 100
   WHERE D.DeptNo = (SELECT E.DeptNo
             FROM EMPLOYEE E
   WHERE E.EmpNo = '123') ;
SET CONSTRAINTS IMMEDIATE ;
```

This procedure defers all constraints. If you insert new rows into DEPT, the primary keys won't be checked; you have removed protection that you may want to keep. Instead, you should specify the constraints that you want to defer. To do this, name the constraints when you create them:

```
CREATE TABLE DEPT
   (DeptNo CHAR(5),
   DeptName CHAR(20),
   Payroll DECIMAL(15,2),
   CONSTRAINT PayEqSumsal
   CHECK (Payroll = SELECT SUM(Salary)
   FROM EMPLOYEE E     WHERE E.DeptNo = DEPT.DeptNo)) ;
```

With constraint names in place, you can then reference your constraints individually:

```
SET CONSTRAINTS PayEqSumsal DEFERRED;
UPDATE EMPLOYEE
    SET Salary = Salary + 100
    WHERE EmpNo = '123' ;
UPDATE DEPT D
    SET Payroll = Payroll + 100
    WHERE D.DeptNo = (SELECT E.DeptNo
                      FROM EMPLOYEE E
                      WHERE E.EmpNo = '123') ;
SET CONSTRAINTS PayEqSumsal IMMEDIATE;
```

Without a constraint name in the CREATE statement, SQL generates one implicitly. That implicit name is in the schema information (catalog) tables. But specifying the names explicitly is more straightforward.

Now suppose that in the second UPDATE statement you mistakenly specified an increment value of 1000. This value is allowed in the UPDATE statement because the constraint has been deferred. But when you execute SET CONSTRAINTS...IMMEDIATE, the specified constraints are checked. If they fail, SET CONSTRAINTS raises an exception. If, instead of a SET CONSTRAINTS...IMMEDIATE statement, you execute COMMIT and the constraints are found to be False, COMMIT instead performs a ROLLBACK.

Bottom line: You can defer the constraints only *within* a transaction. When the transaction is terminated by a ROLLBACK or a COMMIT, the constraints are both enabled and checked. The SQL capability of deferring constraints is meant to be used within a transaction. If used properly, the terminated transaction doesn't create any data that violates a constraint available to other transactions.

Chapter 15

Using SQL within Applications

In This Chapter

▶ Using SQL within an application

▶ Combining SQL with procedural languages

▶ Avoiding interlanguage incompatibilities

▶ Embedding SQL in your procedural code

▶ Calling SQL modules from your procedural code

▶ Invoking SQL from a RAD tool

*P*revious chapters address SQL statements mostly in isolation. For example, questions are asked about data, and SQL queries are developed that retrieve answers to the questions. This mode of operation, *interactive SQL,* is fine for discovering what SQL can do, but that's not how SQL is typically used.

Even though SQL syntax can be described as similar to English, it isn't an easy language to master. The overwhelming majority of computer users are not fluent in SQL. You can reasonably assume that the overwhelming majority of computer users will never be fluent in SQL, even if this book is wildly successful. When a database question comes up, Joe User probably won't sit down at his terminal and enter an SQL SELECT statement to find the answer. Systems analysts and application developers are the people who are likely to be comfortable with SQL, and they typically don't make a career out of entering ad hoc queries into databases. Instead, they develop applications to make those queries.

If you plan to perform the same operation repeatedly, you shouldn't have to rebuild it every time from the console. Write an application to do the job and then run it as often as you like. SQL can be a part of an application, but when it is, it works a little differently than it does in an interactive mode.

SQL in an Application

In Chapter 2, SQL is presented to you as an incomplete programming language. To use SQL in an application, you have to combine it with a *procedural* language such as Visual Basic, C, C++, C#, Java, or COBOL. Because of the way it's structured, SQL has some strengths and weaknesses. Procedural languages are structured differently than SQL, and consequently have *different* strengths and weaknesses.

Happily, the strengths of SQL tend to make up for the weaknesses of procedural languages, and the strengths of the procedural languages are in those areas where SQL is weak. By combining the two, you can build powerful applications with a broad range of capabilities. Recently, *object-oriented rapid application development* (RAD) tools, such as Borland's Delphi, JBuilder, C#Builder, and C++Builder, have appeared, which incorporate SQL code into applications developed by manipulating objects instead of writing procedural code.

Keeping an eye out for the asterisk

In the interactive SQL discussions in previous chapters, the asterisk is used (*) as a shorthand substitute for "all columns in the table." If the table has numerous columns, the asterisk can save a lot of typing. However, using the asterisk this way is problematic when you use SQL in an application program. After your application is written, you or someone else may add new columns to a table or delete old ones. Doing so changes the meaning of "all columns." When your application specifies "all columns" with an asterisk, it may retrieve columns other than those it thinks it's getting.

Such a change to a table doesn't affect existing programs until they have to be recompiled to fix a bug or make some change, perhaps months after the change was made. Then the effect of the * wildcard expands to include all the now-current columns. This change may cause the application to fail in a way unrelated to the bug fix (or other change made), creating your own personal debugging nightmare.

To be safe, specify all column names explicitly in an application instead of using the asterisk.

SQL strengths and weaknesses

SQL is strong in data retrieval. If important information is buried somewhere in a single-table or multitable database, SQL gives you the tools you need to retrieve it. You don't need to know the order of the table's rows or columns because SQL doesn't deal with rows or columns individually. The SQL transaction-processing facilities ensure that your database operations are unaffected by any other users who may be simultaneously accessing the same tables that you are.

A major weakness of SQL is its rudimentary user interface. It has no provision for formatting screens or reports. It accepts command lines from the keyboard and sends retrieved values to the terminal, one row at a time.

Sometimes a strength in one context is a weakness in another. One strength of SQL is that it can operate on an entire table at once. Whether the table has one row, a hundred rows, or a hundred thousand rows, a single SELECT statement can extract the data you want. SQL can't easily operate on one row of a multirow table at a time, however, and sometimes you do want to deal with each row individually. In such cases, you can use SQL's cursor facility, described in Chapter 18, or you can use a procedural host language.

Procedural language strengths and weaknesses

In contrast to SQL, procedural languages are designed for one-row-at-a-time operations, which give the application developer precise control over the way a table is processed. This detailed control is a great strength of procedural languages. But a corresponding weakness is that the application developer must have detailed knowledge about how the data is stored in the database tables. The order of the database's columns and rows is significant and must be taken into account.

Because of the step-by-step nature of procedural languages, they have the flexibility to produce user-friendly screens for data entry and viewing. You can also produce sophisticated printed reports, with any desired layout.

Problems in combining SQL with a procedural language

It makes sense to try to combine SQL and procedural languages in such a way that you can benefit from their mutual strengths and not be penalized by their combined weaknesses. As valuable as such a combination may be, you must overcome some challenges before you can practically achieve this perfect marriage.

Contrasting operating modes

A big problem in combining SQL with a procedural language is that SQL operates on tables a set at a time, whereas procedural languages work on them a row at a time. Sometimes this issue isn't a big deal. You can separate set operations from row operations, doing each with the appropriate tool.

But if you want to search a table for records meeting certain conditions and perform different operations on the records depending on whether they meet the conditions, you may have a problem. Such a process requires both the retrieval power of SQL and the branching capability of a procedural language. Embedded SQL gives you this combination of capabilities. You can simply *embed* SQL statements at strategic locations within a program that you have written in a conventional procedural language (see "Embedded SQL," later in this chapter, for more information).

Data type incompatibilities

Another hurdle to the smooth integration of SQL with any procedural language is that SQL's data types differ from the data types of all the major procedural languages. This circumstance shouldn't be surprising, because the data types defined for any procedural language are different from the types for the other procedural languages.

You can look high and low, but you won't find any standardization of data types across languages. In SQL releases before SQL-92, data type incompatibility was a major concern. In SQL-92 (and also in subsequent releases of the SQL standard), the CAST statement addresses the problem. Chapter 8 explains how you can use CAST to convert a data item from the procedural language's data type to one recognized by SQL, as long as the data item itself is compatible with the new data type.

Hooking SQL into Procedural Languages

Although you potentially face some hurdles when you integrate SQL with procedural languages, mark my word — the integration can be done successfully. In fact, in many instances, you *must* integrate SQL with procedural languages if you intend to produce the desired result in the allotted time — or at all. Luckily, you can use any of several methods for combining SQL with procedural languages. Three of the methods — embedded SQL, module language, and RAD tools — are outlined in the next few sections.

Embedded SQL

The most common method of mixing SQL with procedural languages is called *embedded SQL.* Wondering how embedded SQL works? Take one look at the name and you have the basics down: drop SQL statements into the middle of a procedural program, wherever you need them.

Of course, as you may expect, an SQL statement that suddenly appears in the middle of a C program can present a challenge for a compiler that isn't expecting it. For that reason, programs containing embedded SQL are usually passed through a *preprocessor* before being compiled or interpreted. The preprocessor is warned of the imminent appearance of SQL code by the EXEC SQL directive.

As an example of embedded SQL, look at a program written in Oracle's Pro*C version of the C language. The program, which accesses a company's employee table, prompts the user for an employee name and then displays that employee's salary and commission. It then prompts the user for new salary and commission data and updates the employee table with it:

```
EXEC SQL BEGIN DECLARE SECTION;
    VARCHAR uid[20];
    VARCHAR pwd[20];
    VARCHAR ename[10];
    FLOAT salary, comm;
    SHORT salary_ind, comm_ind;
EXEC SQL END DECLARE SECTION;
main()
{
    int sret;                /* scanf return code */
    /* Log in */
```

```
strcpy(uid.arr,"FRED");     /* copy the user name */
uid.len=strlen(uid.arr);
strcpy(pwd.arr,"TOWER");     /* copy the password */
pwd.len=strlen(pwd.arr);
EXEC SQL WHENEVER SQLERROR STOP;
EXEC SQL WHENEVER NOT FOUND STOP;
EXEC SQL CONNECT :uid;
printf("Connected to user: percents \n",uid.arr);
printf("Enter employee name to update:  ");
scanf("percents",ename.arr);
ename.len=strlen(ename.arr);
EXEC SQL SELECT SALARY,COMM INTO :salary,:comm
           FROM EMPLOY
           WHERE ENAME=:ename;
printf("Employee: percents salary: percent6.2f comm:
     percent6.2f \n",
       ename.arr, salary, comm);
printf("Enter new salary:  ");
sret=scanf("percentf",&salary);
salary_ind = 0;
if (sret == EOF !! sret == 0)    /* set indicator */
     salary_ind =-1;    /* Set indicator for NULL */
printf("Enter new commission:  ");
sret=scanf("percentf",&comm);
comm_ind = 0;     /* set indicator */
if (sret == EOF !! sret == 0)
     comm_ind=-1;       /* Set indicator for NULL */
EXEC SQL UPDATE EMPLOY
           SET SALARY=:salary:salary_ind
           SET COMM=:comm:comm_ind
           WHERE ENAME=:ename;
printf("Employee percents updated. \n",ename.arr);
EXEC SQL COMMIT WORK;
exit(0);
}
```

You don't have to be an expert in C to understand the essence of what this program is doing (and how it intends to do it). Here's a rundown of the order in which the statements execute:

1. SQL declares host variables.

2. C code controls the user login procedure.

3. SQL sets up error handling and connects to the database.

4. C code solicits an employee name from the user and places it in a variable.

5. An SQL SELECT statement retrieves the named employee's salary and commission data and stores them in the host variables :salary and :comm.

6. C then takes over again and displays the employee's name, salary, and commission and then solicits new values for salary and commission. It also checks to see whether an entry has been made, and if one has not, it sets an indicator.

7. SQL updates the database with the new values.

8. C then displays an "operation complete" message.

9. SQL commits the transaction, and C finally exits the program.

You can mix the commands of two languages like this because of the preprocessor. The preprocessor separates the SQL statements from the host language commands, placing the SQL statements in a separate external routine. Each SQL statement is replaced with a host language CALL of the corresponding external routine. The language compiler can now do its job.

The way the SQL part is passed to the database is implementation dependent. You, as the application developer, don't have to worry about any of this. The preprocessor takes care of it. You *should* be concerned about a few things, however, that do not appear in interactive SQL — things such as host variables and incompatible data types.

Declaring host variables

Some information must be passed between the host language program and the SQL segments. You pass this data with *host variables*. In order for SQL to recognize the host variables, you must declare them before you use them. Declarations are included in a declaration segment that precedes the program segment. The declaration segment is announced by the following directive:

```
EXEC SQL BEGIN DECLARE SECTION ;
```

The end of the declaration segment is signaled by:

```
EXEC SQL END DECLARE SECTION ;
```

Every SQL statement must be preceded by an EXEC SQL directive. The end of an SQL segment may or may not be signaled by a terminator directive. In COBOL, the terminator directive is "END-EXEC", and in C, it's a semicolon.

Converting data types

Depending on the compatibility of the data types supported by the host language and those supported by SQL, you may have to use CAST to convert certain types. You can use host variables that have been declared in the

DECLARE SECTION. Remember to prefix host variable names with a colon (:) when you use them in SQL statements, as in the following example:

```
INSERT INTO FOODS
    (FOODNAME, CALORIES, PROTEIN, FAT, CARBOHYDRATE)
    VALUES
    (:foodname, :calories, :protein, :fat, :carbo) ;
```

Module language

Module language provides another method for using SQL with a procedural programming language. With module language, you explicitly put all the SQL statements into a separate SQL module.

An SQL module is simply a list of SQL statements. Each SQL statement is included in an SQL *procedure* and is preceded by a specification of the procedure's name and the number and types of parameters.

Each SQL procedure contains only one SQL statement. In the host program, you explicitly call an SQL procedure at whatever point in the host program you want to execute the SQL statement in that procedure. You call the SQL procedure as if it were a host language subprogram.

Thus, you can use an SQL module and the associated host program to explicitly hand-code the result of the SQL preprocessor for embedded syntax.

Embedded SQL is much more common than module language. Most vendors offer some form of module language, but few emphasize it in their documentation. Module language does have several advantages:

- ✔ **SQL programmers don't have to be experts in the procedural language.** Because the SQL is completely separated from the procedural language, you can hire the best SQL programmers available to write your SQL modules, whether they have any experience with your procedural language or not. In fact, you can even defer deciding which procedural language to use until after your SQL modules are written and debugged.

- ✔ **You can hire the best programmers who work in your procedural language, even if they know nothing about SQL.** It stands to reason that if your SQL experts don't have to be procedural language experts, certainly the procedural language experts don't have to worry themselves over learning SQL.

- ✔ **No SQL is mixed in with the procedural code, so your procedural language debugger works.** This can save you considerable development time.

Once again, what can be looked at as an advantage from one perspective may be a disadvantage from another. Because the SQL modules are separated from the procedural code, following the flow of the logic isn't as easy as it is in embedded SQL when you're trying to understand how the program works.

Module declarations

The syntax for the declarations in a module is as follows:

```
MODULE [module-name]
   [NAMES ARE character-set-name]
   LANGUAGE {ADA|C|COBOL|FORTRAN|MUMPS|PASCAL|PLI|SQL}
   [SCHEMA schema-name]
   [AUTHORIZATION authorization-id]
   [temporary-table-declarations...]
   [cursor-declarations...]
   [dynamic-cursor-declarations...]
   procedures...
```

The square brackets indicate that the module name is optional. Naming it anyway is a good idea if you want to keep things from getting too confusing.

The optional NAMES ARE clause specifies a character set. If you don't include a NAMES ARE clause, the default set of SQL characters for your implementation is used. The LANGUAGE clause tells the module which language it will be called from. The compiler must know what the calling language is, because it will make the SQL statements appear to the calling program as if they are subprograms in that program's language.

Although the SCHEMA clause and the AUTHORIZATION clause are both optional, you must specify at least one of them. Or you can specify both. The SCHEMA clause specifies the default schema, and the AUTHORIZATION clause specifies the authorization identifier. The *authorization identifier* establishes the privileges you have. If you don't specify an authorization ID, the DBMS uses the authorization ID associated with your session to determine the privileges your module is allowed. If you don't have the privilege to perform the operation your procedure calls for, your procedure isn't executed.

If your procedure requires temporary tables, declare them with the temporary table declaration clause. Declare cursors and dynamic cursors before any procedures that use them. Declaring a cursor after a procedure starts executing is permissible as long as that procedure doesn't use the cursor. Doing this for cursors used by later procedures may make sense. You can find more in-depth information on cursors in Chapter 18.

Module procedures

After all the declarations I discuss in the previous section, the functional parts of the module are the procedures. An SQL module language procedure has a name, parameter declarations, and executable SQL statements. The procedural language program calls the procedure by its name and passes values to it through the declared parameters. Procedure syntax looks like this:

```
PROCEDURE procedure-name
    (parameter-declaration [, parameter-declaration ]... )
    SQL statement ;
    [SQL statements] ;
```

The parameter declaration should take the following form:

```
parameter-name data-type
```

or

```
SQLSTATE
```

The parameters you declare may be input parameters, output parameters, or both. SQLSTATE is a status parameter through which errors are reported. You can delve deeper into parameters by heading to Chapter 20.

Object-oriented RAD tools

By using state-of-the-art RAD tools, you can develop sophisticated applications without knowing how to write a single line of code in C, Pascal, COBOL, FORTRAN, or any procedural language for that matter. Instead, you choose objects from a library and place them in appropriate spots on the screen.

Objects of different standard types have characteristic properties, and selected events are appropriate for each object type. You can also associate a method with an object. The *method* is a procedure written in a procedural language. Building useful applications without writing any methods is possible, however.

Although you can build complex applications without using a procedural language, sooner or later you will probably need SQL. SQL has a richness of expression that is difficult, if not impossible, to duplicate with the object paradigm. As a result, full-featured RAD tools offer you a mechanism for injecting SQL statements into your object-oriented applications. Borland C++Builder is an example of an object-oriented development environment that offers SQL capability. Microsoft Access is another application development environment that enables you to use SQL in conjunction with its procedural language VBA.

Chapter 4 shows you how to create database tables with Access. That operation represents only a small fraction of Access's capabilities. Access is a tool and its primary purpose is to develop applications that process the data in database tables. Using Access, you can place objects on forms and then customizes the objects by giving them properties, events, and methods. You can manipulate the forms and objects with VBA code, which can contain embedded SQL.

Although RAD tools such as Access can deliver high-quality applications in less time, they usually don't work across all platforms. Access, for instance, runs only with the Microsoft Windows operating system. You may get lucky and discover that the RAD tool you choose works on a few platforms, but if building platform-independent functionality is important to you, or if you think you may want to eventually migrate your application to a different platform, beware.

RAD tools such as Access represent the beginning of the eventual merger of relational and object-oriented database design. The structural strengths of relational design and SQL will both survive. They will be augmented by the rapid — and comparatively bug-free — development that comes from object-oriented programming.

Using SQL with Microsoft Access

The primary audience for Microsoft Access is people who want to develop relatively simple applications without programming. If that describes you, you might want to put *Access For Dummies* (Wiley) on your shelf as a reference book. The procedural language VBA (Visual Basic for Applications) and SQL are both built into Access, but are not emphasized in either advertising or documentation. If you want to develop more sophisticated applications, using VBA and SQL, try my book, *Access 2003 Power Programming with VBA,* also published by Wiley. Be aware though, that the SQL in Access is not a full implementation, and you almost need the detective skills of Sherlock Holmes to even find it.

I mention the three components of SQL, Data Definition Language, Data Manipulation Language, and Data Control Language ,in Chapter 3. The subset of SQL contained in Access only implements the Data Manipulation Language. You must do your table creation operations with the RAD tool I describe in Chapter 4. The same goes for implementing security features, which I cover in Chapter 13.

To get a look at some Access SQL, you need to sneak up on it from behind. Consider an example taken from the database of the fictitious Oregon Lunar Society, a nonprofit research organization. The Society has several research teams, one of which is the Moon Base Research Team (MBRT). A question has arisen as to which scholarly papers have been written by members of the team. A query was formulated using Access's Query By Example (QBE) facility to retrieve the desired data. The query, shown in Figure 15-1, pulls data from the RESEARCHTEAMS, AUTHORS, and PAPERS tables, with the help of the AUTH-RES and AUTH-PAP intersection tables that were added to break up many-to-many relationships.

You can click the View icon drop-down menu in the upper-left corner of the window to reveal the other available views of the database. One of the choices is SQL View (see Figure 15-2).

When you click SQL View, the SQL editing window appears, showing the SQL statement that Access has generated, based on the choices made using QBE.

This SQL statement, shown in Figure 15-3, is what actually gets sent to the database engine. The database engine, which interfaces directly with the database itself, understands only SQL. Any information entered into the QBE environment must be translated into SQL before it is sent on to the database engine for processing.

Figure 15-1:
The Design View of MBRT Papers query.

Figure 15-2:
One of your
View menu
options is
SQL View.

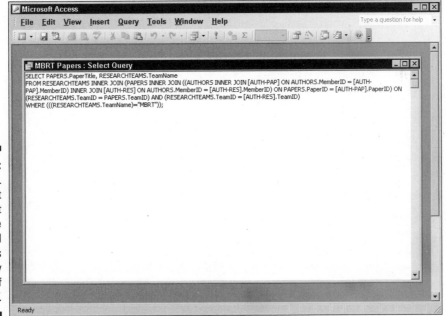

Figure 15-3:
An SQL
statement
that
retrieves the
names of all
the papers
written by
members of
the MBRT.

You may notice that the syntax of the SQL statement shown in Figure 15-3 differs somewhat from the syntax of ANSI/ISO-standard SQL. Take the old adage, "When in Rome, do as the Romans do," to heart here. When working with Access, use the Access dialect of SQL. That advice also goes for any other environment that you may be working in. All implementations of SQL differ from the standard in one respect or another.

If you want to write a new query in Access SQL — one that has not already been created using QBE, that is — you can simply erase some existing query from the SQL editing window and type in a new SQL SELECT statement. Click the Exclamation Point icon in the toolbar at the top of the screen to run your new query. The result appears on-screen in Datasheet View.

Part V
Taking SQL to the Real World

The 5th Wave   By Rich Tennant

In this part . . .

*I*f you've been reading this book from the beginning, enthralled by the unfolding saga of SQL, then you've looked at SQL in isolation — you may even have begun to dream that you can solve all your data-handling problems by using SQL alone. Alas, reality intrudes. Doesn't it always? There are many things you simply can't do with SQL, at least not with SQL by itself. By combining SQL with traditional procedural languages such as COBOL, Java, FORTRAN, Visual Basic, Java, or C++, you can achieve results that you can't get with SQL alone. In this part, I show you how to combine SQL with procedural languages. Then I describe how to operate on external SQL databases that may be located out on the Internet or somewhere on your organizational intranet. Suddenly, reality starts to look pretty good.

Chapter 16

Accessing Data with ODBC and JDBC

In This Chapter

▶ Finding out about ODBC

▶ Taking a look at the parts of ODBC

▶ Using ODBC in a client/server environment

▶ Using ODBC on the Internet

▶ Using ODBC on an intranet

▶ Using JDBC

*I*n the last several years, computers have become increasingly interconnected, both within and between organizations. With this connection comes the need for sharing database information across networks. The major obstacle to the free sharing of information across networks is the incompatibility of the operating software and applications running on different machines. SQL's creation, and its ongoing evolution, has been a major step toward overcoming hardware and software incompatibility.

Unfortunately, "standard" SQL is not all that standard. Even DBMS vendors who claim to comply with the international SQL standard have included proprietary extensions in their implementations that make them incompatible with the proprietary extensions in other vendors' implementations. The vendors are loath to give up their extensions because their customers have designed them into their applications and have become dependent on them. User organizations, particularly large ones, need another way to make cross-DBMS communication possible — a tool that doesn't require vendors to dumb down their implementations to the lowest common denominator. This other way is ODBC (Open DataBase Connectivity).

ODBC

ODBC is a standard interface between a database and an application that accesses the data in the database. Having a standard enables any application front end to access any database back end by using SQL. The only requirement is that the front end and the back end both adhere to the ODBC standard. ODBC 4.0 is the current version of the standard.

An application accesses a database by using a *driver* (the ODBC driver), which is specifically designed to interface with that particular database. The driver's front end, the side that goes to the application, rigidly adheres to the ODBC standard. It looks the same to the application, regardless of what database engine is on the back end. The driver's back end is customized to the specific database engine that it is addressing. With this architecture, applications don't have to be customized to — or even aware of — which back-end database engine controls the data they're using. The driver masks the differences between back ends.

The ODBC interface

The *ODBC interface* is essentially a set of definitions that is accepted as standard. The definitions cover everything needed to establish communication between an application and a database. The ODBC interface defines the following:

- ✔ A function call library
- ✔ Standard SQL syntax
- ✔ Standard SQL data types
- ✔ A standard protocol for connecting to a database engine
- ✔ Standard error codes

The ODBC *function calls* make the connection to a back-end database engine possible; they execute SQL statements and pass results back to the application.

To perform an operation on a database, include the appropriate SQL statement as an argument of an ODBC function call. As long as you use the ODBC-specified standard SQL syntax, the operation works — regardless of what database engine is on the back end.

Components of ODBC

The ODBC interface consists of four functional components, referred to as ODBC layers. Each component plays a role in making ODBC flexible enough to provide transparent communication from any compatible front end to any compatible back end. The four layers of the ODBC interface are between the user and the data that the user wants, as follows:

- **Application:** The application is the part of the ODBC interface that is closest to the user. Of course, even systems that don't use ODBC include an application. Nonetheless, including the application as a part of the ODBC interface makes sense. The application must be cognizant that it is communicating with its data source through ODBC. It must connect smoothly with the ODBC driver manager, in strict accordance with the ODBC standard.

- **Driver manager:** The driver manager is a *dynamic link library (DLL)*, which is generally supplied by Microsoft. It loads appropriate drivers for the system's (possibly multiple) data sources and directs function calls coming in from the application to the appropriate data sources via their drivers. The driver manager also handles some ODBC function calls directly and detects and handles some types of errors.

- **Driver DLL:** Because data sources can be different from each other (in some cases, very different), you need a way to translate standard ODBC function calls into the native language of each data source. Translation is the job of the driver DLL. Each driver DLL accepts function calls through the standard ODBC interface and then translates them into code that is understandable to its associated *data source*. When the data source responds with a result set, the driver reformats it in the reverse direction into a standard ODBC result set. The driver is the key element that enables any ODBC-compatible application to manipulate the structure and the contents of an ODBC-compatible data source.

- **Data source:** The data source may be one of many different things. It may be a relational DBMS and associated database residing on the same computer as the application. It may be such a database on a remote computer. It may be an *indexed sequential access method* (ISAM) file with no DBMS, either on the local or a remote computer. It may or may not include a network. The myriad of different forms that the data source can take requires that a custom driver be available for each one.

ODBC in a Client/Server Environment

In a client/server system, the interface between the client part and the server part is called the *application programming interface* (API). An ODBC driver, for instance, includes an API. APIs can be either proprietary or standard. A *proprietary* API is one in which the client part of the interface has been specifically designed to work with one particular back end on the server. The actual code that forms this interface is a driver, and in a proprietary system, it's called a *native driver*. A native driver is optimized for use with a specific front-end client and its associated back-end data source. Because native drivers are optimized for both the specific front-end application and the specific DBMS back end that they're working with, the drivers tend to pass commands and information back and forth quickly, with a minimum of delay.

If your client/server system always accesses the same type of data source, and you're sure that you'll never need to access data on another type of data source, then you may want to use the native driver that is supplied with your DBMS. However, if you may need to access data that is stored in a different form sometime in the future, then using an ODBC API now could save you from a great deal of rework later.

ODBC drivers are also optimized to work with specific back-end data sources, but they all have the same front-end interface to the driver manager. Any driver that hasn't been optimized for a particular front end, therefore, is probably not as fast as a native driver that is specifically designed for that front end. A major complaint about the first generation of ODBC drivers was their poor performance compared to native drivers. Recent benchmarks, however, have shown that ODBC 4.0 drivers are quite competitive in performance to native drivers. The technology is mature enough that it is no longer necessary to sacrifice performance to gain the advantages of standardization.

ODBC and the Internet

Database operations over the Internet differ in several important ways from database operations on a client/server system. The most visible difference from the user's point of view is the client portion of the system, which includes the user interface. In a client/server system, the user interface is the part of an application that communicates with the data source on the server using ODBC-compatible SQL statements. Over the World Wide Web, the client portion of the system is a Web browser, which communicates with the data source on the server using *HyperText Markup Language* (HTML).

Anyone with a Web browser can access data that is made available on the Web, and putting a database on the Web (called *database publishing*) has many perks, especially if you want to make data available to people outside your LAN. Unfortunately, you usually don't have very strict control over who those people are, so the act of putting data on the Web is more akin to publishing the data to the world than it is to sharing the data with a few co-workers. (Of course, just because your Web browser can access data on the Web doesn't mean your browser can read and translate it. See "Client extensions" for solutions to this problem.) Figure 16-1 compares client/server systems with Web-based systems.

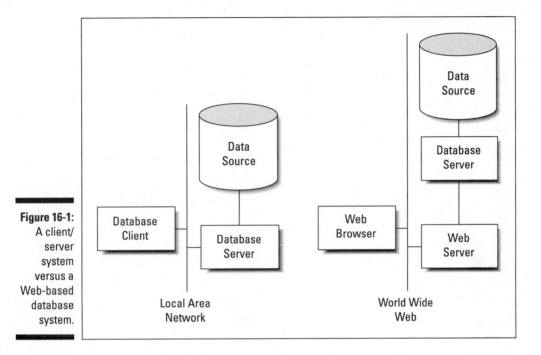

Figure 16-1:
A client/
server
system
versus a
Web-based
database
system.

Server extensions

In the Web-based system, communication between the browser on the client machine and the Web server on the server machine takes place in HTML. A system component called a *server extension* translates the HTML into ODBC-compatible SQL. Then the database server acts on the SQL, which in turn deals directly with the data source. In the reverse direction, the data source sends the result set that is generated by a query through the database server to the server extension, which then translates it into a form that the Web server can handle. The results are then sent over the Web to the Web browser on the client machine, where they're displayed to the user. Figure 16-2 shows the architecture of this type of system.

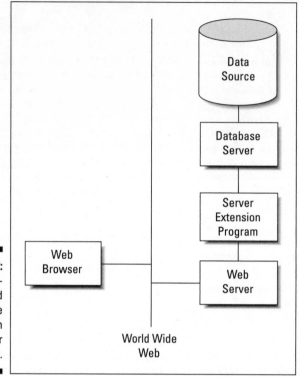

Client extensions

Web browsers were designed — and are now optimized — to provide easy-
to-understand and easy-to-use interfaces to Web sites of all kinds. The most
popular browsers, Mozilla Firefox, Microsoft Internet Explorer, and Apple
Safari, were not designed or optimized to be database front ends. In order for
meaningful interaction with a database to occur over the Internet, the client
side of the system needs functionality that the browser does not provide. To
fill this need, several types of *client extensions* have been developed. These
extensions include helper applications, ActiveX controls, Java applets, and
scripts. The extensions communicate with the server via HTML, which is the
language of the Web. Any HTML code that deals with database access is
translated into ODBC-compatible SQL by the server extension before being
forwarded to the data source.

Helper applications

The first client extensions were called *helper applications*. A helper application is a stand-alone program that runs on the user's PC. It is not integrated with a Web page, and it does not display in a browser window. An example of a helper application is a graphics viewer program that can display graphics file formats that the browser doesn't support.

To use a helper application, the user must first download it from its source site and install it on his or her PC. From then on, when the user downloads a file in that format, the browser automatically prompts the viewer to display the file. One downside to this scheme is that the entire data file must be downloaded into a temporary file before the helper application starts. Thus, for large files, you may have to wait quite a while before you see any part of your downloaded file.

ActiveX controls

Microsoft's ActiveX controls work with Microsoft's Internet Explorer, which is the most popular browser in the world, although recently Firefox has been making inroads to its dominance.

Scripts

Scripts are the most flexible tools for creating client extensions. Using a scripting language, such as the ubiquitous JavaScript or Microsoft's VBScript, gives you maximum control over what happens at the client end. You can put validation checks on data entry fields, thus enabling the rejection or correction of invalid entries without ever going out onto the Web. This can save you time as well as reduce traffic on the Web, thus benefiting other users as well. As with Java applets, scripts are embedded in an HTML page and execute as the user interacts with that page.

ODBC and an Intranet

An *intranet* is a local or wide area network that operates like a simpler version of the Internet. Because an intranet is contained within a single organization, you don't need complex security measures such as firewalls. All the tools that are designed for application development on the World Wide Web operate equally well as development tools for intranet applications. ODBC works on an intranet in the same way that it does on the Internet. If you have multiple data sources, clients using Web browsers and the appropriate client and server extensions can communicate with them with SQL that passes through HTML and ODBC stages. At the driver, the ODBC-compliant SQL is translated into the database's native command language and executed.

JDBC

JDBC (Java DataBase Connectivity) is similar to ODBC, but it differs in a few important respects. One such difference is hinted at by its name. JDBC is a database interface that looks the same to the client program — regardless of what data source is sitting on the server (back end). The difference is that JDBC expects the client application to be written in the Java language, rather than another language such as C++ or Visual Basic. Another difference is that Java and JDBC were both specifically designed to run on the World Wide Web or on an intranet.

Java is a C++-like language that was developed by Sun Microsystems specifically for the development of Web client programs. After a connection is made between a server and a client over the Web, the appropriate Java applet is downloaded to the client, where the applet commences to run. The applet, which is embedded in an HTML page, provides the database-specific functionality that the client needs to provide flexible access to server data. Figure 16-3 is a schematic representation of a Web database application with a Java applet running on the client machine.

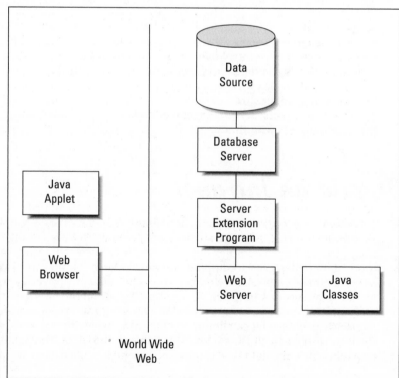

Figure 16-3:
A Web database application using a Java applet.

A major advantage to using Java applets is that they're always up-to-date. Because the applets are downloaded from the server every time they're used (as opposed to being retained on the client), the client is always guaranteed to have the latest version whenever it runs a Java applet.

If you're responsible for maintaining your organization's server, you never have to worry about losing compatibility with some of your clients when you upgrade the server software. Just make sure that your downloadable Java applet is compatible with the new server configuration, and, as long as their Web browsers have been configured to enable Java applets, all your clients automatically become compatible, too. Java is a full-featured programming language, and it is entirely possible to write robust applications with Java that can access databases in some kind of client/server system. When used this way, a Java application that accesses a database via JDBC is similar to a C++ application that accesses a database via ODBC. But a Java application acts quite different from a C++ application when it comes to the Internet (or an intranet).

When the system that you're interested in is on the Net, the operating conditions are different from the conditions in a client/server system. The client side of an application that operates over the Internet is a browser, with minimal computational capabilities. These capabilities must be augmented in order for significant database processing to be done; Java applets provide these capabilities.

An *applet* is a small application that resides on a server. When a client connects to that server over the Web, the applet is downloaded and starts running in the client computer. Java applets are specially designed so that they run in a *sandbox*. A sandbox is a well-defined area in the client computer's memory where the downloaded applet can run. The applet is not allowed to affect anything outside the sandbox. This architecture is designed to protect the client machine from potentially hostile applets that may try to extract sensitive information or cause malicious damage.

You face a certain amount of danger when you download anything from a server that you do not know to be trustworthy. If you download a Java applet, that danger is greatly reduced, but not completely eliminated. Be wary about letting executable code enter your machine from a questionable server.

Like ODBC, JDBC passes SQL statements from the front-end application (applet) running on the client to the data source on the back end. It also serves to pass result sets or error messages from the data source back to the application. The value of using JDBC is that the applet writer can write to the standard JDBC interface, without needing to know or care what database is located at the back end. JDBC performs whatever conversion is necessary for accurate two-way communication to take place.

Chapter 17

Operating on XML Data with SQL

. . . .

In This Chapter

▶ Using SQL with XML

▶ XML, databases, and the Internet

. . . .

*T*he most significant new feature in SQL is its support of XML. XML *(eXtensible Markup Language)* files are rapidly becoming a universally accepted standard for exchanging data between dissimilar platforms. With XML, it doesn't matter if the person you're sharing data with has a different application environment, a different operating system, or even different hardware. XML can form a data bridge between the two of you.

How XML Relates to SQL

XML, like HTML, is a markup language, which means that it's not a full-function language such as C++ or Java. It's not even a data sublanguage such as SQL. However, unlike those languages, it is cognizant of the content of the data it transports. Where HTML deals only with formatting the text and graphics in a document, XML gives structure to the document's content. XML itself does not deal with formatting. To do that, you have to augment XML with a *style sheet*. As it does with HTML, a style sheet applies formatting to an XML document.

SQL and XML provide two different ways of structuring data so that you can save it and retrieve selected information from it:

- ✔ SQL is an excellent tool for dealing with numeric and text data that can be categorized by data type and have a well-defined size. SQL was created as a standard way to maintain and operate on data kept in relational databases.

- ✔ XML is better at dealing with free-form data that cannot be easily categorized. The driving motivations for the creation of XML were to provide a universal standard for transferring data between dissimilar computers and for displaying it on the World Wide Web.

The strengths and goals of SQL and XML are complementary. Each reigns supreme in its own domain and forms alliances with the other to give users the information they want, when they want it, and where they want it.

The XML Data Type

The XML type was introduced with SQL:2003. This means that conforming implementations can store and operate on XML-formatted data directly, without first converting to XML from one of the other SQL data types.

The XML data type, including its subtypes, although intrinsic to any implementation that supports it, acts like a user-defined type (UDT). The XML type brings SQL and XML into close contact because it enables applications to perform SQL operations on XML content, and XML operations on SQL content. You can include a column of the XML type with columns of any of the other predefined types covered in Chapter 2 in a join operation in the WHERE clause of a query. In true relational database fashion, your DBMS will determine the optimal way to execute the query, and then will do it.

When to use the XML type

Whether or not you should store data in XML format depends on what you plan to do with that data. Here are some instances where it makes sense to store data in XML format:

- ✔ When you want to store an entire block of data and retrieve the whole block later.

- ✔ When you want to be able to query the whole XML document. Some implementations have expanded the scope of the EXTRACT operator to enable extracting desired content from an XML document.

- ✔ When you need strong typing of data inside SQL statements. Using the XML type guarantees that data values are valid XML values and not just arbitrary text strings.

- ✔ To ensure compatibility with future, as yet unspecified, storage systems that might not support existing types such as CHARACTER LARGE OBJECT, or CLOB. (See Chapter 2 for more information on CLOB.)

- ✔ To take advantage of future optimizations that will support only the XML type.

Here's an example of how you might use the XML type:

```
CREATE TABLE CLIENT (
     ClientName          CHARACTER (30)      NOT NULL,
     Address1            CHARACTER (30),
     Address2            CHARACTER (30),
     City                CHARACTER (25),
     State               CHARACTER (2),
     PostalCode          CHARACTER (10),
     Phone               CHARACTER (13),
     Fax                 CHARACTER (13),
     ContactPerson       CHARACTER (30),
     Comments            XML(SEQUENCE) ) ;
```

This SQL statement will store an XML document in the `Comments` column of the CLIENT table. The resulting document might look something like the following:

```
<Comments>
     <Comment>
          <CommentNo>1</CommentNo>
          <MessageText>Is VetLab equipped to analyze
          penguin blood?</MessageText>
          <ResponseRequested>Yes</ResponseRequested>
     </Comment>
     <Comment>
          <CommentNo>2</CommentNo>
          <MessageText>Thanks for the fast turnaround on
          the leopard seal sputum sample.</MessageText>
          <ResponseRequested>No</ResponseRequested>
     </Comment>
</Comments>
```

When not to use the XML type

Just because SQL:2003 allows you to use the XML type doesn't mean that you always should. In fact, on many occasions, it doesn't make sense to use the XML type. Most data in relational databases today is better off in its current format than it is in XML format. Here are a couple of examples of when not to use the XML type:

- ✔ When the data breaks down naturally into a relational structure with tables, rows, and columns.
- ✔ When you will need to update pieces of the document, rather than deal with the document as a whole.

Mapping SQL to XML and XML to SQL

To exchange data between SQL databases and XML documents, the various elements of an SQL database must be translatable into equivalent elements of an XML document, and vice versa. I describe which elements need to be translated in the following sections.

Mapping character sets

In SQL, the character sets supported depend on which implementation you're using. This means that IBM's DB2 may support character sets that are not supported by Microsoft's SQL Server. SQL Server may support character sets not supported by Oracle. Although the most common character sets are almost universally supported, if you use a less common character set, migrating your database and application from one RDBMS platform to another may be difficult.

XML has no compatibility issue with character sets — it supports only one, Unicode. This is a good thing from the point of view of exchanging data between any given SQL implementation and XML. All the RDBMS vendors have to define a mapping between strings of each of their character sets and Unicode, as well as a reverse mapping from Unicode to each of their character sets. Luckily, XML doesn't also support multiple character sets. If it did, vendors would have a many-to-many problem that would require several more mappings and reverse mappings to resolve.

Mapping identifiers

XML is much stricter than SQL in the characters it allows in identifiers. Characters that are legal in SQL but illegal in XML must be mapped to something legal before they can become part of an XML document. SQL supports delimited identifiers. This means that all sorts of odd characters such as %, $, and & are legal, as long as they're enclosed within double quotes. Such characters are not legal in XML. Furthermore, XML Names that begin with the characters *XML* in any combination of cases are reserved and thus cannot be used with impunity. If you have any SQL identifiers that begin with those letters, you have to change them.

An agreed-upon mapping bridges the identifier gap between SQL and XML. In moving from SQL to XML, all SQL identifiers are converted to Unicode. From there, any SQL identifiers that are also legal XML Names are left unchanged. SQL identifier characters that are not legal XML Names are replaced with a hexadecimal code that either takes the form "_xNNNN_" or "_xNNNNNNNN_", where N represents an uppercase hexadecimal digit. For example, the underscore "_" will be represented by "_x005F_". The colon will be represented by "_x003A_". These representations are the codes for the Unicode characters for the underscore and colon. The case where an SQL identifier starts with the characters *x, m,* and *l* is handled by prefixing all such instances with a code in the form "_xFFFF_".

Conversion from XML to SQL is much easier. All you need to do is scan the characters of an XML Name for a sequence of "_xNNNN_" or "_xNNNNNNNN_". Whenever you find such a sequence, replace it with the character that the Unicode corresponds to. If an XML Name begins with the characters "_xFFFF_", ignore them.

By following these simple rules, you can map an SQL identifier to an XML Name and then back to an SQL identifier again. However, this happy situation does not hold for a mapping from XML Name to SQL identifier and back to XML Name.

Mapping data types

The SQL standard specifies that an SQL data type must be mapped to the closest possible XML Schema data type. The designation *closest possible* means that all values allowed by the SQL type will be allowed by the XML Schema type, and the fewest possible values not allowed by the SQL type will be allowed by the XML Schema type. XML facets, such as maxInclusive and minInclusive, can restrict the values allowed by the XML Schema type to the values allowed by the corresponding SQL type. For example, if the SQL data type restricts values of the INTEGER type to the range –2157483648<value<2157483647, in XML the maxInclusive value can be set to 2157483647, and the minInclusive value can be set to –2157483648. Here's an example of such a mapping:

```
<xsd:simpleType>
   <xsd:restriction base="xsd:integer">
      <xsd:maxInclusive value="2157483647"/>
      <xsd:minInclusive value="-2157483648"/>
      <xsd:annotation>
         <sqlxml:sqltype name="INTEGER"/>
      </xsd:annotation>
   </xsd:restriction>
</xsd:simpleType>
```

The annotation section retains information from the SQL type definition that is not used by XML, but you may find it valuable later if the document is mapped back to SQL.

Mapping tables

You can map a table to an XML document. Similarly, you can map all the tables in a schema or all the tables in a catalog. Privileges are maintained by the mapping. A person who has the SELECT privilege on only some table columns will be able to map only those columns to the XML document. The mapping actually produces two documents, one that contains the data in the table and the other that contains the XML Schema that describes the first document. Here's an example of the mapping of an SQL table to an XML data-containing document:

```
<CUSTOMER>
    <row>
        <FirstName>Abe</FirstName>
        <LastName>Abelson</LastName>
        <City>Springfield</City>
        <AreaCode>714</AreaCode>
        <Telephone>555-1111</Telephone>
    </row>
    <row>
        <FirstName>Bill</FirstName>
        <LastName>Bailey</LastName>
        <City>Decatur</City>
        <AreaCode>714</AreaCode>
        <Telephone>555-2222</Telephone>
    </row>
    .
    .
    .
</CUSTOMER>
```

The root element of the document has been given the name of the table. Each table row is contained within a <row> element, and each row element contains a sequence of column elements, each named after the corresponding column in the source table. Each column element contains a data value.

Handling null values

Because SQL data might include null values, you must decide how to represent them in an XML document. You can represent a null value either as nil or absent. If you choose the nil option, then the attribute xsi:nil="true" marks the column elements that represent null values. It might be used in the following way:

```
<row>
        <FirstName>Bill</FirstName>
        <LastName>Bailey</LastName>
        <City xsi:nil="true" />
```

```
            <AreaCode>714</AreaCode>
            <Telephone>555-2222</Telephone>
</row>
```

If you choose the absent option, you could implement it as follows:

```
<row>
        <FirstName>Bill</FirstName>
        <LastName>Bailey</LastName>
        <AreaCode>714</AreaCode>
        <Telephone>555-2222</Telephone>
</row>
```

In this case, the row containing the null value is absent. There is no reference to it.

Generating the XML Schema

When mapping from SQL to XML, the first document generated is the one that contains the data. The second contains the schema information. As an example, consider the schema for the CUSTOMER document shown in the "Mapping tables" section, earlier in this chapter.

```
<xsd:schema>
   <xsd:simpleType name="CHAR_15">
      <xsd:restriction base="xsd:string">
         <xsd:length value = "15"/>
      </xsd:restriction>
   </xsd:simpleType>

   <xsd:simpleType name="CHAR_25">
      <xsd:restriction base="xsd:string">
         <xsd:length value = "25"/>
      </xsd:restriction>
   </xsd:simpleType>

   <xsd:simpleType name="CHAR_3">
      <xsd:restriction base="xsd:string">
         <xsd:length value = "3"/>
      </xsd:restriction>
   </xsd:simpleType>

   <xsd:simpleType name="CHAR_8">
      <xsd:restriction base="xsd:string">
         <xsd:length value = "8"/>
      </xsd:restriction>
   </xsd:simpleType>
```

```
<xsd:sequence>
    <xsd:element name="FirstName" type="CHAR_15"/>
    <xsd:element name="LastName" type="CHAR_25"/>
    <xsd:element
        name="City" type="CHAR_25 nillable="true"/>
    <xsd:element
        name="AreaCode" type="CHAR_3" nillable="true"/>
    <xsd:element
        name="Telephone" type="CHAR_8" nillable="true"/>
</xsd:sequence>

</xsd:schema>
```

This schema is appropriate if the nil approach to handling nulls is used. The absent approach requires a slightly different element definition. For example:

```
<xsd:element
    name="City" type="CHAR_25 minOccurs="0"/>
```

SQL Functions that Operate on XML Data

The SQL standard defines a number of operators, functions, and pseudofunctions that, when applied to an SQL database, produce an XML result, or when applied to XML data produce a result in standard SQL form. The functions include XMLELEMENT, XMLFOREST, XMLCONCAT, and XMLAGG. In the following sections, I give brief descriptions of these functions, as well as several others that are frequently used when publishing to the Web. Some of the functions rely heavily on XQuery, a new standard query language designed specifically for querying XML data. XQuery is a huge topic in itself and is beyond the scope of this book. To find out more about XQuery, a good source of information is Jim Melton and Stephen Buxton's *Querying XML,* published by Morgan Kaufmann.

XMLELEMENT

The XMLELEMENT operator translates a relational value into an XML element. You can use the operator in a SELECT statement to pull data in XML format from an SQL database and publish it on the Web. Here's an example:

```
SELECT c.LastName
    XMLELEMENT ( NAME "City", c.City ) AS "Result"
FROM CUSTOMER c
WHERE LastName="Abelson" ;
```

Here is the result returned:

LastName	Result
Abelson	`<City>Springfield</City>`

XMLFOREST

The XMLFOREST operator produces a list, or *forest,* of XML elements from a list of relational values. Each of the operator's values produces a new element. Here's an example of this operator:

```
SELECT c.LastName
   XMLFOREST (c.City,
   c.AreaCode,
   c.Telephone ) AS "Result"
FROM CUSTOMER c
WHERE LastName="Abelson" OR LastName="Bailey" ;
```

This snippet produces the following output:

LastName	Result
Abelson	`<City>Springfield</City>`
	`<AreaCode>714</AreaCode>`
	`<Telephone>555-1111</Telephone>`
Bailey	`<City>Decatur</City>`
	`<AreaCode>714</AreaCode>`
	`<Telephone>555-2222</Telephone>`

XMLCONCAT

XMLCONCAT provides an alternate way to produce a forest of elements by concatenating its XML arguments. For example, the following code:

```
SELECT c.LastName,
   XMLCONCAT(
      XMLELEMENT ( NAME "first", c.FirstName,
      XMLELEMENT ( NAME "last", c.LastName)
      ) AS "Result"
FROM CUSTOMER c ;
```

produces these results:

LastName	*Result*
Abelson	`<first>Abe</first>`
	`<last>Abelson</last>`
Bailey	`<first>Bill</first>`
	`<last>Bailey</last>`

XMLAGG

XMLAGG, the aggregate function, takes XML documents or fragments of XML documents as input and produces a single XML document as output in GROUP BY queries. The aggregation contains a forest of elements. To illustrate the concept:

```
SELECT XMLELEMENT
    ( NAME "City",
        XMLATTRIBUTES ( c.City AS "name" ) ,
        XMLAGG (XMLELEMENT ( NAME "last" c.LastName )
                )
    ) AS "CityList"
FROM CUSTOMER c
GROUP BY City ;
```

When run against the CUSTOMER table, this query produces the following results:

CityList

```
<City name="Decatur">
    <last>Bailey</last>
</City>
<City name="Philo">
    <last>Stetson</last>
    <last>Stetson</last>
    <last>Wood</last>
</City
<City name="Springfield">
    <last>Abelson</last>
</City>
```

XMLCOMMENT

The XMLCOMMENT function enables an application to create an XML comment. Its syntax is:

```
XMLCOMMENT ( 'comment content'
    [RETURNING
        { CONTENT | SEQUENCE } ] )
```

For example:

```
XMLCOMMENT ('Back up database at 2 am every night.')
```

would create an XML comment that looks like:

```
<!--Back up database at 2 am every night. -->
```

XMLPARSE

The XMLPARSE function produces an XML value by performing a nonvalidating parse of a string. You might use it like this:

```
XMLPARSE (DOCUMENT '   GREAT JOB!   '
          PRESERVE WHITESPACE )
```

The above code would produce an XML value that is either XML (UNTYPED DOCUMENT) or XML (ANY DOCUMENT). Which of the two subtypes is chosen depends on the implementation you're using.

XMLPI

The XMLPI function allows applications to create XML processing instructions. The syntax for this function is:

```
XMLPI NAME target
      [ , string-expression ]
      [RETURNING
            { CONTENT | SEQUENCE } ] )
```

The target placeholder represents the identifier of the target of the processing instruction. The string-expression placeholder represents the content of the PI. This function creates an XML comment of the form:

```
<? target string-expression ?>
```

XMLQUERY

The XMLQUERY function evaluates an XQuery expression and returns the result to the SQL application. The syntax of XMLQUERY is:

```
XMLQUERY ( XQuery-expression
      [ PASSING { By REF | BY VALUE }
        argument-list ]
      RETURNING { CONTENT | SEQUENCE }
      { BY REF | BY VALUE } )
```

Here's an example of the use of XMLQUERY:

```
SELECT max_average,
     XMLQUERY (
          'for $batting_average in
               /player/batting_average
          where /player/lastname = $var1
          return $batting_average'
          PASSING BY VALUE
               'Mantle' AS var1,
          RETURNING SEQUENCE BY VALUE )
FROM offensive_stats
```

XMLCAST

The XMLCAST function is similar to an ordinary SQL CAST function, but has some additional restrictions. The XMLCAST function enables an application to cast a value from an XML type to either another XML type or an SQL type. Similarly, you can use it to cast a value from an SQL type to an XML type. Here are a couple of restrictions:

- ✔ At least one of the types involved, either the source type or the destination type, must be an XML type.
- ✔ Neither of the types involved may be an SQL collection type, row type, structured type, or reference type.
- ✔ Only values of one of the XML types or the SQL null type may be cast to XML(UNTYPED DOCUMENT) or to XML(ANY DOCUMENT).

Here's an example:

```
XMLCAST ( CLIENT.ClientName AS XML(UNTYPED CONTENT)
```

The XMLCAST function is transformed into an ordinary SQL CAST. The only reason for using a separate keyword is to enforce the restrictions listed here.

Predicates

Predicates return a value of true or false. Some new predicates have been added that specifically relate to XML.

DOCUMENT

The purpose of the DOCUMENT predicate is to determine whether an XML value is an XML document. It tests to see whether an XML value is an instance of either XML(ANY DOCUMENT) or XML(UNTYPED DOCUMENT). The syntax is:

```
XML-value IS [NOT]
   [ANY | UNTYPED] DOCUMENT
```

If the expression evaluates to a true value, the predicate returns TRUE; otherwise it returns FALSE. If the XML value is null, the predicate returns an UNKNOWN value. If you don't specify either ANY or UNTYPED, the default assumption is ANY.

CONTENT

You use the CONTENT predicate to determine whether an XML value is an instance of XML(ANY CONTENT) or XML(UNTYPED CONTENT). Here's the syntax:

```
XML-value IS [NOT]
   [ANY | UNTYPED] CONTENT
```

If you don't specify either ANY or UNTYPED, ANY is the default.

XMLEXISTS

As the name implies, you can use the XMLEXISTS predicate to determine whether a value exists. Here's the syntax:

```
XMLEXISTS ( XQuery-expression
   [ argument-list ])
```

The XQuery expression is evaluated using the values provided in the argument list. If the value queried by the XQuery expression is the SQL NULL value, the predicate's result is unknown. If the evaluation returns an empty XQuery sequence, then the predicate's result is FALSE; otherwise, it is TRUE. You can use this predicate to determine whether an XML document contains some particular content before you use a portion of that content in an expression.

VALID

The VALID predicate is used to evaluate an XML value to see if it is valid in the context of a registered XML Schema. The syntax of the VALID predicate is more complex than is the case for most predicates:

```
xml-value IS [NOT] VALID
[XML valid identity constraint option]
[XML valid according-to clause]
```

This predicate checks to see whether the XML value is one of the five XML types: XML(SEQUENCE), XML(ANY CONTENT), XML(UNTYPED CONTENT), XML(ANY DOCUMENT), or XML(UNTYPED DOCUMENT). Additionally, it might optionally check to see whether the validity of the XML value depends on identity constraints, and whether it is valid with respect to a particular XML Schema (the validity target).

There are four possibilities for the identify-constraint-option component of the syntax:

- ✔ WITHOUT IDENTITY CONSTRAINTS: If the identity-constraint-option syntax component isn't specified, WITHOUT IDENTITY CONSTRAINTS is assumed. If DOCUMENT is specified, then it acts like a combination of the DOCUMENT predicate and the VALID predicate WITH IDENTITY CONSTRAINTS GLOBAL.

- ✔ WITH IDENTITY CONSTRAINTS GLOBAL: This component of the syntax means the value is checked not only against the XML Schema, but also against the XML rules for ID/IDREF relationships..

  ID and IDREF are XML attribute types that identify elements of a document.

- ✔ WITH IDENTITY CONSTRAINTS LOCAL: This component of the syntax means the value is checked against the XML Schema, but not against the XML rules for ID/IDREF or the XML Schema rules for identify constraints.

- ✔ DOCUMENT: This component of the syntax means the XML value expression is a document and is valid WITH IDENTITY CONSTRAINTS GLOBAL syntax with an XML valid according to clause. The XML valid according to clause identifies the schema that the value will be validated against.

Transforming XML Data into SQL Tables

Until recently, when thinking about the relationship between SQL and XML, the emphasis has been on converting SQL table data into XML to make it accessible on the Internet. The most recent addition to the SQL standard addresses the complementary problem of converting XML data into SQL tables so that it can be easily queried using standard SQL statements. The XMLTABLE pseudo-function performs this operation. The syntax for XMLTABLE is:

```
XMLTABLE ( [namespace-declaration,]
XQuery-expression
[PASSING argument-list]
COLUMNS XMLtbl-column-definitions
```

where the argument-list is:

```
value-expression AS identifier
```

and XMLtbl-column-definitions is a comma-separated list of column definitions, which may contain:

```
column-name FOR ORDINALITY
```

and/or:

```
column-name data-type
[BY REF | BY VALUE]
[default-clause]
[PATH XQuery-expression]
```

Here's an example of how you might use XMLTABLE to extract data from an XML document into an SQL pseudo-table. A pseudo-table isn't persistent, but in every other respect behaves like a regular SQL table. If you want to make it persistent, you can create a table with a CREATE TABLE statement and then insert the XML data into the newly-created table.

```
SELECT clientphone.*
FROM
    clients_xml ,
    XMLTABLE(
        'for $m in
            $col/client
        return
            $m'
    PASSING clients_xml.client AS "col"
    COLUMNS
        "ClientName" CHARACTER (30) PATH 'ClientName' ,
        "Phone" CHARACTER (13) PATH 'phone'
    ) AS clientphone
```

When you run this statement, you see the following result:

```
ClientName                            Phone
------------------------------        -------------
Abe Abelson                           (714)555-1111
Bill Bailey                           (714)555-2222
Chuck Wood                            (714)555-3333

(3 rows in clientphone)
```

Mapping Non-Predefined Data Types to XML

In the SQL standard, the non-predefined data types include domain, distinct UDT, row, array, and multiset. You can map each of these to XML-formatted data, using appropriate XML code. The next few sections show examples of how to map these types.

Domain

To map an SQL domain to XML, you must first have a domain. For this example, create one by using a CREATE DOMAIN statement.

```
CREATE DOMAIN WestCoast AS CHAR (2)
   CHECK (State IN ('CA', 'OR', 'WA', 'AK')) ;
```

Now, create a table that uses that domain.

```
CREATE TABLE WestRegion (
   ClientName           Character (20)        NOT NULL,
   State                WestCoast             NOT NULL
   ) ;
```

Here's the XML Schema to map the domain into XML:

```
<xsd:simpleType>
   Name='DOMAIN.Sales.WestCoast'>

   <xsd:annotation>
     <xsd:appinfo>
        <sqlxml:sqltype kind='DOMAIN'
           schemaName='Sales'
           typeName='WestCoast'
           mappedType='CHAR_2'
           final='true'/>
     <xsd:appinfo>
   </xsd:annotation>

   <xsd:restriction base='CHAR_2'/>

</xsd:simpleType>
```

When this mapping is applied, it results in an XML document that contains something like the following:

```
<WestRegion>
   <row>
```

```
         .
         .
         .
      <State>AK</State>
         .
         .
         .
      </row>
         .
         .
         .
</WestRegion>
```

Distinct UDT

With a distinct UDT, you can do much the same as what you can do with a domain, but with stronger typing. Here's how:

```
CREATE TYPE WestCoast AS Character (2) FINAL ;
```

The XML Schema to map this type to XML is as follows:

```
<xsd:simpleType>
   Name='UDT.Sales.WestCoast'>

   <xsd:annotation>
      <xsd:appinfo>
         <sqlxml:sqltype kind='DISTINCT'
            schemaName='Sales'
            typeName='WestCoast'
            mappedType='CHAR_2'
            final='true'/>
      <xsd:appinfo>
   </xsd:annotation>

   <xsd:restriction base='CHAR_2'/>
</xsd:simpleType>
```

This creates an element that is the same as the one created for the preceding domain.

Row

The ROW type enables you to cram a whole row's worth of information into a single field of a table row. You can create a ROW type as part of the table definition, in the following manner:

```
CREATE TABLE CONTACTINFO (
   Name              CHARACTER (30)
   Phone             ROW (Home CHAR (13), Work CHAR (13))
) ;
```

You can now map this type to XML with the following schema:

```
<xsd:complexType Name='ROW.1'>

   <xsd:annotation>
     <xsd:appinfo>
        <sqlxml:sqltype kind='ROW'>
           <sqlxml:field name='Home'
              mappedType='CHAR_13'/>
           <sqlxml:field name='Work'
              mappedType='CHAR_13'/>
        </sqlxml:sqltype>
     <xsd:appinfo>
   </xsd:annotation>

   <xsd:sequence>
      <xsd:element Name='Home' nillable='true'
         Type='CHAR_13'/>
      <xsd:element Name='Work' nillable='true'
         Type='CHAR_13'/>
   </xsd:sequence>

</xsd:complexType>
```

This mapping could generate the following XML for a column:

```
<Phone>
   <Home>(888)555-1111</Home>
   <Work>(888)555-1212</Work>
</Phone>
```

Array

You can put more than one element in a single field by using an `Array` rather than the `ROW` type. For example, in the CONTACTINFO table, declare `Phone` as an array and then generate the XML Schema that will map the array to XML.

```
CREATE TABLE CONTACTINFO (
   Name              CHARACTER (30),
   Phone             CHARACTER (13) ARRAY [4]
) ;
```

You can now map this type to XML with the following schema:

```
<xsd:complexType Name='ARRAY_4.CHAR_13'>

   <xsd:annotation>
     <xsd:appinfo>
        <sqlxml:sqltype kind='ARRAY'
                          maxElements='4'
                          mappedElementType='CHAR_13'/>
     </xsd:appinfo>
   </xsd:annotation>

   <xsd:sequence>
     <xsd:element Name='element'
     minOccurs='0' maxOccurs='4'
     nillable='true' type='CHAR_13'/>
   </xsd:sequence>

</xsd:complexType>
```

This schema would generate something like this:

```
<Phone>
   <element>(888)555-1111</element>
   <element>xsi:nil='true'/>
   <element>(888)555-3434</element>
</Phone>
```

The element in the array containing xsi:nil='true' reflects the fact that the second phone number in the source table contains a null value.

Multiset

The phone numbers in the preceding example could just as well be stored in a multiset as in an array. To map a multiset, use something akin to the following:

```
CREATE TABLE CONTACTINFO (
   Name           CHARACTER (30),
   Phone          CHARACTER (13) MULTISET
) ;
```

You can now map this type to XML with the following schema:

```
<xsd:complexType Name='MULTISET.CHAR_13'>

   <xsd:annotation>
     <xsd:appinfo>
```

```
            <sqlxml:sqltype kind='MULTISET'
                           mappedElementType='CHAR_13'/>
      </xsd:appinfo>
   </xsd:annotation>

   <xsd:sequence>
      <xsd:element Name='element'
      minOccurs='0' maxOccurs='unbounded'
      nillable='true' type='CHAR_13'/>
   </xsd:sequence>

</xsd:complexType>
```

This schema would generate something like:

```
<Phone>
   <element>(888)555-1111</element>
   <element>xsi:nil='true'/>
   <element>(888)555-3434</element>
</Phone>
```

The Marriage of SQL and XML

SQL provides the worldwide standard method for storing data in a highly structured fashion. The structure enables users to maintain data stores of a wide range of sizes and to efficiently extract from those data stores the information they want. XML has risen from a de-facto standard to an official standard vehicle for transporting data between incompatible systems, particularly over the Internet. By bringing these two powerful methods together, the value of both is greatly increased. SQL can now handle data that doesn't fit nicely into the strict relational paradigm that was originally defined by Dr. Codd. XML can now efficiently take data from SQL databases or send data to them. The result is more readily available information that is easier to share. After all, at its core, sharing is what marriage is all about.

Part VI
Advanced Topics

The 5th Wave   By Rich Tennant

"We're researching molecular/digital technology that moves massive amounts of information across binary pathways that interact with free-agent programs capable of making decisions and performing logical tasks. We see applications in really high-end doorbells."

In this part . . .

You can approach SQL on many levels. In earlier parts of this book, I cover the major topics that you're likely to encounter in most applications. This part deals with subjects that are significantly more complex. SQL deals with data a set at a time. Cursors come into play only if you want to violate that paradigm and grapple with the data a row at a time. Error handling is important to every application, whether simple or sophisticated, but you can approach it either simplistically or on a much deeper level. (Hint: The more depth you give to your error handling, the better off your users are if problems arise.) In this part, I give you a view of the depths as well as of the shallows. The Persistent Stored Modules update that was added in SQL:1999 gives SQL added capability to perform procedural operations without making programmers revert to a host language.

The SQL:2003 international standard continued the object-oriented enhancements added in SQL:1999. Folks who are schooled in traditional procedural programming have to make a major mental shift to handle object-oriented programming. After you make that mental shift, however, you can make your code perform in ways that were not possible when you were playing by the old rules.

Chapter 18

Stepping through a Dataset with Cursors

In This Chapter

▶ Specifying cursor scope with the DECLARE statement

▶ Opening a cursor

▶ Fetching data one row at a time

▶ Closing a cursor

A major incompatibility between SQL and the most popular application development languages is that SQL operates on the data of an entire set of table rows at a time, whereas the procedural languages operate on only a single row at a time. A *cursor* enables SQL to retrieve (or update, or delete) a single row at a time so that you can use SQL in combination with an application written in any of the popular languages.

A cursor is like a pointer that locates a specific table row. When a cursor is active, you can SELECT, UPDATE, or DELETE the row at which the cursor is pointing.

Cursors are valuable if you want to retrieve selected rows from a table, check their contents, and perform different operations based on those contents. SQL can't perform this sequence of operations by itself. SQL can retrieve the rows, but procedural languages are better at making decisions based on field contents. Cursors enable SQL to retrieve rows from a table one at a time and then feed the result to procedural code for processing. By placing the SQL code in a loop, you can process the entire table row by row.

In a pseudocode representation of embedded SQL, the most common flow of execution looks like this:

```
EXEC SQL DECLARE CURSOR statement
EXEC SQL OPEN statement
Test for end of table
Procedural code
```

```
Start loop
    Procedural code
    EXEC SQL FETCH
    Procedural code
    Test for end of table
End loop
EXEC SQL CLOSE statement
Procedural code
```

The SQL statements in this listing are DECLARE, OPEN, FETCH, and CLOSE. Each of these statements is discussed in detail in this chapter.

If you can perform the operation that you want with normal SQL (set-at-a-time) statements, then do so. Declare a cursor, retrieve table rows one at a time, and use your system's host language only when you can't do what you want to do with SQL alone.

Declaring a Cursor

To use a cursor, you first must declare its existence to the DBMS. You do this with a DECLARE CURSOR statement. The DECLARE CURSOR statement doesn't actually cause anything to happen; it just announces the cursor's name to the DBMS and specifies what query the cursor will operate on. A DECLARE CURSOR statement has the following syntax:

```
DECLARE cursor-name [<cursor sensitivity>]
[<cursor scrollability>]
CURSOR [<cursor holdability>] [<cursor returnability>]
FOR query expression
    [ORDER BY order-by expression]
    [FOR updatability expression] ;
```

Note: The cursor name uniquely identifies a cursor, so it must be unlike that of any other cursor name in the current module or compilation unit.

To make your application more readable, give the cursor a meaningful name. Relate it to the data that the query expression requests or to the operation that your procedural code performs on the data.

Here are some characteristics that you must establish when you declare a cursor:

- **Cursor sensitivity:** Choose SENSITIVE, INSENSITIVE, or ASENSITIVE.
- **Cursor scrollability:** Choose either SCROLL or NO SCROLL.
- **Cursor holdability:** Choose either WITH HOLD or WITHOUT HOLD.
- **Cursor returnability:** Choose either WITH RETURN or WITHOUT RETURN.

The query expression

You can use any legal SELECT statement as a *query expression*. The rows that the SELECT statement retrieves are the ones that the cursor steps through one at a time. These rows are the scope of the cursor.

The query is not actually performed when the DECLARE CURSOR statement is read. You can't retrieve data until you execute the OPEN statement. The row-by-row examination of the data starts after you enter the loop that encloses the FETCH statement.

The ORDER BY clause

You may want to process your retrieved data in a particular order, depending on what your procedural code will do with the data. You can sort the retrieved rows before processing them by using the optional ORDER BY clause. The clause has the following syntax:

```
ORDER BY sort-specification [ , sort-specification ]...
```

You can have multiple sort specifications. Each has the following syntax:

```
( column-name ) [ COLLATE BY collation-name ] [ ASC | DESC ]
```

You sort by column name, and to do so, the column must be in the select list of the query expression. Columns that are in the table but not in the query select list do not work as sort specifications. For example, you want to perform an operation that is not supported by SQL on selected rows of the CUSTOMER table. You can use a DECLARE CURSOR statement like this:

```
DECLARE cust1 CURSOR FOR
    SELECT CustID, FirstName, LastName, City, State, Phone
      FROM CUSTOMER
    ORDER BY State, LastName, FirstName ;
```

In this example, the SELECT statement retrieves rows sorted first by state, then by last name, and then by first name. The statement retrieves all customers in Alaska (AK) before it retrieves the first customer from Alabama (AL). The statement then sorts customer records from Alaska by the customer's last name (*Aaron* before *Abbott*). Where the last name is the same, sorting then goes by first name (*George Aaron* before *Henry Aaron*).

Have you ever made 40 copies of a 20-page document on a photocopier without a collator? What a drag! You must make 20 stacks on tables and desks, and then walk by the stacks 40 times, placing a sheet on each stack. This process is called *collation*. A similar process plays a role in SQL.

A collation is a set of rules that determines how strings in a character set compare. A character set has a default collation sequence that defines the order in which elements are sorted. But, you can apply a collation sequence other than the default to a column. To do so, use the optional COLLATE BY clause. Your implementation probably supports several common collations. Pick one and then make the collation *ascending* or *descending* by appending an ASC or DESC keyword to the clause.

In a DECLARE CURSOR statement, you can specify a calculated column that doesn't exist in the underlying table. In this case, the calculated column doesn't have a name that you can use in the ORDER BY clause. You can give it a name in the DECLARE CURSOR query expression, which enables you to identify the column later. Consider the following example:

```
DECLARE revenue CURSOR FOR
    SELECT Model, Units, Price,
           Units * Price AS ExtPrice
      FROM TRANSDETAIL
    ORDER BY Model, ExtPrice DESC ;
```

In this example, no COLLATE BY clause is in the ORDER BY clause, so the default collation sequence is used. Notice that the fourth column in the select list is the result of a calculation of the data in the second and third columns. The fourth column is an extended price named ExtPrice. In my example, the ORDER BY clause is sorted first by model name and then by ExtPrice. The sort on ExtPrice is descending, as specified by the DESC keyword; transactions with the highest dollar value are processed first.

The default sort order in an ORDER BY clause is ascending. If a sort specification list includes a DESC sort and the next sort should also be in descending order, you must explicitly specify DESC for the next sort. For example:

```
ORDER BY A, B DESC, C, D, E, F
```

is equivalent to

```
ORDER BY A ASC, B DESC, C ASC, D ASC, E ASC, F ASC
```

The updatability clause

Sometimes, you may want to update or delete table rows that you access with a cursor. Other times, you may want to guarantee that such updates or deletions can't be made. SQL gives you control over this issue with the updatability clause of the DECLARE CURSOR statement. If you want to prevent updates and deletions within the scope of the cursor, use the clause:

```
FOR READ ONLY
```

For updates of specified columns only — leaving all others protected — use the following:

```
FOR UPDATE OF column-name [ , column-name ]...
```

Any columns listed must appear in the DECLARE CURSOR's query expression. If you don't include an updatability clause, the default assumption is that all columns listed in the query expression are updatable. In that case, an UPDATE statement can update all the columns in the row to which the cursor is pointing, and a DELETE statement can delete that row.

Sensitivity

The query expression in the DECLARE CURSOR statement determines the rows that fall within a cursor's scope. Consider this possible problem: What if a statement in your program, located between the OPEN and the CLOSE statements, changes the contents of some of those rows so that they no longer satisfy the query? What if such a statement deletes some of those rows entirely? Does the cursor continue to process all the rows that originally qualified, or does it recognize the new situation and ignore rows that no longer qualify or that have been deleted?

A normal SQL statement, such as UPDATE, INSERT, or DELETE, operates on a set of rows in a database table (or perhaps the entire table). While such a statement is active, SQL's transaction mechanism protects it from interference by other statements acting concurrently on the same data. If you use a cursor, however, your window of vulnerability to harmful interaction is wide open. When you open a cursor, data is at risk of being the victim of simultaneous, conflicting operations until you close the cursor again. If you open one cursor, start processing through a table, and then open a second cursor while the first is still active, the actions you take with the second cursor can affect what the statement controlled by the first cursor sees.

Changing the data in columns that are part of a DECLARE CURSOR query expression after some — but not all — of the query's rows have been processed results in a big mess. Your results are likely to be inconsistent and misleading. To avoid this problem, make sure that the cursor doesn't change as a result of any of the statements within its scope. Add the INSENSITIVE keyword to your DECLARE CURSOR statement. As long as your cursor is open, it is insensitive to (unaffected by) table changes that affect qualified rows in the cursor's scope. A cursor can't be both insensitive and updatable. An insensitive cursor must be read-only.

For example, suppose that you write these queries:

```
DECLARE C1 CURSOR FOR SELECT * FROM EMPLOYEE
    ORDER BY Salary ;
DECLARE C2 CURSOR FOR SELECT * FROM EMPLOYEE
    FOR UPDATE OF Salary ;
```

Now, suppose you open both cursors and fetch a few rows with C1 and then update a salary with C2 to increase its value. This change can cause a row that you have fetched with C1 to appear again on a later fetch of C1.

The peculiar interactions that are possible with multiple open cursors, or open cursors and set operations, are the sort of concurrency problems that transaction isolation avoids. If you operate this way, you're asking for trouble. So remember: Don't operate with multiple open cursors. For more information about transaction isolation, check out Chapter 14.

The default condition of cursor sensitivity is ASENSITIVE. Although you might think you know what this means, nothing is ever as simple as you'd like it to be. Each implementation has its own definition. For one implementation ASENSITIVE could be equivalent to SENSITIVE in another implementation, and for another it could be equivalent to INSENSITIVE. Check your system documentation for its meaning in your own case.

Scrollability

Scrollability is a capability that cursors didn't have prior to SQL-92. In implementations adhering to SQL-86 or SQL-89, the only allowed cursor movement was sequential, starting at the first row retrieved by the query expression and ending with the last row. With SQL-92's SCROLL keyword in the DECLARE CURSOR statement, you can access rows in any order you want. The current version of SQL retains this capability. The syntax of the FETCH statement controls the cursor's movement. I describe the FETCH statement later in this chapter.

Opening a Cursor

Although the DECLARE CURSOR statement specifies which rows to include in the cursor, it doesn't actually cause anything to happen because DECLARE is a declaration and not an executable statement. The OPEN statement brings the cursor into existence. It has the following form:

```
OPEN cursor-name ;
```

To open the cursor that I use in the discussion of the ORDER BY clause (earlier in this chapter), use the following:

```
DECLARE revenue CURSOR FOR
    SELECT Model, Units, Price,
           Units * Price AS ExtPrice
       FROM TRANSDETAIL
    ORDER BY Model, ExtPrice DESC ;
OPEN revenue ;
```

You can't fetch rows from a cursor until you open the cursor. When you open a cursor, the values of variables referenced in the DECLARE CURSOR statement become fixed, as do all current date-time functions. Consider the following example of SQL embedded in a host language program:

```
EXEC SQL DECLARE CURSOR C1 FOR SELECT * FROM ORDERS
    WHERE ORDERS.Customer = :NAME
        AND DueDate < CURRENT_DATE ;
NAME := 'Acme Co';    //A host language statement
EXEC SQL OPEN C1;
NAME := 'Omega Inc.'; //Another host statement
...
EXEC SQL UPDATE ORDERS SET DueDate = CURRENT_DATE;
```

The fix is in (for date-times)

As I describe in "Opening a Cursor," the OPEN statement fixes the value of all variables referenced in the declare cursor. It also fixes a value for date-time functions. A similar fixing of date-time values exists in set operations. Consider this example:

```
UPDATE ORDERS SET RecheckDate
    = CURRENT_DATE WHERE....;
```

Now suppose that you have a bunch of orders. You begin executing this statement at a minute before midnight. At midnight, the statement is still running, and it doesn't finish executing until five minutes after midnight. It doesn't matter. If a statement has any reference to CURRENT_DATE (or TIME or TIMESTAMP), the value is set to the date and time the statement begins, so all the ORDERS rows in the statement get the same RecheckDate. Similarly, if a statement references TIMESTAMP, the whole statement uses only one timestamp value, no matter how long the statement runs.

Here's an interesting example of an implication of this rule:

```
UPDATE EMPLOYEE SET
    KEY=CURRENT_TIMESTAMP;
```

You may expect that statement to set a unique value in the key column of each employee. You'd be disappointed; it sets the same value in every row.

So when the OPEN statement fixes date-time values for all statements referencing the cursor, it treats all these statements like an extended statement.

The OPEN statement fixes the value of all variables referenced in the declare cursor and also fixes a value for all current date-time functions. As a result, the second assignment to the name variable (NAME := 'Omega Inc.') has no effect on the rows that the cursor fetches. (That value of NAME is used the next time you open C1.) And even if the OPEN statement is executed a minute before midnight and the UPDATE statement is executed a minute after midnight, the value of CURRENT_DATE in the UPDATE statement is the value of that function at the time the OPEN statement executed — even if DECLARE CURSOR doesn't reference the date-time function.

Fetching Data from a Single Row

Processing cursors is a three-step process: The DECLARE CURSOR statement specifies the cursor's name and scope, the OPEN statement collects the table rows selected by the DECLARE CURSOR query expression, and the FETCH statement actually retrieves the data. The cursor may point to one of the rows in the cursor's scope, or to the location immediately before the first row in the scope, or to the location immediately after the last row in the scope, or to the empty space between two rows. You can specify where the cursor points with the orientation clause in the FETCH statement.

Syntax

The syntax for the FETCH statement is

```
FETCH [[orientation] FROM] cursor-name
   INTO target-specification [, target-specification ]...
        ;
```

Seven orientation options are available:

- ✔ NEXT
- ✔ PRIOR
- ✔ FIRST
- ✔ LAST
- ✔ ABSOLUTE
- ✔ RELATIVE
- ✔ <simple value specification>

The default option is NEXT, which, incidentally, was the *only* orientation available in versions of SQL prior to SQL-92. The NEXT orientation moves the cursor from wherever it is to the next row in the set specified by the query expression. That means that if the cursor is located before the first record, it moves to the first record. If it points to record *n,* it moves to record *n*+1. If the cursor points to the last record in the set, it moves beyond that record, and notification of a no data condition is returned in the SQLSTATE system variable. (Chapter 20 details SQLSTATE and the rest of SQL's error-handling facilities.)

The target specifications are either host variables or parameters, respectively, depending on whether embedded SQL or a module language is using the cursor. The number and types of the target specifications must match the number and types of the columns specified by the query expression in the DECLARE CURSOR. So in the case of embedded SQL, when you fetch a list of five values from a row of a table, five host variables must be there to receive those values, and they must be the right types.

Orientation of a scrollable cursor

Because the SQL cursor is scrollable, you have other choices besides NEXT. If you specify PRIOR, the pointer moves to the row immediately preceding its current location. If you specify FIRST, it points to the first record in the set, and if you specify LAST, it points to the last record.

When you use the ABSOLUTE and RELATIVE orientation, you must specify an integer value as well. For example, FETCH ABSOLUTE 7 moves the cursor to the seventh row from the beginning of the set. FETCH RELATIVE 7 moves the cursor seven rows beyond its current position. FETCH RELATIVE 0 doesn't move the cursor.

FETCH RELATIVE 1 has the same effect as FETCH NEXT. FETCH RELATIVE −1 has the same effect as FETCH PRIOR. FETCH ABSOLUTE 1 gives you the first record in the set, FETCH ABSOLUTE 2 gives you the second record in the set, and so on. Similarly, FETCH ABSOLUTE −1 gives you the last record in the set, FETCH ABSOLUTE −2 gives you the next-to-last record, and so on. Specifying FETCH ABSOLUTE 0 returns the no data exception condition code, as does FETCH ABSOLUTE 17 if only 16 rows are in the set. FETCH <simple value specification> gives you the record specified by the simple value specification.

Positioned DELETE and UPDATE statements

You can perform delete and update operations on the row to which a cursor is currently pointing. The syntax of the DELETE statement looks like this:

```
DELETE FROM table-name WHERE CURRENT OF cursor-name ;
```

If the cursor doesn't point to a row, the statement returns an error condition. No deletion occurs.

The syntax of the UPDATE statement is as follows:

```
UPDATE table-name
    SET column-name = value [,column-name = value]...
    WHERE CURRENT OF cursor-name ;
```

The value you place into each specified column must be a value expression or the keyword DEFAULT. If an attempted positioned update operation returns an error, the update isn't performed.

Closing a Cursor

After you finish with a cursor, make a habit of closing it immediately. Leaving a cursor open as your application goes on to other issues may cause harm. Also, open cursors use system resources.

If you close a cursor that was insensitive to changes made while it was open, when you reopen it, the reopened cursor reflects any such changes.

You can close the cursor that I opened earlier in the TRANSDETAIL table with a simple statement such as the following:

```
CLOSE revenue ;
```

Chapter 19

Adding Procedural Capabilities with Persistent Stored Modules

• •

In This Chapter

▶ Tooling up compound statements with atomicity, cursors, variables, and conditions

▶ Regulating the flow of control statements

▶ Doing loops that do loops that do loops

▶ Retrieving and using stored procedures and stored functions

▶ Assigning privileges, creating stored modules, and putting stored modules to good use

• •

Some of the leading practitioners of database technology have been working on the standards process for years. Even after a standard has been issued and accepted by the worldwide database community, progress toward the next standard doesn't slow down. A seven-year gap separated the issuance of SQL-92 and the release of the first component of SQL:1999. During the intervening years, ANSI and ISO issued an addendum to SQL-92, called SQL-92/PSM (Persistent Stored Modules). This addendum formed the basis for a part of SQL:1999 with the same name. SQL/PSM defines a number of statements that give SQL flow of control structures comparable to the flow of control structures available in full-featured programming languages. It enables you to use SQL to perform tasks that programmers were forced to use other tools for. Can you imagine what your life would have been like in the caveman times of 1992, when you'd have to repeatedly swap between SQL and its procedural host language just to do your work?

Compound Statements

Throughout this book, SQL is represented as a nonprocedural language that deals with data a set at a time rather than a record at a time. With the addition of the facilities covered in this chapter, however, this statement is not as true as it used to be. Although SQL still deals with data a set at a time, it is becoming more procedural.

Archaic SQL (that defined by SQL-92) doesn't follow the procedural model — where one instruction follows another in a sequence to produce a desired result — so early SQL statements were stand-alone entities, perhaps embedded in a C++ or Visual Basic program. With these early versions of SQL, posing a query or performing other operations by executing a series of SQL statements was discouraged because these complicated activities resulted in a performance penalty in the form of network traffic. SQL:1999 and all following versions allow compound statements, made up of individual SQL statements that execute as a unit, easing network congestion.

All the statements included in a compound statement are enclosed between a BEGIN keyword at the beginning of the statement and an END keyword at the end of the statement. For example, to insert data into multiple related tables, you use syntax similar to the following:

```
void main {
    EXEC SQL
        BEGIN
            INSERT INTO students (StudentID, Fname, Lname)
                VALUES (:sid, :sfname, :slname) ;
            INSERT INTO roster (ClassID, Class, StudentID)
                VALUES (:cid, :cname, :sid) ;
            INSERT INTO receivable (StudentID, Class, Fee)
                VALUES (:sid, :cname, :cfee)
        END ;
/* Check SQLSTATE for errors */
}
```

This little fragment from a C program includes an embedded compound SQL statement. The comment about SQLSTATE deals with error handling. If the compound statement doesn't execute successfully, an error code is placed in the status parameter SQLSTATE. Of course, placing a comment after the END keyword doesn't correct the error. The comment is placed there simply to remind you that in a real program, error-handling code belongs in that spot. I discuss error handling in detail in Chapter 20.

Atomicity

Compound statements introduce a possibility for error that you don't face when your construct simple SQL statements. A simple SQL statement either completes successfully or doesn't, and if it doesn't complete successfully, the database is unchanged. This is not necessarily the case when a compound statement creates an error.

Consider the example in the preceding section. What if the INSERT to the STUDENTS table and the INSERT to the ROSTER table both took place, but because of interference from another user, the INSERT to the RECEIVABLE table failed? A student would be registered for a class but would not be billed. This kind of error can be hard on a university's finances.

The concept that is missing in this scenario is *atomicity.* An atomic statement is indivisible — it either executes completely or not at all. Simple SQL statements are atomic by nature, but compound SQL statements are not. However, you can make a compound SQL statement atomic by specifying it as such. In the following example, the compound SQL statement is safe by introducing atomicity:

```
void main {
    EXEC SQL
        BEGIN ATOMIC
            INSERT INTO students (StudentID, Fname, Lname)
                VALUES (:sid, :sfname, :slname) ;
            INSERT INTO roster (ClassID, Class, StudentID)
                VALUES (:cid, :cname, :sid) ;
            INSERT INTO receivable (StudentID, Class, Fee)
                VALUES (:sid, :cname, :cfee)
        END ;
/* Check SQLSTATE for errors */
}
```

By adding the keyword ATOMIC after the keyword BEGIN, you can ensure that either the entire statement executes, or — if an error occurs — the entire statement rolls back, leaving the database in the state it was in before the statement began executing.

You can find out whether a statement executed successfully. Read the section, "Conditions," later in this chapter, for more information.

Variables

Full computer languages such as C or BASIC have always offered *variables,* but SQL didn't offer them until the introduction of SQL/PSM. A variable is a symbol that takes on a value of any given data type. Within a compound statement, you can declare a variable, assign it a value, and use it in a compound statement.

After you exit a compound statement, all the variables declared within it are destroyed. Thus, variables in SQL are local to the compound statement within which they are declared.

Here is an example:

```
BEGIN
    DECLARE prezpay NUMERIC ;
    SELECT salary
    INTO prezpay
```

```
      FROM EMPLOYEE
      WHERE jobtitle = 'president' ;
END;
```

Cursors

You can declare a *cursor* within a compound statement. You use cursors to process a table's data one row at a time (see Chapter 18 for details). Within a compound statement, you can declare a cursor, use it, and then forget it because the cursor is destroyed when you exit the compound statement. Here's an example of this usage:

```
BEGIN
      DECLARE ipocandidate CHARACTER(30) ;
      DECLARE cursor1 CURSOR FOR
            SELECT company
            FROM biotech ;
      OPEN CURSOR1 ;
      FETCH cursor1 INTO ipocandidate ;
      CLOSE cursor1 ;
END;
```

Conditions

When people say that a person has a condition, they usually mean that something is wrong with that person — he or she is sick or injured. People usually don't bother to mention that a person is in good condition; rather, we talk about people who are in serious condition or, even worse, in critical condition. This idea is similar to the way programmers talk about the condition of an SQL statement. The execution of an SQL statement leads to a successful result, a questionable result, or an outright erroneous result. Each of these possible results corresponds to a *condition*.

Every time an SQL statement executes, the database server places a value into the status parameter SQLSTATE. SQLSTATE is a five-character field. The value that is placed into SQLSTATE indicates whether the preceding SQL statement executed successfully. If it did not execute successfully, the value of SQLSTATE provides some information about the error.

The first two of the five characters of SQLSTATE (the class value) give you the major news as to whether the preceding SQL statement executed successfully, returned a result that may or may not have been successful, or produced an error. Table 19-1 shows the four possible results.

Table 19-1		SQLSTATE Class Values
Class	*Description*	*Details*
00	Successful completion	The statement executed successfully.
01	Warning	Something unusual happened during the execution of the statement, but the DBMS can't tell whether or not there was an error. Check the preceding SQL statement carefully to ensure that it is operating correctly.
02	Not Found	No data was returned as a result of the execution of the statement. This may or may not be good news, depending on what you were trying to do with the statement. You may be hoping for an empty result table.
Other	Exception	The two characters of the class code, plus the three characters of the subclass code, together comprise the five characters of SQLSTATE. They also give you an inkling about the nature of the error.

Handling conditions

You can have your program look at SQLSTATE after the execution of every SQL statement. What do you do with the knowledge that you gain?

✔ **If you find a class code of** 00**, you probably don't want to do anything.** You want execution to proceed as you originally planned.

✔ **If you find a class code of** 01 **or** 02**, you may or may not want to take special action.** If you expected the "Warning" or "Not Found" indication, then you probably want to let execution proceed. If you didn't expect either of these class codes, then you probably want to have execution branch to a procedure that is specifically designed to handle the unexpected, but not totally unanticipated, warning or not found result.

✔ **If you receive any other class code, something is wrong.** You should branch to an exception-handling procedure. Which procedure you choose to branch to depends on the contents of the three subclass characters, as well as the two class characters of SQLSTATE. If multiple different exceptions are possible, there should be an exception-handling procedure for each one because different exceptions often require different responses. You may be able to correct some errors, or find workarounds. Other errors may be fatal; no one will die, but you may end up having to terminate the application.

Handler declarations

You can put a *condition handler* within a compound statement. To create a condition handler, you must first declare the condition that it will handle. The condition declared can be some sort of exception, or it can just be something that is true. Table 19-2 lists the possible conditions and includes a brief description of what causes each type of condition.

Table 19-2	Conditions That May Be Specified in a Condition Handler
Condition	**Description**
SQLSTATE VALUE 'xxyyy'	Specific SQLSTATE value
SQLEXCEPTION	SQLSTATE class other than 00, 01, or 02
SQLWARNING	SQLSTATE class 01
NOT FOUND	SQLSTATE class 02

The following is an example of a condition declaration:

```
BEGIN
    DECLARE constraint_violation CONDITION
            FOR SQLSTATE VALUE '23000' ;
END ;
```

This example is not realistic, because typically the SQL statement that may cause the condition to occur — as well as the handler that would be invoked if the condition did occur — would also be enclosed within the BEGIN...END structure.

Handler actions and handler effects

If a condition occurs that invokes a handler, the action specified by the handler executes. This action is an SQL statement, which can be a compound statement. If the handler action completes successfully, then the handler effect executes. The following is a list of the three possible handler effects:

✔ CONTINUE: Continue execution immediately after the statement that caused the handler to be invoked.

- ✔ EXIT: Continue execution after the compound statement that contains the handler.

- ✔ UNDO: Undo the work of the previous statements in the compound statement, and continue execution after the statement that contains the handler.

If the handler can correct whatever problem invoked the handler, then the CONTINUE effect may be appropriate. The EXIT effect may be appropriate if the handler didn't fix the problem, but the changes made to the compound statement do not need to be undone. The UNDO effect is appropriate if you want to return the database to the state it was in before the compound statement started execution. Consider the following example:

```
BEGIN ATOMIC
    DECLARE constraint_violation CONDITION
        FOR SQLSTATE VALUE '23000' ;
    DECLARE UNDO HANDLER
        FOR constraint_violation
        RESIGNAL ;
    INSERT INTO students (StudentID, Fname, Lname)
        VALUES (:sid, :sfname, :slname) ;
    INSERT INTO roster (ClassID, Class, StudentID)
        VALUES (:cid, :cname, :sid) ;
END ;
```

If either of the INSERT statements causes a constraint violation, such as adding a record with a primary key that duplicates a primary key already in the table, SQLSTATE assumes a value of '23000', thus setting the constraint_violation condition to a true value. This action causes the handler to UNDO any changes that have been made to any tables by either INSERT command. The RESIGNAL statement transfers control back to the procedure that called the currently executing procedure.

If both INSERT statements execute successfully, execution continues with the statement following the END keyword.

The ATOMIC keyword is mandatory whenever a handler's effect is UNDO. This is not the case for handlers whose effect is either CONTINUE or EXIT.

Conditions that aren't handled

In the example in the preceding section, consider this possibility: What if an exception occurred that returned an SQLSTATE value other than '23000'? Something is definitely wrong, but the exception handler that you coded can't handle it. What happens now?

Because the current procedure doesn't know what to do, a RESIGNAL occurs. This bumps the problem up to the next higher level of control. If the problem isn't handled there, it continues to be elevated to higher levels until either it is handled or it causes an error condition in the main application.

The idea that I want to emphasize here is that if you write an SQL statement that may cause exceptions, then you should write exception handlers for all such possible exceptions. If you don't, you will have more difficulty isolating the source of a problem when it inevitably occurs.

Assignment

With SQL/PSM, SQL gains a function that even the lowliest procedural languages have had since their inception: the ability to assign a value to a variable. Essentially, an assignment statement takes the following form:

```
SET target = source ;
```

In this usage, target is a variable name, and source is an expression. Several examples might include the following:

```
SET vfname = 'Brandon' ;
```

```
SET varea = 3.1416 * :radius * :radius ;
```

```
SET vhiggsmass = NULL ;
```

Flow of Control Statements

Since its original formulation in the SQL-86 standard, one of the main drawbacks that has prevented people from using SQL in a procedural manner has been its lack of flow of control statements. Until SQL/PSM was included in the SQL standard, you couldn't branch out of a strict sequential order of execution without reverting to a host language like C or BASIC. SQL/PSM introduces the traditional flow of control structures that other languages provide, thus allowing SQL programs to perform needed functions without switching back and forth between languages.

IF...THEN...ELSE...END IF

The most basic flow of control statement is the IF...THEN...ELSE...END IF statement. This statement, roughly translated from computerese, means IF a condition is true, then execute the statements following the THEN keyword. Otherwise, execute the statements following the ELSE keyword. For example:

```
IF
    vfname = 'Brandon'
THEN
    UPDATE students
        SET Fname = 'Brandon'
        WHERE StudentID = 314159 ;
ELSE
    DELETE FROM students
        WHERE StudentID = 314159 ;
END IF
```

In this example, if the variable vfname contains the value 'Brandon', then the record for student 314159 is updated with 'Brandon' in the Fname field. If the variable vfname contains any value other than 'Brandon', then the record for student 314159 is deleted from the STUDENTS table.

The IF...THEN...ELSE...END IF statement is great if you want to choose one of two actions based on the value of a condition. Often, however, you want to make a selection from more than two choices. At such times, you should probably use a CASE statement.

CASE...END CASE

CASE statements come in two forms: the simple CASE statement and the searched CASE statement. Both kinds allow you to take different execution paths based on the values of conditions.

Simple CASE statement

A simple CASE statement evaluates a single condition. Based on the value of that condition, execution may take one of several branches. For example:

```
CASE vmajor
    WHEN 'Computer Science'
    THEN INSERT INTO geeks (StudentID, Fname, Lname)
            VALUES (:sid, :sfname, :slname) ;
    WHEN 'Sports Medicine'
    THEN INSERT INTO jocks (StudentID, Fname, Lname)
            VALUES (:sid, :sfname, :slname) ;
    ELSE INSERT INTO undeclared (StudentID, Fname, Lname)
            VALUES (:sid, :sfname, :slname) ;
END CASE
```

The ELSE clause handles everything that doesn't fall into the explicitly named categories in the THEN clauses.

You don't need to use the ELSE clause — it's optional. However, if you don't include it, and the CASE statement's condition is not handled by any of the THEN clauses, SQL returns an exception.

Searched CASE statement

A searched CASE statement is similar to a simple CASE statement, but it evaluates multiple conditions rather than just one. For example:

```
CASE
    WHEN vmajor
        IN ('Computer Science', 'Electrical Engineering')
        THEN INSERT INTO geeks (StudentID, Fname, Lname)
            VALUES (:sid, :sfname, :slname) ;
    WHEN vclub
        IN ('Amateur Radio', 'Rocket', 'Computer')
        THEN INSERT INTO geeks (StudentID, Fname, Lname)
            VALUES (:sid, :sfname, :slname) ;
    ELSE
        INSERT INTO poets (StudentID, Fname, Lname)
            VALUES (:sid, :sfname, :slname) ;
END CASE
```

You avoid an exception by putting all students who are not geeks into the POETS table. Because not all nongeeks are poets, this may not be strictly accurate in all cases. If it isn't, you can always add a few more WHEN clauses.

LOOP...ENDLOOP

The LOOP statement allows you to execute a sequence of SQL statements multiple times. After the last SQL statement enclosed within the LOOP...ENDLOOP statement executes, control loops back to the first such statement and makes another pass through the enclosed statements. The syntax is as follows:

```
SET vcount = 0 ;
LOOP
    SET vcount = vcount + 1 ;
    INSERT INTO asteroid (AsteroidID)
        VALUES (vcount) ;
END LOOP
```

This code fragment preloads your ASTEROID table with unique identifiers. You can fill in other details about the asteroids as you find them, based on what you see through your telescope when you discover them.

Notice the one little problem with the code fragment in the preceding example: It is an infinite loop. No provision is made for leaving the loop, so it will continue inserting rows into the ASTEROID table until the DBMS fills all available storage with ASTEROID table records. If you're lucky, the DBMS will raise an exception at that time. If you're unlucky, the system will merely crash.

For the LOOP statement to be useful, you need a way to exit loops before you raise an exception. That way is the LEAVE statement.

LEAVE

The LEAVE statement works just like you might expect it to work. When execution encounters a LEAVE statement embedded within a labeled statement, it proceeds to the next statement beyond the labeled statement. For example:

```
AsteroidPreload:
SET vcount = 0 ;
LOOP
    SET vcount = vcount + 1 ;
    IF vcount > 10000
        THEN
            LEAVE AsteroidPreload ;
    END IF ;
    INSERT INTO asteroid (AsteroidID)
        VALUES (vcount) ;
END LOOP AsteroidPreload
```

The preceding code inserts 10,000 sequentially numbered records into the ASTEROID table, and then passes out of the loop.

WHILE...DO...END WHILE

The WHILE statement provides another method of executing a series of SQL statements multiple times. While a designated condition is true, the WHILE loop continues to execute. When the condition becomes false, looping stops. For example:

```
AsteroidPreload2:
SET vcount = 0 ;
WHILE
    vcount < 10000 DO
        SET vcount = vcount + 1 ;
        INSERT INTO asteroid (AsteroidID)
            VALUES (vcount) ;
END WHILE AsteroidPreload2
```

This code does exactly the same thing that AsteroidPreload did in the preceding section. This is just another example of the often-cited fact that with SQL, you usually have multiple ways to accomplish any given task. Use whichever method you feel most comfortable with, assuming your implementation allows both.

REPEAT...UNTIL...END REPEAT

The REPEAT loop is very much like the WHILE loop, except that the condition is checked after the embedded statements execute rather than before. Example:

```
AsteroidPreload3 :
SET vcount = 0 ;
REPEAT
    SET vcount = vcount + 1 ;
    INSERT INTO asteroid (AsteroidID)
       VALUES (vcount) ;
    UNTIL X = 10000
END REPEAT AsteroidPreload3
```

Although you can perform the same operation three different ways (with LOOP, WHILE, and REPEAT), you will encounter some instances when one of these structures is clearly better than the other two. Have all three methods in your bag of tricks so that when a situation like this arises you can decide which one is the best tool available for the situation.

FOR...DO...END FOR

The SQL FOR loop declares and opens a cursor, fetches the rows of the cursor, executes the body of the FOR statement once for each row, and then closes the cursor. This loop makes processing possible entirely within SQL, instead of switching out to a host language. If your implementation supports SQL FOR loops, you can use them as a simple alternative to the cursor processing described in Chapter 18. Here's an example:

```
FOR vcount AS Curs1 CURSOR FOR
    SELECT AsteroidID FROM asteroid
DO
    UPDATE asteroid SET Description = 'stony iron'
       WHERE CURRENT OF Curs1 ;
END FOR
```

In this example, you update every row in the ASTEROID table by putting 'stony iron' into the Description field. This is a fast way to identify the compositions of asteroids, but the table may suffer some in the accuracy department. Perhaps you'd be better off checking the spectral signatures of the asteroids and then entering their types individually.

ITERATE

The ITERATE statement provides a way to change the flow of execution within an iterated SQL statement. The iterated SQL statements are LOOP, WHILE,

REPEAT, and FOR. If the iteration condition of the iterated SQL statement is true or not specified, then the next iteration of the loop commences immediately after the ITERATE statement executes. If the iteration condition of the iterated SQL statement is false or unknown, then iteration ceases after the ITERATE statement executes. For example:

```
AsteroidPreload4:
SET vcount = 0 ;
WHILE
    vcount < 10000 DO
        SET vcount = vcount + 1 ;
        INSERT INTO asteroid (AsteroidID)
            VALUES (vcount) ;
        ITERATE AsteroidPreload4 ;
        SET vpreload = 'DONE' ;
END WHILE AsteroidPreload4
```

Execution loops back to the top of the WHILE statement immediately after the ITERATE statement each time through the loop until vcount equals 9999. On that iteration, vcount increments to 10000, the INSERT performs, the ITERATE statement ceases iteration, vpreload is set to 'DONE', and execution proceeds to the next statement after the loop.

Stored Procedures

Stored procedures reside in the database on the server, rather than execute on the client — where all procedures were located before SQL/PSM. After you define a stored procedure, you can invoke it with a CALL statement. Keeping the procedure located on the server rather than the client reduces network traffic, thus speeding performance. The only traffic that needs to pass from the client to the server is the CALL statement. You can create this procedure in the following manner:

```
EXEC SQL
    CREATE PROCEDURE MatchScore
        ( IN result CHAR (3),
          OUT winner CHAR (5) )
    BEGIN ATOMIC
        CASE result
            WHEN '1-0' THEN
                SET winner = 'white' ;
            WHEN '0-1' THEN
                SET winner = 'black' ;
            ELSE
                SET winner = 'draw' ;
        END CASE
    END ;
```

After you have created a stored procedure like the one in this example, you can invoke it with a CALL statement similar to the following statement:

```
CALL MatchScore ('Kasparov', 'Karpov', '1-0', winner) ;
```

The first three arguments are input parameters that are fed to the MatchScore procedure. The fourth argument is the output parameter that the MatchScore procedure uses to return its result to the calling routine. In this case, it returns 'white'.

Stored Functions

A stored function is similar in many ways to a stored procedure. Collectively, the two are referred to as *stored routines.* They are different in several ways, including the way in which they are invoked. A stored procedure is invoked with a CALL statement, and a stored function is invoked with a *function call,* which can replace an argument of an SQL statement. The following is an example of a function definition, followed by an example of a call to that function:

```
CREATE FUNCTION PurchaseHistory (CustID)
   RETURNS CHAR VARYING (200)

   BEGIN
      DECLARE purch CHAR VARYING (200)
         DEFAULT '' ;
      FOR x AS SELECT *
               FROM transactions t
               WHERE t.customerID = CustID
      DO
         IF a <> ''
            THEN SET purch = purch || ', ' ;
         END IF ;
         SET purch = purch || t.description ;
      END FOR
      RETURN purch ;
   END ;
```

This function definition creates a comma-delimited list of purchases made by a customer that has a specified customer number, taken from the TRANSACTIONS table. The following UPDATE statement contains a function call to PurchaseHistory that inserts the latest purchase history for customer number 314259 into her record in the CUSTOMER table:

```
SET customerID = 314259 ;
UPDATE customer
   SET history = PurchaseHistory (customerID)
   WHERE customerID = 314259 ;
```

Privileges

I discuss the various privileges that you can grant to users in Chapter 13. The database owner can grant the following privileges to other users:

- ✔ The right to DELETE rows from a table
- ✔ The right to INSERT rows into a table
- ✔ The right to UPDATE rows in a table
- ✔ The right to create a table that REFERENCES another table
- ✔ The right of USAGE on a domain

SQL/PSM adds one more privilege that can be granted to a user — the EXECUTE privilege. Here are two examples:

```
GRANT EXECUTE on MatchScore to TournamentDirector ;
```

```
GRANT EXECUTE on PurchaseHistory to SalesManager ;
```

These statements allow the tournament director of the chess match to execute the MatchScore procedure, and the sales manager of the company to execute the PurchaseHistory function. People lacking the EXECUTE privilege for a routine aren't able to use it.

Stored Modules

A stored module can contain multiple routines (procedures and/or functions) that can be invoked by SQL. Anyone who has the EXECUTE privilege for a module has access to all the routines in the module. Privileges on routines within a module can't be granted individually. The following is an example of a stored module:

```
CREATE MODULE mod1
    PROCEDURE MatchScore
        ( IN white CHAR (20),
          IN black CHAR (20),
          IN result CHAR (3),
          OUT winner CHAR (5) )
    BEGIN ATOMIC
        CASE result
            WHEN '1-0' THEN
                SET winner = 'white' ;
            WHEN '0-1' THEN
```

```
              SET winner = 'black' ;
          ELSE
              SET winner = 'draw' ;
       END CASE
    END ;
    FUNCTION PurchaseHistory (CustID)
    RETURNS CHAR VARYING (200)
    BEGIN
       DECLARE purch CHAR VARYING (200)
          DEFAULT '' ;
       FOR x AS SELECT *
              FROM transactions t
              WHERE t.customerID = CustID
       DO
          IF a <> ''
             THEN SET purch = purch || ', ' ;
          END IF ;
          SET purch = purch || t.description ;
       END FOR
       RETURN purch ;
    END ;
 END MODULE ;
```

 The two routines in this module don't have much in common, but they don't have to. You can gather related routines into a single module, or you can stick all the routines you are likely to use into a single module, regardless of whether they have anything in common.

Chapter 20

Handling Errors

• •

In This Chapter

▶ Flagging error conditions

▶ Branching to error-handling code

▶ Determining the exact nature of an error

▶ Determining which DBMS generated an error condition

• •

*W*ouldn't it be great if every application you wrote worked perfectly every time? Yeah, and it would also be really cool to win $314.9 million playing Powerball. Unfortunately, both possibilities are equally unlikely to happen. Error conditions of one sort or another are inevitable, so it's helpful to know what causes them. SQL's mechanism for returning error information to you is the *status parameter* (or *host variable*) SQLSTATE. Based on the contents of SQLSTATE, you can take different actions to remedy the error condition.

For example, the WHENEVER directive enables you to take a predetermined action whenever a specified condition (if SQLSTATE has a non-zero value, for example) is met. You can also find detailed status information about the SQL statement that you just executed in the diagnostics area. In this chapter, I explain these helpful error-handling facilities and how to use them.

SQLSTATE

SQLSTATE specifies a large number of anomalous conditions. SQLSTATE is a five-character string in which only the uppercase letters *A* through *Z* and the numerals 0 through 9 are valid characters. The five-character string is divided into two groups: a two-character class code and a three-character subclass code. Figure 20-1 illustrates the SQLSTATE layout.

The SQL standard defines any class code that starts with the letters *A* through *H* or the numerals 0 through 4; therefore, these class codes mean the same thing in any implementation. Class codes that start with the letters *I* through *Z* or the numerals 5 through 9 are left open for implementors (the people who build database management systems) to define because the SQL specification can't anticipate every condition that may come up in every implementation. However, implementors should use these nonstandard class codes as little as possible to avoid migration problems from one DBMS to another. Ideally, implementors should use the standard codes most of the time and the non-standard codes only under the most unusual circumstances.

Figure 20-1:
SQLSTATE
status
parameter
layout.

Class code   Subclass code

I introduce SQLSTATE in Chapter 19, but here's a recap. A class code of 00 indicates successful completion. Class code 01 means that the statement executed successfully but produced a warning. Class code 02 indicates a no data condition. Any SQLSTATE class code other than 00, 01, or 02 indicates that the statement did not execute successfully.

Because SQLSTATE updates after every SQL operation, you can check it after every statement executes. If SQLSTATE contains 00000 (successful completion), you can proceed with the next operation. If it contains anything else, you may want to branch out of the main line of your code to handle the situation. The specific class code and subclass code that an SQLSTATE contains determine which of several possible actions you should take.

To use SQLSTATE in a module language program (which I describe in Chapter 15), include a reference to it in your procedure definitions, as the following example shows:

```
PROCEDURE NUTRIENT
   (SQLSTATE, :foodname CHAR (20), :calories SMALLINT,
      :protein DECIMAL (5,1), :fat DECIMAL (5,1),
      :carbo DECIMAL (5,1))
INSERT INTO FOODS
   (FoodName, Calories, Protein, Fat, Carbohydrate)
   VALUES
   (:foodname, :calories, :protein, :fat, :carbo) ;
```

At the appropriate spot in your procedural language program, you can make values available for the parameters (perhaps by soliciting them from the user) and then call up the procedure. The syntax of this operation varies from one language to another, but it looks something like this:

```
foodname = "Okra, boiled" ;
calories = 29 ;
protein = 2.0 ;
fat = 0.3 ;
carbo = 6.0 ;
NUTRIENT(state, foodname, calories, protein, fat, carbo);
```

The state of SQLSTATE is returned in the variable state. Your program can examine this variable and then take the appropriate action based on the variable's contents.

WHENEVER Clause

What's the point of knowing that an SQL operation didn't execute successfully if you can't do anything about it? If an error occurs, you don't want your application to continue executing as if everything is fine. You need to be able to acknowledge the error and do something to correct it. If you can't correct the error, at the very least you want to inform the user of the problem and bring the application to a graceful termination. The WHENEVER directive is the SQL mechanism for dealing with execution exceptions.

The WHENEVER directive is actually a declaration and is therefore located in your application's SQL declaration section, before the executable SQL code. The syntax is as follows:

```
WHENEVER condition action ;
```

The condition may be either SQLERROR or NOT FOUND. The action may be either CONTINUE or GOTO address. SQLERROR is True if SQLSTATE has a class code other than 00, 01, or 02. NOT FOUND is True if SQLSTATE is 02000.

If the action is CONTINUE, nothing special happens, and the execution continues normally. If the action is GOTO address (or GO TO address), execution branches to the designated address in the program. At the branch address, you can put a conditional statement that examines SQLSTATE and takes different actions based on what it finds. Here are some examples of this scenario:

```
WHENEVER SQLERROR GO TO error_trap ;
```

or

```
WHENEVER NOT FOUND CONTINUE ;
```

The GO TO option is simply a macro: The *implementation* (that is, the embedded language precompiler) inserts the following test after every EXEC SQL statement:

```
IF SQLSTATE <> '00000'
    AND SQLSTATE <> '00001'
    AND SQLSTATE <> '00002'
THEN GOTO error_trap;
```

The CONTINUE option is essentially a NO-OP that says "ignore this."

Diagnostics Areas

Although SQLSTATE can give you some information about why a particular statement failed, the information is pretty brief. So SQL provides for the capture and retention of additional status information in diagnostics areas.

Multiple diagnostics areas are maintained in the form of a *last-in-first-out* (LIFO) stack. That is, information on the most recent error can be found at the top of the stack, with info on older errors farther down in the list. The additional status information in a diagnostics area can be particularly helpful in cases in which the execution of a single SQL statement generates multiple warnings followed by an error. SQLSTATE only reports the occurrence of one error, but the diagnostics area has the capacity to report on multiple (hopefully all) errors.

The diagnostics area is a DBMS-managed data structure that has two components:

- ✔ **Header:** The header contains general information about the last SQL statement that was executed.
- ✔ **Detail area:** The detail area contains information about each code (error, warning, or success) that the statement generated.

The diagnostics header area

In the SET TRANSACTION statement (described in Chapter 14), you can specify DIAGNOSTICS SIZE. The SIZE that you specify is the number of detail areas allocated for status information. If you don't include a DIAGNOSTICS SIZE clause in your SET TRANSACTION statement, your DBMS assigns its default number of detail areas, whatever that happens to be.

The header area contains several items, as listed in Table 20-1.

Table 20-1	Diagnostics Header Area
Fields	*Data Type*
NUMBER	Exact numeric with no fractional part
ROW_COUNT	Exact numeric with no fractional part
COMMAND_FUNCTION	VARCHAR (>=128)
COMMAND_FUNCTION_CODE	Exact numeric with no fractional part
DYNAMIC_FUNCTION	VARCHAR (>=128)
DYNAMIC_FUNCTION_CODE	Exact numeric with no fractional part
MORE	Exact numeric with no fractional part
TRANSACTIONS_COMMITTED	Exact numeric with no fractional part
TRANSACTIONS_ROLLED_BACK	Exact numeric with no fractional part
TRANSACTION_ACTIVE	Exact numeric with no fractional part

The following list describes these items in more detail:

- The NUMBER field is the number of detail areas that have been filled with diagnostic information about the current exception.
- The ROW_COUNT field holds the number of rows affected if the previous SQL statement was an INSERT, UPDATE, or DELETE.
- The COMMAND_FUNCTION field describes the SQL statement that was just executed.
- The COMMAND_FUNCTION_CODE field gives the code number for the SQL statement that was just executed. Every command function has an associated numeric code.
- The DYNAMIC_FUNCTION field contains the dynamic SQL statement.
- The DYNAMIC_FUNCTION_CODE field contains a numeric code corresponding to the dynamic SQL statement.
- The MORE field may be either a 'Y' or an 'N'. 'Y' indicates that there are more status records than the detail area can hold. 'N' indicates that

all the status records generated are present in the detail area. Depending on your implementation, you may be able to expand the number of records you can handle by using the `SET TRANSACTION` statement.

✔ The `TRANSACTIONS_COMMITTED` field holds the number of transactions that have been committed.

✔ The `TRANSACTIONS_ROLLED_BACK` field holds the number of transactions that have been rolled back.

✔ The `TRANSACTION_ACTIVE` field holds a `'1'` if a transaction is currently active and a `'0'` otherwise. A transaction is deemed to be active if a cursor is open or if the DBMS is waiting for a deferred parameter.

The diagnostics detail area

The detail areas contain data on each individual error, warning, or success condition. Each detail area contains 28 items, as Table 20-2 shows.

Table 20-2	Diagnostics Detail Area
Fields	*Data Type*
CONDITION_NUMBER	Exact numeric with no fractional part
RETURNED_SQLSTATE	CHAR (6)
MESSAGE_TEXT	VARCHAR (>=128)
MESSAGE_LENGTH	Exact numeric with no fractional part
MESSAGE_OCTET_LENGTH	Exact numeric with no fractional part
CLASS_ORIGIN	VARCHAR (>=128)
SUBCLASS_ORIGIN	VARCHAR (>=128)
CONNECTION_NAME	VARCHAR (>=128)
SERVER_NAME	VARCHAR (>=128)
CONSTRAINT_CATALOG	VARCHAR (>=128)
CONSTRAINT_SCHEMA	VARCHAR (>=128)
CONSTRAINT_NAME	VARCHAR (>=128)
CATALOG_NAME	VARCHAR (>=128)

Fields	Data Type
SCHEMA_NAME	VARCHAR (>=128)
TABLE_NAME	VARCHAR (>=128)
COLUMN_NAME	VARCHAR (>=128)
CURSOR_NAME	VARCHAR (>=128)
CONDITION_IDENTIFIER	VARCHAR (>=128)
PARAMETER_NAME	VARCHAR (>=128)
PARAMETER_ORDINAL_POSITION	Exact numeric with no fractional part
PARAMETER_MODE	Exact numeric with no fractional part
ROUTINE_CATALOG	VARCHAR (>=128)
ROUTINE_SCHEMA	VARCHAR (>=128)
ROUTINE_NAME	VARCHAR (>=128)
SPECIFIC_NAME	VARCHAR (>=128)
TRIGGER_CATALOG	VARCHAR (>=128)
TRIGGER_SCHEMA	VARCHAR (>=128)
TRIGGER_NAME	VARCHAR (>=128)

CONDITION_NUMBER holds the sequence number of the detail area. If a statement generates five status items that fill up five detail areas, the CONDITION_NUMBER for the fifth detail area is 5. To retrieve a specific detail area for examination, use a GET DIAGNOSTICS statement (described later in this chapter in the "Interpreting the information returned by SQLSTATE" section) with the desired CONDITION_NUMBER. RETURNED_SQLSTATE holds the SQLSTATE value that caused this detail area to be filled.

CLASS_ORIGIN tells you the source of the class code value returned in SQLSTATE. If the SQL standard defines the value, the CLASS_ORIGIN is 'ISO 9075'. If your DBMS implementation defines the value, CLASS_ORIGIN holds a string identifying the source of your DBMS. SUBCLASS_ORIGIN tells you the source of the subclass code value returned in SQLSTATE.

CLASS_ORIGIN is important. If you get an SQLSTATE of '22012', for example, the values indicate that it is in the range of standard SQLSTATEs, so you know that it means the same thing in all SQL implementations. However, if the SQLSTATE is '22500', the first two characters are in the standard range and indicate a data exception, but the last three characters are in the implementation-defined range. And if SQLSTATE is '900001', it's completely in the implementation-defined range. SQLSTATE values in the implementation-defined range can mean different things in different implementations, even though the code itself may be the same.

So how do you find out the detailed meaning of '22500' or the meaning of '900001'? You must look in the implementor's documentation. Which implementor? If you're using CONNECT, you may be connecting to various products. To determine which one produced the error condition, look at CLASS_ORIGIN and SUBCLASS_ORIGIN: They have values that identify each implementation. You can test the CLASS_ORIGIN and SUBCLASS_ORIGIN to see whether they identify implementors for which you have the SQLSTATE listings. The actual values placed in CLASS_ORIGIN and SUBCLASS_ORIGIN are implementor-defined, but they also are expected to be self-explanatory company names.

If the error reported is a constraint violation, the CONSTRAINT_CATALOG, CONSTRAINT_SCHEMA, and CONSTRAINT_NAME identify the constraint being violated.

Constraint violation example

The constraint violation information is probably the most important information that GET DIAGNOSTICS provides. Consider the following EMPLOYEE table:

```
CREATE TABLE EMPLOYEE
(ID CHAR(5) CONSTRAINT EmpPK PRIMARY KEY,
Salary DEC(8,2) CONSTRAINT EmpSal CHECK Salary > 0,
Dept CHAR(5) CONSTRAINT EmpDept,
REFERENCES DEPARTMENT) ;
```

And this DEPARTMENT table:

```
CREATE TABLE DEPARTMENT
    (DeptNo       CHAR(5),
     Budget       DEC(12,2) CONSTRAINT DeptBudget
       CHECK(Budget >= SELECT SUM(Salary)
                        FROM EMPLOYEE
                        WHERE
          EMPLOYEE.Dept=DEPARTMENT.DeptNo),
    ...);
```

Now consider an INSERT as follows:

```
INSERT INTO EMPLOYEE VALUES(:ID_VAR, :SAL_VAR, :DEPT_VAR);
```

Now suppose that you get an SQLSTATE of '23000'. You look it up in your SQL documentation and discover that this means that the statement is committing an "integrity constraint violation." Now what? That SQLSTATE value means that one of the following situations is true:

- ✔ **The value in ID_VAR is a duplicate of an existing ID value:** You have violated the PRIMARY KEY constraint.

- ✔ **The value in SAL_VAR is negative:** You have violated the CHECK constraint on Salary.

- ✔ **The value in DEPT_VAR isn't a valid key value for any existing row of DEPARTMENT:** You have violated the REFERENCES constraint on Dept.

- ✔ **The value in SAL_VAR is large enough that the sum of the employees' salaries in this department exceeds the BUDGET:** You have violated the CHECK constraint in the BUDGET column of DEPARTMENT. (Recall that if you change the database, all constraints that may be affected are checked, not just those defined in the immediate table.)

Under normal circumstances, you would need to do a great deal of testing to figure out what is wrong with that INSERT. But you can find out what you need to know by using GET DIAGNOSTICS as follows:

```
DECLARE ConstNameVar CHAR(18) ;
GET DIAGNOSTICS EXCEPTION 1
   ConstNameVar = CONSTRAINT_NAME ;
```

Assuming that SQLSTATE is '23000', this GET DIAGNOSTICS sets ConstNameVar to 'EmpPK', 'EmpSal', 'EmpDept', or 'DeptBudget'. Notice that, in practice, you also want to obtain the CONSTRAINT_SCHEMA and CONSTRAINT_CATALOG to uniquely identify the constraint given by CONSTRAINT_NAME.

Adding constraints to an existing table

This use of GET DIAGNOSTICS — determining which of several constraints has been violated — is particularly important in the case where ALTER TABLE is used to add constraints that didn't exist when you wrote the program:

```
ALTER TABLE EMPLOYEE
   ADD CONSTRAINT SalLimit CHECK(Salary < 200000) ;
```

Now if you insert data into EMPLOYEE or update the Salary column of EMPLOYEE, you get an SQLSTATE of '23000' if Salary exceeds $200,000. You can program your INSERT statement so that, if you get an SQLSTATE of '23000' and you don't recognize the particular constraint name that GET DIAGNOSTICS returns, you can display a helpful message, such as Invalid INSERT: Violated constraint SalLimit.

Interpreting the information returned by SQLSTATE

CONNECTION_NAME and ENVIRONMENT_NAME identify the connection and environment to which you are connected at the time the SQL statement is executed.

If the report deals with a table operation, CATALOG_NAME, SCHEMA_NAME, and TABLE_NAME identify the table. COLUMN_NAME identifies the column within the table that caused the report to be made. If the situation involves a cursor, CURSOR_NAME gives its name.

Sometimes a DBMS produces a string of natural language text to explain a condition. The MESSAGE_TEXT item is for this kind of information. The contents of this item depend on the implementation; the SQL standard doesn't explicitly define them. If you do have something in MESSAGE_TEXT, its length in characters is recorded in MESSAGE_LENGTH, and its length in octets is recorded in MESSAGE_OCTET_LENGTH. If the message is in normal ASCII characters, MESSAGE_LENGTH equals MESSAGE_OCTET_LENGTH. If, on the other hand, the message is in kanji or some other language whose characters require more than an octet to express, MESSAGE_LENGTH differs from MESSAGE_OCTET_LENGTH.

To retrieve diagnostic information from a diagnostics area header, use the following:

```
GET DIAGNOSTICS status1 = item1 [, status2 = item2]... ;
```

status*n* is a host variable or parameter; item*n* can be any of the keywords NUMBER, MORE, COMMAND_FUNCTION, DYNAMIC_FUNCTION, or ROW_COUNT.

To retrieve diagnostic information from a diagnostics detail area, use the following syntax:

```
GET DIAGNOSTICS EXCEPTION condition-number
    status1 = item1 [, status2 = item2]... ;
```

Again status*n* is a host variable or parameter, and item*n* is any of the 26 keywords for the detail items listed in Table 20-2. The condition number is (surprise!) the detail area's CONDITION_NUMBER item.

Handling Exceptions

When SQLSTATE indicates an exception condition by holding a value other than 00000, 00001, or 00002, you may want to handle the situation by

- Returning control to the parent procedure that called the subprocedure that raised the exception.

- Using a WHENEVER clause (as described earlier in this chapter) to branch to an exception-handling routine or perform some other action.

- Handing the exception on the spot with a *compound* SQL statement (as described in Chapter 19). A compound SQL statement consists of one or more simple SQL statements, sandwiched between BEGIN and END keywords.

The following is an example of a compound-statement exception handler:

```
BEGIN
    DECLARE   ValueOutOfRange EXCEPTION FOR SQLSTATE '73003'
          ;
    INSERT INTO FOODS
       (Calories)
       VALUES
       (:cal) ;
    SIGNAL ValueOutOfRange ;
    MESSAGE 'Process a new calorie value.'
    EXCEPTION
       WHEN ValueOutOfRange THEN
          MESSAGE 'Handling the calorie range error' ;
       WHEN OTHERS THEN
          RESIGNAL ;
END
```

With one or more DECLARE statements, you can give names to specific SQLSTATE values that you suspect may arise. The INSERT statement is the one that might cause an exception to occur. If the value of :cal exceeds the maximum value for a SMALLINT data item, SQLSTATE is set to "73003". The SIGNAL statement signals an exception condition. It clears the top diagnostics area. It sets the RETURNED_SQLSTATE field of the diagnostics area to the SQLSTATE for the named exception. If no exception has occurred, the series of statements represented by the MESSAGE 'Process a new calorie value' statement is executed. However, if an exception has occurred, that series of statements is skipped, and the EXCEPTION statement is executed.

If the exception was a ValueOutOfRange exception, then a series of statements represented by the MESSAGE 'Handling the calorie range error' statement is executed. The RESIGNAL statement is executed if the exception isn't a ValueOutOfRange exception.

RESIGNAL merely passes control of execution to the calling parent procedure. That procedure may have additional error-handling code to deal with exceptions other than the expected value out-of-range error.

Part VII

The Part of Tens

In this part . . .

If you've read all the previous parts of this book, congratulations! You may now consider yourself an SQL weenie (spicy mustard optional). To raise your status that final degree from weenie to wizard, you must master two sets of ten rules. But don't make the mistake of just reading the section headings. Taking some of these headings at face value could have dire consequences. All the tips in this part are short and to the point, so reading them all (in their entirety, if you please) shouldn't be too much trouble. Put them into practice, and you can be a true SQL wizard.

Chapter 21

Ten Common Mistakes

In This Chapter

▶ Assuming that your clients know what they need

▶ Not worrying about project scope

▶ Considering only technical factors

▶ Never asking for user feedback

▶ Only using your favorite development environment or system architecture

▶ Designing database tables in isolation

▶ Skipping design reviews, beta testing, and documentation

*I*f you're reading this book, you must be interested in building relational database systems. Let's face it — nobody studies SQL for the fun of it. You use SQL to build database applications, but before you can build one, you need a database. Unfortunately, many projects go awry before the first line of the application is coded. If you don't get the database definition right, your application is doomed — no matter how well you write it. Here are ten common database-creation mistakes that you should be on the lookout for.

Assuming That Your Clients Know What They Need

Generally, clients call you in to design a database system when they have a problem getting the data they need because their current methods aren't working. Clients often believe that they have identified the problem and its solution. They figure that all they need to do is tell *you* what to do.

Giving clients exactly what they ask for is usually a sure-fire prescription for disaster. Most users (and their managers) don't possess the knowledge or skills necessary to accurately identify the problem, so they have little chance of determining the best solution.

Your job is to tactfully convince your client that you are an expert in systems analysis and design, and that you must do a proper analysis to uncover the real cause of the problem. Usually the real cause of the problem is hidden behind the more obvious symptoms.

Ignoring Project Scope

Your client tells you what he or she expects from the new application at the beginning of the development project. Unfortunately, the client almost always forgets to tell you something — usually several things. Throughout the job, these new requirements crop up and are tacked onto the project. If you're being paid on a project basis rather than an hourly basis, this growth in scope can change what was once a profitable project into a loser. Make sure that everything you're obligated to deliver is specified in writing before you start the project.

Considering Only Technical Factors

Application developers often consider potential projects in terms of their technical feasibility, and they base their time and effort estimates on that determination. However, issues of cost maximums, resource availability, schedule requirements, and organization politics can have a major effect on the project. These issues may turn a project that is technically feasible into a nightmare. Make sure that you understand all relevant nontechnical factors before you start any development project. You may decide that it makes no sense to proceed; you're better off reaching that conclusion at the beginning of the project than after you have expended considerable effort.

Not Asking for Client Feedback

Your first inclination might be to listen to the managers who hire you. After all, the users themselves don't have any clout and they sure as heck don't pay your fee. On the other hand, there may be good reason to ignore the managers, too. They usually don't have a clue about what the users really need. Wait a minute! Don't ignore everyone or assume that you know more than a manager or user about what a database should do and how it should work. Data-entry clerks don't typically have much organizational clout, and many managers have only a dim understanding of some aspects of the work and data-entry clerks do. But isolating yourself from either group is almost certain to result in a system that solves a problem that nobody has. You can learn a lot from managers and from users by asking the right questions.

Always Using Your Favorite Development Environment

You've probably spent months or even years becoming proficient in the use of a particular DBMS or application development environment. But your favorite environment — no matter what it is — has strengths and weaknesses. Occasionally, you come across a development task that makes heavy demands in an area where your preferred development environment is weak. So rather than kludge together something that isn't really the best solution, bite the bullet. You have two options: Either climb the learning curve of a more appropriate tool and then use it, or candidly tell your clients that their job would best be done with a tool that you're not an expert at using. Then suggest that the client hire someone who can be productive with that tool right away. Professional conduct of this sort garners your clients' respect. (Unfortunately, if you work for a company instead of for yourself, that conduct may also get you laid off or fired. Best to go with option one — dive on into a new development environment.)

Using Your Favorite System Architecture Exclusively

Nobody can be an expert at everything. Database management systems that work in a teleprocessing environment are different than systems that work in client/server, resource sharing, or distributed database environments. The one or two systems that you are expert in may not be the best for the job at hand. Choose the best architecture anyway, even if it means passing on the job. Not getting the job is better than getting it and producing a system that doesn't serve the client's needs.

Designing Database Tables in Isolation

If you incorrectly identify data objects and their relationships to each other, your database tables are likely to introduce errors into the data and destroy the validity of any results. To design a sound database, you must consider the overall organization of the data objects and carefully determine how they relate to each other. Usually, no single *right* design exists. You must determine what is appropriate, considering your client's present and projected needs.

Neglecting Design Reviews

Nobody's perfect. Even the best designer and developer can miss important points that are evident to someone looking at the situation from a different perspective. Actually, presenting your work before a formal design review makes you more disciplined in your work — probably helping you avoid numerous problems that you may otherwise have experienced. Have a competent professional review your proposed design before you start development. You should have a database designer check it over, but you may want to show it to the client, as well.

Skipping Beta Testing

Any database application complex enough to be truly useful is also complex enough to contain bugs. Even if you test it in every way you can think of, the application is sure to contain failure modes that you don't uncover. Beta testing means giving the application to people who don't know how it was designed. They're likely to have problems that you never encountered because you know too much about the application. If they're familiar with the data, but not the database, they're also more likely to use the application as they would on a daily basis, so they can pinpoint queries that take a long time to generate results. You can then fix the bugs or performance shortfalls that others find before the product goes officially into use.

Not Documenting Your Process

If you think your application is so perfect that it never needs to be looked at, even once more, think again. The only thing you can be absolutely sure of in this world is change. Count on it. Six months from now, you won't remember why you designed things the way you did, unless you carefully document what you did and why you did it that way. If you transfer to a different department or win the lottery and retire, your replacement has almost no chance of modifying your work to meet new requirements if you didn't document your design.

Without documentation, your replacement may need to scrap the whole thing and start from scratch. Don't just document your work adequately — over-document your work. Put in more detail than you think is reasonable. If you come back to this project after six or eight months away from it, you'll be glad you documented it in detail.

Chapter 22

Ten Retrieval Tips

In This Chapter

▶ Verifying the structure of your database

▶ Using test databases

▶ Scrutinizing any queries containing joins

▶ Examining queries containing subselects

▶ Using GROUP BY with the SET functions

▶ Being aware of restrictions on the GROUP BY clause

▶ Using parentheses in expressions

▶ Protecting your database by controlling privileges

▶ Backing up your database regularly

▶ Anticipating and handling errors

A database can be a virtual treasure trove of information, but like the treasure of the Caribbean pirates of long ago, the stuff that you really want is probably buried and hidden from view. The SQL SELECT statement is your tool for digging up this hidden information. Even if you have a clear idea of what you want to retrieve, translating that idea into SQL can be a challenge. If your formulation is just a little off, you may end up with the wrong results — but results that are so close to what you expected that they mislead you. To reduce your chances of being misled, use the following ten principles.

Verify the Database Structure

If you retrieve data from a database and your results don't seem reasonable, check the database design. Many poorly designed databases are in use, and if you're working with one, fix the design before you try any other remedy. Remember — good design is a prerequisite of data integrity.

Try Queries on a Test Database

Create a test database that has the same structure as your production data-base, but with only a few representative rows in the tables. Choose the data so that you know in advance what the results of your queries should be. Run each test query on the test data and see whether the results match your expectations. If they don't, you may need to reformulate your queries. If a query is properly formulated but you end up with bad results all the same, you may need to restructure your database.

Build several sets of test data and be sure to include odd cases, such as empty tables and extreme values at the very limit of allowable ranges. Try to think of unlikely scenarios and check for proper behavior when they occur. In the course of checking for unlikely cases, you may gain insight into problems that are more likely to happen.

Double-Check Queries That Include Joins

Joins are notoriously counterintuitive. If your query contains one, make sure that it's doing what you expect before you add WHERE clauses or other com-plicating factors.

Triple-Check Queries with Subselects

Queries with subselects take data from one table and, based on what is retrieved, take some data from another table. Therefore, by definition, such queries can really be hard to get right. Make sure the data that the inner SELECT retrieves is the data that the outer SELECT needs to produce the desired result. If you have two or more levels of subselects, you need to be even more careful.

Summarize Data with GROUP BY

Say that you have a table (NATIONAL) that contains the name (Player), team (Team), and number of home runs hit (Homers) by every baseball player in the National League. You can retrieve the team homer total for all teams with a query like this:

```
SELECT Team, SUM (Homers)
    FROM NATIONAL
    GROUP BY Team ;
```

This query lists each team, followed by the total number of home runs hit by all that team's players.

Watch GROUP BY Clause Restrictions

Suppose that you want a list of National League power hitters. Consider the following query:

```
SELECT Player, Team, Homers
    FROM NATIONAL
    WHERE Homers >= 20
    GROUP BY Team ;
```

In most implementations, this query returns an error. Generally, only columns used for grouping or columns used in a set function may appear in the select list. However, if you want to view this data, the following formulation works:

```
SELECT Player, Team, Homers
    FROM NATIONAL
    WHERE Homers >= 20
    GROUP BY Team, Player, Homers ;
```

Because all the columns you want to display appear in the GROUP BY clause, the query succeeds and delivers the desired results. This formulation sorts the resulting list first by Team, then by Player, and finally by Homers.

Use Parentheses with AND, OR, and NOT

Sometimes when you mix AND and OR, SQL doesn't process the expression in the order that you expect. Use parentheses in complex expressions to make sure that you get the desired results. Typing a few extra keystrokes is a small price to pay for better results.

Parentheses also help to ensure that the NOT keyword is applied to the term or expression that you want it to apply to.

Control Retrieval Privileges

Many people don't use the security features available in their DBMS. They don't want to bother with them because they think misuse and misappropriation of data are things that only happen to other people. Don't wait to get burned. Establish and maintain security for all databases that have any value.

Back Up Your Databases Regularly

Understatement alert: Data is hard to retrieve after a power surge, fire, earthquake, or other disaster destroys your hard drive. (Remember, sometimes computers just die for no good reason.) Make frequent backups and put the backup media in a safe place.

What constitutes a safe place depends on how critical your data is. It might be a fireproof safe in the same room as your computer. It might be in another building. It might be in a concrete bunker under a mountain that has been hardened to withstand a nuclear attack. Decide what level of safety is appropriate for your data.

Handle Error Conditions Gracefully

Whether you're making ad hoc queries from the console or embedding queries in an application, occasionally SQL returns an error message rather than the desired results. At the console, you can decide what to do next, based on the message returned. In an application, the situation is different. The application user probably doesn't know what action is appropriate. Put extensive error handling into your applications to cover every conceivable error that may occur. Creating error-handling code takes a great deal of effort, but it's better than having the user stare quizzically at a frozen screen.

Part VIII
Appendixes

The 5th Wave — By Rich Tennant

In this part . . .

For completeness, and as a potentially valuable reference, this part contains an appendix that lists SQL's reserved words. These words are reserved for specific purposes in SQL; you may not use them for any other purpose in your applications. This part also contains a glossary of important terms.

Appendix A

SQL:2003 Reserved Words

ABS	BIGINT	CHECK	CUBE
ABSENT	BINARY	CLOB	CUME_DIST
ALL	BLOB	CLOSE	CURRENT
ALLOCATE	BOOLEAN	COALESCE	CURRENT_COLLATION
ALTER	BOTH	COLLATE	CURRENT_DATE
AND	BY	COLUMN	CURRENT_DEFAULT_TRANSFORM_GROUP
ANY	CALL	COMMIT	
ARE	CALLED	CONDITION	
ARRAY	CARDINALITY	CONNECT	CURRENT_PATH
AS	CASCADED	CONSTRAINT	CURRENT_ROLE
ASENSITIVE	CASE	CONVERT	CURRENT_TIME
ASYMMETRIC	CAST	CORR	CURRENT_TIMESTAMP
AT	CEIL	CORRESPONDING	
ATOMIC	CEILING	COUNT	CURRENT_TRANSFORM_GROUP_FOR_TYPE
AUTHORIZATION	CHAR	COVAR_POP	
AVG	CHAR_LENGTH	COVAR_SAMP	CURRENT_USER
BEGIN	CHARACTER	CREATE	CURSOR
BETWEEN	CHARACTER_LENGTH	CROSS	CYCLE

DATE	ESCAPE	GRANT	LATERAL
DAY	EVERY	GROUP	LEADING
DEALLOCATE	EXCEPT	GROUPING	LEFT
DEC	EXEC	HAVING	LIKE
DECIMAL	EXECUTE	HOLD	LN
DECLARE	EXISTS	HOUR	LOCAL
DEFAULT	EXP	IDENTITY	LOCALTIME
DELETE	EXTERNAL	IN	LOCALTIMESTAMP
DENSE_RANK	EXTRACT	INDICATOR	LOWER
DEREF	FALSE	INNER	MATCH
DESCRIBE	FETCH	INOUT	MAX
DETERMINISTIC	FILTER	INSENSITIVE	MEMBER
DISCONNECT	FLOAT	INSERT	MERGE
DISTINCT	FLOOR	INT	METHOD
DOUBLE	FOR	INTEGER	MIN
DROP	FOREIGN	INTERSECT	MINUTE
DYNAMIC	FREE	INTERSECTION	MOD
EACH	FROM	INTERVAL	MODIFIERS
ELEMENT	FULL	INTO	MODULE
ELSE	FUNCTION	IS	MONTH
EMPTY	FUSION	JOIN	MULTISET
END	GET	LANGUAGE	NATIONAL
END-EXEC	GLOBAL	LARGE	NATURAL

NCHAR	OVERLAY	REGR_COUNT	SECOND
NCLOB	PARAMETER	REGR_ INTERCEPT	SELECT
NEW	PARTITION		SENSITIVE
NIL	PERCENT_RANK	REGR_R2	SESSION_USER
NO	PERCENTILE_ CONT	REGR_SLOPE	SET
NONE		REGR_SXX	SIMILAR
NORMALIZE	PERCENTILE_ DISC	REGR_SXY	SMALLINT
NOT	POSITION	REGR_SYY	SOME
NULL	POWER	RELEASE	SPECIFIC
NULLIF	PRECISION	RESULT	SPECIFICTYPE
NUMERIC	PREPARE	RETURN	SQL
OCTET_LENGTH	PRIMARY	RETURNS	SQLEXCEPTION
OF	PROCEDURE	REVOKE	SQLSTATE
OLD	RANGE	RIGHT	SQLWARNING
ON	RANK	ROLLBACK	SQRT
ONLY	READS	ROLLUP	START
OPEN	REAL	ROW	STATIC
OR	RECURSIVE	ROW_NUMBER	STDDEV_POP
ORDER	REF	ROWS	STDDEV_SAMP
OUT	REFERENCES	SAVEPOINT	SUBMULTISET
OUTER	REFERENCING	SCOPE	SUBSTRING
OVER	REGR_AVGX	SCROLL	SUM
OVERLAPS	REGR_AVGY	SEARCH	SYMMETRIC

SYSTEM	TRIGGER	VARCHAR	XMLCOMMENT
SYSTEM_USER	TRIM	VARYING	XMLCONCAT
TABLE	TRUE	WHEN	XMLELEMENT
TABLESAMPLE	UNION	WHENEVER	XMLEXISTS
THEN	UNIQUE	WHERE	XMLFOREST
TIME	UNKNOWN	WIDTH_BUCKET	XMLITERATE
TIMESTAMP	UNNEST	WINDOW	XMLNAMESPACES
TIMEZONE_HOUR	UPDATE	WITH	XMLPARSE
TIMEZONE_ MINUTE	UPPER	WITHIN	XMLPI
TO	USER	WITHOUT	XMLQUERY
TRAILING	USING	XML	XMLSERIALIZE
TRANSLATE	VALUE	XMLAGG	XMLTABLE
TRANSLATION	VALUES	XMLATTRIBUTES	YEAR
TREAT	VAR_POP	XMLBINARY	
	VAR_SAMP	XMLCAST	

Appendix B

Glossary

ActiveX control: A reusable software component that can be added to an application, reducing development time in the process. ActiveX is a Microsoft technology; ActiveX components can be used only by developers who work on Windows development systems.

aggregate function: A function that produces a single result based on the contents of an entire set of table rows. Also called a *set function*.

alias: A short substitute or nickname for a table name.

applet: A small application, written in the *Java* language, stored on a Web server that is downloaded to and executed on a Web client that connects to the server.

application program interface (API): A standard means of communicating between an application and a database or other system resource.

assertion: A constraint that is specified by a CREATE ASSERTION statement (rather than by a clause of a CREATE TABLE statement). Assertions commonly apply to more than one table.

atomic: Incapable of being subdivided.

attribute: A component of a structured type or relation.

back end: That part of a DBMS that interacts directly with the database.

catalog: A named collection of *schemas*.

client: An individual user workstation that represents the *front end* of a DBMS — the part that displays information on a screen and responds to user input.

client/server system: A multiuser system in which a central processor (the server) is connected to multiple intelligent user workstations (the clients).

cluster: A named collection of *catalogs*.

CODASYL DBTG database model: The network database model. *Note:* This use of the term *network* refers to the structuring of the data (*network* as opposed to *hierarchy*), rather than to network communications.

collating sequence: The ordering of characters in a character set. All collating sequences for character sets that have the Latin characters (a, b, c) define the obvious ordering (a, b, c, . . .). They differ, however, in the ordering of special characters (+, −, <, ?, and so on) and in the relative ordering of the digits and the letters.

collection type: A data type that allows a field of a table row to contain multiple objects.

column: A table component that holds a single attribute of the table.

composite key: A key made up of two or more table columns.

conceptual view: The *schema* of a database.

concurrent access: Two or more users operating on the same rows in a database table at the same time.

constraint: A restriction you specify on the data in a database.

constraint, deferred: A constraint that is not applied until you change its status to *immediate* or until you `COMMIT` the encapsulating transaction.

cursor: An SQL feature that specifies a set of rows, an ordering of those rows, and a current row within that ordering.

Data Control Language (DCL): That part of SQL that protects the database from harm.

Data Definition Language (DDL): That part of SQL used to define, modify, and eradicate database structures.

Data Manipulation Language (DML): That part of SQL that operates on database data.

data redundancy: Having the same data stored in more than one place in a database.

data source: A source of data used by a database application. It may be a database or a flat data file.

data sublanguage: A subset of a complete computer language that deals specifically with data handling. SQL is a data sublanguage.

data type: A set of representable values.

database: A self-describing collection of integrated records.

database, enterprise: A database containing information used by an entire enterprise.

database, personal: A database designed for use by one person on a single computer.

database, workgroup: A database designed to be used by a department or workgroup within an organization.

database administrator (DBA): The person ultimately responsible for the functionality, integrity, and safety of a database.

database engine: That part of a DBMS that directly interacts with the database (serving as part of the *back end*).

database publishing: The act of making the database contents available on the Internet or over an intranet.

database server: The server component of a *client/server* system.

DB2: A relational database management system marketed by IBM Corporation.

DBMS: A database management system.

deletion anomaly: An inconsistency in a multitable database that occurs when a row is deleted from one of its tables.

descriptor: An area in memory used to pass information between an application's procedural code and its dynamic SQL code.

diagnostics area: A data structure, managed by the DBMS, that contains detailed information about the last SQL statement executed and any errors that occurred during its execution.

distributed data processing: A system in which multiple servers handle data processing.

domain: The set of all values that a database item can assume.

domain integrity: A property of a database table column where all data items in that column fall within the domain of the column.

driver manager: A component of an *ODBC*-compliant database interface. On Windows machines, the driver manager is a dynamic link library (DLL) that coordinates the linking of data sources with appropriate drivers.

driver: That part of a database management system that interfaces directly with a database. Drivers are part of the *back end*.

entity integrity: A property of a database table that is entirely consistent with the real-world object that it models.

file server: The server component of a resource-sharing system. It does not contain any database management software.

firewall: A piece of software (or a combination of hardware and software) that isolates an *intranet* from the Internet, allowing only trusted traffic to travel between them.

flat file: A collection of data records having minimal structure.

foreign key: A column or combination of columns in a database table that references the primary key of another table in the database.

forest: A collection of elements in an XML document.

front end: That part of a DBMS (such as the client in a *client/server* system) that interacts directly with the user.

functional dependency: A relationship between or among attributes of a relation.

hierarchical database model: A tree-structured model of data.

host variable: A variable passed between an application written in a procedural host language and embedded SQL.

HTML (HyperText Markup Language): A standard formatting language for Web documents.

implementation: A particular relational DBMS running on a specific hardware platform.

index: A table of pointers used to locate rows rapidly in a data table.

information schema: The system tables, which hold the database's *metadata*.

insertion anomaly: An inconsistency introduced into a multitable database when a new row is inserted into one of its tables.

Internet: The worldwide network of computers.

intranet: A network that uses World Wide Web hardware and software, but restricts access to users within a single organization.

IPX/SPX: A local area network protocol.

Java: A platform-independent compiled language designed specifically for Web application development.

JavaScript: A script language that gives some measure of programmability to HTML-based Web pages.

JDBC (Java DataBase Connectivity): A standard interface between a Java *applet* or application and a database. The JDBC standard is modeled after the ODBC standard.

join: A relational operator that combines data from multiple tables into a single result table.

logical connectives: Used to connect or change the truth value of predicates to produce more complex predicates.

mapping: The translation of data in one format to another format.

metadata: Data about the structure of the data in a database.

modification anomaly: A problem introduced into a database when a modification (insertion, deletion, or update) is made to one of the database tables.

module language: A form of SQL in which SQL statements are placed in modules, which are called by an application program written in a host language.

mutator function: A function associated with a user-defined type (UDT), having two parameters whose definition is implied by the definition of some attribute of the type. The first parameter (the result) is of the same type as the UDT. The second parameter has the same type as the defining attribute.

nested query: A statement that contains one or more subqueries.

NetBEUI: A local area network protocol.

network database model: A way of organizing a database to get minimum redundancy of data items by allowing any data item (node) to be directly connected to any other.

normalization: A technique that reduces or eliminates the possibility that a database is subject to modification anomalies.

object: Any uniquely identifiable thing.

ODBC (Open DataBase Connectivity): A standard interface between a database and an application that is trying to access the data in that database. ODBC is defined by an international (ISO) and a national (ANSI) standard.

Oracle: A relational database management system marketed by Oracle Corporation.

parameter: A variable within an application written in SQL module language.

precision: The maximum number of digits allowed in a numeric data item.

predicate: A statement that may be either logically true or logically false.

primary key: A column or combination of columns in a database table that uniquely identifies each row in the table.

procedural language: A computer language that solves a problem by executing a procedure in the form of a sequence of steps.

query: A question you ask about the data in a database.

rapid application development (RAD) tool: A proprietary, graphically oriented alternative to SQL. A number of such tools are on the market.

record: A representation of some physical or conceptual object.

reference type: A data type whose values are all potential references to sites of one specified data type.

referential integrity: A state in which all the tables in a database are consistent with each other.

relation: A two-dimensional array of rows and columns, containing single-valued entries and no duplicate rows.

reserved words: Words that have a special significance in SQL and cannot be used as variable names or in any other way that differs from their intended use.

row: A sequence of `(field name, value)` pairs.

row value expression: A list of value expressions enclosed in parentheses and separated by commas.

scale: The number of digits in the fractional part of a numeric data item.

schema: The structure of an entire database. The information that describes the schema is the database's *metadata*.

schema owner: The person who was designated as the owner when the schema was created.

SEQUEL: A data sublanguage created by IBM that was a precursor of SQL.

set function: A function that produces a single result based on the contents of an entire set of table rows. Also called an *aggregate function.*

SQL: An industry standard data sublanguage, specifically designed to create, manipulate, and control relational databases.

SQL, dynamic: A means of building compiled applications that does not require all data items to be identifiable at compile time.

SQL, embedded: An application structure in which SQL statements are embedded within programs written in a host language.

SQL, interactive: A real-time conversation with a database.

SQL/DS: A relational database management system marketed by IBM Corporation.

structured type: A user-defined type that is expressed as a list of attribute definitions and methods rather than being based on a single predefined source type.

subquery: A query within a query.

subtype: A data type is a subtype of a second data type if every value of the first type is also a value of the second type.

supertype: A data type is a supertype of a second data type if every value of the second type is also a value of the first type.

table: A relation.

TCP/IP (Transmission Control Protocol/Internet Protocol): The network protocol used by the Internet and intranets.

teleprocessing system: A powerful central processor connected to multiple dumb terminals.

transaction: A sequence of SQL statements whose effect is not accessible to other transactions until all the statements are executed.

transitive dependency: One attribute of a relation depends on a second attribute, which in turn depends on a third attribute.

translation table: Tool for converting character strings from one character set to another.

trigger: A small piece of code that tells a DBMS what other actions to perform after certain SQL statements have been executed.

update anomaly: A problem introduced into a database when a table row is updated.

user-defined type: A type whose characteristics are defined by a type descriptor specified by the user.

value expression: An expression that combines two or more values.

value expression, conditional: A value expression that assigns different values to arguments, based on whether a condition is logically true.

value expression, datetime: A value expression that deals with DATE, TIME, TIMESTAMP, or INTERVAL data.

value expression, numeric: A value expression that combines numeric values using the addition, subtraction, multiplication, or division operator.

value expression, string: A value expression that combines character strings with the concatenation operator.

value function: A function that performs an operation on a single character string, number, or date/time.

view: A database component that behaves exactly like a table but has no independent existence of its own.

virtual table: A view.

World Wide Web: An aspect of the Internet that has a graphical user interface. The Web is accessed by applications called *Web browsers,* and information is provided to the Web by installations called *Web servers.*

XML: A widely accepted markup language used as a means of exchanging data between dissimilar systems.

Index

• *Symbols and Numerics* •

+ (addition operator), 60, 149
* (asterisk)
  applications, 288
  as multiplication operator, 60, 149
  wildcard character, 124, 202
|| (concatenation operator), 60–61, 148
/ (division operator), 60, 149
= (equal to comparison operator),
      63, 178, 232
> (greater than comparison operator),
      63, 178
>= (greater than or equal to comparison
      operator), 63
< (less than comparison operator), 63, 178
<= (less than or equal to comparison
      operator), 63
* (multiplication operator)
  applying, 149
  described, 60
<> (not equal to comparison operator),
      63, 178
( ) (parentheses), 196
% (percent sign), 182–184
[ ] (square brackets), 155, 176
– (subtraction operator), 60, 149
_ (underscore character), 182–184
1NF (first normal form), 116–117
2NF (second normal form), 117–118
3NF (third normal form), 49, 118–119
4GLs (fourth-generation languages), 75

• *A* •

abnormal form, 120
absolute value expression function (ABS),
      157, 160
abstract data types (ADTs), 37

access level
  DBA, 256–257
  foreign keys, limiting, 68
  security, database, 255
Access (Microsoft)
  applications, creating, 297
  database table, creating single, 78–79
  deleting tables, 85–86
  opening screen, 77
  platform limitations, 297
  saving single database table, 80
  SQL editor, opening, 87
  SQL statements, entering, 162
ACID database, 280
actions, error handler, 350–351
ActiveX control, 309, 389
ad hoc query, 22
adding
  block of rows to table, 132–135
  columns, 109
  data to selected columns, 132
  one row at a time, 130–132
  values in specified column (SUM
      function), 65, 154
addition operator (+), 60, 149
ADTs (abstract data types), 37
aggregate function
  described, 389
  with GROUP BY clause, 196
  operators, 232
alias, 389
ALL
  quantifier, 233–235
  WHERE clauses, 185–188
all rows, changing (UPDATE
      statement), 137
alphabetical order, displaying in (ORDER
      BY clauses), 198–199
ALTER TABLE command
  constraint violations, detecting, 369
  data, loading tables with, 49

ALTER TABLE command *(continued)*
  exact numeric data type, 59
  table structure, altering, 89
AND
  logical connective, 64, 194–195
  parentheses, using with, 381
ANSI (American National Standards
    Institute), 23, 24
ANY, 185–188, 233–235
API (application programming interface),
    305, 389
applet, 310–311, 389
applications
  asterisk (*), 288
  damage during transactions, 67
  described, 287
  embedded SQL, 291–294
  Java applets, 311
  Microsoft Access with SQL, 297–300
  module language, 294–296
  object-oriented RAD tools, 296–297
  ODBC, 305
  problems combining SQL with procedural
    language, 290
  procedural language strengths and
    weaknesses, 289
  SQL strengths and weaknesses, 289
  SQL transactions, 274
approximate numeric data type
  DOUBLE PRECISION, 29, 41
  FLOAT, 29–30, 41, 142
  REAL, 28, 41, 142
Aristotle, logical system of thought by,
    185–186
array
  collection value expressions, 62
  two-dimensional, of rows and columns
    (relation), 14
ARRAY data type, 36–37
ARRAY XML data, 41, 330–331
ASENSITIVE keyword, cursors, 340
assertion, 43, 113, 389
assignment, compound statement, 352
asterisk (*)
  applications, 288
  as multiplication operator, 60, 149
  wildcard character, 124, 202
AT LOCAL keywords, 61

atom, 142
atomic
  ACID database requirement, 280
  compound statements, SQL-92/PSM,
    346–347, 389
  value of field, 142
ATOMIC keyword, UNDO error handling, 351
attribute
  described, 8, 389
  domain of, 18
  entities, associated, 93
  keys, 98
  public versus private, 38
  views with modified, 128–129
automatic entry of block of rows to
    table, 132
average sale, computing, 66
averaging values in specified column
  described, 65–66, 153
  GROUP BY clause, 196–197

• B •

back end, 389
backing up data, 281, 382
bad input data, 110
base tables, 125
basic join, 206–208, 393
BCNF (Boyce-Codd normal form), 116
beta testing, importance of, 378
BETWEEN, WHERE clause, 180–181
BIGINT data type, 27, 41
blanks, character field, 31, 156–157
BLOB data type, 41
block of rows, adding to table, 132–135
BOOLEAN data type, 32, 41
Boolean value expressions, 62
Boyce-Codd normal form (BCNF), 116
byte, 159

• C •

C program, 346
cardinality expression function,
    157, 159–160
Cartesian product, 177
cascade deletions, 106–108

CASE conditional expressions
  COALESCE, 170
  described, 163–164
  NULLIF, 168–169
  with search conditions, 164–166
  with values, 166–168
CASE...END CASE statement, 353–354
CAST data-type conversions
  described, 170–171
  row value expressions, 173–174
  within SQL, 172
  between SQL and host language, 172–173
catalog, 57, 389
CEIL or CEILING function, 157, 161
chain of dependency, 267
character sets
  languages, 159
  multitable relational database, 97–98
  NAMES ARE clause, 295
  users, granting privileges to, 263–264
  XML data, mapping, 316
character string
  blanks, trimming, 156–157
  listed, 31–32, 41, 142
  substring, extracting from source,
    154–155
  value functions, 154
CHARACTER VARYING (VARCHAR)
    function, 31, 41, 155
CHARACTER_LENGTH function, 158
CHAR_LENGTH expression function, 157
clients (persons), 375–376
client/server system, 44–45, 305–306, 389
CLOB (CHARACTER LARGE OBJECT),
    31, 41
cluster, 389
COALESCE conditional expression, 170
CODASYL DBTG database model, 390
Codd, Dr. E. F. (inventor)
  normalization, rules of, 35, 116
  relational database model, origins of, 12
  repeating groups, 37
collating sequence, 59, 390
collations
  multitable relational database, 97–98
  users, granting privileges to, 263–264

collection data types
  ARRAY, 36–37
  described, 390
  multiset, 37, 41
collection value expressions, 62
columns
  adding and deleting, 109
  adding data to selected, 132
  adding values in specified (SUM function),
    65, 154
  ALTER TABLE commands, 59
  averaging values in specified, 65–66, 153
  constraints, 18–19, 112
  cursor, ORDER BY clause, 337–338
  data, adding to selected, 132
  identifying, 49
  maximum value in specified, 65, 153
  in Microsoft Access terminology, 78
  minimum value in specified, 65, 153
  multitable relational database, 92–93, 390
  name join, relational operators, 211–212
  references, 146–147
  self-consistent, in array, 14
  transferring selected between tables,
    133–135
  two-dimensional array, 14
comma-delimited data entry, 130
comments, XML, 315, 322–323
COMMIT statement
  dirty read, 276, 278
  protecting data, 279
  transactions, 66
comparison operators, 63, 237–239
comparison predicates, 178–179
complete logical view, 18
complexity, database, 9
composite key, 117, 390
compound statements, SQL-92/PSM
  assignment, 352
  atomic, 346–347, 389
  conditions, 348–349
  cursors, 348
  described, 345–346
  exceptions, 351–352
  handling conditions, 349–351
  variables, 347–348
computer console, 22

concatenating XML arguments, 321–322
concatenation operator (| |), 60–61, 148
conceptual view, 18, 390
concurrent access, 390
conditional join, 211
conditional value expressions, 150
conditions, compound statements, 348–349
consistency, ACID database, 280
console, computer, 22
constant, value of, 142
constraints
    assertion, 58, 113, 389
    column, 112
    data types, SQL, 42–43
    deferred, 390
    described, 18–19, 111, 113, 390
    diagnostics, 366
    INSERT statement violations,
        351, 368–369
    referenced tables, controlling access
        with, 68
    table, 113
    within transactions, 282–286
    user access, controlling, 68
constructors, structured UDTs, 39
containment hierarchy, 48
CONTENT predicate, 325
conversions, CAST data-type
    described, 170–171
    row value expressions, 173–174
    within SQL, 172
    between SQL and host language, 172–173
CONVERT string value function, 157
copying data, 133
correlated subqueries
    with comparison operators, 237–239
    described, 235
    HAVING clause, 239
    IN, 236–237
    UPDATE, DELETE, and INSERT
        statements, 240–242
CORRESPONDING relational operator,
    203–204
COUNT function, 64, 152–153
crashes, 8
CREATE ASSERTION command, 58

CREATE command
    constraints, 58
    described, 49
    foreign keys, 100
CREATE INDEX command, 89
CREATE TABLE command
    constraints, 58
    Microsoft Access, inability to use, 87
    syntax, 88
CROSS JOIN relational operator, 210
cursors
    closing, 344
    compound statements, SQL-92/PSM, 348
    declaring, 336
    described, 335–336, 390
    fetching from single row (FETCH
        statement), 342–344
    opening, 340–342
    ORDER BY clause, 337–338
    query expression, 337
    scrollability, 340
    sensitivity, 339–340
    updatability clause, 338–339

data
    access alternative, 303
    DEFERRABLE constraint, 283
    defined, 8
    deleting obsolete, 139–140
    entry methods, 130
    foreign file, copying block of rows
        from, 133
    loading tables with, 49
    table, creating and filling with, 50
    transferring, 138–139
Data Control Language. See DCL; DCL
    security
Data Definition Language. See DDL
data dictionary, 9
data integrity problem areas
    bad input data, 110
    data redundancy, 110–111, 390
    DBMS capacity, exceeding, 111
    described, 269–273

importance of recognizing, 109
malice, 110
mechanical failure, 110
modification anomalies, 114, 393
operator error, 110
Data Manipulation Language. *See* DML
data redundancy, 110–111, 390
data source, 305, 390
data types, SQL
  approximate numerics, 28–30
  BOOLEAN, 32, 41
  character strings, 30–32
  collection, 36–37
  constraints, 42–43
  datetimes, 32–33
  described, 390
  exact numerics, 26–28
  intervals, 34
  listed with conforming literals, 40–41
  null values, 42
  predefined, 26
  REF, 37, 41
  ROW, 35–36, 41
  UDTs, 37–40
  XML type, 34–35
data types, XML, 317
database
  constraints, 18–19, 111, 113, 390
  data dictionary, 9
  DBMS, 9–10, 391
  described, 8, 391
  design considerations, 20
  domains, 18
  enterprise, 391
  flat files, 9–12, 392
  hierarchical model, 12, 392
  metadata, 9, 393
  network model, 12
  object-relational model, 19–20
  personal, 391
  queries, trying, 380
  record, 8, 394
  relational model, 12–15
  retrieval tips, 379
  schemas, 18, 394
  size and complexity, 9
  views (virtual tables), 15–17
  workgroup, 391

database administrator (DBA),
    256–257, 391
database engine, 391
database management system (DBMS)
  capacity, exceeding, 111
  described, 9–10, 391
database publishing, 306, 391
database server. *See* server
DATE data types, 32, 41, 142
datetime data types, 32–33, 41, 142
datetime expressions, DML, 61–62
date-time functions, cursors, 341
datetime value
  expressions, 149–150
  functions, 162
days, ordering results by, 199
day-time interval, 34, 41, 150
DB2 (IBM), 391
DBA (database administrator),
    256–257, 391
DBMS (database management system)
  capacity, exceeding, 111
  described, 9–10, 391
DCL (Data Control Language)
  described, 47, 390
  referential integrity constraints, data and,
    70–72
  transactions, 66–67
  users and privileges, 67–70
DCL (Data Control Language) security
  database, 256
  delegating responsibility for, 72
DDL (Data Definition Language)
  catalog, ordering by, 57
  containment hierarchy, 48
  CREATE command, 58–59
  described, 47, 86, 390
  index, creating, 88–89
  index, deleting, 90
  Microsoft Access, 87
  planning, 48–49
  portability considerations, 90
  schemas, collecting tables into, 56
  table structure, altering, 89
  tables, creating, 49–50, 87–88
  tables, deleting, 89–90
  views, 51–56
DECIMAL data type, 28, 41

decimal point, number containing, 28
default transaction, 275
DEFERRABLE constraint, 283
deferred constraints, 390
DELETE statement
  access, limiting, 68
  correlated subqueries, 240–242
  cursor sensitivity, 339
  fetching from single row (FETCH
    statement), 343–344
  table columns, 59
deleting
  columns, 109
  DDL index, 90
  DDL table, 89–90
  duplicate rows, 202
  Microsoft Access tables, 85–86
  obsolete data, 139–140
  obsolete rows from table, 262
deletion anomaly, 114, 391
deletions
  cascading, 106–108
  privileges, 359
departmental database, 9
descriptor, 391
diagnostics area
  DBMS, 391
  error handling, 366–368
DIAGNOSTICS SIZE, error handling, 275
dirty read, 276, 278
distinct types, UDTs, 38–39, 329
DISTINCT, WHERE clause, 189
distributed data processing, 391
division operator (/), 60, 149
DK/NF (domain-key normal form),
    116, 119–120
DML (Data Manipulation Language)
  AVG set function, 65–66, 153
  Boolean value expressions, 62
  collection value expressions, 62
  COUNT set function, 64, 152–153
  datetime and interval value expressions,
    61–62
  described, 47, 59, 390
  logical connectives, 64
  MAX set function, 65, 153
  MIN set function, 65, 153
  numeric value expressions, 60

predicates, 63
reference value expressions, 63
row value expressions, 62
string value expressions, 60–61
subqueries, 66
SUM set function, 65, 154
user-defined type value expressions, 62
DOCUMENT predicate, XML data, 325
documentation, importance of, 378
domain
  described, 18, 391
  INSERT statement problems, 105
  integrity, 391
  users, granting privileges to, 263–264
  XML data, mapping to, 328–329
domain-key normal form (DK/NF),
    116, 119–120
dormant, 146
DOUBLE PRECISION approximate numeric
    data type, 29, 41
driver, 392
driver
  DLL, 305
  ODBC, 304
driver manager, 305, 391
DROP command, 49, 71
DROP domains, 264
DROP TABLE command, 59, 89–90
duplicate rows, eliminating, 202
duplicating primary keys, constraint
    violation, 351
durability, ACID database, 280

• E •

effects, error handler, 350–351
embedded SQL, 145, 291–294
end points, using with BETWEEN
    predicate, 180
enterprise database, 9
entities
  attributes, associated, 93
  integrity, multitable relational database,
    104–105, 392
ENVIRONMENT_NAME field, diagnostics, 370
equal to comparison operator (=),
    63, 178, 232
equi-join relational operators, 208–210

error handling
  conditions, 348–349
  constraint violation information, 368–369
  diagnostics detail area, 366–368
  diagnostics header area, 364–366
  exception handling, 371–372
  existing table, adding constraints, 369
  importance of, 382
  interpreting SQLSTATE information, 370
  number prepared to save information
    (DIAGNOSTICS SIZE), 275
  SQLSTATE, 361–363
  WHENEVER clause, 363–364
escape characters, 159
Euros, 39
exact numeric data type
  ALTER TABLE command, 59
  BIGINT, 27, 41
  DECIMAL, 28, 41
  DROP TABLE command, 59
  NUMERIC, 27–28, 41
  SMALLINT, 27, 41
EXCEPT relational operator, 205–206
exceptions, conditions that aren't handled,
    351–352
executing SQL statements, granting users
    privileges to, 264–265
existence test, nested queries, 235–236
EXISTS
  nested query, 235–236
  WHERE clauses, 188–189
EXIT effect, error handling, 351
exponential function value expression
    function (EXP), 157, 160
expressions, 141
eXtensible Markup Language. *See*
    XML data
extensions
  ODBC client, 308–309
  ODBC server, 307–308
  portability considerations, 90
extract expression function (EXTRACT),
    157, 158

• *F* •

Fagin, Ronald (DK/NF inventor), 116
feedback, clients, 376

fetching from single row (FETCH
    statement)
  orientation of scrollable, 343
  positioned DELETE and UPDATE
    statements, 343–344
  syntax, 342–343
field
  as column in Microsoft Access
    terminology, 78
  described, 142
  fixed length, 11
  null values, 42
  single field, extracting (EXTRACT
    function), 158
file server, 392
filtering comparison predicates, 178–179
1NF (first normal form), 116–117
fixed length field, 11
flat file system, 9, 133
FLOAT data type, 29–30, 41, 142
floating-point number, 28
floor value expression function (FLOOR),
    157, 161
flow of control statements, 353–356
foreign data file, copying block of rows
    from, 133
foreign keys
  access, limiting, 68
  CREATE command, 100
  hackers, corrupting database with, 71
  multitable relational database, 100, 392
  referential integrity rules, 192
forest, 392
forms, data entry by, 130
fourth-generation languages (4GLs), 75
FROM clause, 175–176, 177
front end, 125, 392
full outer joins, 216
function calls, 304, 358
functional dependency, 117, 392
functions
  datetime value, 162
  described, 141
  numeric value, 157–161
  recursion, 243
  set, summarizing with, 151–154
  stored, 358
  string value, 154–157

• G •

German character set, 97–98
GRANT DELETE statement, 69, 70
GRANT INSERT statement, 69, 70
GRANT REFERENCES statement, 68, 69, 71
GRANT SELECT statement, 69–70
GRANT statement, 68, 258–259
GRANT UPDATE statement, 69, 70, 72
GRANT USAGE statements, 68–69
GRANT, using with REVOKE, 268
greater than comparison operator (>), 63, 178
greater than or equal to comparison operator (>=), 63
Greenwich Mean Time, 149
GROUP BY clause
  aggregate function, 196
  clause restrictions, monitoring, 381
  data summaries, importance of using, 380–381
  described, 175–176, 196–197
  ORDER BY clauses versus, 198
  subqueries, 239

• H •

hackers, corrupting database with foreign key, 71
handling conditions
  handler actions and handler effects, 350–351
  handler declarations, 350
  knowledge gained, 349–350
handling errors
  conditions, 348–349
  constraint violation information, 368–369
  diagnostics detail area, 366–368
  diagnostics header area, 364–366
  exception handling, 371–372
  existing table, adding constraints, 369
  importance of, 382
  interpreting SQLSTATE information, 370
  number prepared to save information (DIAGNOSTICS SIZE), 275
  SQLSTATE, 361–363
  WHENEVER clause, 363–364
hard drive crash, 8

hard-coded database structure, 13
hardware
  computer console, 22
  single-precision circuitry, 29–30
  transactions, damage during, 67
HAVING clause
  correlated subqueries, 239
  with GROUP BY clause, 175–176, 197–198
helper applications, ODBC client, 309
hierarchical database model, 12, 110, 392
host language, CAST data-type conversions, 172–173
host variable, 145, 392
HTML (HyperText Markup Language)
  applets, embedded, 310–311
  database publishing, 306
  described, 392

• I •

IBM
  relational database model, invention of, 12
  SQL, origins of, 23
ID columns, result of union joins, 220
identifiers, mapping to XML data, 316–317
IF...THEN...ELSE...END IF statement, 352–353
impedance mismatch, 38
implementation, 23, 392
implicit transaction-starting statement, 278
IN keyword
  correlated subqueries, 236–237
  subqueries introduced by, 228–229
IN predicate, WHERE clauses, 181–182
inconsistent date, keeping out, 108
indexed sequential access method (ISAM), 305
indexes
  benefits of using, 102–103
  creating, 88–89
  deleting, 90
  described, 101–102, 392
  effective, creating, 84–85
  maintaining, 103
  RAD, creating, 82–85
  SQL support, 100
information schema, 57, 392
inner join, 212–213

INSENSITIVE keyword, cursors, 339
INSERT statement
  constraint violations, 351, 368–369
  copying data from table, 134–135
  correlated subqueries, 240–242
  cursor sensitivity, 339
  domain integrity concerns, 105
  privileges, 359
  table columns, 59
  user access, limiting, 68, 260
insertion anomaly, 392
INTEGER data type, 26–27, 41
integrity, referential
  constraints, DCL, 70–72
  foreign keys, 192
  multitable relational database,
    106–108, 394
interface
  client computer, 44–45
  ODBC, 304
  SQL, 289
Internet
  described, 392
  ODBC, 306–309
  SQL, 45–46
INTERSECT relational operator, 204–205
intervals
  DML value expressions, 61–62
  SQL data types, 34
  time, overlapping (OVERLAPS
    predicate), 190
intranet
  described, 392
  ODBC, 309
  SQL, 45–46
IPX/SPX, 393
ISAM (indexed sequential access
  method), 305
ISO/IEC international standard SQL, 20, 24
isolation
  ACID database, 280
  levels, 276–278
ITERATE statement, 356–357

• J •

Java, 393
JavaScript, 393
joining text strings, 60–61

joins
  basic, 206–208, 393
  Cartesian product, 177
  column-name, 211–212
  conditional, 211
  described, 393
  double-checking, 380
  inner, 212–213
  left outer, 213–215
  natural, 210–211
  right outer, 215–216
  union, 216–223

• K •

keys, 98. *See also* foreign keys; primary
  keys; UNIQUE key

• L •

language
  character sets, 159
  non-English, converting, 97
  sublanguage versus, 44
  two, mixing with preprocessor, 293
LEAVE statement, 355
length expression functions
    (CHAR_LENGTH,
    CHARACTER_LENGTH,
    OCTET_LENGTH), 157
less than comparison operator (<), 63, 178
less than or equal to comparison operator
  (<=), 63
letter sets. *See* character sets
LIKE
  WHERE clauses, 182–184
  wildcard characters, 182
literals
  data types listed with conforming, 40–41
  values, 142–144
LN natural logarithm value expression
  function, 157, 160
locking database objects, 280
log file, transactions, 66–67
logarithm, natural, 160
logical connectives
  AND, 194–195
  described, 393
  DML, 64

logical connectives *(continued)*
NOT, 195–196
OR, 195
logical schema, 56
LOOP...ENDLOOP statement, 354–355
LOWER string value functions, 156

• M •

maintaining indexes, 103
major entities, 92
malice, data integrity problems, 110
manipulating data
block of rows to table, 132–135
deleting obsolete data, 139–140
described, 123
one row at a time, 130–132
retrieving, 124–125
selected columns, adding to, 132
transferring data, 138–139
updating existing data, 135–138
updating views, 129
views, creating, 125–126
views from tables, 126–127
views with modified attribute, 128–129
views with selection condition, 127–128
mantissa, 29
mapping
character sets, 316
data types, 317
described, 393
domain to, 328–329
identifiers, 316–317
tables, 318
MATCH clause
described, 190–191
referential integrity, 192–193
maximum value in specified column
(MAX function), 65, 153
mechanical failure, data integrity
problems, 110
MERGE statement, transferring data,
138–139
metadata, 9, 393
method, object-oriented RAD tools, 296
Microsoft Access
applications, creating, 297
database table, creating single, 78–79
deleting tables, 85–86

opening screen, 77
platform limitations, 297
saving single database table, 80
SQL editor, opening, 87
SQL statements, entering, 162
Microsoft Office Online panel, 77
minimum value in specified column
(MIN function), 65, 153
modification abnormalities, normalizing,
114–115
modification anomalies
correlated subqueries, 242
deletion anomalies, 114, 391
described, 393
modifying clauses, 175–177
modifying table data, 261
module language, 294–296, 393
modules, SQL-92/PSM, 359–360
modulus value expression function (MOD),
157, 160
multiple rows, changing (UPDATE
statement), 136
multiplication operator (*)
applying, 149
described, 60
multiset data types, 37, 41
multiset XML data, 41, 331–332
multitable relational database. *See also*
normalizing multitable relational
database
columns, 109, 390
constraints, 111–113
data integrity problem areas, 109–111
design steps, 91–92
domain integrity, 105–106
domains, character sets, collations, and
translations, 97–98
entity integrity, 104–105, 392
foreign keys, 100, 392
indexes, 100–103
keys, advantages of using, 98
objects, defining, 92, 393
primary keys, 49, 98–99, 394
referential integrity, 106–108, 394
tables and columns, identifying, 92–93
tables, defining, 93–97
multitable views, 51
mutator function, 39, 393

• N •

NAMES ARE clause, 295
NATIONAL CHARACTER, NATIONAL
    CHARACTER VARYING, and NATIONAL
    CHARACTER LARGE OBJECT
    character strings, 31–32
natural join, 210–211
natural logarithm value expression
    function (LN), 157
needs, assuming clients know, 375–376
nested queries
    ALL, SOME and ANY quantifiers, 233–235
    copying data from table, 134
    described, 225–226, 393
    existence test, 235–236
    sets of rows, returning, 227–230
    single value, returning, 230–233
    subqueries, 226
NetBEUI, 393
network database model, 12, 393
non-English languages, converting, 97
non-existent values, 42
nonprocedural language, SQL as, 21–22
nonrepeatable read isolation level, 276–277
normalizing multitable relational database
    abnormal form, 120
    described, 393
    DK/NF, 119–120
    1NF, 116–117
    modification abnormalities, 114–115
    normal forms, intention of, 35
    2NF, 117–118
    3NF, 49, 118–119
NOT DEFERRABLE constraint, 282
not equal to comparison operator (<>),
    63, 178
NOT EXISTS nested query, 236
NOT IN keyword, subqueries introduced
    by, 229–230
NOT IN predicate, WHERE clauses, 181–182
NOT LIKE, WHERE clauses, 182–184
NOT LIKE wildcard character, 182
NOT logical connective, 64, 195–196
NOT NULL constraint
    columns, applying, 112
    one-to-many relationship, 53
    primary keys, 99, 104
NOT, using parentheses with, 381

null values
    average sale, computing, 66
    reasons for using, 152
    SQL data types, 42
    XML data, handling, 318–319
NULL, WHERE clauses, 184–185
NULLIF, CASE conditional expressions,
    168–169
number of characters in character string
    (CHARACTER_LENGTH), 158
NUMERIC data type, 27–28, 41
numeric value expressions, 60, 149
numeric value functions
    ABS, 160
    CARDINALITY, 159–160
    CEIL or CEILING, 161
    CHARACTER_LENGTH, 158
    EXP, 160
    EXTRACT, 158
    FLOOR, 161
    listed, 157
    LN, 160
    MOD, 160
    OCTET_LENGTH, 159
    POSITION, 158
    POWER, 160–161
    SQRT, 161
    WIDTH_BUCKET, 161

• O •

object database, 19
object model, 7
object-oriented programming (OOP), 37
object-oriented RAD tools, 296
object-relational database model, 19–20
objects
    locking database, 280
    multitable relational database, defining,
        92, 393
observer functions, SELECT statements,
    including, 39
observers, structured UDTs, 39
obsolete data, deleting, 139–140
obsolete rows, privilege of deleting from
    table, 262
OCTET_LENGTH expression function,
    157, 159
ODBC. *See* Open DataBase Connectivity

Office (Microsoft) Online panel, 77
ON clause, 219, 223
one-to-many relationships, 53, 96
online application processing (OLAP), 161
OOP (object-oriented programming), 37
Open DataBase Connectivity (ODBC)
    client/server environment, 305–306
    components, 304–305
    data access alternative, 303
    described, 393
    interface, 304
    Internet, 306–309
    intranet, 309
    JDBC, 310–311, 393
OPEN statement, 341–342
opening
    cursors, 340–342
    Microsoft Access screen, 77
operand, 156
operator error, data integrity
        problems, 110
operators, relational. *See* relational
        operators
OR
    logical connective, 64, 195
    parentheses, using with, 381
Oracle, 12, 23, 394
ORDER BY clauses
    alphabetical order, displaying in, 198–199
    cursors, 337–338
    with GROUP BY clauses, 175–176
    GROUP BY clauses versus, 198
outer joins
    full, 216
    left, 213–215
    right, 215–216
OVERLAPS, time intervals, 190

● *P* ●

parameters, 145, 394
parent-child table relationships,
        13, 106–108
parentheses (()), 196
PARTIAL rules, 194
percent sign (%), 182–184
performance, 103, 277
Persistent Stored Molecules. *See*
    SQL-92/PSM

personal database, 9
phantom read isolation level, 277, 278
physical schema, 56
planning, DDL, 48–49
platforms
    Microsoft Access limitations, 297
    scalable DBMS, 9
portability, DDL, 90
position expression function (POSITION),
        157, 158
power function value expression function
        (POWER), 157, 160–161
power to grant privileges, 265–266
precision, number, 27, 394
predicates
    described, 394
    DML, 63
    in WHERE clauses, 178–179
    XML data, 324
preprocessor, mixing languages with, 293
preserving duplicate rows, 203
previous session, 146
primary keys
    duplicating, constraint violation, 351
    multitable relational database,
        49, 98–99, 394
    NOT NULL constraint, 99, 104
    RAD tool, identifying, 49, 82
    referential integrity rules, 192
private attributes, 38
privileges, granting to users. *See* users,
        granting privileges to
procedural language
    described, 394
    problems combining SQL with, 290
    SQL isn't, 21
    strengths and weaknesses, 289
programs. *See* applications
project scope, ignoring, 376
protecting data
    ACID database, 280
    backing up data, 281
    COMMIT, 279
    constraints within transactions, 282–286
    default transaction, 275
    implicit transaction-starting
        statement, 278
    isolation levels, 276–278
    locking database objects, 280

principles, 273
ROLLBACK, 279
savepoints and subtransactions, 281–282
SET TRANSACTION, 278–279
SQL transactions, using, 274–275
threats to data integrity, 269–273
public access level, database security,
    257–258
public attributes, 38

• Q •

queries. *See also* nested queries; recursive
    queries
described, 22, 394
joins, double-checking, 380
subselects, checking, 380
Query Analyzer, SQL, 162
query expression, 337

• R •

RAD (rapid application development) tool
deleting a table, 85–86
described, 75, 394
index, creating, 82–85
object-oriented tools, 296–297
primary key, identifying, 49, 82
table, creating with Design View, 77–80
table structure, altering, 80–82
track, deciding what to, 76–77
range check, 110
range, value out of, 42
RDBMS (relational database management
    system), 23
READ UNCOMMITTED isolation level,
    276, 278
REAL data type, 28, 41, 142
record, 8, 14, 394
recursive queries
airline flight problem outlined, 247–248
described, 243–244, 246
other uses, 252
problem, 244
saving time, 249–252
series, 248–249
termination condition, 245–246
redundancy, 270

REF data type, 37, 41
reference type, 359, 394
reference value expression, 63
referenced tables
controlling access with constraints, 68
related tables, privileges for, 262–263
references, column, 146–147
referential integrity
constraints, DCL, 70–72
foreign keys, 192
multitable relational database,
    106–108, 394
register sizes, numerics, 28
related tables, granting users privileges
    for, 262–263
relation
among tables, referential integrity, 106
defined, 14, 394
tables, correspondence to, 14
relational database management system
    (RDBMS), 23
relational model, 7, 12
relational operators
basic join, 206–208, 393
column-name join, 211–212
conditional join, 211
CORRESPONDING, 203–204
CROSS JOIN, 210
equi-join, 208–210
inner join, 212–213
INTERSECT, 204–205
natural join, 210–211
ON versus WHERE clauses, 223
outer join, 213–216
UNION, 201–203
UNION ALL, 203
union join, 216–223
Relational Software, Inc., 23
REPEATABLE READ isolation level,
    277, 278
repeating groups, 37
REPEAT...UNTIL...END REPEAT
    statement, 356
reports, monthly or quarterly, 103
reserved words
described, 394
SQL, 25
SQL:2003, 385–388

RESIGNAL, error-handling, 352, 372
RESTRICT option, 267
retrieval
 privileges, controlling, 381
 tips, database structure, 379
reviews, design, 378
REVOKE statements, 69, 266–268
roles, granting users privileges
  through, 260
ROLLBACK statement, 66, 279
root element, mapping tables, 318
routines, multiple, 359–360
ROW data type
 SQL, 35–36, 41
 XML, 329–330
row value expressions
 CAST data-type conversions, 173–174
 described, 394
 DML, 62
rows
 adding one at a time, 130–132
 all, changing, 137
 automatic entry of block to table, 132
 deleting obsolete from table, privilege
  of, 262
 multiple, changing, 136
 retrieving all in specified table, 124
 sets, returning, 227–230
 single, changing, 135–136
 transferring all between tables, 133
 transferring selected between tables,
  133–135
 two-dimensional array, 14
 values, 142
rows, selecting. *See also* cursors
 cascading deletions, 106–108
 columns, 14
 described, 394
 eliminating duplicate, 202
 number in specified table, 64, 152–153
 preserving duplicate, 203
 uniqueness, need for, 98

• *S* •

sandbox, Java applet, 311
savepoints, 281–282

saving time, recursive queries, 249–252
scalable DBMS, 9
scale, 27, 394
schema
 CREATE command, 58
 DDL, collecting tables into, 56
 described, 18, 394
 multiple, in catalogs, 57
 owner, 394
 user access, limiting, 68
 XML data, generating, 319–320
scripts, ODBC client, 309
scrollability, cursors, 340
search conditions, CASE conditional
  expressions, 164–166
2NF (second normal form), 117–118
security, database. *See also* users, granting
  privileges to
 access levels, 255, 256
 database object owners access level, 257
 DBA access level, 256–257
 delegating responsibility for, 72
 public access level, 257–258
 views, 129
SELECT statements
 access, controlling, 68
 all rows in specified table, retrieving, 124
 columns, specifying, 134
 compound conditions inside, 124–125
 described, 59
 observer functions, including, 39
 virtual table, 125
 with WHERE clause, 124
 XMLELEMENT, 320
selection condition, views with, 127–128
self-consistent columns, 14
sensitivity, cursors, 339–340
SEQUEL (Structured English QUEry
  Language), 22, 394
serialization, 272–273
series, recursive queries, 248–249
server
 database, defined, 391
 downloading from, 311
 ODBC extensions, 307–308
 SQL, 43–44
SESSION_USER variable, 146

set functions
    AVG, 153, 196–197
    COUNT, 64, 152–153
    MAX, 153
    MIN, 153
    returning rows, 227–230
    SUM, 154
    summarizing, 151–154
    uses, 151–152
SET TRANSACTION statement,
        275, 278–279
SIMILAR, WHERE clauses, 184
single field, extracting (EXTRACT
        function), 158
single-precision hardware circuitry, 29–30
single-table view, 51–52
size, database, 9
slower read, 277
SMALLINT data type, 27, 41
software. *See* applications
SOME quantifier, 185–188, 233–235
source type, 38
special variables, 146
spreadsheets, electronic, 14
SQL. *See also* data types, SQL
    client, 44–45
    commands, 24–25
    editor, opening in Microsoft Access, 87
    extracting information from database,
        22–23
    history, 23–24
    on Internet/intranet, 45–46
    as nonprocedural language, 21–22
    procedural language, problems
        combining, 290
    reserved words, 25
    server, 43–44
    statements, entering with Microsoft
        Access, 162
    strengths and weaknesses, 289
    as sublanguage, 22
    users, granting privileges to execute
        statements, 264–265
SQL-86, 23, 340
SQL-89
    adoption, 23
    cursor scrollability, 340
    UNIQUE rule, 194

SQL-92, 23
SQL-92/PSM (Persistent Stored Molecules).
        See also compound statements,
        SQL-92/PSM
    described, 345
    flow of control statements, 352–357
    privileges, 359
    stored functions, 358–359
    stored modules, 359–360
    stored procedures, 357–358
SQL:2003
    core commands, 24–25
    reserved words, 385–388
    as standard for book, 24
    XML data type, introduction of, 314
square brackets ([ ]), 155, 176
square root value expression function
        (SQRT), 157, 161
stored functions, 358–359
stored modules, 359–360
stored procedures, 357–358
storing data, 8
string. *See also* character string
    percent sign or underscore, searching,
        183–184
    value expressions, 60–61, 148
    value functions, 154–157
    XML, parsing, 323
Structured English QUEry Language
        (SEQUEL), 22, 394
structured UDTs
    constructors, 39
    example, 40
    mutator function, 39, 393
    observers, 39
    subtypes and supertypes, 39
sublanguage, 22, 44, 390
subqueries. *See also* correlated subqueries
    baseball statistics example, 234–235
    DML, 66
    EXISTS predicate, 188–189
    GROUP BY, 239
    IN keyword, introduced by, 228–229
    nested queries, 226
subselect method, 134, 380
SUBSTRING string value function, 154–155
subtraction operator (–), 60, 149
subtransactions, 281–282

subtypes, structured UDTs, 39
SUM function, 65, 154
summarizing data, baseball statistics example, 380–381
Sun Microsystems, 310
super user, 257
supertypes, structured UDTs, 39
system architecture, using favorite, 377
SYSTEM_USER variable, 146

● *T* ●

tables. *See also* views (virtual tables)
  ALTER TABLE statement, 59
  automatic entry of block of rows, 132
  CREATE TABLE statement, 58
  DDL, 49–50, 56, 87–88
  deleting, 85–86
  designing in isolation, 377
  existing, adding constraints, 369
  identifying, 49
  multitable relational database, 92–97
  RAD, creating with Design View, 77–80
  referenced, controlling access with constraints, 68
  relation among, referential integrity, 106
  restrictions for multiple (assertions), 113
  saving single database, 80
  structure, altering in DDL, 89
  transferring all rows between, 133
  transferring selected columns and rows, 133–135
  users, granting privileges to modify, 261
  XML data, 318, 326–327
technical factors, considering only, 376
temporary table declaration clause, 295
termination condition, recursive queries, 245–246
testing, importance of beta, 378
text strings, joining two, 60–61
3NF (third normal form), 49, 118–119
time intervals, overlapping (OVERLAPS predicate), 190
TIME WITH TIME ZONE data type, 33, 41
TIME WITHOUT TIME ZONE data type, 32–33, 41
TIMESTAMP WITH TIME ZONE data types, 33, 41, 142
TIMESTAMP WITHOUT TIME ZONE data type, 33, 41, 142
transaction interaction trouble, 271–272
transaction processing, 270
transactions
  constraints within, 282–286
  DCL, 66–67
  log file, 66–67
transferring all rows between tables, 133
transferring data, 138–139
transitive dependency, 118
TRANSLATE string value function, 157
translation tables, 59
translations
  multitable relational database, 97–98
  users, granting privileges to, 263–264
TRIM string value functions, 156–157
truth test, Boolean value expressions, 62
tuple, 14
two-dimensional arrays, 14

● *U* ●

UDTs (user-defined types)
  benefits of using, 62
  described, 37–38, 41
  distinct types, 38–39
  structured types, 39–40
underscore character (_), 182–184
UNDO error handling, 351
UNION ALL relational operator, 203
union join relational operator, 216–223
UNION relational operator, 133, 134, 201–203
union-compatible tables, 201–202
UNIQUE key
  entity integrity, 104–105
  referential integrity, 192, 193
UNIQUE rule, SQL-89, 194
UNIQUE, WHERE clauses, 189
uniqueness, need for, 98
Universal Time Coordinated (UTC), 149
updatability clause, cursors, 338–339
update anomalies, 106

UPDATE statement
  access privileges, 68
  all rows, changing, 137
  altering tables, 59
  correlated subqueries, 240–242
  cursor sensitivity, 339
  domain integrity concerns, 105
  fetching from single row, 343–344
  multiple rows, changing, 136
  privileges, 359
  single row, changing, 135–136
  stored functions, 358–359
updating views, 129
UPPER string value functions, 156
U.S. dollar, 39
user interface
  client computer, 44–45
  SQL, 289
user name, 260
user-defined types (UDTs)
  benefits of using, 62
  described, 37–38, 41
  distinct types, 38–39
  structured types, 39–40
users, granting privileges to
  constraints, applying, 18–19
  DCL, 67–70
  deleting obsolete rows from table, 262
  deletions, 359
  domains, character sets, collations,
    and translations, 263–264
  executing SQL statements, 264–265
  GRANT and REVOKE, using together, 268
  GRANT statement, 258–259
  inserting data, 260
  mapping tables, 318
  modifying table data, 261
  power to grant, granting, 265–266
  referencing related tables, 262–263
  retrieval, controlling, 381
  revoking, 266–267
  roles, 260
  schema, 68
  viewing data, 260–261
UTC (Universal Time Coordinated), 149

• V •

VALID predicate, XML data, 326
value expressions. *See also* CASE
    conditional expressions
  conditional, 150
  datetime, 149–150
  described, 147–148
  numeric, 149
  string, 148
value functions, character strings, 154
values
  CASE conditional expressions, 166–168
  column references, 146–147
  listed, 141
  literal, 142–144
  row, 142
  special variables, 146
  variables, 144–145
VARCHAR (CHARACTER VARYING)
    function, 31, 41, 155
variables
  compound statements, SQL-92/PSM,
    347–348
  values, 144–145
views (virtual tables)
  creating, 125–126
  database, 15–17
  DDL, 51–56
  with modified attribute, 128–129
  multitable, 51
  security, database, 129
  SELECT statements, 125
  with selection condition, 127–128
  from tables, 126–127
  updating, 129
  users, granting privileges to, 260–261

• W •

WHERE clause
  ALL, SOME, ANY, 185–188
  BETWEEN, 180–181
  comparison predicates described, 179
  with DELETE statement, 139–140

WHERE clause *(continued)*
  described, 175–179
  DISTINCT, 189
  EXISTS, 188–189
  IN and NOT IN predicates, 181–182
  LIKE and NOT LIKE, 182–184
  MATCH, 190–193
  ON clause versus, 223
  NULL, 184–185
  OVERLAPS, 190
  restricting rows, 134
  SELECT statements, 124
  SIMILAR, 184
  UNIQUE, 189
  with UPDATE statement, 135, 137
WHILE...DO...END WHILE
    statement, 355
width bucket function, 157, 161
wildcard characters
  asterisk (*), 124, 202
  LIKE or NOT LIKE, 182
WITH GRANT OPTION clause, 265–266
wizard, Microsoft Access, 78
words, reserved
  described, 394
  SQL, 25
  SQL:2003, 385–388
workgroup database, 9

XML data
  ARRAY, 41, 330–331
  character sets, mapping, 316
  data types, mapping, 317
  distinct UDT, 329
  domain, mapping to, 328–329
  forest, 392
  functions, 322–326
  identifiers, mapping, 316–317
  multiset, 41, 331–332
  null values, handling, 318–319
  predicates described, 324
  ROW, 329–330
  schema, generating, 319–320
  SQL, relating with, 313–314
  tables, 318, 326–327
  types, 34–35, 314–315
XQuery expression, 323–324

year-month interval, 34, 150